James Murray

An impartial history of the present war in America

containing an account of the rise and progress, the political springs thereof, with

its various successes and disappointments, on both sides

James Murray

An impartial history of the present war in America
containing an account of the rise and progress, the political springs thereof, with its various successes and disappointments, on both sides

ISBN/EAN: 9783742821058

Manufactured in Europe, USA, Canada, Australia, Japa

Cover: Foto ©ninafisch / pixelio.de

Manufactured and distributed by brebook publishing software (www.brebook.com)

James Murray

An impartial history of the present war in America

AN IMPARTIAL

HISTORY

OF THE PRESENT

WAR in AMERICA;

CONTAINING

An ACCOUNT of its RISE and PROGRESS,

The POLITICAL SPRINGS thereof,

WITH ITS VARIOUS

SUCCESSES and DISAPPOINTMENTS,

ON BOTH SIDES.

By the Rev. JAMES MURRAY, *of* NEWCASTLE.

Arma Virumque cano———
——————— Bella, horrida Bella !
Et Tybrim multo spumantem sanguine cerno.
  VIRGIL. *Æneid.* VI. 86.

NEWCASTLE UPON TYNE:

Printed for T. ROBSON, Head of the GROAT-MARKET;
R. Baldwin, No. 47. Pater-noster-Row, London; N. Frobisher, York;

TO THE KING.

SIR,

As it is the happy privilege of all the dutiful subjects of the British empire, without regard to rank or distinction, to address their sovereign, it can be no presumption in one who wishes well to the Revolution, and the illustrious family of Brunswick, though remote from the throne, thus to address your Majesty. To wish well to the rightful sovereign of these kingdoms, is the duty of all Protestants; and the happiness of a Prince ruling by law, *ought to be* the prayer of all good subjects. A reflection upon the unhappiness of former times, when *tyranny*, and the *iron rod of arbitrary power*, ruled over these realms, makes the dutiful subjects of your Majesty rejoice, that they are, by the *glorious Hanoverian succession*, set free from the apprehensions of *civil and religious slavery*.

Your Majesty's *true* friends will always join the glorious Revolution, and the succession of your family to the throne of these kingdoms, in their united thanksgivings to Heaven; and never forget the 5th of November, and the glorious first of August, when Popery and arbitrary power were *so effectually baffled*.

The warm expressions of heart-felt joy, which your subjects loudly manifested at your accession to the crown of Great Britain, could not but declare to all the world, how happy they were, in having a Protestant Prince born among them, to be their King. Your Majesty's gracious speech on that occasion was received with raptures throughout the whole empire, and all ranks and degrees of your subjects were transported with your royal sentiments.

There have few sovereigns, since the first institution of government, that have had all the satisfaction they could have desired: *Misunderstandings* and *mismanagements*, in *high* and *low*, are common in the present state of human nature. It requires a more exalted state of existence, than any rank of beings in this system arrive at, to be perfect. The subject of this history, thus addressed to your Majesty, is a palpable proof of the *weakness* and *imperfection* of mortals in this world.

The far greater part of your Majesty's good subjects, are much afflicted for the *causes* and *occasion* of the present unhappy contention in the British empire, and from *their hearts* earnestly pray, that it may be speedily at an end; that your Majesty may enjoy the sweets of peace, and the real pleasure of ruling a dutiful and happy people.

History

[iv]

History must record the events that happen in time, that future ages may know what has passed in former periods of the world, and take an example and warning from the transactions of their predecessors. An historian should know no party, but record truth. *Adulation* and *flattery* as well as *rancor* and *prejudice*, are inconsistent with the character of an honest historian. The author presumes that your Majesty will meet with none of these in his history. Love of liberty, and of his sovereign, has made him write freely; and if he have any ruling prejudice, it is in favour of his *Country*, his *King*, and *the Law*. Your Majesty will be graciously pleased to accept of this humble address of a subject, who is sincerely attached to the Brunswick family; who loves his King and country, values liberty and religion, and reveres the British constitution; who sincerely wishes that your Majesty, your royal consort, and family, may live long, that it may be your happiness to rule with wisdom, live in tranquillity, and make your subjects happy;—and at last enjoy a kingdom, incorruptible, undefiled, and that fadeth not away;

Such is the sincere prayer,

Of your Majesty's most humble,

And most dutiful Subject,

JAMES MURRAY.

Newcastle upon Tyne
Dec. 22, 1780.

BOOK I.

CHAP. I.

War more celebrated in history than the arts of peace—the American War proceeded from two causes—an account of the Cyder Act—the Stamp Act—debates concerning it—an abridgement thereof—arguments for, and against it—the proceeding of the Colonists against it—the Americans would have defended themselves without our help—the parliament would not suffer them—Doctor Franklin's letter to Governor Shirley.

WAR, though of all things the most destructive to the human species, and contrary to the original dictates of nature, has in all ages of the world filled up a great part of the history of nations. The laws and constitutions of kingdoms, and the improvements of virtue and science, make a small figure in the annals of empires, when compared with the ponderous volumes that contain the achievements of soldiers, and the rise and progress of war. The works of Archimedes, Socrates, and Plato; the laws of Solon, and other eminent legislators, fill up but a few pages in comparison of the history of the wars of Greece and Rome. It is custom that renders the most disagreeable things familiar, makes things disgustful at

first

first, afterwards pleasant; and stamps the most abandoned of all actions with the epithet of glory. The glory of war is a creature of the imagination; often formed by caprice, nursed by policy, and manumitted by public authority; when yet this unnatural creature of fancy, instead of promoting public or private happiness, is the torment of the possessor, and the universal bane of all society. A thirst after this glory, and a propensity for renown in martial exploits, have made fruitful countries a wilderness, cities a desolation, and empires scenes of slaughter; this unnatural appetite drags the parent from his family, the children from their parents, renders the widow desolate, their children fatherless, and the father without offspring. Hence it becomes glorious to thirst for blood, an honour to spoil our neighbours, and the dignity of men to live by rapine. It is magnanimity to fall at the command of princes; and to return maimed from battle, though in an unjust cause, is accounted bravery in the lowest individual. By giving false names and epithets to things, and by frequently repeating them as matters of the highest importance, they at last leave an impression which becomes a principle of action in the minds of such as do not examine them.

The present war in America seems to have proceeded from two general causes; an excessive desire of dominion in government, and an exceeding great jealousy in the people of the colonies, of ministerial designs against their natural rights and liberties.—— It cannot be disputed that the legislature in Great Britain, as well as the executive power, by modern statutes of parliament, which had all the appearance of selfishness and domination, gave sufficient ground of jealousy to the colonies. From the pretence of expences and disbursements, laid out for the defence of America, the government of the mother country claimed a right of internal taxation, unknown to the English constitution; and proceeded to frame new laws, which in their own nature declared that the sole right of legislation remained in the parliament of England. In this case the subjects of the empire in that western part of the world, were considered, not as other subjects, but as vassals, under absolute authority, to a legislature, in which they had none to represent them, and who were not under sufficient obligations to pay regard to their interest. The late war with France and Spain, had added an enormous weight of debt to our former national burdens, and the peace that was but lately concluded had given us an addition of territory, without making us any richer than we were before. As soon as peace gave the nation time to reflect, it was found that the flattering ideas of conquest could not remove the feelings, which the pressure of so many millions of debt, had impressed on our national constitution. It was expected that our debts would have been lessened, our taxes reduced, and our burdens lightened; but the hot fever of war had so relaxed the solids of the body politic, and weakened the whole frame of the constitution, that the nation soon after the ratification of the peace, appeared in the second stage of a consumption. The conductors of the last stages of the war, who had only proceeded upon the plan which a minister, the glory of his country, had formed before, were obliged ignominiously to drop it, for want of credit and capacity to carry it on; and ratified a peace as inglorious as the war had been successful. Though an indifferent peace is preferable to even a successful state of war, yet when a nation is laden with a burden of enormous debt, contracted for its own defence against a perverse enemy, wisdom and political prudence, will certainly vindicate a nation, in making their enemies, when they are in their power, pay as much of the debt contracted as it is possible to obtain from them. The negociators of the peace were considered by the nation as men unfriendly to the common interest, and persons, who when they were sensible of their incapacity to carry on the war, were determined to conclude a peace, with as much advantage to their own private interest as possible. Demands which might have protracted a war, which they neither had genius nor credit to carry on, were industriously avoided, and the more mild requisitions of private douceurs were supposed to have been adopted. Whether this jealousy of the nation proceeded from a suspicion founded in distrust, or from signatures which implied moral certainty, I will not pretend to determine; but it was the general opinion of the people at that period, that the French ministry purchased the peace, and that some persons of no small distinction in England, received the price thereof. What gave more weight to these suspicions of the people on this occasion was, that their favourite minister, who had recovered the nation from disgrace, and exalted it to an high pitch of glory and renown, had for some time been displaced, through the influence of the royal favourite, who now was supposed to manage all the springs of government. It is so seldom that a prime minister is universally esteemed, and when such a phænomenon happens in the political world, it must be an unpopular action in a sovereign, to turn him out of office, without setting forth some conspicuous acts of his mal-administration. The whole transactions concerning the peace, being carried on by men of different complexions and characters from their former minister, afforded ground of suspicion, that neither the inclinations of the subjects, nor the interest of the nation, were regarded by the sovereign and his ministers. On this account, many things inconsistent with candour and charity, were surmised, and oftentimes publicly affirmed, for which there was no certain proof, nor the least public evidence. It will not from hence follow, that the opposition of the nation to the measures of the minister, proceeded from a spirit of faction and restlesness; for while the people saw a man at the helm who knew to steer his course with wisdom and success, they voluntarily gave both him and his master all due honour and applause. They considered the removal of this favourite from his majesty's service as a public disrespect shewn to the national approbation; and concluded, that some new ideas of favouritism ruled in the cabinet, unknown in the two former reigns. It was said that the former minister was haughty, that his ambition was boundless, that he wanted to rule both the king and the nation, and that he had not shewn that respect to his sovereign which became a servant. These reflections were grounded upon his refusing to serve jointly in the cabinet, and in the ministry, with men whose principles he abhorred, and of whose abilities he had no opinion. He had proposed to reach a blow to Spain at a time when her behaviour was equivocal, that would have instantly made her feel, and prevented a tedious war, which afterwards was carried on at a great expence of blood and treasure: But this proposal was rejected as unfair and ungenerous, and not consistent with the laws of nations. Fruitless queries were sent, and equivocal answers returned, till the Spanish flota arrived, and then the court of Madrid pulled off the mask. From this Lord Chatham concluded, that it was impossible to carry on a war with success, or to manage the national affairs with honour, jointly with men, who either through partiality or want of capacity, were on every occasion to be a clog to his measures; and as responsibility was connected with his office, he found it dangerous to unite with partners who would be ready to impute their own blunders to his management, and then shelter themselves under the protection of the royal favour. What, therefore, many have attributed to his pride, would rather appear to have proceeded from his sagacity, and his discernment of the character of those that were proposed to be joined with him in the management of public affairs.

The discontent which had for some time raged in the nation on account of so disadvantageous a peace, after a successful war, was scarcely abated, when another alarm was given by a new duty imposed on cyder and perry, at the rate of four shillings the hogshead. This, though as reasonable as many other taxes upon the necessaries of life, raised a prodigious ferment in those counties in England, where these commodities are in the greatest abundance. Such was the opposition made to this new law, that the legislature was obliged, for the sake of the quiet of the nation, three years after, to repeal it. This condescension of the parliament and the legislative powers, though it assuaged the torrent of clamour and outrage, which was increased to a great pitch, had not all the effects that might have been expected. The nation considered the repeal of this law to proceed more from the weakness of the ministry, than from a sincere desire in the legislature to make the subjects easy: The rescinding this act therefore, rather increased their presumption, than conciliated their affections: They were still ready to join in new clamours when the smallest occasion was given. When ministers of state once fall under a suspicion of behaving in an arbitrary manner, there is scarcely any of their actions, however innocent, that pass without censure from those in opposition: And the public at large, who are always jealous of their own liberties, are for the most part ready to support such as appear to be on their side.

The government, since the conclusion of the peace had been casting about and projecting several schemes, for raising a revenue to support the credit of the mother country, by contriving ways and means to raise sums to pay the interest of the national debt; but as the number of pensioners were not reduced, and many enormous sums were paid to place of sinecure, all the methods that had as yet been devised were found ineffectual to answer the intentions of the ministry. They began at last to turn their attention to a new subject, which in conclusion brought on disorders in the empire, and has at last issued in a civil war and revolt of thirteen colonies. As the merchants in Britain had been enriched by their traffic in America, and government had for many years received a large revenue from the trade of that country; the ministers began to imagine that there was an inexhaustible fund of riches and wealth in the colonies, to answer their present purpose, as well as to be adequate for future emergencies. Without examining strictly into the consequences which might follow a too precipitate determination in a point so new and so delicate, they agreed to raise a new revenue in the colonies from an inland taxation. But before they proceeded to this dangerous and critical point, the legislature of Great Britain in 1764, impose a new tax upon America, to the amount of 431,577l. 0s. 1d. This was to be totally raised by new imposts and duties upon her trade and commerce; and though the several duties imposed were principally raised from articles of luxury, yet this law was a great restraint upon the trade of America. But what is the worst part of this new act of parliament, it permits litigious informations and law suits, where the persons whose property has been unjustly seized, have no damages, provided the court shall determine that there was a probability of the charge brought against them being true. This was a mean to give an handle to ill-natured persons, who knew they were in no danger, to distress innocent people, and put them to a great deal of unnecessary expences.

There is one proceeding of parliament which cannot be reconciled with the principles of either justice or sound policy. After assessing all the foreign articles of luxury imported into America, they proceeded to restrain the colonists from exporting their superfluous commodities to the Spanish and French colonies.—— This trade, which had been formerly winked at, though not strictly agreeable to the laws of trade and navigation, was of great advantage to both the colonies and the mother country. Those articles which would have been as lumber upon their hands, and could not have been useful to Great Britain, were sold to the Spaniards and French for ready money, or bartered for valuable commodities, for which there is always a demand in Europe. This enabled the colonies to pay their bills in specie to the merchants at home, or to afford them such merchandize as was equivalent to ready money. The advantage in this case was mutual, and both Great Britain and her colonies were profited by the traffic. What were the secret springs of action which moved the British legislature flature to prefer this impolitic flatute, is not easy to perceive, unless by liftening to the reports of British West-India merchants, who might conceive that it would enable the French and Spaniards to underfell them at foreign markets, and of confequence reduce their profits, they were feduced to give way to their folicitations. It is fufficiently evident that this trade was a real benefit to all the three parties concerned. In the time of war it had been carried on by flags of truce between Great Britain and France, as a public benefit to both, till the French Weft-India iflands being fhut up by our fleets, it was conceived that the French had more advantage by it than England, and for that reafon it was reftrained as a treafonable practice. But this laft reafon of reftraint had no exiftence after the peace was concluded, and ought therefore to have been taken off inftead of receiving frefh parliamentary confirmation.

Unreafonable as this law may appear to be, the method of putting it in execution was ftill more abfurd and oppreffive. A number of armed cutters were fitted out and ftationed upon the coafts of America, to prevent this fuppofed contraband trade, the captains of which were to act in the character of revenue officers, and to determine what fhips were liable to the penalties of this act, and what exempt from them. The greateft part of thefe new naval revenue officers, were totally ftrangers to the nature of their employment. They were ready frequently to detain fhips which came not within the defcription of the act, as being unacquainted with the character of the commodities with which they were loaded: And by unneceffary detention of trading veffels; interrupted trade, without bringing any thing into the treafury. When, through their ignorance, or infolence, a lawful

ful trader was injured, it was not easy to obtain redress; the offenders lived upon an element where justice and law has often little influence: and when they came ashore, it was in bodies too numerous to be called to an account by the civil officers; or in places where their actions were not cognizable by the law, and where they were certain they should not meet their accusers. The lords of the admiralty, or of the treasury, in England, could only remove this grievance; but considering the distance of place, and the manner of application, the whole trade might have been ruined before redress could have been obtained. This was a grievance which the American subjects felt severely, and was likely to produce no favourable ideas in their minds concerning the British legislature. The many unjust acts of violence that happened on this occasion, tended much to irritate the minds of both parties, and when they represented their cases, it was frequently with great acrimony and aggravations. Self interest had a powerful sway on both sides, and the truth was not easily discovered by comparing such opposite representations. The English parliament might have easily foreseen these consequences, had they not been infatuated with the ideas of revenue, and exasperated by some late irritating events. The majority in the house of commons, but especially the ministry, were yet smarting sore, from the blows they had received from the North Britain and other political pasquinades. A secretary of state had been also the year before, legally fined in a court of justice in the penalty of a thousand pounds, for issuing a general warrant, which government was supposed to have disbursed; and considering the lowness of the exchequer, every such touch increased the painful feelings of the ministry. They seemed in a state of of distraction, when they passed this law of restraint upon the trade of America; and it had more the appearance of an act of political fury, than the marks of judicious legislation. It could answer no other purposes than to assert the dominion of parliament over America, and to irritate the colonies against the mother country. Ever since the ministry of Mr. Pitt, the nation had been in a state of confusion, with regard to political sentiments, and the opposition in parliament against Lord Bute, was echoed through all England. In 1763 his lordship resigned his office as first lord of the treasury, and was succeeded by Mr Grenville; but the contentions continued, and during this new ministry, political animosity came to a great height. It was at this time that the American colonies began to feel the oppressive hand of the mother country. She had not only prevented the Americans from procuring the necessaries of life, with the superfluities of their own country, but obliged them to make payment in specie to the Exchequer in England for the duty on such goods as they were allowed to trade in. This was an effectual method of draining the whole money from the colonies, and leaving them nothing for circulation: and what was still more oppressive, two weeks after the bill now mentioned was passed, another was preferred to hinder the distressed colonies from supplying the demand of money for their internal necessities with paper bills of credit, and that no such bills should be a legal tender for payment; to this was added that such paper bills as were passing in currency should after a limited time be called in and sunk. This was an exertion of authority beyond all bounds of justice and equity; for it was impossible that the Americans without trade, money, or paper credit, could pay any thing at all. It was indeed affirmed that all the money raised from the above mentioned duties, was to be applied for defraying the expences of protecting the colonies where it was levied, and that at the same time that a law was made to restrain the increase of paper currency, several new laws were preferred to encourage and encrease the commerce of the colonies with the mother country. The laws here referred to were, an act for granting leave for a limited time for carrying rice from the provinces of South Carolina and Georgia to other parts of America, on paying British duties:——an act for granting a bounty upon the importation of hemp, and rough and undressed flax, from the American colonies into Great Britain; and another to encourage the whale fishery on their coasts. All this supposed in the first instance, that the Americans were either not judges of their own affairs, or that they had no just or legal right to judge of, or interfere with, their own trade. A more abject and servile situation can scarcely well be imagined, than is implied in this idea. The whole of this proceeding implies that nothing in course of trade and commerce was to be allowed to the Americans, except what brought immediate profit, and advantage to Great-Britain. The laws that were at this time made in behalf of the colonies, had no proportion in their influence, as to any advantage, in comparison of those restraints that were laid upon their trade by the other statutes. The effects of the one were slow and progressive, but the other was instantaneous and immediately felt. The colonies could not help feeling immediately the effects of cramping their domestic business, and foreign commerce, by not only hindering them from receiving money from strangers, for their superfluities, to supply their immediate calls, but for bidding them to make any at home; whereas the laws pretended to compensate these disadvantages, were both uncertain and remote in their effects; so distant that it might be many years before any benefit could arise from them, and might; in conclusion, produce no effect at all. This was a partiality in the legislature, sufficient to create a jealousy in the minds of the colonists, that the parliament of Britain considered them not as fellow subjects, but inferior vassals, not to be regarded in the same manner as the subjects of the mother country. A people that are restrained from gaining money by trading with others, and are not permitted to have any of their own, are in such a situation as the constitution of England to ally disapproves. Unless the Americans had lost all sense of right and wrong, it was impossible but they should have considered these acts of the legislature as *unjust* and *oppressive*.

It has been alledged, that the greatest part of the money, if not the whole of it, arising from these duties, would return to the colonies, to pay the troops quartered there for their defence. This is a mere allegation; for if the money collected from duties in America had been intended merely for paying the troops quartered there, there was no occasion to send it to the British exchequer to risk the danger of seas in sending it back again to America. This would have been a piece of mere wantonness, first to distress the colonies in collecting a revenue, to shew the power of the British parliament, and then to order the money to be paid to the troops residing among them. It would have been more easy to have given orders to their assemblies to have paid them at first hand, without so much risk and unnecessary expence. This was such a trial of the affections of the colonies as was not easy

easy to be endured, and yet they bore it with great patience. These proceedings in the parliament had as bad an effect upon the mother country as the colonies: it hindered the Americans from bringing any cloathing from England, except what was absolutely necessary, and made them enter into associations to encourage manufactures among themselves. The more severe the laws of the mother country towards the Americans were, the more were the colonists united, and the more they exerted all their vigour to bear their present burdens with fortitude. It was a thing not at all to be expected, that the colonies out of mere compliment to great Britain, should submit to perish for want of the necessaries of life, when they had a great abundance within themselves. Their sufferings already were of the severest sort; for, like the children of Jacob, in the land of bondage, they were required to make brick without straw;—to carry on trade and manufactures, without either money or paper currency to promote their course.

It was easy to perceive the effects that this restriction upon the American commerce would have upon both the trade and revenue of the mother country; in proportion to the quantity of goods the colonies manufactured themselves, or as far as they restrained themselves to things merely necessary, so much would the trade of Great Britain decrease, and the duty upon goods exported to America be lessened. It has been computed that the colonies, besides the foreign goods which they purchased from our merchants, took annually of our produce and manufactures to the amount of three millions. A very great multitude of people were employed in manufacturing, in buying, selling, and transporting these goods: So that from the sowing of the seeds, till they were landed in

some

some port in America, the people of Great Britain were constantly employed, and in conclusion were paid by the colonies. When this trade was stopped, or when it did not go on in its proper course, it is natural to conceive that all the thousands who were employed in preparing these manufactures, must have some way or other been supported at the expence of the community, as it was impossible that in a short time they could find any new kind of employment to pursue. This was at one stroke striking off from business a multitude of useful members of society, and throwing them upon the public for present supply. The government could not help feeling the effects of this impolitic proceeding by a decrease of revenue; for they both lost the duty payable upon the goods exported to America, and the import duties payable on goods we received from foreign countries, in return for what were sent them by the colonies; and however small all this may appear to some, it could not but amount to more than any thing that could possibly be raised by the unhappy restriction.

It is somewhat surprizing that the wisdom of both the ministry and parliament should have at this time so far forsaken them, as to prefer a law, so absurd in its own nature, and ruinous in its consequences; which every one by paying the smallest attention to the subject, might have easily discerned to be a dangerous expedient, as well as an irrational project for raising money. It appears to have been a time of political infatuation, and the ministry were bent both upon their own ruin and that of the nation. The present reign has been the most unfortunate, for unhappy measures of government, under a good constitution and a religious sovereign, of any since the reign of Charles the first. The ministry, as if all the possessions of the subjects in America

America had been totally at their difpofal, proceeded a ftep ftill farther to make themfelves ridiculous. Before they had enjoyed the profits and fruits of this obnoxious bill, they proceeded to another fcheme, pregnant with folly, oppreffion, and defpotifm. After having laid new reftraints on the traffic of the colonies, ftopt their fources of procuring fpecie, and rendered their paper money in a great meafure ufelefs, they proceeded to impofe a new tax, unknown and unheard of on the other fide of the Atlantic. A bill was brought into parliament, and paffed both houfes, for laying a duty upon ftamps in all the American colonies. This law impofed no lefs than fifty-three different forts of ftamps and other duties upon the colonies and plantations in America, fome of them extremely exorbitant and heavy, and none of them favourable to the interefts of the colonies except one, which impofes ten pounds per fheet upon the licenfes of attornies, folicitors, and counfellors: This would probably have been a check upon the progrefs of a profeffion, which, when much encouraged, is rather the bane than the benefit of fociety.— But many other articles were highly oppreffive and burdenfome to the fubject.

The

* ABSTRACT of STAMP DUTIES.

(1) All declarations, pleas, replications, rejoinders, demurrers, &c. in courts of law to pay 3d per fheet. (2) Special bail and appearances in the faid courts 2s. per fheet. (3) Petitions, bills, anfwers, claims, pleas, replications, rejoinders, demurrers, &c. In the courts of chancery, 1s. 6d. per fheet. (4) Copies of petitions, bills, &c. In the faid courts, 3 l. per fheet. (5) Monitions, libels, anfwers, allegations, inventories, or renunciations, in courts exerciting ecclefiaftical jurifdiction, 1s. per fheet. (6) Copies of wills, monitions, &c. in the faid courts, 6d. per fheet. (7) Donations, prefentations, collations, inftitutions, regifters, entries, teftimonials, certificates of degrees, 2l. per fheet. (8) Monitions, libels, claims, anfwers, allegations, informations, letters of requeft execution, renunciations, inventories in the courts of admiralty, 1s. per fheet. (9) Copies of fuch, &c. 6d. per fheet.

The transactions in the British parliament were not so secretly carried on but they reached America before they were ready to be put in execution. After this stamp bill was read in parliament the first time, before it was read a second time, a petition was offered to the Commons by Edward Montague, agent for the province of Virginia, praying to take their unhappy circumstances into consideration; and that their house of burgesses might be continued in the rights and privileges they had so long enjoyed; and they might be heard by their council against a bill that might be intended to charge stamp or any other duties on the colony of Virginia. A petition was also offered to be presented by the governor and company of the English colony of Connecticut, in North America, praying that the colony might be indulged in the exercise of the power of laying all internal taxes on the said colony,

---

sheet. (10) Appeals, writs of error and of dower, ad quod damnum, certiorari, statute merchant, statute staple, attestations, certificates, exemplifications of records or proceedings in any courts, except appeals, &c. from proceedings before a single justice. 10s. per sheet. (11) Writs of covenant or of entry, attachment, &c. in any of the said courts, 5s. per sheet. (12) Judgements, decrees, sentences, dismissions, records of nisi prius, or pullea in any of the courts, 4s. per sheet. (13) Affidavits, common bail for appearance, interrogatory depositions, rules, orders, warrants of court, dedimus protestatem, apur, subpœnas, summonses, compulsory citations, commissions, recognisances, 1s. per sheet. (14) Licences, appointments, admissions of councellors, solicitors, &c. to practise in any court, 10l. per sheet. (15) Bills of lading, cockets, clearances, 4d. per sheet. (16) Letters of mart, commissions for private ships of war, 20s. per sheet. [17] Grants, appointments, admissions to public beneficial offices, &c, of 20l. per annum value or upwards (army, navy, judges, and justices of the peace excepted) 10s. per sheet. [18] Grants of liberties, privileges, of franchises, under the seal of any of the colonies, or sign manual of any governor, &c. or any exemplifications thereof, 6l. per sheet. [19] Licences for retailing spirituous liquors 20s. per sheet. [20] Licence for retailing wine only 4l. per sheet. [21] Licences for retailing wine, where a licence has been granted for retailing spirituous liquors, 3l. per sheet. [22] Probates of wills, letters of administration or guardianship, &c. on the continent, and the Bermuda and Bahama islands, 5s. per sheet.

lony, and that the resolution of that house in the last session of parliament, might not be carried into execution, by a bill for imposing stamp duties on the colonies. William Middleton, Esq. Daniel Hughes, Esq. and Joseph Nitt, Esq. also offered a petition in behalf of themselves, and the rest of the inhabitants, owners of property, in his Majesty's province of South Carolina, praying that the house should not approve of any bill that might be offered, charging stamp duties in the province of Carolina. A motion was made with respect to each of these questions, that they should be brought in, but upon each of the questions respectively a negative was put. Upon a division it was carried by 245 against 49 that the petitions should not be heard. The bill, after going through all its stages and forms, was at last passed, and received the royal sanction.

It

sheet. [23] Probates, letters of administration or guardianship, in other parts of America, 10s. per sheet. [24] Bonds for any sum not exceeding 10l. on the continent and islands of Bermuda and Bahama, 6d. per sheet. [25] Bonds for any sum above 10l. and not exceeding 20l. within the said places, 1s. per sheet. [26] Bonds for any sum above 20l. and not exceeding 40l. within the same places 1s. 6d. per sheet. [27] Warrants for surveying or setting out any lands not exceeding 100 acres, 6d. per sheet. [28] Warrants for surveying and setting out any land above 100 acres, and not exceeding 200, 1s. per sheet. [29] Warrants for surveying or setting out any lands above 200 acres and not exceeding 300, 1s. 6d. per sheet. [30] Original grants, or deeds, mesne conveyances, &c. of lands not exceeding 100 acres upon the continent or islands of Bermuda and Bahama, 1s. 6d. per sheet. [31] Original grants, &c. of lands above 100 acres, and not exceeding 200 in the said places, 2s. per sheet. [32] Original grants, &c. of land above 200 acres, and not exceeding 300 in the said places, 2s. 6d. per sheet. [33] Original grants, &c. of lands not exceeding 100 acres within all other parts of America, 3s. per sheet. [34] Original grants, &c. of lands above 100 acres, and not exceeding 300 acres, 4s. per sheet. [35] Grants, appointments, or admissions to any public beneficial office, not before charged, above 20l. per annum value, or exemplifications thereof, army, navy, and justices of the peace excepted upon the continent, or Bermuda and Bahama Islands.

It must be acknowledged to the honour of the British parliament, that this bill did not pass without opposition; the friends of liberty, and of the constitution,—the sincere lovers of the Brunswick family, opposed it, in all its stages, and offered such arguments against it as their opponents were not able to answer. The jurisdiction of parliament over the colonies, was combated with arguments, which every sober person, under no influence except truth, must confess in their hearts to be forcible and conclusive. It was argued in behalf of the colonies, that those who first planted them, were driven from their native country by violent persecutions, and had left their mother country for conscience sake, at their own risque and expence; that being both persecuted and forsaken by her, all ties, except what are common to mankind, were dissolved between them. That as England had ceased to give them

---

4l. per sheet. [36] Grants, or admission to such offices in any other part of America, 6l. per sheet. [37] Indentures, leases, conveyances, contracts, stipulation——— of sale, charter-parties, protests, articles of apprenticeship or covenants, except for the hiring of servants, and other matters before charged, 2s. 6d. per sheet. [38] Warrants for auditing public accounts, beneficial warrants, orders, grants, certificates, under the public seal or sign manual of the governors, &c. not before charged, (passports, surrenders of offices, policies of assurance, warrants for the navy or army, or grants of offices under 20l. per annum value excepted) 5s. per sheet. [39] Notorial acts, bonds, deeds, letters of attorney, procuration, mortgage, release, or obligatory instrument, [not charged before] 2s. 3d. per sheet. [40] Registers, entries or inrolments of grants, deeds &c. (before charged) 3d. per sheet. [41] Registers, entries or inrolments of grants, deeds, &c. [not before charged] 2s. per sheet. [42] Duties payable upon cards and dice, viz. on cards, 1s. per pack, dice 10s. per pack. [43] Duties on pamphlets, newspapers, viz. pamphlets, half a sheet or less, one half-penny on every printed copy; larger than half a sheet and not exceeding a whole sheet, 1d. for every copy; being larger than one sheet and not exceeding 6 in octavo or under, or not exceeding 12 sheets in quarto or 20 sheets in folio, 1s. per sheet for one printed copy; for every advertisement in any gazette or other paper 12s. for every almanack, &c. to serve for one year 4d. for every almanack to serve for several years, duties to the sums amount respectively for each year; on instruments, process,

them legal protection, they were absolved from all duty of obedience to her. That their charters only bound them to the common duty of subjects, to the sovereign, as the supreme head of the empire, but did not oblige them to submit to the dictates of the legislature, in which they had no share. That it was unreasonable that the people of Britain should pretend to exercise rights over their brethren in America, which they themselves declare to be oppressive and illegal at home, when claimed by others among them.

It was further urged that it could not reasonably be imagined that when the people of Great Britain contended with the crown, for the sake of their own rights, that they considered it might be lawful for the sovereign to usurp a power over others, which they denied could be lawfully exercised over themselves. And that however binding their charters might have been, yet as they had been deprived of them by an arbitrary exertion of government, which the people at home would not suffer, they ought to be still considered as entitled to them, and the benefits arising from them; that as their charters gave them full privilege to make their own laws, provided they did not make any contrary to the fundamental principles of the English constitution, and as they had not been

---

ings, &c. aforesaid, engrossed, written, or printed, in any other than the English language, double the amount of the respective duties before charged thereon.——On clerks fees, or apprentices, not exceeding 60l. a duty of 6d. for every 20s. so paid, and 1s. on every 20s. exceeding 50l. The penalties in case of non-observance of this act, are heavy and grievous, like the act itself. All persons who should sign, write, or seal any thing that was liable to be stamped, before being stamped, was to be fined 10l. and no instrument could be admitted in evidence, in any cause, unless stamped. It was made death to counterfeit a stamp, inrolling any deed unstampt, the fine 50l. Counsellors or others, neglecting to file or record in due time any matter for which duty is payable, the forfeit 50l.

been charged with any such misdemeanours, they were undoubtedly entitled to their original chartered rights, of which the bill, then in agitation, was a manifest perversion. It was added that it was the birth-right of Englishmen, and their dependants, not to be taxed by any except their representatives; but that the colonies were so far from being represented in the parliament of Great Britain, that they were not virtually represented, as the meanest inhabitants of the mother country were. That the people of Ireland, were more virtually represented in the parliament of Great Britain, than it was possible for the colonies to be; that many Irish gentlemen and peers possessed estates in England, and Englishmen in Ireland, so that there were numbers of Irish noblemen and gentlemen, in both houses of parliament, and the parliament of Britain never claimed a right to tax the people of Ireland, in consequence of this virtual representation.

It was objected that the mother country had given great assistance to the colonies, expended great sums of money in protecting them, and that it was reasonable to tax them for the sake of being reimbursed for that expence. To this it was answered, that Britain either assisted the colonies from principles of humanity, or with a view of being repaid; if from principles of humanity and brotherly affection, their liberty was too dear a price for such a favour; and provided they expected to be repaid, they ought first to settle accompts, and see how much the balance was that was due to Great Britain. That as the colonies had frequently assisted the mother country, and suffered great loss by giving Britain an exclusive trade, by which they were prevented from selling their goods to others, at a much higher price than they could sell them to her, and were obliged to buy from her what they

they could have purchased much cheaper from others, it was presumed, that, upon a fair reckoning, the accompts would appear nearly even, and there would be little to pay. On the side of government, it was urged, that the colonies had submitted to laws made by the mother country for their internal government, and that the British parliament had now a prescriptive right of legislation. It was answered that this could no more be brought as a precedent against the colonies, than against England, which tamely submitted to the arbitrary dictates of King Henry, and the authority of the star-chamber; the tyranny of many being as grievous as that of a single person. That if freedom was due to those who had sense enough to value it, and courage to expose themselves to every danger and fatigue to acquire it, the descendants of those who had suffered so much in the wilds of America from dreadful enemies, were better entitled to it, than their brethren in Great Britain. But it was urged against the arguments drawn from their charters, that all the corporations in England might plead the privileges of their charters, to be exempted from parliamentary taxation. But this, of all other arguments was the most frivolous and insignificant. The corporations in England send members to parliament, and are represented, and many of them received their charters for that very purpose; they therefore make their own laws, which makes the cases very unlike to one another.

There is one argument which the writer of the historical part of the *Annual Register* offers against the claim of the Americans, to be represented in the British parliament, which, at first view, has more force than several others, and it is founded upon their keeping of slaves. He imagines it would not be safe to truſt men with making of laws, who have been accuſtomed to have an unlimited right over the lives and liberties of others. This is undoubtedly true; but I am afraid that this will exclude a great number in England from being repreſented in the Britiſh parliament. If there is any truth at all in the ſtories of the ſlave trade, there are not a few in Britain that are concerned in it, to their diſgrace; and whatever colonies continue in the practice they will not long enjoy their liberty.—But the colonies do not deſire to be repreſented in the Britiſh parliament; they only want to have their own repreſentatives at home, and to make laws for themſelves, as we do in England. It would be unreaſonable for them to expect to be repreſented in the parliament of England. But this is not any part of the controverſy. The above writer ſeems to hint that Britain ſhould claim a right to make laws to the Americans, becauſe they are unfit to make laws to themſelves, for want of feelings of humanity; and that this entitles Britain to an abſolute right of empire over the colonies If this argument were fairly analyſed, it would be found to go a great length, and much farther than the writer ſeems to intend; for it ſuppoſes that all the colonies are alike in this reſpect, which is contrary to fact, and alſo that the parliament of England ought to have abſolute empire over a people whom they encourage in a trade that makes them ſubject to ſlavery. It is very manifeſt that if thoſe whom he has confined to the abſolute empire of the Britiſh legiſlature, were to come to England, they could not be denied a ſhare in the government of this country; provided they had property to qualify them; and ſuppoſe they employed thouſands in the ſlave trade, it would be no objection to their ſitting in parliament. But it is a point to be ſoberly conſidered,

whether

whether Great Britain is not as guilty as Virginia in this particular; for amongst all the laws for regulating the trade of the colonies, the British parliament has not yet made a law against this most infamous traffic. It is no uncommon thing to see a British member of parliament have his *Negro slave* following him, which plainly shews that this practice, is not peculiar to America. The first settlers who went to America, knew nothing of this business. It began in some other place where it does not disqualify men from being represented.

The ministry at this time, whatever their intentions were, acted very impolitically: They acted with a great degree of positiveness, yet wavered in pursuing their measures. They would neither give up their plans, nor would they pursue them with firmness: their whole designs were known over all America, before ever they were able to execute them.

While our ministry and parliament were deliberating concerning the methods to pursue the stamp act, the leaders among the American colonies had time to paint it in the most formidable point of light, to the lower ranks of people, and to kindle a flame in their tempers against it, that neither the art nor power of the King's ministers were afterwards able to quench. Wherever the news of this impolitic and oppressive law reached, it spread discontent like a conflagration and blazed from one colony to another. The tempers of all the colonies being alike affected, it was easy to stir up the same aversion in them all, against a law which was against their interest, and had much the appearance of oppression. One thing with which the ministry then, and since have deceived themselves, is, that they were persuaded that the aversion to this law was not universal: It was alledged that only a few

of

of the colonies, and but some in each of them, were disposed to pursue opposition, or that like the people at home, they would raise a little clamour for a season, and then submit to the authority of the mother country, in the point of taxation. This was only surmise, without any real shadow of foundation, or so much as a partial understanding of the temper of the colonies, which ought to have been fully investigated before such a dangerous expedient had been tried. The managers at home appear to have been ignorant of the real state and disposition of the colonists, and seem to have judged of a people, not yet corrupted with luxury, nor initiated in a system of dissipation, from the examples they had observed in the mother country, where corruption and venality is almost universal. In this they were greatly mistaken, and found by experience, that a people that still retained the spirit and temper of the last century, and were in many respects formed upon the principles of their ancestors, were not to be managed in the same manner as people rendered soft and effeminate, by importing the luxuries and vices of all nations under the sun. The ministry were unfortunate in the beginning of this scheme, and unsuccessful in the conclusion of it. The news of passing the stamp act came first to New England, a colony the most tenacious of their liberty, and jealous to the last degree, of every appearance of despotism. This colony considered itself as the offspring of progenitors, who had suffered both severely and unjustly at the hands of the mother country, and who had asserted their natural rights and privileges at the risque of their lives, and the expence of much blood. They had not forgot how their fathers had, for the sake of civil and religious liberty, fled to a wilderness, which they had now converted into a

fruitful

fruitful field, from an intolerable spiritual persecution, which could not be borne and they were not disposed to surrender the fruits of their own labour, and that of their ancestors, to the children of those that had banished their fathers from their native country. The first colonists succeeded in their undertakings without any expence or charge to the state; which was acknowledged by a vote of the house of commons as early as 1642; and it was not to be expected that their children were tamely to give up rights, that were both founded in nature, and the principles of common justice.

When the news of the stamp act having received the royal signature, reached New England, the melancholy that had taken possession of their minds before, upon hearing that it was voted a proper measure to lay it upon them, broke out into fury and outrage. The ships in the harbours hung out their colours half mast high, in token of deep mourning; the bells were muffled; the act was printed with a death's head to it, in the place where it is customary to affix the new acts of parliament, and called publicly about the streets, by the name of the *Folly of England*, and the ruin of America. Several essays were written, not only against the expediency, but against the justice, of this law, in several news-papers: one in particular had the title of the *Constitutional Courant*, containing matters interesting to liberty, and no wise repugnant to loyalty, printed by Andrew Marvel, at the sign of the Bribe Refused, on Constitutional Hill, North America. This had a more significant frontispiece than any of the rest: It had a snake cut in pieces with the initial letters of the names of the several colonies, from New-England to South Carolina inclusively, fixed to each piece, and above them Join or Die. To these were
added

added several characters, and sententious aphorisms, suited to the occasion, which were easily circulated, and as easily committed to memory; and being exceedingly expressive, they had all the force of a great many arguments. Many of the papers were written with great acrimony, and threw forth severe reflections against the British ministry, and the leaders in these impolitic and arbitrary measures; and it must be granted by every judicious and candid person, that they had great provocation. There were two things exceedingly grievous in this act to the colonies. The first was, that the persons that acted under this law, had in their power to bring an action, the cause of which had arisen at one extremity of North America, to the other, at the distance of near two thousand miles, without the traders being intitled to recover damages, in case the judge should certify that there was any probable cause for the prosecution. The second was, the judge had an interest in giving a sentence in favour of the party suing for the penalties of the act, by being allowed, by way of commission, a very large share in these penalties. This was injustice that the greatest slaves could not easily endure without murmuring; and it was not to be expected that a free people, who have the most strict ideas of liberty, would, without repining, submit to such flagrant oppression and tyranny. By the time the act reached the colonies, they were wrought up to the highest pitch of aversion against it, and treated it with the greatest contempt: In many places it was publicly burnt, together with the effigies of the chief promoters thereof, who, provided they had been present, would have met with abundant disgrace. On the other hand they praised and applauded, with eulogiums of the highest strain, the persons who had op-

posed

posed this obnoxious bill. In several of their meetings they voted thanks to General Conway and Colonel Barre, two gentlemen who had used their influence to prevent this arbitrary statute, in the British house of commons. Their speeches against it, and their pictures were requested from England; the pictures to be hung up in their places of meeting, and the speeches to be inserted in the books designed to record their principal transactions.

The government was now much embarrassed how to have this new act put into execution; for when the tidings of this discontent in America arrived in England, there were but few masters of ships found, who were willing to take on board such an obnoxious and unpopular cargo; and it was soon discovered that this precaution was founded in prudence, and the principles of self-preservation. Such as were so adventurous as to carry any quantity of these tickets of taxation to America, were made sadly to repent, when they arrived at their destined port; where, to save their vessels from fire, and themselves from an ignominious death, the most of these adventurers were obliged to deliver up their execrated cargoes into the hands of the enraged populace, to be treated with as much ignominy as the act itself had been treated before:— Others were obliged to shelter themselves under such of the King's ships, as happened to be nearest to protect them. The glorious harvest that was now expected to be reaped by English tax-gatherers, to be sent over to collect this revenue, was by this storm soon blasted, and those gentlemen who came from England with commissions to act as distributors of stamps, were made to repent severely of engaging in such an enterprize. Many of them were made to renounce, now and for ever, in the most public manner, and upon
oath,

oath, all manner of concern in them, and others cautiously returned to the places from whence they came; while some of a more froward disposition, persisting strenuously in putting the act in execution, were treated by the people as enemies of their country, who meant to enslave America for the sake of paltry emoluments from the court of Britain. Some of this character were severely handled; their houses were burnt, and their effects plundered and destroyed; and such was the rage of the multitude against this unpopular and oppressive statute, that some who had been appointed without their consent or solicitation, to superintend the distribution of the stamped paper, by virtue of their bearing the office of governors, were treated in the same manner, and with the like severity. Mr Hutchinson who was suspected, and according to the best accounts, not without reason, of misrepresenting the colonies in his letters to government, was severely used. The people obliged him to deliver up copies of his own letters which he had sent to England, and by this means made him evidence against himself. This was as illegal as the general warrant that was issued by a secretary of state against Mr Wilkes, and it is not improbable that the colonies on this occasion formed their practice upon some modern British precedents, pretended to have been used through the law of necessity. Had the Americans at this time been in the same situation with the subjects of the mother-country, and agreed by representation to the framing of this law, their present proceedings would have been *traitorous* and *rebellious*; but as all was done without their consent, and contrary to the essential constitution of the empire, their conduct may be accounted rash and severe, but cannot be justly pronounced *treason* or *rebellion*. People in this country who are partly self-interested, and lie also at a distance from the scene of action, are ready to censure the colonists more through partiality and attachment to some party, than from a principle of judgment and true discernment: Had they been in the same situation, they would have probably determined otherwise.

The colonists shewed that they were determined not to submit to the stamp act upon any account; for when ships which came from these colonies that had submitted to this law, brought stamps to the custom-houses, for the sake of their own vindication, they were seized and stuck up in taverns and coffee-houses in scorn, and afterwards committed to the flames with the usual ceremony. This was not merely the device and operation of a fickle mob of unthinking people: Persons of *wisdom* and *character* were concerned both in the plan and its operation, and frequently mingled with the populace, to direct the execution of their main design. Some of the leading men in the opposition, not only countenanced the people in their outrages against this act, privately, but some of them gave an open defiance to the authority that imposed this act, by publicly advertising that those who were employed to enforce that law, might save themselves the trouble of applying to them, for they were resolved not to pay any duty, except what was laid on by their representatives. The provincial assemblies were of the same sentiments with the many individuals, in the opposition, which they at first shewed, by declining giving the governors any advice concerning their behaviour, in such a critical juncture of affairs: They knew that without their assistance and concurrence, the governors could not proceed far, and were determined to give them no aid in executing a law which they considered as altogether unconstitutional. Some of the governors of the provinces, and the provincial assemblies, were not very cordial in their affections to one another; they proceeded upon different principles, and were influenced by different ideas of interest. The governors who had formerly had their salaries paid by the provinces, were now paid by the crown, which gave them a bias towards the side of the ministry, which was not always consistent with the advantage of the colonies. While the governors were paid by the provinces, the colonills were often ready to reward their good services, with singular tokens of favour and esteem, which made the legislative part of the constitution, and that of the executive, keep up a good understanding with one another; but when their interests were separated, their affections soon became disunited, and frequently the governors disapproved what the assemblies were pleased to recommend. This in process of time created jarring between the houses of representatives and their governors, which had proceeded to an uncharitable length about the time of the stamp act. These assemblies were not displeased to see men embarrassed in the execution of an office, which they considered as not discharged for the purpose of its first institution. They therefore gave them very small assistance on this pressing occasion. They disavowed the riotous proceedings of the multitude, and went so far as to promise rewards for seizing the rioters who had plundered the house of one of their chief justices, who was obliged to appear on the seat of justice without the insignia of his office, and the badges of his authority. When some of these rioters were brought to their trial, the juries would not proceed so far as the friends of the stamp act were inclined they should. The writer of the Annual Register affirms that they could be brought to condemn them no farther than decency required, and would not promise to strengthen the hands of government so far as to prevent commotions about the stamp-act; nor did they account these commotions were objects of military restraint. When once a controversy is begun, there are often errors on both sides, and there is no question but the colonists did several things that they ought not to have done*; but when the reasons and causes of their opposition to this law are considered, it must be allowed that their provocations were not small. It may be easy for persons who are biassed by interest and party attachments, to form a specious shew of reasoning to condemn the colonists, and vindicate the government of this country; but an impartial historian with nothing but truth in his eye, will be obliged to draw his inferences from pure facts, and the natural reasons of them, without paying any regard to party or persuasions.

On this occasion, when the debates and quarrels of the parties ran very high, some persons, from caution or some other principle, privately spiked up the cannon belonging to the forts and ship-yards, lest any use should be made of them by either party; and though this might be construed an illegal interference with his Majesty's stores and arms, was a ready mean to prevent bloo[d]shed in case of a sudden rencounter, through the irritation of party spirit. What was determined in the provincial assemblies, with regard to the stamp-act, was approved by several assemblies of the principal

---

* The plundering of Governor Hutchinson's house on the 16th of August, was cruel, barbarous, and unjust. His papers were all burnt, his house unroofed, and all his clothes, with those of his daughter and

cipal inhabitants of some places, who instructed their representatives not to agree in any measures for the protection of the stamp papers, or stamp officers. They granted there had been some tumults and disorders on that account, but that these must be laid to the charge of those who wanted to urge unconstitutional laws upon them, contrary to their charters, and their rights as English subjects, who ought to enjoy the equal privileges of the empire in making their own laws, and taxing themselves. They also cautioned their representatives against all unconstitutional drafts on the public treasury, for fear that the governors should endeavour to strengthen their hands by that means, without their consent. These were proceedings which, though at first view they may appear precipitate and too determined, argued yet a political foresight, which shewed they were not disposed to trifle.

The general assemblies proceeded still further. Instead of winking at the opposition of the people, they began to patronize it, and in express terms, affirmed that the British legislature had no right to tax them. This had been often asserted, and even proved by the strongest arguments, to be founded in reason and the British constitution. It was granted that they were subjects of the empire under one sovereign, or one executive power; but that they had as good a right to make their own laws as the subjects at home, and that none but themselves had a right to give away their property. They came at last to a resolution to petition the legislature of Britain against the stamp act, and pleaded their incapacity to pay any such tax as was now imposed upon them; but at the same time they asked the favour, they did not acknowledge that they were dependent upon the parliament of Britain. This

was

was considered as only asking a favour of equals, without making the submission the parliament required, which rendered their petition offensive to the majority of the legislature. From the manner of their proceedings, some wise men foresaw what would be the consequence of the mother country's asserting a right of legislation over the colonists; they opposed the stamp act because they considered it both unconstitutional in its nature, and detrimental to the real interest of the empire.

On this trying occasion the colonists were not wanting to themselves in any measure that might promote unanimity of designs and execution in the different colonies: They formed associations, and appointed committees, for the sake of a general correspondence in carrying on the common affairs of the whole body. From these committees deputies were appointed to meet in congress at New-York; and what shewed the unanimity of their sentiments in this general cause, and that they were all of one mind is, that when the deputies met at New-York, they were so well agreed, that they had little more to do than to congratulate one another, and set their hands to one general declaration of their rights, and the grievances they laboured under, and to a petition expressing a sense of these grievances to the king, lords, and commons of great Britain. It was not long till the magistrates subordinate to the king began to join the legislative part. The justices of Westmoreland in Virginia, gave public notice under their hands, that they had resigned their office, and declined acting in that capacity; that they would not any longer be instrumental to the destruction of their country, which their oath as justices of the peace

now

now obliged them to, provided they continued in the discharge of their offices. The gentlemen of the law also declared that they would lay down their offices rather than be obliged to practice upon stamp paper. This is an instance of patriotism rarely to be met with, and to which the mother country cannot afford a parallel. Those that are acquainted with the general character of a people of that profession in Great Britain, will be ready to conclude, that the lawyers in Virginia have had a very different education, or that they are not descendants of the natives of this country. How far they may have been in the right or in the wrong in this particular I will not pretend to say; it however argued a great degree of self-denial, to give up their business for the sake of the public interest. Before the 1st of November, when the act was to take place, there was not a sheet of stamp paper to be had throughout the several colonies of New England, New York, New Jersey, Pennsylvania, Virginia, Maryland, or the two Carolinas, except a parcel at New York, which the government through fear was obliged to surrender to the corporation, upon condition that they would not destroy it like the rest. Thus, all business that could not be carried on without stamps, was put to a stand, except newspapers, which the printers, for fear of the populace, were obliged to continue without stamps. But in Canada, where stamps were made use of, the printers were in a worse situation, for few, or none would buy a newspaper on account of its being stamped, and the whole lay upon their hands. The courts of justice were now shut up as well as the ports; and even in those colonies where stamps were used, the people of the best rank submitted to be called in the churches rather than take out licenses for
private

private marriages. This shews us how far the English ministry have deceived themselves and the public, in representing that where any colony had not totally joined with the rest in opposition to government, that they were all satisfied and unanimous. In those places where some leading people had rule, matters were for some time smoothed over, and kept in a temper; when at the same time the far greater part were wholly dissatisfied with the public measures.

The evil consequences of such a stagnation in business began to be felt severely, and would have cooled a moderate zeal for liberty, where distress was so manifest. The friends of government raised their hopes, that from feeling such inconveniences, the deluded multitude would return to a due sense of their duty, and in a short time opposition would totally subside.— Men who set no value upon liberty, are ready to imagine that all others view it in the same light, and that is general mankind. mean no more by opposition to power, and by the name of liberty, than to worm themselves into preferment or places of profit and emolument: This may be the case with a few, or with some designing politicians; but when a whole country catches the flame, there is always more than the hope of court preferment in the case. Demagogues may on a particular occasion, mislead some unthinking people, but it requires more than is in the power of any human address, to lead a continent, unless they have some rational principle to proceed upon. It is a very common thing for both parties on each side of a question, to impute the worst designs to their antagonists, but wherever truth and wisdom are pursued, whatever names may be ascribed to the agents, time will determine both the nature of the cause, and the principles of the actors.

During this interruption of public business, some fruitful expedients were tried to evade the influence of this new law, and among others, the bark of a tree was discovered, which answered for a succedaneum instead of paper, and was sent to the printers at Boston for their approbation; and as it was neither paper, parchment, nor vellum, the discoverer wanted to know whether deeds written upon this bark might not be valid though they were not stamped. In this case he was ready to serve with good writing bark, all those whose consciences were bound by the late act of parliament. This invention was certainly ingenious, but the proposal was not altogether honest; for such as were free to use this vegetable paper, without scruple of conscience, ought not to have laid a snare before the consciences of others.*

While these transactions were going on, the assembly of South Carolina, whose lieutenant governor refused to transact business without stamps, addressed him to know through what channel the stamp act had been transmitted to him. His answer was, that he had it first from the attorney-general, and next from Mr Boone, governor of that province. They said, as that

---

* The writer of the *Annual Register* says, "At last the governors of some of the provinces, though bound by the act to swear to see it observed, under the severest penalties, thinking the total stoppage of all public business, of such bad consequence to the community, as to render lawful the non-compliance with any injunctions laid on them, or even the breach of any oath taken by them, in consequence of injunctions, merely for the sake of that community, thought proper to dispense with the usual stamps, grounding their dispensation on the impossibility of procuring any vessels to protect them from the penalties of the act in the other parts of his Majesty's dominions." Though the act bound the governors to see it observed upon severe penalties, yet while they had not sworn, they only broke the statue, but not their oath. Their making use of paper even without its npn, would have been disobedience to the law, but could be no breach of their oath.

that was the case, he had not received it legally, nor were those *true* notifications of the act, as the governor when out of the province, and the attorney-general when in it, could not, with regard to this communication, be considered in any other light than a private persons. They gave several instances of the province having suffered from the accidental detention of government information, sufficient to prove that certain forms were absolutely to be used in all matters of government, especially such as related to authenticating new laws of such immense consequence to that province. It is highly probable that they had received many laws through channels not more authentic than this now mentioned, but as this was more contrary to their inclination, they were disposed to make the more objections to it.

But the colonists devised a better method to avoid the stamp act. The merchants throughout all these colonies entered into the most solemn engagements to each other, to order no more goods from great Britain, whatever should be the consequence, and to recal the orders they had already given, if not executed before the 1st of January, 1766; and they resolved further, not even to dispose of any British goods sent them upon commission, that were not shipped before that day; or if they consented to any relaxation from these engagements, it was not to take place till the stamp act, sugar act, and paper money acts were repealed. The people of Philadelphia also resolved by a large majority, that till such a repeal should happen, no lawyer should put in suit for a demand for money, owing by a resident in America to any one in England; nor any person in America, however indebted in England, make any remittances there. This resolution was adopted by the retailers, who unanimously agreed not to buy any more English goods shipped contrary to these resolutions. Ages to come will be amazed that separate governments, and so many colonies distinct from each other, should have united so speedily in one interest, notwithstanding the influence of government agents among them, who both opposed all their measures, and endeavoured to frustrate all their designs. Ideas of freedom, when people are not too much vitiated through the power of venality and dissipation, will produce marvellous effects on the behaviour of a people.

This controversy between the mother country and the colonists was for a season of great service to Ireland. What goods the Americans could not possibly want, they ordered from that country, in exchange for their hemp and flax-feed, of which they sent yearly a great quantity.——But in the mean time they pursued every rational method to free themselves from that dependence. A society of arts, manufactures, and commerce, was instituted at New-York in imitation of that of London, and markets were opened for the sale of home-made manufactures. It soon appeared that neither the natives nor those manufacturers which they had invited from Britain and other nations, were idle; they gave good encouragement, and they found workmen in abundance. They made progress in the woollen and linen manufactures, in several species of coarse iron-ware, malt, spirits, and paper-hangings. These were shewn to the society and approved, and when brought to the market, were greedily purchased: and to furnish materials for the woollen work, most of the inhabitants came to a resolution to eat no lamb;—and to extend this design more universally, they determined not to deal with any butcher that should kill or expose any lamb to sale for a limited time. The spirit of industry prevailed to such a degree, and so far took place of idleness and profusion, that the most substantial people were among the first to set an example to their countrymen, by wearing home-spun or old clothes, rather than make use of any British manufactures, of which they were wont to be madly fond. Such were the efforts of all ranks, and such wise and prudent measures did they pursue, that many began to think what they formerly had imagined impossible, was exceedingly probable, and that in a little time the colonies would be able to supply themselves with every necessary of life. Where ideas of freedom once prevail, the arts, sciences, and every other branch of profitable knowledge will attend them. Slavery enfeebles the mind, and renders all the faculties thereof stupid, dull, and inactive: Men who know not the nature of freedom, may toil like beasts of burden, or chaunt like birds in a cage, at the pleasure of their masters; but they enjoy no rational pleasure, nor possess the enjoyment of creatures, dignified with reason and divine understanding. It is something amazing that men who profess to be great and wise, should not take pleasure in seeing others as wise, great, and happy as themselves, but should have the ambition to think that the Deity gave all men the same faculties, with a design to make them the servants of a few, and never to be their own masters.

As one thing generally leads to another, the Americans began to enter into a resolution, which in its consequences would have made the mother country feel the fruits of her folly effectually. It was proposed to stop the exportation of tobacco from Virginia and South Carolina to Great Britain; which considering the great quantities of that article which are re-exported from Great Britain, and the immense sums

sums so insensibly raised, by home consumption, her trade, and especially her revenue, could not fail of being greatly affected. These were notices to the mother country of what a resolute people will determine; and had she been so wise as to have profited by those warnings, she and her colonies might have for ages to come lived in friendship and dependance upon each other.

As the rise and spring of the present war in America ought first to be investigated before we can determine on either side of the question, it must be observed here, that one pretence for beginning and carrying it on is groundless and frivolous. It has often been affirmed that the taxes intended to be imposed on the colonies, were only designed to indemnify the mother country for the expence of protecting them in the last war. To set this point in a clear light, it may be remembered, that in the year 1754, when the French were making encroachments on the crown lands in America, and interrupted the trade of that country with the Indians, a war was apprehended, and commissioners from a number of the colonies met at Albany, to form a plan of union for their mutual defence. The plan they agreed to was this, 'That a grand council be chosen by the assemblies and sent from all the colonies; which council, together with a governor-general to be appointed by the crown, should be empowered to make general laws to raise money in all the colonies for the defence of the whole. This plan was sent to the government in England for their approbation, and had it been approved and established by authority, English America at that time thought itself sufficiently able to defend itself against the French without any assistance. Several of the colonies in former wars withstood

stood the whole power of the French without assistance from Britain, or any other quarter. The plan was rejected, and a new one formed in its stead; in which it was proposed that the governors of all the colonies, attended by one or two members of their respective councils, should assemble and concert measures for the defence of the whole, erect forts where they thought proper, and raise what troops they thought necessary, with power to draw on the treasury in England for the sums that should be wanted; and the treasury to be reimbursed by a tax laid on the colonies by act of parliament. This new plan was communicated by Governor Shirley to Doctor Franklin, who was then at Boston, whose thoughts at that time on the subject will throw considerable light upon this controverted point. The enemies of this renowned philosopher must confess, that it is impossible to answer his arguments; but the reader shall judge for himself.

Tuesday morning.

" SIR,

" I return the loose sheets of the plan, with thanks, to your excellency for communicating them.

" I apprehend, that excluding the *people* of the colonies from all share in the choice of the grand council, will give extreme dissatisfaction, as well as the taxing them by act of parliament where they have no representative. It is very possible, that this general government might be as well and faithfully administered without the people as with them; but where heavy burdens have been laid upon them, it has been found useful to make it, as much as possible, their own act; for they bear better when they have, or think they have share in the direction; and, when any public

BENJAMIN FRANKLIN,
L.L.D.F.R.S.
One of the American Plenipotentiaries at the Court of France.

lic measures are generally grievous or even distasteful to the people, the wheels of government must move more heavily."

Wednesday morning.

SIR,

"I mentioned in yesterday to your excellency, as my opinion, that excluding the *people* of the colonies from all share in the choice of the grand council, would probably give extreme dissatisfaction, as well as the taxing them by act of parliament, where they have no representative. In matters of general concern to the people, and especially where burdens are to be laid upon them, it is of use to consider, as well what they will be apt to think and say; I shall therefore, as your excellency requires it of me, briefly mention what of either kind occurs to me on this occasion.

"First they will say, and perhaps with justice, that the body of the people in the colonies are as loyal, and as firmly attached to the present constitution, and reigning family, as any subjects in the king's dominions.

"That there is no reason to doubt the readiness and willingness of the representatives they may chuse, to grant from time to time such supplies for the defence of the country, as shall be judged necessary, so far as their abilities will allow.

"That the people in the colonies, who are to feel the immediate mischiefs of invasion and conquest by an enemy in the loss of their estates, lives and liberties, are likely to be better judges of the quantity of forces necessary to be raised and maintained, forts to be built and supported, and of their own abilities to bear the expence, than the parliament of England at so great a

"That governors often come to the colonies merely to make fortunes, with which they intend to return to Britain; are not always men of the best abilities or integrity, have many of them no estates here, nor any natural connections with us, that should make them heartily concerned for our welfare; and might possibly be fond of raising and keeping up more forces than necessary, from the profits accruing to themselves, and to make provision for their friends and dependants.

"That the counsellors in the most of the colonies being appointed by the crown, or the recommendation of governors, are often of small estates, frequently dependant on governors for offices, and therefore too much under influence.

"That there is, therefore, great reason to be jealous of a power in such governors and councils, to raise such sums as they shall judge necessary, by draft on the lords of the treasury, to be afterwards laid on the colonies by act of parliament, and paid by the people here; since they might abuse it by projecting useless expeditions, harrassing the people, and taking them from their labour to execute such projects, merely to create offices and employments, and gratify their dependents, and divide profits.

"That the parliament of England is at a great distance, subject to by misinformed and misled by such governors and councils, whose united interests might probably secure them against the effect of any complaint from hence.

"That it is supposed an undoubted right of Englishmen, not to be taxed but by their own consent given through their representatives.

"That the colonies have no representatives in parliament.

That

"That to propose taxing them by parliament, and refusing them the liberty of chusing a representative council, to meet in the colonies, and consider and judge of the necessity of any general tax, and the quantum, shews suspicion of their loyalty to the crown, of their regard for their country, or of their common sense and understanding, which they have not deserved.

"That compelling the colonies to pay money without their consent, would be rather like raising contributions in an enemy's country, than taxing of Englishmen for their own public benefit.

"That it would be treating them as a conquered people, and not as true British subjects.

"That a tax laid by the representatives of the colonies might easily be lessened as the occasions should lessen, but being once laid by parliament under the influence of the representations made by governors, would probably be kept up and continued for the benefit of governors, to the grievous burden and discouragement of the colonies, and prevention of their growth and increase.

"That a power in governors to march the inhabitants from one end of the British and French colonies to the other, being a country of at least 1500 square miles, without the approbation or consent of their representatives first obtained, such expeditions might be grievous and ruinous to the people, and would put them on a footing with the subjects of France in Canada, that now groan under such oppression from their governor, who for two years past has harrassed them with long and destructive marches to the Ohio.

"That if the colonies in a body may be well governed by governors and councils appointed by the crown, without representatives, particular colonies may as well or better be so governed; a tax may be laid on them all by act of parliament for support of government, and their assemblies may be dismissed as an useless part of the constitution.

"That the powers proposed by the Albany plan of union, to be vested in a grand council representative of the people, even with regard to military matters, are not so great as those the colonies of Rhode Island and Connecticut are trusted with by their charter, and have never abused; for by this plan, the president-general is appointed by the crown, and controuls all by his negative; but in these governments the people chuse the governor, and yet allow him no negative.

"That the British colonies bordering on the French, are properly frontiers of the British empire; and the frontiers of an empire are properly defended at the joint expence of the body of the people in such empire: It would now be thought hard by act of parliament to oblige the Cinque ports or sea-coasts of Britain to maintain the whole navy, because they are more immediately defended by it, not allowing them at the same time a vote in chusing members of the parliament; and if the frontiers in America must bear the expence of their own defence, it seems hard to allow them no share in voting the money, judging of the necessity and sum, or advising the measures.

"That besides the taxes necessary for the defence of the frontiers, the colonies pay yearly great sums to the mother-country unnoticed: For taxes paid in Britain by the landholder or artificer, must enter into and increase the price of the produce of land and of manufactures made of it; and great part of this is

paid

paid by consumers in the colonies, who thereby pay a considerable part of the British taxes.

"We are restrained in our trade with foreign nations; and where we could be supplied with any manufacture cheaper from them, but must buy the same dearer from Britain, the difference of price is as a clear tax to Britain. We are obliged to carry great part of our produce directly to Britain, and where the duties there laid upon it lessen its price to the planter, or it sells for less than it would in foreign markets, the difference is a tax paid to Britain.

"Some manufactures we could make, but are forbidden, and must take them of British merchants; the whole price of these is a tax paid to Britain.

"By our greatly increasing the demand and consumption of British manufactures, their price is considerably raised of late years; their advance is clear profit to Britain, and enables its people better to pay great taxes; and much of it being paid by us, is a clear tax to Britain.

"In short, as we are not suffered to regulate our trade, and restrain the importation and consumption of British superfluities (as Britain can the consumption of foreign superfluities) our whole wealth centers finally among the merchants and inhabitants of Britain, and if we make them richer, and enable them better to pay their taxes, it is nearly the same as being saved ourselves, and equally beneficial to the crown.

"These kind of secondary taxes, however, we do not complain of, though we have no share in the laying or disposing of them; but to pay immediate heavy taxes, in the laying, approbation, and disposition of which we have no part, and which perhaps we may know to be as unnecessary as grievous,

ous, must seem a hard measure to Englishmen, who cannot conceive, that by hazarding their lives and fortunes, in subduing and settling new countries, extending the dominion and increasing the commerce of their mother nation, they have forfeited the native right of Britons, which they think ought rather to be given them as due to such merit, if they had been before in a state of slavery.

"These, and such kind of things as these, I apprehend, will be said and thought by the people, if the proposed alteration of the Albany plan should take place. Then the administration of the board of governors and councils so appointed, not having any representative body of the people to approve and unite in its measures, and conciliate the minds of the people to them, will probably become suspected and odious; dangerous animosities and feuds will arise between the governors and the governed, and every thing go into confusion.

"Perhaps I am too apprehensive in this matter; but having freely given my opinions and reasons, your excellency can judge better than I whether there be any weight in them, and the shortness of the time allowed me, will, I hope, in some degree, excuse the imperfections of this scrawl.

"With the greatest respect and fidelity, I have the honour to be, your excellency's most obedient and most humble servant."

Boston, December 22, 1754.

SIR,

"Since the conversation your excellency was pleased to honour me with, on the subject of uniting the colonies more intimately with Great Britain, by allowing them representatives in parliament, I have
some.

something further considered that matter, and am of opinion, that such an union would be very acceptable to the colonies, provided they had a reasonable number of representatives allowed them; and that all the old acts of parliament restraining the trade or cramping the manufactures of the colonies, be at the same time repealed, and the British subjects on this side the water put, in those respects, on the same footing with those in Great Britain, till the new parliament, representing the whole, shall think it for the interest of the whole to re-enact some or all of them: It is not that I imagine so many representatives will be allowed the colonies, as to have any great weight by their numbers; but I think there might by sufficient to occasion those laws to be better and more impartially considered, and perhaps to overcome the private interest of a petty corporation, or of any particular set of artificers or traders in England, who heretofore seem, in some instances, to have been more regarded than all the colonies, or than was consistent with the general interest, or best national good. I think too, that the government of the colonies by a parliament, in which they are fairly represented, would be vastly more agreeable to the people, than the method lately attempted to be introduced by royal instructions, as well as more agreeable to the nature of an English constitution, and to English liberty; and that such laws as now seem to bear hard on the colonies, would (when judged by such a parliament for the best interest of the whole) be more chearfully submitted to, and more easily executed.

"I should hope too, that by such an union, the people of Great Britain, and the people of the colonies, would learn to consider themselves, not as belonging to a different community, with different interests,

terests, but to one community with one interest, which I imagine would contribute to strengthen the whole, and greatly lessen the danger of future separations.

"It is, I suppose, agreed to be the general interest of any state, that its people be numerous and rich; men enough to fight in its defence, and enough to pay sufficient taxes to defray the charge; for these circumstances tend to the security of the state, and its protection from foreign power: But it seems not of so much importance whether the fighting be done by John or Thomas, or the tax paid by William or Charles. The iron manufacture employs and enriches British subjects, but is it of any importance to the state, whether the manufacturers live at Brimingham or Sheffield, or both, since they are still within its bounds, and their wealth and persons at its command? Could the Goodwin Sands be laid dry by banks, and land equal to a large country thereby gained to England, and presently filled with English inhabitants, would it be right to deprive such inhabitants of the common privileges enjoyed by other Englishmen, the right of vending their produce in the same ports, and of making their own shoes, because a merchant, or a shoemaker, living on the old land, might fancy it more for his advantage to trade or make shoes for them? Would this be right, even if the land were gained at the expence of the state? And would it not seem less right, if the charge and labour of gaining the additional territory to Britain had been borne by the settlers themselves? And would not the hardship appear yet greater, if the people of the new country should be allowed no representatives in the parliament enacting such impositions? Now I look on the colonies as so many counties gained to Great Britain, and more advantageous to it than if

they

they had been gained out of the sea around its coasts, and joined to its land: For being in different climates, they afford greater variety of produce, and materials for more manufactures; and being separated by the ocean, they increase much more its shipping and seamen; and since they are included in the British empire, which has only extended itself by their means; and the strength and wealth of the parts is the strength and wealth of the whole; what imports it to the general state, whether a merchant, a smith, or a hatter, grow rich in Old or New England? And if, through increase of people, two smiths are wanted for one employed before, why may not the *new* smith be allowed to live and thrive in the *new country*, as well as the *old* one in the *old*? In fine, why should the countenance of a state be *partially* afforded to its people, unless it be most in favour of those, who have most merit? And if there be any difference, those who have most contributed to enlarge Britain's empire and commerce, encrease her strength, her wealth, and the numbers of her people, at the risk of their own lives and private fortunes, in new and strange countries, methinks ought rather to expect some preference.

"With the greatest respect and esteem, I have the honour to be.

Your excellency's most obedient,
And most humble servant."

It is plain from the above account, which Governor Shirley was intimately acquainted with, that the reason why the English colonists received assistance from Britain, was because the English parliament would not suffer them to defend themselves, but wanted to form plans of operation in a country they not know, to drain a perpetual tax from the colonies for an occafional affiftance. They were fo far from fupplicating government for affiftance, that they would willingly have done without it, provided they had been permitted to have purfued their own meafures. Arguments in favour of a war between the members of the fame empire, ought to be exceedingly plain and felf-evident, and the reafons of engaging in it fo convincing to indifferent perfons, and bye-ftanders, on the fide of the party which pretends a right to profecute the other, that there fhould be nothing doubtful or fufpicious in the premifes or the conclufion. Partiality and felf-intereft may blind the eyes of the parties concerned; but the public at large, or fuch as are not engaged in the controverfy, will judge according to truth. We fhall find in the fequel of this hiftory, how differently men have reafoned upon the fprings, and caufe of this unhappy and ruinous war, and how different parties have coloured that fide of the queftion they have efpoufed. Arguments, when they are brought to fupport fanguinary meafures, had much need to be ftrong and well founded: every one of them ought to be as felf-evidently true, and as confiftent with the dictates of the divine mind, as the precepts of the decalogue, otherwife they ought never to be put in practice.

CHAP.

Chap. II.

The distress of the nation through the stoppage of trade—Debates in parliament concerning the repeal of the Stamp Act—the arguments used on both sides of the question—the joy of the nation upon repealing the act—the right of taxation confirmed, &c.

ANNO DOMINI 1766.

IT is no wonder when we consider the transactions of the preceeding two years, that both this country and the colonies were in a distracted and an uneasy situation; commerce was sunk, and the manufactures were in a great measure at a stand; provisions exceedingly dear, and many labourers without employment. Thousands had no visible methods of providing for themselves and families, however willing they were to work to supply their necessities. That source of supply which supported our manufacturers at home was now stopped: The colonists were neither able nor willing to pay for the goods they had received, nor were they disposed to continue their usual trade with the mother country. In America every thing was in a state of anarchy and confusion: The laws were suspended, and the lawless committed many outrages with impunity. Under a pretence of liberty, bad men gave full reins to their vicious inclinations, as is common in a state of universal commotion. The common people, who though they are not in general the most vicious, yet are often easiest misled; when they assembled in bodies went into extravagances of the most licentious kind. The sober part were not able to restrain the impetuosity of a multitude, without law, magistracy, or order; nor did they find it convenient to use means to restrain a temper, which they perceived might on some future occasion, serve the purposes they had in view. They were designed to oppose the stamp act, and they cold do nothing without the aid of the people.

There were two things which gave the colonists an advantage over our manufacturers at home, they were in possession of large quantities of British goods, which were yet unpaid, and they had an extensive country abounding with many necessary articles fitted for all the conveniences of life. These prevented them from feeling so smartly the immediate effects of this universal stagnation in business, occasioned by the stamp act. To these may be added the flame of zeal for liberty being put in such a strong agitation by this new law, made them bear difficulties which in other cases would have been intolerable. Our manufacturers at home not being under the influence of the same enthusiasm, were ready to despond and sink at the prospect of their future distresses; and as many of them had lavishly squandered what they had earned by their labour, they had laid nothing up for a time of calamity. They were therefore oppressed, without having the same source of animation which supported the colonists. The million of debt which the Americans owed the merchants in this country, rendered them incapable to carry on business as formerly, and the effects of this evil were soon felt severely. The poor rates encreased; the poor were ill provided for, and the nation complained; universal discontent reigned in every quarter of the empire, and the ministry were blamed for all. Some at home were for enforcing the stamp act by military power at once, and for sending a powerful armament to give sanction to this new act of parliament. Others considered this measure as both unpolitic and unnatural; like making one member of the body destroy another, and affirmed that it would be better to repeal the act than waste any part of the empire with fire and sword. This was undoubtedly both a rational and judicious opinion; for though they should have forced the Americans to have suffered the stamps to have continued, they could not have forced them to have used them, except they had pleased, unless in certain cases; for provided they had been disposed to have trusted one another upon common paper, they would have had no need of stamps to make their deeds legal; nor could they have forced them to have taken all their necessaries from Britain, when they could have, and make them at home, without reducing them to a state of mere slavery.

The ministry on this occasion were much perplexed: They were pressed on the one hand to enforce the law by coercive measures, and on the other hand desired to repeal the stamp act. The promoters of the stamp law meant to embarrass the ministry by persuading them to use violent measures, and then the reproach would have fallen upon the minister, and they would have been forgotten in the general odium. On the other hand, the courtiers, and their instruments were ready to charge them with sacrificing the honour of the nation and the dignity of the crown. This ministry, which has since gone by the name of the Rockingham ministry, met with much opposition in all their proceedings, both from some popular men, and many of another character; but they pursued such measures as gained

them

them credit with the nation, and when they were changed gave up without *penfion, place,* or *emolument.* I cannot help here reciting a paffage from the Annual Regifter, which fhews what the miniftry had to ftruggle with at this critical period. Says the author, "There were not few that kept aloof from, and in "due time declared againft the miniftry, upon fome "fymptoms which appeared early, of their wanting "that countenance, which as it has been favoura-"ble or adverfe, has determined the fortune of the "feveral fucceffive fyftems of adminiftration for fome "years paft. This part of the oppofition for very "obvious reafons, was by much the moft danger-"ous."

But the miniftry had, what few fince can pretend to, fair and clear characters, and though they were young in office, were in high efteem with the nation; their integrity was above fufpicion, and their abilities feemed to encreafe with the difficulties of their employment. Their conftant attachment to the caufe of liberty had procured them the confidence and goodwill of the people, both which they enjoyed in a very exalted degree. This fhewed both their good fenfe, and the foundnefs of their principles, that though they were in an immediate fenfe the fervants of the fovereign, yet they would not employ their power and authority for any other purpofe except the good of the fubjects. Confidering the difficulties they had to combat, they fhewed as much political wifdom and fagacity as any minifters have done for many years. And it is no reproach to the memory of Mr Pitt, to affirm that they behaved with as much wifdom and fteadinefs, in as difficult a fituation, as ever was exemplified in his miniftry. They had a multitude of jarring interefts to reconcile, a divided

empire

empire to unite, and the miscarriages of the past ministry to rectify; and besides an animosity among brethren to overcome, which is worse to remove then even to conquer an enemy.

What their enemies imagined was impossible for them to accomplish, they effected; they both preserved the dignity of the crown and nation, and prevented the subjects from destroying one another. All their dispatches to the different governors, were delivered with firmness and temper, which, when they were examined before the commons did them great honour; they were found neither to have driven the colonies to desperation, nor to have yielded up the dignity of the crown and nation in any particular. In this administration the Duke of Richmond was one of the secretaries of state, whose abilities as well as integrity has since shone forth conspicuously on the side of true patriotism. It may be presumed that he had a share in the wise direction of measures at this time.

The prudent management of the ministry on this occasion, was severely censured by those who were then and have been since for violent measures; their conduct was called weak, pusillanimous, and feeble, their measures undetermined and without design. But the reason of this censure was obvious; they saw that by the repeal of measures which they had promoted, disgrace would fall upon them, and they wanted to see the executive power embarrassed before the meeting of parliament so far, that the legislature could not in honour recede from supporting it. For this reason the moderation of the Rockingham administration was most severely censured by the opposition. The controversy began now to be discussed at large, and many pamphlets were published on both sides of the question, with very little temper. Had the

cause

cause depended upon the clearness and force of argument, or had each party put themselves in the others place for a little time, the controversy might soon have been ended. But when persons in power form arguments concerning the rights of other men, they are often ready to be so blinded with the intoxicating idea of dominion, that they cannot perceive the truth clearly; and those who defend their own rights when they have a jealousy of government, are ready to mingle envy with sound reasoning. It is not to be supposed that men under the influence of the spirit of party, will clearly see and admit all the force of their opponents arguments; after times will determine with more impartiality and justness which of the arguments used in this dispute are the most solid and convincing. The impartial historian cannot help in his own judgment to take a side; but with regard to his determinations for others, ought not to be too positive. I shall as briefly as possible give an abstract of the arguments on both sides of the question, and leave the reader to determine for himself on which side the truth rests. But it must be observed that while the colonies carry their ideas of liberty to the highest pitch, their opponents seem to imagine that a person by becoming a colonist, forfeits every birthright and privilege of an Englishman.

When the point concerning the right of taxation came to be debated in parliament, it was said upon the side of the colonies, "That by going up to magna charta, and referring to several writs upon record, issued out for the purpose of raising taxes for the crown, and sending representatives to parliament, as well as from the bill of rights, it appears throughout the whole history of our constitution, that no British subject can be taxed except *per communem*

con-

consensum parliamenti, that is, of himself or his own representative; and this is that first and general right as British subjects, with which the first inhabitants of the colonies emigrated; for the right does not depend upon their charters: the charters were but the exterior modeling of the constitution of the colonies: but the great interior fundamental of their constitution, is this general right of a British subject, which is the very first principle of British liberty,—No man shall be taxed but by himself, or by his representative.

"That the counties palatine of Chester, Durham, and Lancaster, were not taxed but in their own assemblies or parliament; till at different periods in our history they were melted into our present form of parliamentary representation. That the body of the clergy till very lately taxed themselves, and granted the king benevolences. That the marches of Wales had a right of taxing themselves, till they had sent members to parliament. And from this circumstance has continued the stile of the king's proclamations and of our acts of parliament to this day, although unnecessarily to be named, especially the principality of Wales, and the town of Monmouth, as they do that of Berwick.

"That many people carry their idea of a parliament too far, in supposing that a parliament can do every thing: but that is not true, and if it were, it is not right constitutionally, for there might be an arbitrary power in parliament as well as in one man. There are many things a parliament cannot do. It cannot make itself executive, nor dispose of offices that belong to the crown. It cannot take any man's property, even that of the meanest cottager, as in the cases of inclosures, without his being heard.

"The lords cannot reject a money bill from the commons, nor the commons erect themselves into a court of justice. The parliament could not tax the clergy, till such time as they were represented in parliament. Nor can the parliament of England tax Ireland. The charters of the colonies, which are derived from the prerogative, are in fact only so many grants from the crown, are not the only rights the colonies have to being represented before they are taxed: they as British subjects take up their rights and liberties from a higher origin than their charters only. They take them up from the same origin and foundation, from whence they flow to all Englishmen, from magna charta, and the natural right of the subject. By that rule of right, the charters of the colonies, like all other crown grants, are to be restricted and interpreted, for the benefit, not the prejudice of the subjects. Had the first inhabitants of the colonies renounced all connection with their mother country, they might have renounced their original right; but when they emigrated under the authority of the crown, and the national sanction, they went out from hence at the hazard of their lives and fortunes, with all the first great privileges of Englishmen on their backs. But at the same they were not bound, nor could be bound by the penal laws of this country, from the severity of which they fled, to climates remote from the heavy hand of power; and which they hoped to find more friendly to their principles of civil and religious liberty. It is upon this ground that it has been universally received as law, that no acts of parliament made here, and particularly those which enact any penalties, are binding upon the colonists, unless they are expressly named. The inhabitants of the colonies once removed from the domestic legislation of the mother country, are no more dependent upon it in the general system, than the *Isle of Man* is, or than in the feudal system of Europe. many subordinate principalities are dependent on the jurisdiction of the *Seignior Suzerain*, or Lord Paramount, but owing only a limited obedience.

"It is not meant by what has been said, to effect the case of any external duties laid upon their ports, or of any restrictions, which by the act of navigation, or other acts, are laid upon their commerce; for they are in the same case as all other colonies belonging to the rest of the maritime powers in Europe, who have shut up their colonies, which out-grew their mother countries, such as Carthage, the northern emigrants, &c. Precedents were also quoted from what happened in the Netherlands, and other places, which should serve as a beacon to warn us from pursuing such measures as brought about those revolutions."

The arguments that were used without doors on both sides were much of the same nature with the following: "What a noise," says an advocate on the one side, "have we had of late about American charters, American legislation, American freeholders, and the privileges of those freeholders? But is there any legislation in America? Are there any freeholders there? No man who knows any thing of the law of England will assert that there is any legislation in America, or one freeholder in that part of the world. The king has no power of legislation, and he cannot by his charters convey to any class of his subjects a power not resident in the crown. The parliament, including his majesty, as the head thereof, has a power of legislation, but they possess that power unalienably.

"The power of legislation is not a chattle to be disposed of by grant or other conveyance. It is a trust granted by the common law for the good of the community, and for their good must remain with the august body in which it resides. The power of making bye-laws, for the utility of subordinate bodies politic, is a quite different affair. That power is often created by the parliament, which has essentially, in itself, all the powers of government. But charters from the crown, not confirmed in parliament, can convey no jurisdiction whatever, because the king is not the fountain of law, as he is of honour.

"All our courts, from those in Westminster-hall to those in manors, are founded on the custom of England, *time out of mind*, or upon the law of the land; that is, *statutes made in parliament* The parliament only can create new courts and new jurisdictions. But as the king must govern by the law, he cannot make that law upon which his authority rests, nor by his charters convey to others a power which he enjoys not.

"Every foot of ground in England lies in some manor, which is itself the creature of custom *time out of mind*. These manors anciently possessed all jurisdiction civil and criminal; and this jurisdiction was exerted in the court of freeholders, in which the lord, or his steward, was the judge, the freeholders serving as jurors, by virtue of their freeholds. Thus you see that our freeholders are, by virtue of their freehold, possessed of a radical judicative authority in manors; which they are entitled to by the common law, and possess their estates by the same tenure by which his majesty holds his crown. They are indebted to no prince for this estate and judicative authority thereto appendant. Their title to their lands is a tide of independence, and in every respect equal to the royal title by which the crown is held.

"And as these freehold estates are of a very particular nature with respect to their origin, so they are conveyed in a very particular manner. They cannot be taken by a writ of *fieri facias*. And if they are seized by a writ of *elegit*, one moiety only of the estate can be applied, for payment of the debt and costs on which the judgment is founded, the other moiety must remain for his support and maintenance. The freehold descends to the heir, discharged of all debts, or specialties.

"Now, we have seen what an English freehold is. Are there any such estates in America? I am certain there are not. There can be no manors in that part of the world, for we can shew the origin of their tenures. Their properties, pretended legislative authority, and the existence of what they call freeholds can be traced from prerogative. Are our freeholds owing to human beneficence? No; We can name several persons who oppressed us; but the Americans can point out none who have conferred upon us our estates, or any privileges whatever. Is there an estate in America which may not be taken by the same writ that takes in execution a negro or a horse? The whole course of chancery proves that their estates are only commercial chattles, subject to the disposition of the last will of the owner, and chargeable with all the debts of the deceased proprietor. And lest any doubt should arise about the propriety of these decrees in equity, equalizing a foreign plantation to a personal estate, there was a statute made in the fifth year of the preceding reign, declarative of the common law in this respect, and statuting that foreign plantations should only be regarded in the light of personal estates

After that law, what man in his right senses can dignify those estates with the name of freeholds?

"The American estates are destitute of the principal characteristic of a freehold. They are derived from royal grants for the improvement of commerce. The pretended American freeholders are not original members of any court, by virtue of their freeholds. They have no manors, nor manor-courts in America, and consequently no courts to which the pretended American freeholders repair, by virtue of their freeholds, and in consequence of a title paramount to all human laws. Why then should they pretend to equalize their supposed freeholds with ours? An absolute ignorance of all and common-sense could only give birth to such injudicious conduct. Our freeholders have a share in the legislation; because by customs as ancient as those that establish government, they are entitled to rule in a certain district of the kingdom. Can the Americans boast of the existence of any such customs among them, or of estates and judicative authority derived out of these customs? Why then should the pretend to be freeholders, and as such only subject to the legislation of their own election.

"The Americans will, perhaps, reply, that they serve on juries when called by the King's writ into the supreme court of their respective provinces. But this happens not as with us by the excellency of tenures, whose origin is unknown, but is owing to the grace of those princes who, without the authority of law, granted them that constitution. Are tenures flowing from the prince equal to tenures held independent of the crown? Surely not. The Americans have no rights but from royal grants; and of consequence those rights must not be extended beyond their natural meaning, or interpreted to the prejudice of those

those who by an inherent right, independent of the crown, govern the whole kingdom. The privileges of persons claiming under so high a tenure, cannot be impaired by deeds from the crown, and consequently the government of our parliament must reach over all the English dominions, as if no such grants had been made, and no estates derived out of them."

A Writer on the other side says, "The question if properly understood, is not concerning a *three-penny stamp*, but liberty. Not *that* liberty which is the tool of contending parties, the key to power, or the reviler of a minister's cradle; but *that* true and genuine liberty which expands and ennobles the heart of the poorest freeholder, and prevents his property from being touched, but by the permission of those who by the constitution are his representatives in parliament.

"The infatuation of some people here, while they endeavour by the most frivolous arguments, to establish a right to tax America, in direct violation of this animating principle of their constitution, is to the last degree deplorable. It shall be my endeavours to shew here in a few words, how such a right would be directly subversive of our constitution, and therefore of our liberties. And here, I shall not enter into the question whether America be in the manor of East-Greenwich, (a frivolous equivocation derived from the casual use of this expression in the Massachusett's charter of King Charles the second) nor yet whether American corn be *indigestible* or *unpalatable*, (though I profess I think it exceedingly palatable) because these do not seem to me to be quite pertinent to the dispute, and are indeed unworthy refutation or animadversion. The lands in America are as much freehold and derive that tenure from the same hand, as are the lands of England; and the holders of them, on the same tenure,

are

are as much freeholders as those of England. Now it must be known to every one, that, at this day, there is not a freeholder in England who does not give his vote for a representative in the assembly of the commons of England; who from thence derive their name, and their sole right of taxing the property of the people. Nor is there any freeholder in the nation so ignorant of his right, and of the foundation of his liberty, that he would not complain of a violation of it if he were deprived of the privilege of voting for such a representative; yet we are subjecting the American freeholders to that very grievance, of which we ourselves would complain as destructive of our freedom; we are subjecting them to be taxed by representatives, in the election of whom they have not one voice. They are freeholders as we are, they choose representatives to tax them as we do; and it seems inconsistent with the nature of the British constitution, and subversive of the freedom of the common people, that the property of a freeholder should be taxed by any representatives but those for which he votes, and thereby empowers to tax him. Let the case, for a moment, be our own, and suppose ourselves liable to be taxed by representatives chosen by the freeholders of America; should we hesitate an instant in declaring it an absolute violation of our libery, and a slavish imposition? Therefore the right of taxing the American freeholders, which some would establish here, must needs seem as unconstitutional and arbitrary with respect to the Americans. With what justice then can we thus attempt to violate the liberty of the Americans? Is not this the height of infatuation?

"Having thus proved, upon fair and unquestionable principles, that we can have no right to tax the freeholders in America, I shall add a word or two upon what is termed a *rebellion* in America. The only occurrences there, which can have given the least ground for such a charge, are the tumultuous proceedings of the mob, and the resolves of the assemblies. With regard to the former, I would only beg leave to ask, whether it is usual to call the riotous actions of a mob rebellion? Were the weavers, when they assembled together, surrounded the parliament-house, offered most dangerous violence to the coach of a noble peer, and if I mistake not, did him a personal injury, attempted to pull down his house, and assaulted his majesty's guards with stones, so as to occasion the death of some of them, were they called *rebels*, or *rioters?* Has the American mob been more outrageous? and are they and the whole colonists of America, who never were guilty of any such riots, to be branded with the most odious and detested name of *rebels?* Let us now consider how far the resolves of the American assemblies can be called rebellious. I have already proved, that England can have no right to tax America. The stamp-act seemed to them therefore unconstitutional, and a direct violation of the rights of the American assemblies, who are the true and only representatives of the freeholders, and have the sole constitutional right of taxing their property. The assemblies, by their resolves, immediately asserted their rights, and remonstrated against this infringement of them, with a spirit and freedom which was well worthy the free representatives of a free people; and can this be termed rebellion? In France, in Germany, in Asia, it might have been esteemed such; and is it not a melancholy proof, that this country is degenerating into their servile state and abject sentiments, when

the

the voice of freedom, and the assertion of liberty, meets with the same estimation? The American assemblies were impelled to these resolves by the strongest motives of justice to themselves, to their constituents, and to their posterity. Had they tamely surrendered their liberties, they had been the most contemptible of mankind; they bravely asserted them, and are——"

There is no other method to convince either party of the weakness of their arguments, than first to make them consider whether the authority to tax belongs to England or to Englishmen, and provided the present inhabitants who are now in England were in America, and the colonists in England, would the right of taxation be continued or altered? If it belong to this country, in consequence of the right of manorship, who ever succeeds to the manors must have a claim of right to liberty, and nobody else; and if the colonists were to change with the present inhabitants, they would have a right to tax them, which they would not be ready to submit to. The claims of so extensive liberty as the colonists require, appear inconsistent with their former connections with their mother country, and the authority which the mother country claims as her right over the colonists, makes her rather a step-mother than a kind parent. Were they to change situations, neither the one nor the other should incline to have such treatment, as they on this occasion were disposed to give each other. Upon the principles of nature and reason the colonists main arguments cannot be confuted; upon the mutual policy of the present government of the empire they have no force. It is a part of the unhappiness of all the present systems of government, that in them reason and policy are frequently at variance, and the passions and interests of leading men, prevail more powerfully, than the general good of society. It is the best government where a just balance is kept,—where the interest of every man is the general good of the whole. This is a maxim that might be practised provided policy was founded upon morality: but in the present state of nations it is only a speculation, which is a great pity.

Two bills were brought in this session of parliament, one for securing the dependency of the colonies upon the mother country, and another for repealing the stamp-act. The first met with no opposition, the latter was warmly disputed.

The enemies of the ministry, who were many of them, under a secret influence, which some think has been baneful to these kingdoms, strained every nerve to prevent the repeal of the stamp-act. Arguments were drawn from the outrageousness of the behaviour of the Americans, and the insult they had offered to the dignity of the English government, and the consequences that would follow provided the act was repealed.—That it would shew such weakness and pusillanimity in government, as would encourage the Colonists to give fresh affronts, and lessen the respect of the King's subjects to the dignity of the crown, and the authority of the laws. It was urged further, that as the power of taxation was an essential branch of authority, it ought in justice to be exercised over all the members of the empire, in proportion to their several abilities; that it would shew a degree of partiality unworthy of good government, to exempt one part of the subjects from a duty which others were obliged to pay, and from burdens which the rest of the community were under a necessity to bear.—That it was contrary to the trust reposed by the people in the legislature, and tended to deftroy all confidence upon which government is founded. It was denied that the colonifts were unable to bear the weight of the tax impofed by the ftamp-act, and it was afferted as an inftance to the contrary, that if the debt contracted by them in the late war, 1,755,000l. had been already paid in the courfe of only three years, that the far greater part of their remaining burden, amounting to 760.000l. would be difcharged in two years more. Other arguments were ufed; the general burden of the mother country, the ability of the Colonifts, their exemption from all taxation, and their peremptory refufal to contribute to any relief from the public load of debt that the nation groaned under.

It was replied that feveral of thefe objections had no weight in them, as all the confequences they fuppofed were guarded againft by the bill for fecuring the dependence of the colonies upon the mother country, which both fecured the dignity of Great-Britain, and her conftitutional fuperiority over America. In fupport of the repeal, it was argued that the colonifts had really borne their proper fhare of the public burdens according to the confeffion of the other party; for the heavy debt which they had contracted during the war was a fufficient proof that they had contributed largely to the public expence; and their being paid back a part of it fince, was a convincing evidence that the parliament were perfuaded they had done more than they were well able to do. It was further urged that nothing could be more diftant from the fact, than the affertion that they paid no taxes; for they even paid many which the parliament had impofed upon them. They paid port duties, which lay heavy upon their trade; before ties laid on by the authority of the provinces; many excises; a land tax in many provinces; an heavy poll-tax; besides a faculty-tax upon all personal estates and acquisitions, amounting in some provinces to five or six shillings in the pound; so that the assertion of their not being taxed, or contributing to the public expence, was totally without foundation.

The friends of the ministry, and of the colonists, demonstrated that the Americans were poor, and were indebted four millions to the merchants in Britain; who, as they were creditors to such an amount, were really the proprietors of a great part of what the Americans seemed to possess: That the suppression of manufactures in America, by obliging them to take every sort which they used, from Britain, was making them pay, in one species of taxation, all other kinds of taxes; and in fact, making them the chief supporters of public burdens. Considering their great distance from this country, it was urged that it was impossible for the people here to be so well acquainted with the state of American affairs, as to be able to judge minutely concerning the propriety of a revenue tax: That without being well acquainted with the state of the colonists, we, in this country might be ready to oppress them, which government should above all things, endeavour to avoid: That it was the best policy to keep to commercial views, and pursue the advantages that attended them, which would less oppress the colonists, and would enable them sooner to pay their debts to our merchants.— These are a few of the arguments on both sides, on this occasion, and it will be allowed by all who are clear of prejudice, that the ministry had the better in this dispute. *Justice, sound policy, clemency,* and *humanity* were united in their reasonings; whereas the

opposition

opposition breathed *domination tyranny*, and *destruction* through the whole of this debate.

Notwithstanding the violence and vigour of those in opposition, and all the secret influence of an invisible power, the bill passed, upon a division, by a majority of 275 to 167, and was carried up to the lords by above two hundred members of the house of commons. The approbation with which it was introduced into the upper house, did not secure it from a vigorous opposition: Thirty-three lords entered a protest against it at the second reading, and twenty-eight at the third reading: It was however carried by a majority of thirty-four lords, and in three days received the royal assent. The repeal of this law, was the cause of more universal joy through the dominions of Britain, than probably ever was known by any one event. It could not but do the hearts of the promoters of this appeal good, to see and hear of so many millions of their fellow subjects rejoicing and exulting at an event which proceeded from the wisdom, benevolence, justice, and clemency, of men whom they had entrusted with their concerns. There was more true glory to the king, the parliament, and the ministry, in repealing this act, than if they had all united to enforce it by fleets and armes, fire and sword. There can be little true glory in forcing laws by military execution, but there is much honour in making such statutes or repealing them, as give joy to a whole empire. This is one of the glories of the present reign, and for the sake of this noble act of wisdom, every humane person will be ready to forgive an hundred faults. Whatever may happen in future times, it may be said that George the Third had once a wise ministry, and put his hand to a noble and illustrious deed. In all cases that are problematical

nothing

nothing displays the wisdom of a legislature more than the pursuing measures that are lenient in their own nature, and tend to conciliate the affections of the subjects to government. The infirmities of human nature require that the exertions of government should be tender, and that power which is lodged in the hands of governors to preserve men's lives, should never be employed to destroy them, as long as any other method can be adopted.

There was also this sessions a bill brought in and passed, for securing the dependance of the colonies upon Great Britain; and another for granting indemnity to such as had incurred penalties on account of the stamp-act, and an order made by government, that the provinces of North America should indemnify such as had suffered by the late riots, by making a compensation for the losses they had sustained, which they some time after accordingly did. The cyder-act was also repealed, and another duty laid on in the place of it, so that one popular law succeeded another, and the ministry encreased in popularity as they were envied by those in opposition. The satisfaction arising from the repeal of this act was heightened in proportion to the degree of discontent that had arisen from the passing of it, and the cyder counties tasted the same pleasure with their brethren in America, which they enjoyed at the same time, and testified their thankfulness by universal joy. As men in growing really wiser generally grow better, so as the ministry encreased in wisdom, they proceeded in promoting acts of utility. By their conferences with the merchants in North America, and those of the West Indies, they acquired more knowledge of their trade, and the method of conducting it, and by virtue of some petitions from trading towns in England, a bill was passed for opening free ports in the West Indies

dies under certain limitations and restrictions. Several new and important regulations were likewise made in the general system of commerce in the colonies, and some restrictions taken off, that had been long complained of, as an heavy clog upon trade and business. These popular acts made the ministry the idol of the mercantile part of the nation, who could not help being highly pleased at the attention which had been paid to their interests, so different, from what former administrations had generally practised.

Some other acts and resolutions were passed this session, which all tended either to ease, or remove the burdens of the people; among which may be reckoned the repeal of the old duties upon houses and windows, and the new bill, by which the duties are much more equitably laid on, and more easy to the lower and middling degrees of people. It was also resolved that the taking up of people by general warrants, or the seizing of their papers, except in such cases as are prescribed by acts of parliament are illegal.

The ministry had hitherto succeeded in the most prosperous manner; they had weathered the storm of opposition during this session, and gained every point they had attempted in parliament. They had secured the confidence and good will of the public, in the highest degree; they also had aquired some credit in their foreign transactions: an advantageous commercial treaty had been concluded with the empress of Russia, and the long contested Canada bills, were settled, to the satisfaction of the owners; and they had made some progress in reviving the long neglected affair of the Manilla ransom. Such was the success of the ministry, that it was now thought that they were

were securely settled and fixed in their present situation. It was at this time, to the surprise of the whole nation, that notwithstanding these appearances the ministry was changed. The present reign had hitherto been remarkable for changes of this sort, and the reason generally assigned for this political phænomonon was, that a secret influence of an invisible agent which did not appear publickly directed the springs of government, and produced so many and various revolutions in the ministry. Whether this opinion proceeded from jealousy or some other cause I will not pretend to determine, but it was the general belief of the public at that time, upon whatever principle it might be founded. Such a sudden overturn in the ministerial department, when all the nation applauded the measures of government, could not be accounted for, upon any rational principle of operation; for as the ministry were the servants whom the king had appointed to manage the public affairs of the nation, and they had discharged their duty with universal approbation, the turning them out of office when they were so agreeable to the public, seemed to declare, that the interests of the king and the nation were different, or that the sovereign did not sustain the people proper judges of their own interests. The ministry finished their career with so much honour to themselves, and satisfaction to the nation, and withal, behaved in such a disinterested manner, that their popularity increased after their dismission from their office. They had gained nothing to themselves, and secured nothing to their friends, and retired without place, pension, or emolument. The public expressed the sense they had of their services, by numerous addresses presented to the marquis of Rockingham on this occasion, while they shewed their displeasure at displacing men, who had behaved so worthily in the execution of the trust reposed in them. Upon the 30th of July the Duke of Grafton was appointed first Lord of the Treasury, in the place of the Marquis of Rockingham; the Earl of Shelburne, secretary of state in the room of the Duke of Richmond; Lord Cambden, lord high chancellor, in the place of the Earl of Northington, the Right Honourable Charles Townshend, in the room of the Right Honourable William Dowdeswell, and the Right Honourable Willam Pitt, lately created Viscount Pinsent, and Earl of Chatham, lord privy seal. Many other changes took place, in the different departments of government, which by no means seemed to ensure a long continuance of this new administration. Though some popular men were now admitted into administration, the public considered this only as a scheme of the favourite, to lessen their popularity, and bring them into disesteem with the nation. This ministry was something like the king of Babylon's image, which he saw in his dream, partly iron and partly clay. It was foreseen that men of such different principles, would not long unite, in carrying on a system of government. Lord Chatham, by dividing the interests of those that were the favourites of the nation, sunk greatly in his popularity, and his receiving a place, pension, and title, contributed not a little to deface, his former greatness. Such is the uncertainty of human applause and popularity, that what is gained by diligence and hard application, may be lost in an instant of time beyond recovery.

The new ministry came to their office at a time, when circumstances combined to render their duty a task of great difficulty; they not only succeeded a set of men who were popular and successful, but found new difficulties arise which they had not foreseen, or would perceive. The prices of provisions were now come to an exorbitant height, and the poor of the nation were in great distress; there was no just proportion between the price of those articles that are essentially necessary to human life, and the value of the money that could be obtained by daily labour. The corn was exported to other countries, and the poor at home were greatly distressed: this occasioned mobs, riots and disorders in the nation, and produced many unhappy consequences. In the month of September a proclamation was issued, to prohibit the exportation of corn, and messengers were sent to the sea-ports to see that the terms of the proclamation were observed, and to prevent such ships as were loaded from sailing with their cargoes. The proclamation, though it was well intended, was illegal, and was an assuming of a power which the constitution does not permit to the crown; it was therefore the foundation of several severe debates in parliament. Though the expedient at the time was both necessary and popular, yet the mode of the transaction was considered by the more discerning as a thing dangerous, as thereby the crown assumed a power to dispense with the laws of the land. This was one of those evils which had been most effectually provided against at the revolution; at which time, it had been declared to be utterly inconsistent with the English constitution, and contrary to the known laws, statutes, and freedom of the kingdom. The advisers and executors of this proclamation, were therefore exposed to a severe censure: but as their intention was good, and the effects of their proceedings salutary, it would have been justice in extreme to have taken the advantage of the statutes against men who had done all in their power to relieve the present distress of the kingdom. A bill was therefore brought in to indemnify all persons who had acted in obedience to the late act of council, concerning the embargo.

This bill, when it was brought in, secured the inferior officers against prosecution for their acting contrary to law, but left out the council who had advised the proclamation; and it also wanted an introduction to point out the illegality of the measure. This was the occasion of much altercation, in which some of the ministry who had been formerly very popular, and admired as the friends of liberty, deserted its cause, and advanced doctrines entirely contrary to the principles of the revolution. They not only vindicated the measure concerning the embargo as a necessary expedient, in a critical situation, but defended it as a matter of right; and maintained, that a dispensing power, in cases of state necessity, was one of the prerogatives of the crown. That which rendered this proclamation more suspicious and unpopular, was, that a proclamation had been issued before, against forestalling upon the same day that the parliament was prorogued, from the sixteenth of September, till the eleventh of November following. It was argued on this occasion, that provided the ministry had not had some intention to introduce an arbitrary power, they would have advised the King to have called the parliament, and laid on the embargo by an act of the legislature; for by such a long and unnecessary prorogation, all advice of parliament was precluded; that the reason given for the proclamation was that his Majesty had not an opportunity to take the advice of parliament, while yet the proclamation for the embargo was issued sixteen days after that for proroguing the parliament. All this was urged, to prove against the ministry some design of pursuing arbitrary measures. After many strong arguments had been used against the measure concerning the embargo, it was inferred, that if the doctrine of the suspension of the laws was admitted on a plea of state necessity, as constitutional, the revolution could be deemed nothing but a successful rebellion, and a lawless and wicked invasion of the rights of the crown; the bill of rights, a false and scandalous libel, and an infamous imposition upon both prince and people; and James the second neither abdicated nor forfeited, but was robbed of his crown. Consistency is a thing not always to be found universally observed in the practice of politicians; they often make use of government to serve their own purposes, and when they have once committed an error, they endeavour to find arguments to defend it. There is no reason to believe that the ministry at this time had the smallest intention of violating the constitution, and therefore the arguments brought against their proceedings, could not have the same force that they had in the case of James the second; whose designs to subvert the constitution were palpable and evident; but it must be allowed that when they defended, as a right, this stretch of prerogative, it was but fair to shew them the inconsistency of their arguments and proceedings.

1767. The operations of the human passions, in the systems of policy, are a mystery not easily unveiled; it often happens that when simple and undesigning people have given their plaudit to measures, which from the best evidence they could obtain, they thought deserved approbation, that persons of refinement will presently attempt to prove that they were absurd, ridiculous, and inconsistent. The repealing of the stamp act, which obtained so much praise to the former ministry, was attacked by a set of venal writers, as a piece of the worst policy, and the most inconsistent with the dignity of Britain, of any thing that had happened for many years. Mildness in government was interpreted pusillanimity and weakness; and an aversion to hostility, and bloodshed, was considered as a want of concern or indifference, for the welfare of the mother country. Topics of this sort now became common, which made persons of discernment conclude that the measures adopted by those who promoted the repeal of the stamp act, were not agreeable to an invisible agent, who now intended to direct the springs of government; and that another plan of operation would be adopted. The Marquis of Rockingham and his friends had been turned out of their offices before that the disturbances in America were totally settled, and some offensive acts yet remained, to which they had as much aversion as the stamp act. But before we proceed to consider the new disturbances that arose this year, and their causes, it may be necessary to consider the pre-monitions that were given to this nation and the government concerning their proceedings towards the colonists; and this I shall do in the words of the writers themselves.

"The British empire on the continent of America is well known to be extremely extensive, and is, by our late conquests, and the cessions that have been made to us, become entirely compact. In the variety of colonies which it comprehends, there are all kinds of soils and climates; so that there can be no doubt entertained, but that with a farther clearance of the country (as yet abounding with wild forests) fertility of soil, and salubrity of air, will become improved, and even perfected, particularly in the moderating of heat and of cold, while to improvements and population there can hardly any end be foreseen.

"Little doubt can be entertained, that this vast

country will in time become the the greatest and most prosperous empire that perhaps the world has ever seen. The earth is well known to contain abundance of mines, and probably of every species that can be said to enrich a country; so likewise, in time, all products whatever may be expected from the soil. Its seas, banks, bays, coasts and rivers, we also know have the most abundant fisheries, so that their can be no natural impediment to its becoming greatly powerful and prosperous.

"The least computation of white inhabitants, at present, is two millions of souls: and if thereto are added the Indian tribes, Negroes and Mulattoes, perhaps the whole number of inhabitants lately mentioned in the public papers, may not be an exaggeration, in their being estimated at five millions. But in considering the progress of population, I shall consider the white inhabitants only; because in proportion is they increase it may probably be conjectured, that those of the other colours will diminish.

"The American writers all agree in acknowledging, that from the encouragements which are given to early marriage, from the facility of acquiring settlements on lands, and the temptations there are to make them, in the inexhaustible sources of improvement in those kinds of property, that the numbers of white inhabitants become doubled in five and twenty years. Let us then consider, upon the bottom on which the colonies stand at present, at how rapid a rate their population must increase. In twenty-five years their numbers will probably have grown from two millions to four, in fifty years, eight, in seventy-five years to sixteen, and in an hundred years to thirty-two millions; which is such a striking prospect of increasing population in those regions, as should induce

induce us to desert the idea of being long able to subject them by our power, and make us adopt, as its substitute, true policy, for that purpose which, perhaps, for many ages may preserve what mere power might fail to secure for a few years.

"There are no subjects so frequently handled as those of government, policy, and trade, but in which there is discoverable much ignorance and prepossession, and those often among such as should best understand them; for many judgments are continually seen to be framed, without right information, and too many false ones are often obtruded on government, and the world, from self-interested motives; so that dishonesty and ignorance appear co-operating together, to our great national injury.

"Some late unfortunate transactions that have proved greatly irritating to our colonists, have set them, as we see, upon estimating for themselves; and that turn, which has perhaps been injudiciously given to their contemplations, has served to convince them of their utility to us, which they seem inclinable to rate at its very utmost estimation, and accordingly thereon set a value on themselves; and we ought to be aware how very strongly the estimations of their own utility, will, on all occasions, operate on the minds of individuals, or bodies of men.

"The North-Americans now say and write, that they have ever been toiling for the benefit of the mother country, in which, if they are not considered as children, their treatment is that of slaves; and therefore, if attempted to be oppressed, they must unite in their own defence. They accordingly cry out for union; and we even see, by the public papers, that there is to be a conference, or congress of deputies for that purpose, which is first proposed for reprefentation only; but fhould they not therein fucceed, ought we not to be aware of what they next may proceed to confult on, and what may prove the confequences of either rooted hatred, or rafh defperation?

"I, who was never in the colonies, nor have any particular connections with them, do not take upon my felf to vindicate their opinions or proceedings, or to plead partially in their behalf; but have endeavoured to regulate my thoughts by the principles of right policy, when I venture to cenfure thofe, who are preffing for a rigid exertion of authority; becaufe I am well convinced, that there are occafions when every kind of authority may find it prudent to yield upon critical exigencies, as every intelligent man muft know, is occafionally the cafe in all countries upon earth. The higheft authority has often done it with true wifdom in this kingdom, as I need but inftance in the year 1733, with regard to the propofed excife on wine and tobacco, and in the year 1755, with refpect to the law for allowing the naturalizing of Jews; concerning the utility or propriety of which ftate meafures, any more than of thefe regarding America, I deliver no opinions of my own; but I muft applaud every relaxation for the fake of reftoring harmony, or preventing defperation.

"From true principles of policy and commerce, I, however, venture to pronounce, that whatever reftrictions tend to prevent our colonifts, either of North-America, or the Weft-Indies, from enriching themfelves by other ftates, are of prejudice to the mother-country, becaufe all the riches which they acquire, muft, in one fhape or another, finally center among us, for which conviction, I defire no better authority, than thofe barometers of balances the courfes of exchange; and how immensely they are against every one of our colonies, must by all men be known. If therefore, from whatever they are capable by any means to get, they only subsist themselves, with being kept in a state of deep debt to us, what have we to desire more, and whom can we so much injure by restrictions as ourselves?

"Restraints on their trade must then, in their nature, be impolitic; or whatever trade they carry-on, if they get but a balance in their favour, which one way or other they must do, it will turn out to our advantage; and surely, of all instruments for suppressing trade, if otherwise, the military and marine are the last to be employed, because their arbitrary laws and principles are quite incompatible with commerce, which can never flourish but with mildness and encouragement; nor ought vice-admiralty-courts to be entrusted with powers over commerce; so likewise, in proportion to the remoteness of the scene of transactions from the seat of government, will ever be the degrees of the danger from trusting them therewith.

"So, with regard to a medium of traffic, what could we desire more, than that our colonies should content themselves with a paper currency; in order to be enabled to send all the bullion they could possibly acquire, in payments to us? Was not this contenting themselves with working for money, or effects, to purchase manufactures, and commodities of us? And should not we have been contented with getting all their real wealth, and leaving them with such a substitute as a paper currency?

"With regard to their taxes likewise, if they have not money to pay them, and also to purchase our manufactures whatever is gained in one way, must be lost to us in another: and surely it need not be rehow ruinous the loss of that trade of our supply to them, must prove to us. It surely would be time enough for us to think of taxing the Americans, when they had found the means of getting more money than they wanted to pay us in the way of trade, but the demanding it of them while they had it not, was reducing them to the branded Egyptain slavery, of making bricks without straw.

"In short, our great object, with regard to North America, is that of vending our manufactures, which the more they are enabled to buy, so much the better it must be for us, in the employment of our people at home, and in the returns we receive: and the more we adhere to this general scheme of common interest, and the less we perplex ourselves with particular and intricate ones, the safer and more advantageous will be the course we shall take, as well for the peace, as the prosperity of both countries.

"But I am afraid the true fact is, in this country of self-interested bodies and individuals, all pursuing their own good to the hurt and danger of the community, that we are more jealous of the trade than of the power of the North Americans, which is a solecism in policy that is founded in short-sighted self-interest, to which, in the end, it will be found to prove fatal.

"To form a right judgment * concerning the state of the colonies, we should, in the first place, consider the produce of their agriculture in enumerated commodities; which, with all their other products, sent to Britain are well known, both from the accounts of the custom-house, merchants, and planters; all which have been carefully examined for many years past, and from these it appears, that the value of all their

* Present State of Great Britain and America.

their enumerated commodities is but 767,000 l. *per annum*; even the highest computation does not bring it to 800,000 l. meaning in neat proceeds to the planters. Their value has indeed always been computed at 600,000 l. till within these few years past. But every one, who is acquainted with the colonies, may see, that their enumerated commodities, are the chief part of their produce ; every thing they make, indeed, is for remittances to Britain, in order to purchase their necessaries, and to pay their debts ; whence we may be very certain, that their non-enumerated commodities, sold in other countries, are not equal in value to the enumerated, which are sent to Britain. Accordingly, the first are computed at 700,000 l. a year at most ; and if we were to enter into the particulars, no one could make them amount to that sum. Thus the produce of all the colonies in North America amounts at most to 1,500,000 l. per annum, above what they consume among themselves ; and we shall see below, that it cannot well exceed 1,400,000 l. All that they import into Great Britain, both in enumerated commodities, and what they purchase with their, amounts at most, by the rates at the custom-house, but to 1,066,491 l. per annum.

" By the custom-house accounts, from the year 1756 to 1761 inclusive, the state of the trade between Great Britain and North America, during these six years of war, was as follows :

		£.
" Annual exports from Britain to North America on an average	- -	2045144
Imports into Britain	- - -	752338
Balance due to Britain	- -	1292806

" By the same accounts from 1762 to 1764, both

included, since the peace, that trade is thus stated:

	£.
Exports from Britain on an average	2022445
Imports into Britain	1066491
Balance due to Britain	955954

"In these nine years, since the commencement of the war, from 1756 to 1764 inclusive, the following is the state of the whole on an average:

	£.
Exports from Britain	2037577
Imports into Britain	856756
Balance due to Britain	1180521
Total exports in the nine years	18338199
Total imports	7713506
Total balance due to Britain in nine years	10624693

"Now, as the colonies exported to the value of eighteen millions, and owe five or six millions to Britain, they cannot have paid more than thirteen millions in these nine years, which is 1,444,000 l. *per annum*; and as people who are so much in debt, are obliged to pay their all, this must be their annual income, and agrees with the above account of their produce.

	£.
Now, as their enumerated commodities amount to	767000
The value of their non-enumerated commodities must be	977000
Total	1444000

"But as the entries at the custom-house are too well known

known to exceed the real value of the exports, this income of the colonies cannot be so much as these accounts make it, and cannot exceed 1,400,000 l. per annum. It is indeed impossible to bring such accounts to a certain precision; but from this state of them we may be well assured, that the annual income of all the North American colonies cannot exceed a million and a half a year, and it is probably not so much.

"From these accounts it appears, that the annual balance of trade against North America in favour of Britain has been for the last nine years 1,180,000 l. but as that balance was greater in the time of war, it may be reckoned now in the time of peace about a million a year, so long as they export to the value of two millions from Britain. In the last nine years this balance has amounted to ten millions, which is certainly more than they could pay, if we consider their income. This confirms the accounts of the merchants, who make the colonies so much indebted to them. By these accounts, this balance has accumulated to a debt of five millions; and as many accounts have not been received, it is computed, that the whole debt due to Britain in North America, amounts at least to five millions and a half, if not six millions.

"Besides this, they owe a public debt of 797,000 l. Thus their public and private debts amount to more than six millions of money; the interest of which alone, at five per cent. comes to 350,000 l. but as many of them pay eight per cent. according to the custom of the trade, the interest of their debts may be reckoned at half a million a-year; especially if we add the loss they sustain in the exchange by making remittances of money, which has of late been thirty and forty per cent. and the ten per cent. they pay on protested bills, with six per cent. per annum, till they are discharged,

charged. If we add this to the balance of trade they owe to Britain, the two amount to their whole income.

"If we deduct this interest of their debts, loss of exchange, and protested bills, from their income above mentioned, their neat income is but 900,000l. a year; which is the whole of what all the colonies in North America have to purchase their necessaries from Britain. This sum divided among three millions of people is but six shillings a head *per annum*.—Even if we allow their income to be a million and a half a year, it is but ten shillings a head.

"Thus the colonies have to discharge a debt of six or seven millions, to pay an annual balance of nigh one million; and to maintain three millions of people, out of an income of a million and a half a year at most, which is certainly impracticable.—If their whole income were to be appropriated to the payment of their debts alone, and they were to take nothing either from Britain, or the West-Indies, it would not discharge their debts, with interest, in five years.—It is commonly computed, that all their personal estates are not worth above six millions; that they would hardly pay their debts to Britain; and that their current cash would not pay the interest of their debts alone for half a year.—How then does it appear, "they can certainly bear more, they ought to pay more?" as we are told by the author of the late regulations concerning the colonies.

"If we allow these colonies to have ten shillings a head *per annum* to expend in Britain, it would not purchase a sixth part of their necessaries; and as their neat income is but six shillings a head, it will not purchase a tenth part of them. To supply them with necessaries from Britain, not to mention many other articles,

articles would require at least three pounds a head, as appears from many particular estimates. At this rate of three pounds a head, three millions of people would spend nine millions a year; but as their income is only a million and a half, the difference of seven millions and a half must be looked upon as a national loss; which we not only encrease, but render irreparable, by taxes, duties, confinement of their settlements, &c. all which oblige them to supply themselves. By these proceedings we deprive the nation of such advantages, which might be reaped from the colonies, for the sake, or rather the impracticable attempt, of raising 100,000l. to maintain Canada and Florida.

"This bad state of the colonies is owing to three causes; the first and chief is, the wearing out of the lands, and great increase of the people, who consume twice or thrice as much as they used to do, while their lands do not produce half as much, although that is the source of their whole support. They now likewise require, for their own consumption, most of the articles imported by their trade, which they used formerly to sell, and to make money by them, particularly sugar. Now as these causes, are daily growing more prevalent, we may see the necessity of extending their settlements, and improving their old plantations; without which this state of the colonies is never likely to be remedied, but must daily grow worse.

"Their expences in the war have likewise involved them in great part of this debt. It appears from the certificate of the commander in chief, that he had twenty thousand provincial troops under his command, besides what they had in other services; to pay these troops, they raised about six millions, and owe that sum to Britain. Hence they seem to have run in debt to Britain for all their expences in the war, and if they were to raise any more money, it could only be by the same means, or by diminishing their exports from Britain.

"In these circumstances it is impossible that they should have any money. The balance of trade they owe to Britain, would in one year drain them of all the money they have, were it five times more than it is.--- They have no way to get money but by a trade to the West Indies, the balance of which is against them; so that it is impossible to make money by it. By that trade they rather lose then gain.—Hence in all these colonies you hardly meet with any thing but paper for money. This paper occasions trade and circulation, it is true, but as the balance of that trade is so much against them, it drains them of their current cash, and leaves nothing but paper behind. Thus their trade and paper currency drain them of that money, which their agriculture brings in. And when their cash is gone, so that they have none to exchange their paper, so it is no longer of any value, if it be not for an internal commerce among themselves; this ruins their credit in Britain, and puts them upon manufactures———It is therefore more prejudical to the nation at home, than to the colonies, to drain them entirely of money, and to leave them no medium of trade with Britain. That only obliges them to make their own necessaries, instead of purchasing them here; and let any one judge, which is the greatest gainer by that alternative.

"They who imagine, that the colonies have money, seem not to know what they are, or should be.— It is expected, they should purchase all their manufactures from Britain, which alone is impossible. If they were to purchase one half of them, they could never have

have any money. The raw and unwrought materials, by which they should purchase their manufactures, if they could make them, are of so much less value, that the one will never pay for the other. There are no people in the world who purchase all their manufactures; or if they were to do it, they could never have money. The mere and unmanufactured produce of lands will never purchase manufactures. Suppose we were to make no manufactures in Britain, how should we be supplied with them? It is by manufactures, that this nation gains its wealth; and if you would have the colonies to get money, or pay taxes, they must do the same, and not only supply themselves, but vend their manufactures in order to raise that money; which these proceedings will soon drive them to. Thus the very thought of raising money in the colonies, is contrary to the first principles of colonization, and to the interest of Britain in them. It must infallibly make them her rivals both in trade and manufactures.

"But if this is the case of the most fruitful countries, what can we expect from North America? Or from the produce of the poor and mean lands there, the greatest part of which will hardly yield the bare necessaries of life! What could any one ever expect from a little tobacco, rice, pitch and tar, or fish, the chief products of North America, or any thing else it produces, to maintain two or three milions of people and to raise money? They who could expect this, must be totally unacquainted with the value of these commodities. If the colonies could purchase half their necessaries from Britain, it would be a very considerable income, and worth four or five millions a year to Britain; but on the lands they now possess, if they are confined to them, they will never be able to purchase a fourth, if a tenth part of the necessaries they want. There are but two ways for any people to subsist, to wit, by the produce of lands, or of labour; that is, by agriculture, or manufactures; and if they can make nothing by the first, they must necessarily apply to the other, which is the present state of the colonies. They now consume the chief part of what their lands produce, and have no way to get manufactures but by making them.—To these two resources many will add trade; but that can only be carried on in the produce of lands, or manufactures; without which, you lose by trade, as the colonies do; which will soon oblige them to trade in their own manufactures, if they depend on that, instead of agriculture.

" The plenty which many perceive in the colonies proceeds from their land, and not from wealth; they are only rich in flocks and herds, like the patriarchs of old, and not in money. If any man shew a greater sign of opulence, it all proceeds from the labour of slaves; who are so chargeable, that they rather give their owners credit than wealth, till they are no longer able to pay their debts, which is their present condition. Hence they who go to the colonies, and see signs of opulence in them, as they imagine, only deceive themselves, and impose upon the whole nation, when they pretend to be mighty well acquainted with them.

" Upon all these accounts, it must appear to be absolutely impracticable ever to raise a revenue in the colonies in *sterling cash*, in which they were to have paid their taxes. They pay their own taxes either in staple commodities, or their paper currency; and no one can expect to get money, where there is none. If they may have a little current cash, it is not properly theirs, but belongs to the Merchants of Britain, to whom it is due. This is a stock of the nation in trade, left there by the merchants, in order to improve it; and to apply that to any other purpose, is like a merchant who lives upon his capital, instead of improving it by trade, which soon brings them both to an end. But if Britain thus ruins her trade, in order to maintain *standing armies* in time of peace, this must become a very different nation from what it ever has been, or cease to be one.

"The advantages of the North American trade seem not to be considered in a public light; their commodities are of so small value, that they are very unprofitable either to make, or to trade in them, but they are on that account more profitable to the public; if they are vile and cheap, it is because they are gross and bulky, by which they are sources of navigation, and support the maritime power of the nation. If you caculate the freight, commission, and charges, on the products of North America, they amount to half their value; which is all gain to Britain, but is so much deducted from the income of the colonies. From a particular account of the whole trade of North America, too long to be here inserted it appears, that the gross proceeds, including freight and all charges, amount in value, to Britain, to three millions a year, when the net proceeds to the planters do not exceed a million and a half: and as these charges, are all paid by the planters, out of the first produce of their commodities, this nation certainly does not enjoy any trade so profitable as this —"If we examine into the circumstances of the inhabitants of our plantations, and our own," says a very good judge [*], " it will appear, that not one

fourth

---

[*] Gee on Trade, P. 149.

fourth part of their product redounds to their own profit."

"Thus the colonies, which produce staple commodities for Britain, are a much greater advantage to the nation than seems to be apprehended. They pay, one with another, one half of all that they make, for transporting and vending the rest, which is all expended, in Britian. By that means you get their all, and cannot possibly have any more. Neither can it be expected, that any people can ever be worth money in their situation. Were they to have the profits only of transporting and vending their own products, their income would be double of what it is; but as these are now all reaped by Britain, it is to rob the nation of its best income, to deprive it of this. This is the advantage of the colonies, and the tax which they pay for their protection; which must, appear a very considerable one, as it amounts to one half of all they make; and is much more advantageous to the nation than a petty revenue, which they cannot possibly have money to pay, as that all centers in Britain.

"Besides this deduction on their products, and the heavy duties upon them, the colonies pay all the taxes of Britain on every thing they consume; as it is well known, all taxes fall on the consumers whoever may first pay them. Now, as these taxes on British goods amount at least to fifty or sixty *per cent.* and the colonies pay such a great part of what they purchase them with, is not this much more advantageous to the nation than a petty revenue? Were they to pay 100,000l. in taxes, they must supply themselves with manufactures to that value; this would establish manufactures among them; the public would lose the taxes and duties on these goods; the merchants their profits, and the nation the benefit of the trade

trade and navigation; which losses would amount to twice or thrice as much as the tax. And this loss would fall much heavier on the landed interest than the mercantile; the profits of the merchants in the trade to North America are but small: they are reckoned not to exceed ten *per cent.* but allowing them to be twenty-five *per cent.* the other seventy-five is expended on the manufactures of the kingdom, and chiefly such as are made of British materials, which are all gain to the land-owners. Let not the landed gentlemen therefore, expect to relieve the burdens on their estates, by taxes on the colonies; that is a certain way to entail their taxes on them and their posterity for ever, and render them unable to bear the burden. They must than pay their taxes themselves, instead of having them paid by the colonies, who consume the produce of their lands, and employ their tradesmen who are maintained on the land."

CHAP.

Chap. III.

An account of the first settlements in New-England—their hardships—their progress—their religion and churches—Massachuset charter—Harvard college, &c.

As in the course of this history, many arguments will arise, concerning the rights of the colonists, and the principles of the English government, with regard to them; it may be necessary, after we have hinted a few reasons of the present contest, to give some account of the origin of these colonies, with which we are now contending. Whether all the accounts of the ancients concerning the peopling of America are apocryphical or true, I will not pretend to affirm or deny. At so great a distance from the original of a people, so far separated from the rest of the world, many things that have been written are unknown, many things are uncertain, and very few that can be fully depended upon as matters of fact. From some circumstances acknowledged by creditable writers, it is highly probable that there were parts of America inhabited by Britons, three hundred years before the Spaniards knew any thing of these western parts. Modern writers, by adopting a new theory of history, have, by one dash of the pen, struck out all the very ancient accounts of nations, and their manners as fabulous; and at once freed themselves both of the truth and falsehood of ancient records. The authority of *Diodorus Siculus*, *Plato*, and others, are now considered as mere dreams, and the more modern accounts of Spanish and Portuguese Papists received as the data and first principles of American history. Columbus is allowed in general to be the first discoverer of America in these latter times, though De la Vega informs us, that one *Sanchez*, a native of *Helva*, in Spain, discovered these regions before him. It was in the year 1492 that Columbus entered upon his enterprize, and discovered the northern parts of America; and in 1497 that Americus Vesputius discovered the southern parts. In this same year, the two *Cabots*, the father and son, under the commission of King Henry the seventh, made further discoveries than either Americus or Columbus, for which they were highly honoured by the king of England. What gives the preference to the two Englishmen, above the Genoese and the Florentine is, that the Britons discovered the continent, when the others only discovered some islands, and did not discover the main land till a year after it had been discovered by the Cabots. *Americus* came after them both, and gave a name to the whole western world, to which, as a discoverer, he was no ways entitled. It was in consequence of the discoveries which the *Cabots* made, that after adventurers in England, made their acquaintance with the western parts of the globe. Most of the attempts to settle colonies in America were unsuccessful at first, which happened either through the ignorance of the adventurers, or the treachery of some particular persons among them; who, for selfish and interested purposes, betrayed the trust reposed in them. Sir Walter Raliegh, Willoughby, Frobisher, Gilbert, and Gosnold, made several bold and unsuccessful attempts before they succeeded, and

their

their utmost efforts proceeded little farther than to discover the possiblity of settling colonies in those parts of the world. The greatest part of the western continent, towards the north, was called at first Virginia, either because the first white person that was born there was a female, or in honour of the Queen of England, under whose sanction they had made the discovery. This country was at first distinguished by the names of North and South Virginia, till Captain Smith, in the year 1614, by presenting a map of North Virginia had its name changed to that of New-England.

The violence of the Laudean party in England in a great measure promoted the population of America: and without any design of advancing the interests of adventurers, gave existence to schemes that planted an English race of people in the wilds of the west. In the year 1620, some persons, who at that time were called Puritans, to avoid the violence of religious persecution fled to Holland, and settled at Leyden, where they were allowed the free exercise of their religion. After they had continued there for some years, they began to find a lukewarmness of temper, and callousness of disposition gradually encrease upon them, and were afraid, that by constant intercourse with the lukewarm Dutchmen, their posterity would in process of time lose all that zeal which they thought necessary to support that form of religion they approved of. Their children had married into Dutch families, and their congregation began to decline: they therefore projected the scheme of emigration to America, chiefly with a design to plant a church according to that form which they had now set up in Holland. This congregation of Christians were called Independents, because they maintained that congregational churches are independent on all Episcopal or Presbyterian jurisdiction, and held that professed believers of the Gospel, uniting in the faith and worship of the New Testament, have a just right to exercise all religious discipline within their congregation, without being accountable to any foreign jurisdiction. After much deliberation, it was resolved that the younger part should go and settle in America, under the protection of the King of England, where they might enjoy the liberty of their consciences, and be capable of encouraging their friends and countrymen to follow them.

They sent their agents into England, and obtained a patent from the crown, and agreed with several merchants to become adventurers in the undertaking. Several members of the church, over whom the famous Mr Robinson was pastor, sold their estates, and made a common bank, with which they purchased a small ship of sixty tons, and hired another of one hundred and eighty. The agents sailed into Holland with their own ship, to take in as many of the congregation as were willing to embark while the other vessel was freighting with all necessaries for the new plantation. All things being ready, Mr Robinson kept a day of fasting and praying with his congregation, and took his leave of the adventurers with the following exhortation:

'Brethren, we are now quickly to part from one
'another. and whither I may ever live to see your
'faces on earth any more, the God of heaven only
'knows; but whether the Lord has appointed that
'or no, I charge you before God, and his blessed
'angels, that ye follow me no farther than you have
'seen me follow the Lord Jesus Christ.

'If God reveal any thing to you, by any other in-

'strument of his, be as ready to receive it as ever
' you were to receive any truth by my ministry; for
' I am verily persuaded, the Lord has more truth
' yet to break forth out of his holy word. For my
' part, I cannot sufficiently bewail the condition of
' the reformed churches, who are come to a period
' in religion, and will go at present no farther than
' the instruments of their reformation. The Lu-
' therans cannot be drawn to go beyond what
' Luther saw; whatever part of his will our God
' has revealed to Calvin, they will rather die then
' embrace it; and the Calvinists, you see, stuck fast
' where they were left by that great man of God,
' who yet saw not all things.

' This is a misery much to be lamented, for though
' they were burning and shining lights in their times,
' yet they penetrated not into the whole council of
' God, but were they now living, would be as wil-
' ling to embrace further light as that which they first
' received. I beseech you, remember 'tis an article
' of our church covenants, that you be ready to re-
' ceive whatever truth shall be made known to you
' from the written word of God. Remember that
' and every other article of your sacred covenant.
' But I must here withal exhort you, to take heed
' what you receive as truth, examine it, consider it,
' and compare it with other scriptures of truth, before
' you receive it, for it is not possible that the christi-
' an world should come so lately out of such thick an-
' tichristian darkness, and that perfection of know-
' ledge should break forth at once.'

On the first of July, the adventurers went from Leyden to Delfthaven, whither Mr Robinson and the ancients of his congregation accompanied them; they continued

continued together all night, and next morning, after mutual embraces, Mr Robinson kneeled down on the sea-shore, and with a fervent prayer, committed them to the protection and blessing of heaven. The adventurers were about one hundred and twenty, who having joined their other ship, sailed for New-England on the fifth of August; but one of their vessels proving leaky, they left it, and embarked in one vessel, which arrived at Cape Cod on the ninth of November, one thousand six hundred and twenty. Sad was the condition of these poor men, who had winter before them, and no accommodations on land for their entertainment: most of them were in a weak and sickly condition with the voyage, but there was no remedy: they therefore manned their long-boat, and having coasted the shore, at length found a tolerable harbour, where they landed their effects, and on the twenty-fifth of December, began to build a store-house, and some small cottages to preserve them from the weather. Their company was divided into nineteen families, each family having an allotment of land for lodging and gardens, in proportion to the number of persons of which it consisted; and to prevent disputes, the situation of each family was decided by lot. They agreed likewise upon some laws for their civil and military government, and having chosen a governor, they called the place of their settlement by the name of *New Plymouth*.

These new planters underwent great hardships when they first went over, and many of them died through the fatigues of their voyage, and a distemper which raged among them. Their friends in England sent them supplies, and notwithstanding all difficulties they maintained their station, and laid the foundation of one of the noblest settlements in America; which

has

has proved an asylum to many Non-conformists since that time.

In the first spring after these new settlers had weathered out a severe winter, when they began to look after what things were necessary for their further sustenance, they were suddenly surprised with the appearance of two Indians, who, in broken English, bad them welcome. One of these Indians had been acquainted with some of the English who had been fishing on the eastern parts of New-England, and the other had been seduced by a shipmaster aboard his vessel, and carried to Europe, with some others, and there sold a slave, but had made his escape to England, out of Spain, and become servant to one Mr. Slany, from whom he had found a way to return to his own country. This Indian's name was Squanto. He performed many good offices to this infant colony, and instructed them how to plant Indian corn, and made them acquainted with one of the principal Sachems in the country, who came with some of his people from a great distance to pay them a visit, entered into a league with them, and became subjects of England. Historians inform us of a strange device that this Squanto observed, to bring the Sachems and Indians into friendship with the colonists, and under the government of the English. He persuaded them that the King of England kept the plague locked up in a cellar, and could let it out when he pleased, to destroy them all. This had a great effect upon the apprehensions of those ignorant savages, who had seen the greatest part of their neighbours a few years before swept away by a most terrible plague. This friendly stratagem of Squanto was a happy mean of preserving this infant colony, and was by the pious and religious people of these times, considered

as

as a special interposition of providence in their favour.

In the midst of many trials, dangers, and disappointments, those colonists continued to support themselves, and maintain their religion, as their circumstances would permit, till a company of gentlemen in England gave them further relief and assistance.

From the time that the first adventurers went over to America, the losses that those at home had sustained in their substance in supporting them, made them turn sick of those adventures. But there were other noblemen and gentlemen who were ready to engage in this cause, and obtained a new grant, 1620, of all the country between the latitudes 40 and 48, and had a patent made out to them, under the title of " the Council established at Plymouth, in the county of Devon, for the planting, ruling, ordering, and governing of New-England in America, their heirs and assigns." This afterwards received the name of the grand Plymouth Patent.

Mr White a clergyman of Dorchester, having projected a scheme of a new settlement of, and asylum for ejected ministers, entered into a treaty with these new patentees. In consequence of this, the council of Plymouth, by a deed under their common seal, gave, granted, bargained, and sold to Henry Boswell, and five others, gentlemen of Dorsetshire, their heirs and assigns, and their associates for ever, all that part of New-England therein described, at the bottom of a certain bay there, commonly called Massachusetts bay. In this deed, there was granted, all rights, jurisdictions, royalties, liberties, freedoms, immunities, privileges, franchises, pre-eminences, and commodities whatsoever, which they themselves had or might exercise, or enjoy within the said lands. Some years after

after, this company was joined with several gentlemen in London, the principal of whom was Sir Richard Saltonstall, and a new draught of the former patent was made out, and the names of the new adventurers inserted in it. It was confirmed by the King, and passed the seals March 4th 1628. By the royal charter, this company was created a corporation, and had governors and assistants appointed, and were impowered to chuse annually their successors upon the first day of Easter term. They accordingly met, and for the first time, on the 13th of May 1628, chose a governor, deputy-governor, and eighteen assistants. At this time the court agreed that every one of the company who should subscribe 50 l. should have 200 acres of land for their dividend, and in proportion for a greater sum. A list of the names of subscribers, and the sums subscribed, was transmitted to Mr Endicot, whom they had just a little before sent over as governor in the plantation. This was the first royal charter, and the original of settling the Massachusetts bay. This company was formed upon a plan similar to that of the East-India company. The gentlemen who formed this company were resident in England, and chose their governor, deputy-governor, and assistants out of their own body, resident among themselves, and then sent out a person under their authority, as governor, to dispose of the new settlement. The first of these was Mr Endicot, whom they sent away as soon as the charter was executed, to take care of the colony, and to prevent the new settlers from returning home, who were in great distress, and intended to have returned to England.

Among the several debates concerning the nature of charters, it has never been yet fairly determined, whether such royal patents, granted for ever, to corporate bodies, fulfilling the conditions of their charters, can be dissolved at the pleasure of the legislature. The only difficulty concerning this charter is, whether, after the company removed from Old-England to New-England, the acts and proceedings of that company had the same force as before? Reason and justice will readily determine this point in the affirmative; but what it may be as a point of law, I will not affirm. If the sovereign has a right to grant charters, according to the laws of the empire, one charter must be as good as another; and if an act of parliament be necessary to make them legal and certain, then all the charters of incorporated bodies must have that sanction, otherwise they are not good tenures for any privileges. It would appear that the above-mentioned charter was a charter to hold lands within certain latitudes, and to authorise these settlers to chuse a governor and assistants. From whence it is natural to infer, that it gave them authority within those districts, when the inhabitants should encrease, to encrease the number of assistants; or at least to grant to all who should incorporate with them, according to the intention of the grant, the same privileges, according to their charters, as members of the corporation. These adventurers did not intend to set up any independent government, but meant to continue members of the British empire; but they certainly believed that their removing from one place of the empire to another, did not deprive them of that privilege which other subjects of the sovereign enjoyed. When they purchased lands under the sanction of their charter, they did not imagine that they were not their own, but might be taken from them at the pleasure of the British legislature without their consent. They certainly understood that their estates were freeholds,

held

held upon condition of their fulfilling the allegiance to the sovereign implied in their charter, and that no power in Britain could take them from them, without manifest injustice, and breach of faith. As to the difference between Old and New-England freeholds, lawyers and casuists may have such to say; but by tracing matters to their original, it will be found that the greatest part of those estates called freeholds, and the tenures of corporations, are only founded upon the grants of princes, and the charters of sovereigns. When royal charters are granted, which are understood to give a title to certain privileges of freedom it is also understood that this freedom is the same in all parts of the same empire; and that though there is no new government granted, yet all the new privileged subjects have as good a right as the old ones, to enjoy the same freedom. The colonists, by going to America, were not freed from the jurisdiction of the British parliament, nor did they pretend to any such liberty; but they imagined that when they were made free by charter, that a foundation was laid, for their having some share in the legislature. All acts of parliament are certainly binding upon every part of the empire; but this arises from either an expressed or implied representation of the subjects in parliament: and though the king cannot give a charter to abolish acts of parliament, he may, notwithstanding, according to the laws, give a new qualification to subjects, to make them a part of the same legislature. The colonists who were freemen of the empire were bound by the laws thereof; but in so far as they were freemen, they were also entitled to a share in the legislature; to refuse them the latter, would be loosing them from all obligation to the former, or subjecting them

to

to an arbitrary power, againſt which they had no remedy.

The firſt coloniſts ſeem to have had but very different ideas of civil and religious liberty; for the colony of Maſſachuſetts bay confined their civil liberty to their church-members, and permitted none to a ſhare in their government, who were not joined members in their congregations. And with regard to religious freedom, they were exceedingly narrow minded, and inſtead of tolerating people of different ſentiments, they perſecuted the innocent Quakers with unrelenting rigour. They were, no doubt, much fretted and chagrined in their tempers, with the uſage they had met with in their own country; and had imbibed the temper of the times, which was very far from being mild. It does not appear that their profeſſed principles taught them the practices they founded upon them, but their behaviour was rather a perverſion of their principles. They, through long oppreſſion, had acquired a ſourneſs of temper, and a ſolemnity of manners, of which their religion and whole behaviour was ſeaſoned; ſo that their religion was more under the government of their manners, than became the purity of their profeſſion. The people were much to be blamed, though their religion deſerves commendation. It was a boiſterous age in which they lived, and it could not well be expected that men who had ſuffered ſo many hardſhips and ſeverities would be exceeding mild in their tempers.

The people who at this time emigrated to America, were generally of two ſorts: ſuch as fled from perſecution, on account of their religion; and ſuch as were influenced by the love of worldly advantage: Theſe, as their motives were different, frequently purſued different meaſures to obtain their ends. But every reader

reader of their history must confess that an unanimity was maintained beyond what could have been expected, in such singular circumstances. The force of religion was such a bond of union in the minds of the majority, that amidst all the various jarrings and contentions which happened among them, they never proceeded so far as to come to any considerable rupture. They bore one another's infirmities, and overlooked many faults, which in ordinary cases they would not have done; their mutual hardships cemented them together, and made them shew compassion to each other, as strangers in a foreign land.

After the government, together with their first charter, were removed from England to the colony, they began to increase exceedingly fast; persons of rank and fortune not only patronized them, but bore them company into the wilderness of America. The Lady Arabella Johnston, and several others of rank and condition, forsook their own native homes, and crossed the Atlantick, where they might enjoy the free exercise of their religion. Their governor, John Wintrop, Esq; and their deputy-governor, Thomas Dudley, Esq; were men of character and abilities, who did not leave England for the sake of gain, but to maintain a good conscience: they possessed all the enjoyments in their native country that most people are fond of, but they wanted liberty of conscience, which is one of the greatest enjoyments. They therefore committed their lives and their fortunes to the mercy of winds and seas, for the hope of enjoying liberty in a country they never saw, and where they could promise themselves nothing but hardships and difficulties. A fleet of eleven ships, of which the Arabella was the admiral's ship, a vessel of three hundred and fifty tons, landed safe in New-England in the middle of July 1630. Two thousand passengers came over in this fleet, carrying with them as much of their fortunes as they could command, with all things they thought necessary for the climate in which they designed to settle.

Soon after their arrival, Lady Arabella died of a distemper which she had contracted in the voyage, to the great grief of her friends, and of the colonists; and many of the company were likewise carried off by diseases common to the climate. There were two things which at this time alarmed them greatly; scarcity of provisions and fear of the Indians: scorching droughts had in a great measure consumed the fruits of the ground; so that the necessaries of life became exceedingly scarce, and the whole colony were in danger of perishing. From this fear they were happily delivered, by the arrival of several ships from Ireland, laden with various sorts of provisions, which supplied their necessity for the present, till more supplies could be provided. The same providence that delivered them from the dread of famine, removed also their other ground of fear. A most dreadful plague, together with the small pox, had swept away nine out of ten of the natives, so that the few that remained, fled from the infection, to more distant places of the country. These new settlers after their arrival, did not consider the patent of the King to be a sufficient title to give them possession of the lands of the original natives; they therefore, before they pretended to possess any tracts of ground, made a lawful purchase thereof from the true proprietors, and paid them a price for what they afterwards possessed. To reason, it is an high absurdity, for a king of Britain, or any other sovereign, to pretend to give charters of right to other people's possessions, because
some

some of their subjects, when scampering round the globe, should chance to see their country as they are passing along. With as much justice might some other nations grant charters to their subjects, of possessions in England and France, because some adventurers of their nations happened to sail along their coasts, as the people in England and France grant charters to their subjects in America. It was a fair acknowledgment of those settlers, that they did not believe their charters gave them a lawful title, when they purchased their lands from the natives of the country; and it is certainly no more than an act of justice, which all nations should observe towards those that are giving them no trouble, to purchase what they mean to possess in their country. If, after they have made their purchase, they intend to hold of their native country as subjects for protection, they ought undoubtedly to pay the ordinary respects due to its government, and enjoy the common rights of others of the community. A charter can never lawfully proceed any farther than a promise of protection of those lawful possessions which the subjects of a government have acquired: for no government can give a right to a soil which does not belong thereto. It is plain from this observation, that this Massachusetts colony did not derive their right of manorship from any sovereign, but from purchase; for at no time can it be said, that ever the lands of the Indians belonged to either king or parliament of any nation in Europe. Their charter affirms that they were to hold their title to the soil in common, and free soccage, as of the manor of East-Greenwich in Kent*,

but

---

* MASSACHUSETS COLONY CHARTER.

Whereas our most dear and royal Father King James of blessed memory, by his Highness's letters patent bearing date at Westminster

but how a title could be given to a soil by those to whom it did not belong, appears rather whimsical and absurd. It may be an amusement for lawyers to trifle with, but justice and equity will remove all such ideas. One would think the colonists, though they were flying from oppression, had at this time very mean ideas of justice and liberty; to solicit a patent to carry in their pockets, to a foreign country, to claim a right to other people's lawful possessions. It would appear they saw the inconsistency, and claimed

the third day of November, in the eighteenth year of his reign, hath given and granted unto the Councel established at Plymouth in the county of Devon, for the planting, ruling, ordering, and governing of New-England in America, and to their heirs, successours, and assignes for ever: All that part of America lying and being in breadth from forty degrees of northerly latitude from the equinoxtiall line to fourty eight degrees of the said northerly latitude inclusively, and in length of and within all the breadth aforesaid throughout the maine lands from sea to sea, together also with all the firme lands, soyles, grounds, havens, ports, rivers, waters, fishing, mines and mineralls, as well royall mines of gould and silver, as other mines and mineralls, precious stones, quarries, and all and singular other commodities, jurisdictions, privileges, franchises and preheminences both within the said tract of land upon the maine, and also within the islands and seas adjoining. Provided alwaye that the said islands or any the premisses by the said letters patent intended and meant to be granted were not then actually possessed or inhabited by any other christian prince, or state, nor within the bounds limits or territories of the southern colonies then before granted by our said deare father to be planted by such of his loving subjects in the southern parts. To have and to hold, possess and enjoy all and singular the aforesaid continent, lands, territories, islands, hereditaments and precincts, seas, waters, fishings, with all and all manner their commodities, royalties, liberties, preheminences, and profits that should from thenceforth arise from thence with all and singular their appurtenances, and every part and parcel thereof, unto the said Councel, and their successors and assignes for ever, to the sole and proper use, benefit and behoof of them the said Councel and their successors and assignes for ever: To be houlden of our said most dear and royal Father, his heirs and successors, as of his manor of East-Greenwich in the county of Kent, in free and common soccage, and not in Capite nor by knights service. Yielding and paying therefore to the said late King, his heirs and successors the fifth part of the ore of gould and silver which should from time to time and at all times thereafter happen to be found, gotten, had and obtained in, at, or within any of the said lands, limits, territories and precincts, or in or within any part or parcel thereof, for or in respect of all and all manner

ed no right till they had firſt made a bargain, and paid the purchaſe. Thoſe who at preſent debate concerning theſe old parchments on either ſide of the queſtion, will never be able to draw an honourable concluſion from them, worthy of the true friends of liberty. In the hiſtory of human nature, it is difficult to find conſiſtency, when men's intereſts and paſſions become counſellors for their actions.

The charms of a charter under the great ſeal of England wrought powerfully upon perſons of ſeveral degrees;

ver of duties, demands and ſervices whatſoever to be done made or paid to our ſaid dear Father the late King his heirs and ſucceſſors; as in and by the ſaid letters patent (amongſt ſundry other clauſes, powers, privileges and grants therein contained) more at large appeareth.

And whereas the ſaid Councel eſtabliſhed at Plymouth in the county of Devon, for the planting, ruling, ordering and governing of New England in America, have by their deed indented under their common ſeal bearing date the nineteenth day of March laſt paſt, in the third year of our reign, given, granted, bargained, ſold, enfeoffed, aliened and confirmed to Sir Henry Roſewell, Sir John Young, knights, Thomas Southcott, John Humfrey, John Endicott and Symon Whetcomb, their heirs and aſſociates forever, all that part of New England in America aforeſaid which lieth and extendeth between a great river there called Monomack, alias Merrimack, and a certain other river there called Charles river, being the bottom of a certain bay there commonly called Maſſachuſetts, alias Mattachuſetts, alias Mattatuſetts bay, and alſo all and ſingular thoſe lands and hereditaments whatſoever lying and being within the ſpace of three Engliſh miles on the ſouth part of the ſaid Charles river, or of any or every part thereof, and alſo all and ſingular the lands and hereditaments whatſoever, lying and being within the ſpace of three Engliſh miles to the ſouthward of the ſouthermoſt part of the ſaid bay called Maſſachuſetts, alias Mattachuſetts, alias Mattatuſetts bay, and alſo all thoſe lands and hereditaments which lye and be within the ſpace of three Engliſh miles to the northward of the ſaid river called Monomack, alias Merrimack, or to the northward of any and every part thereof, and all lands and hereditaments whatſoever, lyeing within the limits aforeſaid, north and ſouth, in latitude and breadth, and in length and longitude, of and within all the breadth aforeſaid, throughout the main lands, there from the Atlantic and weſtern ſea and ocean on the eaſt part to the ſouth ſea on the weſt part, and all lands and grounds, place and places, ſoils woods and wood crowds, havens, ports, rivers, waters, fiſhings and hereditaments whatſoever, lying within the ſaid bounds, and limits, and every part and parcel thereof, and alſo all iſlands in America aforeſaid in the ſaid ſeas or either of them on the weſtern or eaſtern coaſts or parts of the ſaid tracts of lands by the ſaid indenture mentioned

degrees; the diftreffed, the religious, and the avaricious, from different motives, flocked to New-England. Perfons defcended of ancient families, minifters of the Gofpel, merchants, hufbandmen, artificers, during the fpace of twelve years, went over in large bodies to fettle in America. The expence of thofe migrations was truly extraordinary; it was computed that the paffage of the emigrants coft at leaft ninety thoufand pounds; the tranfportation of the firft fmall cattle, befides their price, coft twelve thoufand

mentioned to be given, granted, bargained, fold, enfeoffed, aliened and confirmed or any of them: And alfo all mines and mineralls, as well royall mines of gould and filver, as other mines and mineralls whatfoever in the faid lands and premiffes or any part thereof, and all Jurifdiction, rights, royalties, liberties, freedoms, immunities, priviledges, franchifes, preheminences and commodities whatfoever, which they the faid Councel eftablifhed at Plymouth in the county of Devon for the planting ruling ordering and governing of New-England in America then had or might ufe exercife or enjoy, in and within the faid lands and premiffes by the faid indenture mentioned to be given, granted, bargained, fould, enfeoffed and confirmed, or in or within any part or parcel thereof. To have and to hould the faid part of New England in America which lyeth and extends and is abutted as aforefaid, and every part and parcel thereof; And all the faid iflands, rivers, ports, havens, waters, fifhings, mines and mineralls, Jurifdiction, franchifes, royalties, liberties, privileges, commodities, hereditaments and premiffes whatfoever, with the appurtenances, unto the faid Sir Henry Rofewell, Sir John Younge, Thomas Southcott, John Humfrey, John Endecott and Symon Whetcomb, their heirs and affignes, and their affociates, to the only proper and abfolute ufe and behoof of the faid Sir Henry Rofewell, Sir John Younge, Thomas Southcott, John Humfrey, John Endecott and Symon Whetcomb, their heirs and affignes, and affociates forevermore. To be houlden of us, our heirs and fucceffors, as of our maner of Eaft-Greenwich in the County of Kent, in free and common foccage, and not in Capite, nor by knights fervice, yielding and paying therefore unto us, our heirs and fucceffors, the fifth part of the oare of gould and filver which fhall from time to time and at all times hereafter happen to be found, gotten, had and obtained, in any of the faid lands within the faid limits, or in or within any part thereof, for and in fatisfaction of all manner of duties, demands and fervices whatfoever, to be done, made or paid to us, our heirs or fucceffors, as in and by the faid recited indenture more at large may appear.

Now know ye, that we, at the humble fuite and petition of the faid Sir Henry Rofewell, Sir John Younge, Thomas Southcott, John Humfrey, John Endecott and Symon Whetcomb, and of others whom they have affociated unto them. Have, for divers good caufes and

sand pounds: the provisions laid in, till more could be provided, cost forty-five thousand pounds; the materials for building their first cottages, cost eighteen thousand pounds: their arms and ammunition, including their artillery, twenty-two thousand pounds. Besides these vast sums, the adventurers laid out many other considerable ones; and no fewer than an hundred and ninety-eight ships were employed in carrying men, women, children, cattle, and other commodities to this new settlement. It must have been

an

and considerations us moving granted and confirmed, and by these presents of our especiall grace, certain knowledge, and mere motion do grant and confirm unto the said Sir Henry Rosewell, Sir John Younge, Thomas Southcott, John Humfrey, John Endecott, and Symon Whetcomb, and to their associates hereafter named (videlicet) Sir Richard Saltonstall, Knt. Isaac Johnson, Samuel Aldersey, John Ven, Matthew Cradlock, George Harwood, Increase Nowell, Richard Bellingham, Nathaniel Wright, Samuel Vassall, Theophilus Eaton, Thomas Goffe, Thomas Adams, John Browne, Samuel Browne, Thomas Hutchins, William Vassall, William Pinchon, and George Foxcroft their heirs and assignes, all the said part of New England in America, lyeing and extending betweene the bounds and limits in the said recited indenture expressed, and all lands and grounds, place and places, soyles, wood and wood grounds, havens, ports, rivers, waters, mines, mineralls, jurisdictions, rights, royalties, liberties, freedoms, immunities, priviledges franchises, preheminences, hereditaments and commodities whatsoever to them the said Sir Henry Rosewell, Sir John Younge, Thomas Southcott, John Humfrey, John Endecott and Symon Whet-

combe, their heirs and assignes, and to their associates by the said recited Indenture given, granted, bargained, sould, enfeoffed, aliened, or confirmed, or mentioned, or intended thereby to be given, granted, bargained, sould, enfeoffed, aliened, and confirmed. To have and to hould the said part of New England in America and other the premisses hereby mentioned to be granted and confirmed and every part or parcell thereof with the appurtenances unto the said Sir Henry Rosewell, Sir John Younge, Sir Richard Saltonstall, Thomas Southcott, John Humfrey, John Endecott, Symon Whetcomb, Isaac Johnson, Samuel Aldersey, John Ven, Matthew Cradlock, George Harwood, Increase Nowell, Richard Perry, Richard Bellingham, Nathaniel Wright, Samuel Vassall, Theophilus Eaton, Thomas Goffe, Thomas Adams, John Browne, Samuel Browne, Thomas Hutchins, William Vassall, William Pinchon, and George Foxcroft, their heirs and assignes for ever, to their only proper and absolute use and behoof for evermore. To be houlden of us our heirs and successors as of our mannor of East Greenwich aforesaid in free and common soccage, and not in Capite nor by knights service, and also yielding and paying therefore

to

an amazing impulse that wrought so powerfully upon such numbers of people, to make them forsake their native country to go to reside in the midst of a wilderness.

What declared the principal design of those emigrants, was their practice; for they had no sooner arrived in New England, than they began to pursue that reformation in religion, which they had projected before they left their native country. On August the 27th 1630, they kept a solemn fast, and chose a minister

to us our heirs and successours the fifth part only of all oare of gould and silver, which from time to time and at all times hereafter shall be there gotten, had or obtained, for all services, exactions and demands whatsoever, according to the tenure and reservation in the said recited indenture expressed.

And further know ye that of our more especiall grace, certain knowledge and meer motion, we have given and granted, and by these presents do, for us, our heirs, and successours give and grant unto the said Sir Henry Rosewell, Sir John Younge, Sir Richard Saltonstall, Thomas Southcott, John Humfrey, John Endecott, Symon Whetcombe, Isaac Johnson, Samuel Aldersey, John Ven, Matthew Craddock, George Harwood, Increase Nowell, Richard Perry, Richard Bellingham, Nathaniel Wright, Samuel Vassal, Theophilus Eaton, Thomas Goffe, Thomas Adams, John Browne, Samuel Browne, Thomas Hutchins, William Vassal, William Pinchon, and George Foxcroft, their heirs and assignes, all that part of New England in America which lies and extends between a great river there commonly called Monomack river, alias Merrymack river, and a certain other river there called Charles river, being in the bottom of a certain bay there commonly called Massachusets, alias Mattachusets, alias Mattatusets bay, and also all and singular those lands and hereditaments whatsoever lying within the space of three English miles on the south part of the said river called Charles river, or of any or every part thereof, and also all and singular the lands and hereditaments whatsoever lyeing and being within the space of three English miles to the southward of the southermost part of the said bay called Massachusetts, alias Mattachusetts, alias Mattatusets bay. And also all those lands and hereditaments whatsoever which lye and be within the space of three English miles to the northward of the said river called Monomack alias Merrymack, or to the northward of any and every part thereof, and all lands and hereditaments whatsoever lyeing within the limits aforesaid north and south in latitude and breadth, and in length and longitude of and within all the breadth aforesaid throughout the maine lands there from the Atlantick and western sea and ocean on the east part to the south sea on the west part, and all lands and grounds, place and places, soyles, wood and wood grounds, havens, ports, rivers, waters and hereditaments whatsoever lyeing within the said bounds and limits

nister to preside in their public worship. One Mr Wilson, formerly a minister of Sudbury, in the county of Suffolk, was appointed their pastor. This new church was formed at Charlestown, on the north side of Charles'-river, not far from Boston, which at that time did not exist. In a very short time there were seven churches formed in Massachusett's-Bay, all observing the same order, worship, and discipline*, which the writers of the New-England history compare to the seven

* Charlestown, Dorchester, Boston, Roxbury, Lyn, Watertown, Plymouth.

limits and every part and parcel thereof, and also all islands in America aforesaid in the said seas or either of them on the western or eastern coasts or parts of the said tracts of lands hereby mentioned to be given or granted or any of them, and all mines and mineralls as well royal mines of gould and silver as other mines and mineralls whatsoever, in the said lands and premisses or any part thereof, and free liberty of fishing in or within any the rivers or waters within the bounds and limits aforesaid and the seas thereunto adjoining, and all fishes, royal fishes, whales, balan, sturgeon, and other fishes of what kind or nature soever that shall at any time hereafter be taken in or within the said seas or waters or any of them, by the said Sir Henry Roswell, Sir John Younge, Sir Richard Saltonstall, Tho. Southcott, John Humfrey, John Endecott, Symon Whetcombe, Isaac Johnson, Samuel Aldersey, John Ven, Matthew Cradduck, George Harwood, Increase Nowell, Richard Perry, Richard Bellingham, Nathaniel Wright, Samuel Vassal, Theopilus Eaton, Thomas Goffe, Thomas Adams, John Browne, Samuel Browne, Thomas Hutchins, William Vassal, William Pinchon, and George Foxcroft their heirs and assignes, or by any other person or persons whatsoever there inhabiting, by them, or any of them, appointed to fish therein. Provided always that, if the said lands, islands, or any other the premisses herein before mentioned, and by these presents intended and meant to be granted, were at the time of the granting of the said former letters patent dated the third day of November, in the eighteenth yeare of our said deare fathers reigne aforesaid, actually possessed or inhabited, by any other christian prince or state, or were within the bounds, limits, or territories of that southerne colonie then before granted by our said late father to be planted by divers of his loving subjects in the south parts of America, that then this present grant shall not extend to any such parts or parcells thereof, so formerly inhabited or lying within the bounds of the southern plantation as aforesaid, but as to those parts or parcells so possessed or inhabited by such christian prince or state, or being within the bounds aforesaid, shall be utterly voide, these presents or any thing therein contained to the contrary notwithstanding. To have and to hould, possess and enjoy the said parts of New-England in America, which lye, extend and are abutted

seven churches in Asia, which in some things they endeavoured to imitate.

The colony of Massachusetts-Bay soon became numerous, and it was resolved to plant other colonies in that country, as near one another as was possible to settle them. For this purpose in the year 1635, Mr Thomas Hooker, and a company that joined with him, sent agents from Cambridge, Connecticut, who purchased lands of the natives, where they settled, and formed another colony. Those new colonists finding

abutted as aforesaid and every part and parcell the. eaf, and all the islands, rivers, ports, havens, waters, fithings, fishes, mines, minerals, jurisdictions, franchises, royalties, liberties, priviledges, commodities and premisses whatsoever, with the appurtenances unto the said Sir Henry Rosewell, Sir John Younge, Sir Richard Saltonstall, Thomas Southcoat, John Humfrey, John Endecott, Symon Whetcombe, Isaac Johnson, Samuel Aldersey, John Ven, Matthew Craddock, George Harwood, Increase Nowell, Richard Perry, Richard Bellingham, Nathaniel Wright, Samuel Vassal, Theophilus Eaton, Thomas Goffe, Thomas Adams, John Browne, Samuel Browne, Thomas Hutchins, William Vassal, William Pinchon and George Foxcroft, their heirs and assignes forever, to the only proper and absolute use and behoofe of the said Sir Henry Rosewell, Sir John Younge, Sir Richard Saltonstall, Thomas Southcoat, John Humfrey, John Endecott, Symon Whetcombe, Isaac Johnson, Samuel Aldersey, John Ven, Matthew Craddock, George Harwood, Increase Nowell, Richard Perry, Richard Bellingham, Nathaniel Wright, Samuel Vassall, Theophilus Eaton, Thomas Goffe, Thomas Adams, John Browne, Samuel Browne, Thomas Hutchins, William Vassall, William Pinchon, and George Foxcroft, their heirs and assigns forevermore. To be houlden of us our heirs and successours, as our manner of East Greenwich in the county of Kent within our realme of England, in free and common soccage, and not in Capite, nor by knights service, and also yielding and paying therefore to us, our heirs and successours the fifth part only of all oare of gould and silver which from time to time and at all times hereafter shall be there gotten, had, or obtained, for all services, exactions, and demands whatsoever. Provided alwayes and our expresse will and meaneing is, that onely one fifth part of the the gould and silver oare abovementioned in the whole, and no more, be reserved or payeable unto us, our heirs and successthurs, by colour or vertue of these presents, the double reservations or recitals aforesaid, or any thing therein contained notwithstanding.

And for as much as the good and prosperous successe of the plantation of the said parts of New-England aforesaid intended by the said Sir Henry Rosewell, Sir John Younge, Sir Richard Saltonstall, Thomas Southcott, John Humfrey, John Endecott, Symon Whetcombe, Isaac Johnson, Samuel Aldersey finding themselves without the bounds of the Massachusetts charter, formed a government of their own, in imitation of that which they had seen observed in the colony they had left. They afterwards received an ample charter from the King of England, and became a flourishing colony. But what extended this colony more, and made it more considerable was, Messrs Davenport and Eaton, two of the first settlers in Massachusetts bay, desired their friends that were now gone to Connecticut, to purchase for them, of

dersey, John Ven, Matthew Craddock, George Harwood, Increase Nowell, Richard Perry, Richard Bellingham, Nathaniel Wright, Samuel Vassal, Theophilus Eaton, Thomas Goffe, Thomas Adams, John Browne, Samuel Browne, Thomas Hutchins, William Vassall, William Pinchon, and George Foxcroft, to be speedily set upon, cannot but chiefly depend, next under the blessing of Almighty God, and the support of our royal authority, upon the good government of the same, to the end that the affairs and business which from time to time shall happen and arise concerning the said lands and the plantation of the same, may be the better managed and ordered. We have further hereby of our especiall grace, certain knowledge and meere motion, given, granted and confirmed, and for us, our heires and successours, do give, grant and confirme unto our said trustie and well-beloved subjects Sir Henry Rosewell, Sir John Younge, Sir Richard Saltonstall, Thomas Southcott, John Humfrey, John Endecott, Symon Whetcombe, Isaac Johnson, Samuel Aldersey, John Ven, Matthew Craddock, George Harwood, Increase Nowell, Richard Perry, Richard Bellingham, Nathaniel Wright, Samuel Vassall, Theophilus Eaton, Thomas Goffe, Thomas Adams, John Browne, Samuel Browne, Thomas Hutchins, William Vassall, William Pinchon, and George Foxcroft, and for us, our heires and successours, wee will and ordaine, That the said Sir Henry Rosewell, Sir John Younge, Sir Richard Saltonstall, Thomas Southcott, John Humfrey, John Endecott, Symon Whetcombe, Isaac Johnson, Samuel Aldersey, John Ven, Matthew Craddock, George Harwood, Increase Nowell, Richard Perry, Richard Bellingham, Nathaniel Wright, Samuel Vassall, Theophilus Eaton, Thomas Goffe, Thomas Adams, John Browne, Samuel Browne, Thomas Hutchins, William Vassall, William Pinchon, and George Foxcroft, and all such others as shall hereafter be admitted and made free of the company and society hereafter mentioned shall from time to time and at all times forever hereafter be by virtue of these presents one body corporate politique in fact and name, by the name of *the Governor and Companie of the Massachusetts Bay in New-England*: And them by the name *of the Governor and Companie of the Massachusetts bay in New-England*, one body politique and corporate in deed, fact, and name, wee doe, for us, our heirs, and successours, make, ordaine, constitute, and confirme

of the native proprietors, all the lands that lay between them and Hudson's river. This accordingly done, and the purchasers in the year 1637 removed thither, and planted a beautiful colony, in a pleasant bay along the sea coast, where they built the towns of New-Haven, Guildford, Milford, Stampford, and Braintree. Soon after the colony of Long Island was settled, an Island of 18 miles in breadth, and 120 miles in length. This is a very pleasant Island, stretching itself along Fairfield county, in New-England, near the mouth

firme by these presents; and that by that name they shall have perpetuall succession; and that by the same name they and their successors shall and may be capable and enabled, as well to impleade and to be impleaded, and to prosecute, demand, and answer, and be answered unto, in all and singular suits, causes, quarrells, and actions of what kind and nature soever; and also to have, take, possesse, acquire, and purchase any lands, tenements, or hereditaments, or any goods or chattels, the same to lease, grant, demise, alien, bargain, sell, and dispose of, as other our lege people of this our realme of England, or any other corporation or body politique of the same, may lawfully doe. And further that the said Governor and Companie and their successors may have forever one common seale to be used in all causes and occasions of the said Companie, and the same seale may alter, change, break and new make from time to time at their pleasures.

And our will and pleasure is, and we do hereby, for us, our heirs, and successors, ordaine and grant, that from henceforth for ever there shall be one Governor, one deputy Governor, and eighteen Assistants of the same Companie to be from time to time constituted, elected and chosen out of the freemen of the said Companie for the time being, in such manner and forme as hereafter in these presents is expressed. Which said officers shall apply themselves to take care for the best disposing and ordering of the generall businesse and affairs of for and concerning the said lands and premisses hereby mentioned to be granted, and the plantation thereof and the government of the people there.

And for the better execution of our royall pleasure and grant in this behalfe, we do by these presents, for us, our heires, and successors, nominate, ordaine, make, and constitute our well beloved the said Matthew Craddock, to be the first and present Governor of the said Companie, and the said Thomas Goffe to be deputy Governor of the said Companie, and the said Sir Richard Saltonstall, Isaac Johnson, Samuel Aldersey, John Ven, John Humfrey, John Endecott, Symon Whetcombe, Increase Nowell, Richard Perry, Nathaniel Wright, Samuel Vassall, Theophilus Eaton, Thomas Adams, Thomas Hutchins, John Browne, George Foxcroft, William Vassall, and William Pinchon to be the present Assistants of the said Companie, to continue in the said severall offices respectively for such time and

mouth of Hudson's river, and is well furnished every where with convenient harbours. The fourth colony was called New-Haven, which being Londoners, intended to pursue trade, but failed in their enterprise; their fortunes sunk so fast, that they lost all hope, and many of them in returning to England, perished at sea, and never more saw their native country. As many, however, still remained as supported the colony, which afterwards became considerable, and was joined in one charter with Connecticut, in the reign of Charles the second, 1664; it is

in such manner as is and by these presents is hereafter declared and appointed.

And further we will and by these presents, for us our heires and successors do ordaine and grant that the Governor of the said Companie for the time being, or in his absence, by occasion of sicknefs or otherwise, the deputy Governor for the time being shall have authority from time to time upon all occasions to give order for the assembling of the said Companie, and calling them together to consult and advise of the business and affaires of the said Companie.

And that the said Governor, deputy Governor and Assistants of the said Companie for the time being shall or may once every month or oftener at their pleasures assemble and hould and keep a court or assembly of themselves for the better ordering and directing of their affaires. And that any seven or more persons of the Assistants together with the Governor or deputy Governor so assembled shall be said, taken, held, and reputed to be, and shall be a full and sufficient court and assembly of the said Companie, for the handling, ordering, and dispatching of all such businesses and occurrents, as shall from time to time happen, touching or concerning the said Companie or plantation. And that there shall or may be held and kept by the Governor or deputy Governor of the said Companie, and seven or more of the said Assistants for the time being upon every last Wednesday in Hillary, Easter, Trinity and Michaelmas Terms respectively for ever, one great generall and solemn assembly, which four generall assemblies shall be styled and called *the foure greate and generall courts of the said Company*: In all or any of which said greate and generall courts so assembled, We do, for us, our heires and successors, give and grant to the said Governor and Companie and theire successors, that the Governor, or in his absence the deputy Governor of the said Companie for the time being, and such of the Assistants and Freemen of the said Companie as shall be present or the greater number of them so assembled, whereof the Governour or deputy Governour and six of the Assistants at the least to be seven, shall have full power and authority to choose, nominate and appoint such and so many others as they shall thinke fitt, and that shall be willing to accept the same, to be free of the said Company and Body, and them into the same to admit: And to elect and constitute such officers as they shall thinke fitt

is the capital of a country of the same name, and was in a very flourishing condition before the present war. In all these colonies, the first settlers were careful to form independent churches; which, though they did consider themselves as accountable to each other for their conduct, yet lived in full fellowship and communion, walking in love with one another, and in the fear of God. Their strictness and severities to those that offended or dissured from them, in more enlightened times, may have the appearance of a real want of charity;

fitt and requisite for the ordering, managing and dispatching of the affaires of the said Governor and Companie and theire successours: And to make lawes and ordinances for the good and welfare of the said Companie, and for the government and ordering of the said lands and plantation, and the people inhabiteing an is to inhabite the same, as to them from time to time shall be thought meete. So as such lawes and ordinances be not contrary or repugnant to the lawes and statutes of this our realme of England.

And our will and pleasure is, and we do hereby for us, our heires and successours, establish and ordaine, That yearely once in the yeare forever hereafter, namely the last Wednesday in Easter terme yearely, the Governor, deputy Governor and Assistants of the said Companie, and all other officers of the said Companie shall be in the generall court, or assemblie, to be held for that day of time, newly chosen for the yeare ensueing by such greater part of the said Companie for the time being, then and there present, as is aforesaid.

And if it shall happen the present Governor, deputy Governor and Assistants by these presents appointed, or such as shall hereafter be newly chosen into their roomes,

or any of them or any other of the officers to be appointed for the said Companie, to dye, or to be removed from his or their severall offices or places before the said generall day of election (whom we do hereby declare for any misdemeanor or defect to be removeable by the Governor, deputy Governor, Assistants and Companie, or such greater part of them in any of the publick courts to be assembled as is aforesaid) that then and in every such case it shall and may be lawful to and for the Governor, deputy Governor, Assistants, and Companie aforesaid, or such greater part of them so to be assembled as is aforesaid, in any of their assemblies to proceed to a new election of one or more others of their Companie, in the roome or places, roome or places of such officer or officers so dyeing or removed, according to their discretions. And immediately after and upon such election and elections made of such Governor, deputy Governor, Assistant or Assistants, or any other officer of the said Companie in manner and forme aforesaid, the authority, office, and power before given to the former Governor, deputy Governor, other officer, and officers, so removed, in whose stead and place new shall be chosen, shall as to him and them and every

rity; but such were the manners of those times, that there was little forbearance among professors of any denomination. Whatever may have been their various defects and imperfections, they had, notwithstanding, a sense of religion upon their minds, which shews at least they were in earnest in what they professed. Their follies, weaknesses, and extravagances, when compared with their virtues, bear less proportion, than perhaps may he found in the case of their successors either in the mother country or in the colonies.

Just every of them cease and determine.

Provided also, and our will and pleasure is that as well such as are by these presents appointed to be the present Governour, deputy Governour and Assistants of the said Companie, as those that shall succeed them, and all other officers to be appointed and chosen as aforesaid shall, before they undertake the execution of their said offices and places respectively, take their corporall oathes for their due and faithfull performance of their duties in their severall offices and places, before such person or persons as are by these presents hereunder appointed to take and receive the same, that is to say, the said Matthew Craddock, who is hereby nominated and appointed the present Governour of the said Companie, shall take said oathes before one or more of the Masters of our court of chancery for the time being unto which Master or Masters of the Chancery we do by these presents give full power and authority to take and administer the said oath to the said Governour accordingly. And after the said Governour shall be sworne, then the said deputy Governour and Assistants before by these presents nominated and appointed shall take the said severall othes, to their offices and places respectively belonging; before the said Matthew Craddock the present Governour so sworne as aforesaid. And every such person as shall at the time of the annuall election, or other wise upon Death or removall, be appointed to be the new Governour of the said Companie, shall take the oathe to that place belonging before the deputy Governour or two of the Assistants of the said Companie at the least for the time being. And the new elected Deputy-Governour and Assistants, and all other officers to be hereafter chosen as aforesaid from time to time shall take the oaths to their places respectively belonging before the Governour of the said Companie for the time being, Unto which said Governour, Deputy-Governour, and Assistants, we do by these presents give full power and authority to give and administer the said oathes respectively, according to the true meaning herein before declared, without any commission or further warrant to be had and obtained of us, our heirs and successors in that behalfe.

And we do further of our especiall grace, certain knowledge, and meere motion, for us, our heires, and successors, give and grant to the said Governour and Companie and their successours for ever by these

Just sentiments of civil and religious liberty have always been friendly to learning, and though there might be several blemishes in the conduct of the first settlers in America; yet it must be granted even by their enemies, that they were friends both to liberty and learning. The colonists had scarcely been one year in New-England after they received their charter, when they began to contemplate a scheme for erecting a college or university among them, where youth might be instructed in the liberal arts, and persons

these presents, that shall be lawful and free for them and their assignes at all and every time and times hereafter, out of any of our realmes and dominions whatsoever, to take, leade, carry and transport for, in, and into their voyages, and for and towards the said plantation in New-England, all such and so many of our loving subjects or any other strangers that will become our loving subjects and live under our allegiance, as shall willingly accompany them in the same voyages and plantation, and also shipping, armour, weapons, ordinance, ammunition, powder, shott, corne, victuals, and all manner of cloathing, implements, furniture beasts, cattle, horses, mares, merchandizes, and all other things necessary for the said plantation, and for their use and defence, and for trade with the people there, and in passing and returning to and fro, any law or statute to the contrary hereof in any wise notwithstanding, and without paying or yeilding any custom or subsidie, either inwards or outward, to us, our heires or successours, for the same, by the space of seven years from the day of the date of these presents. Provided that none of the said persons be such as shall be hereafter by speciall name restrained by us, our heires or successours.

And for theire further incouragement, of our especial grace and favour, we do by these presents for us, our heires, and successours, yeeld and grant to the said Governor and Companie and theire successours and every of them, their factors and assignes, that they and every of them shall be free and quiet from all taxes, subsidies and customes in New-England for the like space of seven years, and from all taxes and impositions for the space of twenty and one yeares upon all goods and merchandises at any time or times hereafter, either upon importation thither, or exportation from thence, into our realme of England, or into any other of our dominions, by the said Governour and Companie and their successours, their deputies, factors and assignes, or any of them, except only the five pounds per centum due for customs upon all such goods and merchandises, as after the said seven yeares shall be expired shall be brought or imported into our realme of England, or any other of our dominions, according to the ancient trade of merchants: which five pounds per centum onely being paid, it shall be thenceforth lawfull and free for the said adventurers the same goods and merchandizes to export and carry out of our said dominions

THE WAR IN AMERICA.   129

sons fitted for all public offices, both for the magistracy and ministry. Accordingly at a general court, held at Boston September 8th, 1630, a subscription was opened for building a college at New Town, the name of which they changed to Cambridge. The subscriptions were at first but small, but such was the zeal and emulation of those colonists, that in a short time the money raised was considerable. Mr John Harvard, minister at Carlestown, by his last will, bequeathed 779l. 17s. 2d. for the purpose of building a college, which was presently

ons into foreign parts, without any custome, taxe or other duty to be paid to us, our heires or successours, or to any other officers or ministers of us, our heires and successours. Provided that the said goods and merchandises be shipped out within thirteen months after their first landing within any part of the said dominions.

And we do for us, our heirs and successours give and grant unto the said Governour and Companie and their successours, that whensoever, or so often as any custome or subsidie shall grow due or payable unto us, our heirs, or successours, according to the limitation and appointment aforesaid, by reason of any goods, wares, or merchandises to be shipped out, or any return to be made of any goods, wares, or merchandises, unto or from the said parts of New England hereby mentioned to be granted at aforesaid, or any of the lands and territories aforesaid, that then and so often and in such case the farmers, customers, and officers of our customs of England and Ireland and every of them for the time being, upon request made to them by the said Governor and Companie or their successours, factors, or assignes, and upon convenient security to be given in that behalfe, shall give and allowe unto the said

Governour and Companie and their successours, and to all and every person and persons free of that Companie as aforesaid, six months time for the payment of one halfe of all such custome and subsidie as shall be payable unto us, our heirs and successours, for the same, for which these our letters patents, or the duplicate or the inrollment thereof, shall be unto our said officer, a sufficient warrant and discharge. Nevertheless, our will and pleasure is, that any of the said goods, wares, and merchandises which be or shall be at any time hereafter landed or exported out of any of our realmes aforesaid, and shall be shipped with a purpose not to be carried to the parts of New England aforesaid, but to some other place, that then such payment, dutie, custome, imposition, or forfeiture shall be paid or belong to us, our heirs and successours, for the said goods, wares and merchandise so fradulently sought to be transported, as if this our grant had not been made or granted.

And wee do further will and by these presents for us, our heirs and successours firmly enjoine and commande, as well the Treasurer, Chancellor and Barons of the Exchequer of us, our heirs and successors, as also all and singular the customers, farmers, and collectors of

sently begun, and a committee appointed to promote this noble design. This academy received the name of Harvard college from one of its first and principal benefactors. While this college was building, a number of scholars were preparing under one Nathaniel Eaton, an excellent scholar, but a man of bad morals, and a great tyrant. Cotton Mather, in his History of New-England, observes of him, that it might be truly said, that such as were educated under him, received their education in the school of Tyrannus.

On

of the customes, subsidies and imposts, and other the officers and ministers of us, our heires and successors, whatsoever for the time being, that they and every of them, upon the shewing forth unto them of these letters patents, or the duplicate or exemplification of the same, without any other writt or warrant whatsoever from us, our heires or successours, to be obtained or sued forth, do and shall make full, whole, entire and due allowance and cleare discharge unto the said Governour and Companie and theire successours, of all customs, subsidies, impositions, taxes, and duties whatsoever that shall or may be claymed by us, our heires and successours, of or from the said Governour and Companie and their successours, for or by reason of the said goods, chattels, wares, merchandises and premisses, to be exported out of our said dominions, or any of them, into any part of the said lands or premisses hereby mentioned to be given, granted, and confirmed, or for, or by reason of any of the said goods, chattels, wares or merchandises to be imported from the said lands and premisses hereby mentioned to be given, granted and confirmed, into any of our said dominions, or any part thereof, as aforesaid, excepting only the said five pounds per centum hereby reserved and payable after the expiration of the said terme of seven yeares as aforesaid and not before. And these our letters patents, or the inrollment, duplicate or exemplification of the same shall for ever hereafter from time to time, as well to the Treasurer, Chancellor and Barons of the Exchequer of us, our heires, and successours, as to all and singular the customers, Farmers and Collectors of the customes subsidies and imposts, of us, our heires and successours, and all searchers and other the officers and ministers whatsoever of us, our heires, and successours, for the time being, be a sufficient warrant and discharge in this behalfe.

And further our will and pleasure is, and we doe hereby for us, our heires and successours, ordaine, declare and grant to the said Governour and Companie and theire successours, That all and every the subjects of us our heires and successours, which shall goe to and inhabite within the said lands and premisses hereby mentioned to be granted, and every of theire children which shall happen to be borne there, or on the seas in going thither or returning from thence, shall have and enjoy all liberties and immunities of free and naturall subjects within any of the dominions

On August 27th, 1640, the magistrates and ministers of the colony chose Mr Henry Dunstar, president of this new college; and afterwards the general assembly endowed it with a charter, and made it a corporation consisting of a president, two fellows, and a treasurer; reserving unto the governor, deputy governor and all the magistrates of the colonies, and the ministers of the six nearest towns for the time being, to be overseers or visitors of this society. The languages and arts were now taught in the college and great regularity

dominions of us, our heires or successours, to all intents constructions and purposes whatsoever, as if they and every of them were borne within the realme of England. And that the Governour and Deputy-Governour of the said Companie for the time being, or either of them, and any two, or more, of such of the said Assistants as shall be thereunto appointed by the said Governour and Companie, at any of their courts or assemblies, to be held as aforesaid, shall and may at all tymes, and from tyme to tyme, hereafter have full power and authority to administer and give the oath and oaths of supremacie and allegiance, or either of them, to all and every person and persons which shall at any tyme or tymes, hereafter goe or passe to the lands and premisses hereby mentioned to be granted, to inhabite in the same.

And wee do of our further grace, certain knowledge and meere motion give and grant to the said Governour and Companie and their successours, that it shall and may be lawfull to and for the Governour Deputy Governour and such of the Assistants and Freemen of the said Company for the tyme being as shall be assembled in any of their generall courts aforesaid, or in any other courts to be specially summoned and assembled for that purpose, or the greater part of them (whereof the Governour or Deputy Governour and sixe of the Assistants to be always seven) from tyme to tyme to make, ordaine, and establish all manner of wholesome and reasonable orders, lawes, statutes and ordinances, directions and instructions not contrary to the lawes of this our realme of England, as well for the setling of the formes and ceremonies of government and magistracie fitt and necessary for the said plantation and the inhabitants there, and for nameing and styling of all sorts of officers both superior and inferiour which they shall find needfull for that government and plantation, and the distinguishing and setting forth of the severall duties, powers, and limits of every such office and place, and the formes of such oathes warrantable by the lawes and statutes of this our realme of England, as shall be respectively ministered unto them, for the execution of the said severall offices and places, as also for the disposing and ordering of the elections of such of the said officers as shall be annuall, and of such others as shall be to succeed in case of death or removall, and ministering the said oathes to the new elected officers; and for imposition

regularity was observed. To support this college, the revenues of Charlestown Ferry were appropriated by an act of a general court, but the benefactions at last were so numerous, that the funds thereof became exceedingly strong. A good library was set up, and enriched by many donations of books from gentlemen in England, among whom were Sir Knelem Digby, Sir John Maynard, Mr Richard Baxter, and Mr Joseph Hill. To all these benefactions the famous Theophilus Gale, who wrote the Court of

tion of lawful fynes, mulcts, imprisonment, or other lawful correction, according to the courſe of other Corporations of this our realme of England, and for the directing, ruleing and diſpoſing of all other matters and things whereby our ſaid people inhabiteing there may be ſo religiouſly, peaceably and civilly governed, as theire good life and orderly converſation may winne and invite the natives of that country to the knowledge and obedience of the onely true God and Saviour of mankind, and the chriſtian faith, which in our royall intention and the adventurers free profeſſion is the principal end of this plantation. Willing, commanding and requiring, and by theſe preſents for us, our heires and ſucceſſours, ordaining and appointing, that all ſuch orders, lawes, ſtatutes and ordinances, inſtructions and directions as ſhall be made by the Governour or Deputy Governour of the ſaid Company and ſuch of the Aſſiſtants and Freemen as aforeſaid, and publiſhed in writing under theire common ſeale, ſhall be carefully and and duly obſerved, kept performed and put in execution according to the true intent and meaneing of the ſame. And theſe our letters patents, or the duplicate or exemplification thereof,

ſhall be to all and every ſuch officers, ſuperiour and inferiour, from tyme to tyme, for the putting of the ſame orders, lawes, ſtatutes and ordinances, inſtructions and directions in due execution, againſt us, our heirs and ſucceſſours, a ſufficient warrant and diſcharge.

And wee doe further, for us, our heirs and ſucceſſours, give and grant to the ſaid Governour and Companie and their ſucceſſours, by theſe preſents, That all and every ſuch chiefe commanders, captains, governours and other officers and miniſters, as by the ſaid orders, lawes, ſtatutes, ordinances, inſtructions or directions of the ſaid Governour and Companie "for the tyme being, ſhall be from time to time hereafter employed either in the government of the ſaid inhabitants and plantation, or in the way by ſea thither or from thence, according to the natures and limits of theire offices and places reſpectively, ſhall from tyme to tyme hereafter forever within the precincts and parts of New England hereby mentioned to be granted and confirmed, or in the way by ſea thither, or from thence, have full and abſolute power and authority to correct, puniſh, pardon, governe and rule, ſuch the ſubjects of us, our heirs and ſucceſſours, as ſhall from tyme to tyme adventure

of the Gentiles, added his own library which he left to Harvard college. Thus was the academy furnished with mathematical instruments, and books of all sorts, and supplied with the best of masters. Dunstar, who was the first president, lost his place by turning Anabaptist, and Mr Charles Chancey was appointed in his stead. Both the manner of admission and the method of teaching in this college were very exact and particular.

Those who had attended a grammar-school till they could

ture themselves in any voyage thither or from thence, or that shall at any time hereafter inhabite within the precincts and parts of New-England aforesaid, according to the orders, laws, ordinances, instructions and directions aforesaid, not being repugnant to the laws and statutes of our realme of England as aforesaid.

And we do further, for us our heires and successors, give and grant to the said Governour and Companie and their successors, by these presents, That it shall and may be lawful to and for the chief commanders, governours and officers of the said companie for the tyme being, who shall be resident in the said part of New England in America by these presents granted, and others there inhabiting, by their appointment and direction from tyme to tyme and at all tymes hereafter, for their speciall defence and safety to encounter, repulse, repell and resist by force of armies, as well by sea as by land, and by all fitting wayes and meanes whatsoever, all such person and persons as shall at any tyme hereafter attempt or enterprise the destruction, invasion, detriment or annoyance of the said plantation or inhabitants: And to take and surprize by all wayes and means whatsoever all and every such person and persons, with their shipps, armour, ammunition, and other goods, as shall in hostile manner invade and attempt the defeatinge of the said plantation, or the hurt of the said Companie and inhabitants. Neverthelefs, our will and pleasure is, and we do hereby declare to all Christian Kings, Princes and States, That if any person or persons which shall hereafter be of the said Companie or plantation, or any other by lycence or appointment of the said Governour and Companie for the tyme being, shall at any tyme or tymes hereafter, robb or spoyle by sea or by land, or do any hurt, violence, or unlawfull hostility to any of the subjects of us, our heirs or successours, or any of the subjects of any Prince or State being then in league and amity with us, our heirs and successours, and that upon such injury done, and upon just complaint of such Prince or State or theire subjects, Wee, our heirs or successors, shall make open proclamation within any of the parts within our realme of England commodious for that purpose, that the person or persons having committed any such robbery or spoyle, shall, within the term limited by such a proclamation, make full restitution or satisfaction of all such injuries done, so as the said Princes or others so

complaining

could read any classical author, and turn it into English, could readily make and speak Latin, and write it in prose or verse, and could decline Greek nouns and verbs, were judged qualified for admission, and upon examination, were accordingly admitted by the president and fellows: After that, they signed the college laws, which they were to transcribe and preserve as continual monitors of the duties which they were obliged by their privileges to observe. The president inspected the manners of the students, and

every

complaining may hould themselves fully satisfied and contented. And that if the said person or persons having committed such robbery or spoyle shall not make, or cause to be made, satisfaction accordingly, within such tyme so to be lymited, that then it shall be lawfull for us, our heires and successors, to putt the said person or persons out of our allegiance and protection; and that it shall be lawfull and free for all Princes to prosecute with hostility the said offenders and every of them theire procurers, ayders, abettors and comforters in that behalfe.

Provided also, and our expresse will and pleasure is, and wee doe by these presents for us, our heires and successors, ordaine and appoint, that these presents shall not in any manner enure, or be taken to abridge, barre or hinder any of our loving subjects whatsoever to use and exercise the trade of fishing upon that coast of New-England in America by these presents mentioned to be granted: But that they or any and every or any of them shall have full and free power and liberty to continue and use their said trade of fishing upon the said coast in any of the seas thereunto adjoineing, or any armes of the seas or salt-water rivers where they have beene wont to fish, and to build and set upon the lands

by these presents granted such wharfes, stages, and workhouses as shall be necessary for the salting, drying, keeping and packing up of their fish to be taken or gotten upon that coast; and to cut downe and take such trees and other materials there growing, or being, as shall be needful for that purpose, and for other necessary easements, helps and advantage concerning theire said trade of fishing there, in such manner and forme as they have been heretofore at any tyme accustomed to doe, without makeing any wilfull waste or spoyle, any thing in these presents contained to the contrary notwithstanding.

And we doe further for us, our heirs and successours, ordaine and grant the said Governour and Companie and theire successours by these presents, that these our letters patents shall be firme, good, effectuall and available in all things and to all intents and constructions of lawe, according to our true meaning herein before declared, and shall be construed, reputed, and adjudged in all cases most favourably on the behalfe and for the benefit and behoofe of the said Governour and Companie and their successors; Although expresse mention of the true yearely value, or certainty of the premises, or any of them, or of any other gifts or

grants

THE WAR IN AMERICA.

every morning and evening said prayers in the common hall; to which was joined an exposition of some chapters of the old testament, which the students read out of Hebrew into Greek in the morning: and in the evening some part of the New Testament out of English into Greek. He also preached upon Sunday upon what subjects he judged most proper in the church in Cambridge, where the students had a gallery allotted them, and where they usually attended. The fellows resident were also tutors in the college; who, after they had taught the students Hebrew, instructed them in the liberal arts, before the first four years were expired. During this time they had their weekly declamations, and disputes, in the college hall, every Friday, where either the president or the fellows acted as moderators. Such as stood candidates for degrees, were obliged to attend in the hall for certain hours, on Mondays and on Tuesdays, for three weeks together, in the middle of June. These were called visitation weeks, when all who pleased, might ask them any questions, and examine them concerning their skill in the languages, or the sciences, which they professed

grants, by us or any other of our progenitors or predecessors, to the foresaid Governor and Companie before this time made, in these presents is not made, or any statute, act, ordinance, provision, proclamation or restraint to the contrary thereof heretofore had, made, published, ordained or provided, or any other matter, cause, or thing whatsoever to the contrary thereof in any wise notwithstanding. In witness whereof we have caused these our letters to be made patent. Witness ourselves at Westminster, the fourth day of March in the fourth yeare of our reigne.

This is a true copy of such letters patents under the great seal of England. In testimony whereof I John Winthrop governour of the Massachusetts aforesaid have caused the publick seal of the same to be here-

Loc.
Sigilli.

professed to understand. On this occasion, it was common for some of the overseers, while they were sitting solstice, as it was called, to visit them, with a design of seeing their improvement. When the time of commencement began, which was at first, the second Tuesday of August; but afterwards the first Wednesday of July, those who were to proceed batchelors, held their act publicly in Cambridge, where both the magistrates, and ministers, attended, to confer honour upon their exercises. These exercises were, besides an oration delivered by the president, orations delivered by the commencers, wherein suitable compliments were paid to the audience, according to their characters, dignities, and offices. These academical orations were made not only in latin, but sometimes in Greek and Hebrew. But the principal exercises were disputations upon questions, where the respondents exhibited a thesis which might be impugned by any who pleased. In conclusion, the president delivered a book into the hands of the candidates, and gave them their first degree. Those who were admitted to the degree of Masters of Arts, were obliged to undergo a new trial, and dispute upon some question suited to the time they had studied. When this was finished, they received their degree with the same formality as in the first. Such diligence and strictness could not but have great influence in promoting learning, and preventing many from wasting their time idly, as happens in many European universities, where such discipline is not observed. Whether this order is still observed, I will not pretend to say; but according to the laws and statutes of the college, it ought to be kept up. The statutes are so express, that they must expose themselves greatly, to depart from them.

There are twenty-three rules in their statutes very express, * and strong, that would be thought rather too severe for either of the two universities in Old England.

S   What

* Statutes and Privileges of the Harvard College.

I. Such as are capable to read Cicero, or any such like classic authors, and can speak and write latin in prose and verse, and can also decline the Greek nouns and verbs, may be admitted into the college. None can be admitted otherwise.

II. All that are admitted into this college are to be received into a fellowship, and pay three pounds to the steward at theire admission, and at the end of every quarter of a year, pay what expences are due for their board. No student shall be allowed to dine or sup out of the college without leave from the president or tutors. But if any student shall, for the sake of receiving instruction which cannot be had in the college, go out of it, he shall forfeit no privilege.

III. While they continue in the college they must attend all the proper times appointed for instruction, and improve their time diligently in study.

IV. All students shall be obliged to perform every religious, as well as school exercise, peculiar to his station, both publicly and privately. And while they are pupils they shall deliver a public oration six times every year. The masters of arts are to be twice a weak present at the public disputations, and both Bachelors and Masters make an analysis of some part of sacred literature. Once in the half year, the Bachelors shall publicly discuss some philosophical questions under the government of the president, or in his absence, under the direction of the senior tutors in their turns.

V. No student under any pretence whatever, shall keep company with persons of loose and corrupt morals.

VI. No student, without leave from the president and tutors, shall go out of the town; nor shall any one, whatever be his rank and degree, be allowed to eat and drink in taverns or ordinaries, unless called by his parents, guardians, or such like near relations.

VII. No scholar, without the approbation of his parents, guardians or tutors, shall give away, sell, or lend any thing. If he does he shall be fined by the president and tutors, according to the nature of the offence.

VIII. All scholars must wear decent apparel, and abstain from gaudy dress, nor must any go out of the college without his gown or cloak.

IX. Every scholar who is not a graduate, shall only be called by his own name, unless he is a fellow commoner, the eldest son of a knight, or of some noble family.

X. Every commoner shall pay five pounds for the constant use of the college before he is admitted.

XI. Every student, in the condition of a pupil, shall pay two pounds to his tutor every year: but if he is a commoner, he shall pay three pounds.

XII. None of the older students, except the tutors or fellows shall be allowed to force any of the younger ones to go errands, or do

Whatever might be the errors and absurdities in the conduct of these colonists, it must be allowed that they were at great pains, both to support learning and religion;

do any other thing by threatenings, words, or blows. If any one, not a graduate, break this rule, he shall be punished by bodily correction, expulsion, or otherwise as the president and fellows shall think fit.

XIII. None of the students shall be allowed to play at cards, dice, or any kind of game for money, under the penalty of twenty shillings, as often as he shall offend, if he is a graduate, if he is not, he shall be fined according to the pleasure of the president and tutors.

XIV. If any student is absent from the prayers or lessons, without being obliged by necessity, or having obtained leave from the president or tutors, he shall be admonished according to the wisdom of the president or tutors, and if he offend more than once a week, he shall be liable to punishment.

XV. No student, for any cause whatever, unless first given notice of, and approved by the president and master, shall be absent from the stated studies and exercises of the college, except an half hour at breakfast, and an hour and an half at dinner; at nine o'clock at night they shall be called to supper.

XVI. If any student transgress any divine law, or rule of the college wilfully, or through mere negligence, after being twice admonished, he shall be corrected by severer punishments, according as the wisdom of the president and masters shall think proper. But for atrocious crimes, the punishment shall be more summarily executed.

XVII. Every scholar who, upon trial, can interpret the Holy Scriptures from the original text into Latin, and understands logic, natural and moral philosophy, and is blameless in his conversation, may, by the consent of the president, at some public meeting, be admitted to the first degree. Otherwise, not till after three years and ten months.

XVIII. Every student who has a common place and synopsis of logic, natural or moral philosophy, arithmetic, geometry, or astronomy, shall exhibit and defend his own Thesis, and also being found skilled in the original tongues, provided his morals are good, and he is approved by the college, shall be judged worthy of the second degree.

XIX. It is ordained, that if any student shall apply himself to the study of divinity before he has taken a bachelors degree, he shall take a degree of master of arts, and apply carefully to the study of divinity and Hebrew, which he shall study seven years, during which time, he shall dispute against a bachelor of divinity, and once be a respondent, he shall preach once in Latin, and once in English, either in the church, or in the college hall; and provided he has made sufficient progress, he shall be made a Bachelor by a solemn inauguration; with this proviso, that no one shall be admitted to this privilege before he has studied

five

religion; and many persons, eminent both for learning and abilities, were brought up and tutored among them. Their churches were filled with learned and religious ministers, and their chief magistrates were men of great abilities, and of good character. The greatest number of both their magistrates and clergy, in the reign of King William, had been bred in the Harvard college, and were persons of no mean character in their country. A list of those who had taken degrees in the Harvard college from 1642 to 1696, and of their churches and their pastors may be seen in the notes *.

This

five years from the time that he has taken his degree of master of arts.

XX. It is ordained, that such as shall desire the degree of doctor in divinity, shall study divinity five years from the time of taking the bachelors degree, and before he be admitted to this privilege, he shall once be opponent and once respondent, in some Theological questions, and if possible, to a doctor in divinity. He shall preach once in Latin and once in English, either in some church, or in the college hall: he must six times read and expound some portion of Scripture, and within a year after a solemn introduction, he must propose a question, the doubts and difficulties thereof he must resolve in the college hall publicly.

XXI. It is ordained, that besides those exercises to be performed for degrees in divinity, such as shall become a candidate for a degree of bachelor in divinity shall be obliged to publish some tract, according to the direction of the masters of the college, against some gross error or heresy, for the benefit of the church.

XXII. The academical degrees, formerly conferred by the president and masters of the Harvard college, are to be held valid and sufficient.

XXII. Every scholar shall procure a copy of these laws, signed by the president, and some of the tutors, before he is admitted into the college.

* A Catalogue of Gentlemen who had taken degrees in the Harvard College, from 1641 to 1658.

1642.	Samuel Bellingham	Samuel Danford fellow
Benjamin Woodridge	Henry Saltonstall	John Allen
George Douning	Tobias Bernard	1644. 1645.
John Bukely	Nathaniel Brewster	John Oliver
William Hubbard	1643.	Jeremiah Holand
John Wilson	John Jones	William Ames
	Samuel Mather fello.	John Russel

Samuel

HISTORY OF

This colony, during the reign of Charles the second, and his brother James, met with much trouble, though Charles had actually confirmed their charter, and promised them all encouragement. But the disputes concerning religion had almost ruined all their liberties. When this sovereign promised to preserve their patent, and confirm their charter, he also required, among other things, a rescinding of all their laws, and a repeal of every thing contrary to the King's authority; the allowance of the use of the Com-

mon

Samuel Stow	Henry Butler	Thomas Grave
Jacob Ward	Nathaniel Pelham	John Emerson
Samuel Johnson	John Davies	1657.
1646.	Isaac Chancey	Zechariah Syms
John Alcock	Ichabod Chauncey	Zechariah Brigdon
John Brock	Jonathan Burr	John Cotton
George Stirk	1652.	John Hale
Nathaniel White	Joseph Rowlandson	Elisha Cook
1647.	1653.	John Whiting
Jonathan Mitchel	Samuel Willis	Barnabas Chauncey
Nathaniel Mather	John Angier	1658.
Constant Star	Thomas Shepherd	Joseph Elliot
John Barden	Samuel Nowel	Joseph Haynes
Abraham Walver	Richard Hubbard	Benjamin Bunker
George Hadden	John Whiting	Jonah Fordham
William Mildmay	Samuel Hooker	John Burnham
1648, 1649.	John Stone	Samuel Talcot
John Roger president	William Thompson	Samuel Shepherd
Samuel Eaton	Edward Rawson	1659.
Urian Oaks	Samuel Badsireet	Nathaniel Saltonstall
John Collins	John Long	Samuel Alcock
John Bowers	Samuel Whiting	Abijah Savage
1650.	John Moody	Samuel Willard
William Stoughton	Joshua Ambrose	Thomas Parish
John Glover	Thomas Crosby	Samuel Cheever
Joshua Hobbart	1654.	Ezek. Rogers
Jeremiah Hobbart	Philip Nelson	Samuel Belcher
Edmund Wild	1655.	Jacob Nopes
Samuel Philips	Gershom Bulley	1660.
Leonard Hoar	Mordicai Matheson	Simon Bradstreet
Isaac Alerton	1656.	Nathaniel Collins
Jonathan Ince	Eleazer Mather	Samuel Elliot
1651.	Increase Mather	William Whitingham
Michael Wigglesworth	Robert Paine	Joseph Cook
Margena Cotton	Subal Dummer	Samuel Carter
Thomas Dudley	John Hensie	Manassah Armitage
John Glover	John Elliot	Peter Buckley
		1661

THE WAR IN AMERICA.

mon Prayer, and the permission of persons of all persuasions to vote at their elections. These were requisitions they were not ready to comply with, though the latter was exceedingly reasonable; and for their non-compliance, lost the King's favour, and fell under his displeasure, which they suffered during the whole course of his reign.

In consequence of this disobedience, the King, 1664, issued a special commission under the great seal, impowering Colonel Nichols, and three others, therein named

1661.
John Bellingham
Nathaniel Chancey
Jonathan Chancey
Compenfat Osborn
Daniel Weld
Joseph Cook
Joseph Whiting
John Parker
Thomas Johnson
Boraland Sherman
1662.
John Hoboke
Benjamin Thompson
Soloman Stodart
Moses Tusk
Ephraim Savage
Thomas Oaks
1663.
Samuel Symonds
Samuel Cabbot
John Ryper
Benjamin Blackman
Thomas Mighil
Nathaniel Cutler
1664.
Alexander Nowell
John Flint
Joseph Pynchon
Samuel Brakenbur
John Woodbridge
Joseph Easterbrook
Samuel Street
1665.
Benjamin Elliot
Joseph Dudley
Samuel Bishop

Edward Mitchelfon
Samuel Mann
Spertus Arthurton
Jabez Fox
Caleb Cheesemnick
1666.
Joseph Brown
John Richardson
Daniel Mason
John Filer
1667.
John Harriman
Nathaniel Atkinson
John Foster
Gershom Hobbart
Japeth Hobbart
Nehemiah Hobbart
Nehemiah Noyes
1668.
Adam Winthrop
John Cullick
Zecheriah Whitman
Abraham Pierson
John Prodden
1669.
Samuel Epps
Daniel Epps
Jeremiah Shepherd
Daniel Gookin
John Bridgham
Daniel Russel
Jacob Bagley
Joseph Gerrish
Samuel Treat
1670.
Nathaniel Higgison
Ammi Ruhamah Cobet

Thomas Clarke
George Burrough
1671.
Ifaac Foster
Samuel Phipps
Samuel Sewell
Samuel Mather
Samuel Danforth
Peter Thacker
William Adam
Thomas Wild
John Bowles
John Norton
Edward Taylor
1672, 1673.
Edward Pelham
George Hancock
Samuel Angier
John Nifs
1674.
Edmund Davie
Thomas Serjeant
1675.
Joseph Hanley
John Pike
Jonathan Russel
Peter Oliver
Samuel Andrew
James Minot
Timothy Woodbridge
Daniel Allen
John Emerson
Nathaniel Gookin
1676.
Thomas Shepherd
Thomas Brattle
Jeremiah Cushing
1677

HISTORY OF

named, to go over and enquire into the state of the colony, and to hear and determine all complaints, and appeals in all causes, and matters civil, military, or criminal, according to their good and sound discretion, and to such instructions as they had or should receive. Upon the return and report of these commissioners various complaints and suits were brought against this colony, till at last they ended in the condemnation of the charter, and the total dissolution of their government, in the year 1684, Charles gave the finishing

1677.
Thomas Cheven
John Danforth
Edward Payson
Samuel Sweetman
Joseph Copper
Thomas Scotlow
1678.
John Cotton
Cotton Mather
Grandal Rawson
Urian Oaks
1679.
Jonathan Danforth
Edward Oaks
James Allen
Thomas Barnard
1680.
Richard Martin
John Leveret
James Oliver
William Brattle
Perleval Green
1681.
Samuel Mitchel
John Cotton
John Hasting
Noadiah Russel
Joseph Pierpont
John Davie
Samuel Russel
William Danison
Joseph Elliot
1682, 1683.
Samuel Danforth
John Williams
William Williams
1684.

John Denison
John Rogers
Gordon Saltonshall
Richard Wentley
Samuel Miles
Nehemiah Walters
Joseph Web
Edward Thompson
Benjamin Rolf
1685.
Thomas Dudley
Warham Mather
Nathaniel Mather
Rowland Cotton
Henry Gibs
Thomas Ferry
John Whiting
Edward Mills
John Elliot
Samuel Shepherd
Peter Ruck
Isaac Greenwood
John White
Jonathan Pierpont
1686.
Francis Wainwright
Benjamin Lynd
Daniel Rogers
George Philips
Robert Hale
Charles Chancey
Nicholas Morton
1687.
John Davenport
John Clark
Nathaniel Roger
John Mitchel
Daniel Brewer

Timothy Stephens
Nathaniel Welsh
Joseph Daffel
Henry Newman
Josias Dwight
Seth Shove
1688, 1689.
James Allen
Samuel Moody
William Payne
Addington Davenport
John Haynes
William Partridge
Richard Whitingham
John Emerson
John Sparrowhauk
Benjamin Marston
John Eveleth
Benjamin Pierpont
John Hancock
Thomas Swan
1690.
Paul Dudley
Samuel Mather
John Willard
Daniel Denison
John Jones
Joseph Whiting
Nathaniel Clap
Joseph Belcher
Nathaniel Stone
John Clark
Thomas Buckingham
Samuel Mansfield
Peter Burr
John Seleck
John Newmarch
Thomas

THE WAR IN AMERICA. 145

ing stroke to their charter, and his brother James succeeded, to exercise a despotism over them in its outmost extent. Sir Edmund Andros was appointed to be their governor, who would not suffer them to select an assembly or council, or to have any other government than what depended upon his arbitrary pleasure. He himself made laws, raised troops, levied taxes, and managed all things with a council of his own creatures, whom he made the instruments of his tyranny, and the promoters of the ends of his covetousness.

New-

Thomas Greenwood	Benjamin Ruggle	Samuel Whitman
Benjamin Wadworth	William Grosvenor	Samuel Estabrook
Thomas Ruggles	1694.	Andrew Gardiner
Stephen Mix	Adam Winthrop	Samuel Melyen
Edmund Goff	John Woodbridge	1697.
Nicholas Lynd	Dudley Woodbridge	Elisha Cook
Ben. Easterbrook	Elephelet Adams	Anthony Stodart
1691.	John Savage	Anthony Stodart
John Tyng	John Ralantine	Jabez Wakeman
Ebenezer Pemberton	Salmon Treat	Nathaniel Collins
Thomas Mackarty	John Filch	Samuel Borr
Joseph Lord	1695.	John Read
Christopher Tappon	Samuel Vassal	Samuel Moody
Samuel Emmery	Walter Price	Richard Brown
Thomas Atkinson	Richard Saltonstal	Hugh Adams
Timothy Edwards	John Hubbard	John Swift
1662.	Simon Willard	John Southmakl
Benjamin Coleman	Hubijah Savage	Joseph Coil
Zechariah Alder	Oliver Noyse	Joseph Persons
Ebenezer White	Thomas Phips	1698.
James Townshend	Timothy Lyndall	Thomas Symms
John Mors	Jonathan Law	John Cotton
Caleb Cushing	Ezekiel Lewis	Samuel Mather
1693.	Thomas Blowers	Josiah Willard
Isaac Chancry	Thomas Little	Dudley Bradstreet
Stephen Buckingham	John Perkin	Peter Cutler
Henry Flint	Jedediah Andrews	John Fox
Simon Bradstreet	John Smith	Nathaniel Hubbard
John Wade	John Robinson	Henry Swan
Nathaniel Hodson	Joseph Green	John White
Pen Townsend	Joseph Mors	Josiah Torry
Nathaniel Williams	Nicholas Webster	Oxenbridge Thacker
George Denison	1696.	Richard Billings.
John Woodward	George Vaughan	This is the Catalogue
Joseph Baxter	Peter Thacher	as it stood in the sixth
William Vesey	Dudley Woodbridge	of August 1698.
Nathaniel Hunting	Jonathan Remington	

At

HISTORY OF

New-England was now in a most dismal situation; their charters were dissolved, and the whole province brought into a state of absolute subjection. They were told that their charters being dissolved, their titles to their lands were forefeited therewith, and now belonged to the King. Under this pretence, they were called upon to take out new patents for their lands, subject to such fines as should be imposed; and writs of ejectment were brought against such as refused, to put them out of their possession. This was tyranny with a witness, but exceedingly consistent with the other measures of the government at that time. The colony deserved to feel some chastisement for their spirit of intolerance; but this was chastisement beyond all measure, and from hands that were guilty of higher transgressions. A general exception was also made to all titles, in consequence of the disolving of the charter, and the towns were declared to be incapable of receiving any estates; this rendered their situation truly abject. The town of Ipswich remonstrated against paying taxes levied by the governers's sole authority, without the consent of an assembly, or of the parliament, and the select men voted, "That in as much as it is against the privilege of English subjects, to have money raised without their consent, in an assembly or parliament, they therefore

At the time of the collecting the above catalogue, there were in the three colonies of Plymouth, Massachusetts, and Connecticut, an hundred and thirty-nine congregations, and of the ministers of these, there were above eighty, graduates of the Harvard college, and many of them men of good learning, and excellent parts.

Plymouth county,	7	Hampshire and Piscataqua	15
Barnstable,	6	Hartford,	12
Bristol,	6	London county,	9
Marthas Vineyard, Nantucket, and Rhode Island,	4	New-Haven,	6
Suffolk county,	20	Fairfield,	9
Middlesex	22		139

therefore will petition the King for liberty of an assembly, before they make any rates." For this, two of them were imprisoned, and the rest fined twenty, thirty, and fifty pounds a man.

In this condition of oppression, did this colony, and some others remain, till the accession of King William to the throne of Great Britain, when the people of Boston seized upon their governor, and called a convention. This assembly added two new agents to the two that were in England, and sent them over with instructions, to solicit the continuance of their ancient charter, and all its rights and privileges; and if there should be an opportunity, to endeavour the obtaining such further privileges as might be of benefit to the colony. It had been resolved in the house of commons, that the seizing of the charters of the corporations and colonies, in the reign of Charles the second, was illegal, and a bill had been brought in for the renewal of them, but it did not pass, though it was the general sense of the best friends of the constitution, that it ought to have passed. From this consideration, the agents, however, concluded, that they might be allowed to resume their charter, which according to the opinion of the most noted lawyers, could have been of very little service to them, whenever an arbitrary ministry should think fit to confine them to the letter thereof. The reader will judge for himself when he considers the charter, whether it is liable to the defects which are imputed to it. The opinion of council, which was taken at that time, was, "That a bare restitution of the Massachusetts charter could be of no service at all, because it was defective in five particulars. They had no power thereby to call a select assembly,—no power to lay taxes, and raise money on inhabitants, whether freemen, or strangers trading with them;—they had no admiralty,—no power to keep a prerogative court, to prove wills, nor to erect courts of judicature, especially chancery-courts. Some of their agents were very zealous to have the old charter renewed, but it would appear, they either did not understand the nature of it, nor were aware of the consequences which might arise from the quirks of lawyers, concerning their not literally fulfilling the conditions thereof. This charter did, indeed, affirm that they had power to imprison, or inflict punishment in criminal cases, according to the course of corporations in England; but the lawyers said, that unless capital cases, were expressly mentioned, the power could not reach *them*: That they had no power to erect judicatories, or courts for probates of wills, or with admiralty jurisdiction; nor had they power to constitute an house of representatives, nor impose taxes on the inhabitants; nor to incorporate towns, colleges, or schools, which power and privileges they had, notwithstanding, usurped; and of consequence, by law, had forefeited their charter. An historian who reads the transactions of those times, and judges upon the principles of common sense, finds himself greatly at a loss, when he finds a power granted to a people to make laws to themselves, provided they are consistent with the laws of England, and yet men who pretend to know the law better than others, declaring that there are many things which the subjects in England may do, that those in America may not do; were mankind divested of selfishness and prejudice, they would certainly infer, that an authority to make laws suited to any society, agreeable to the laws of another society, implied a right to make as many as they pleased, provided they were consistent with that general rule. If this is not the meaning of the words of the charter, it will be difficult to say what is the meaning of words. It has been alledged that the American charters cannot be infifted upon, as giving them a right of exemption from the jurifdiction of parliament; and it is certainly true; but it is also true, that all incorporated towns in England have a share in the legiflature, which the colonists have not; which right they have by their charters. It does not appear that thefe colonifts wanted to be free from the jurifdiction of parliament, but to have a fhare in the legiflature which pretends to tax them, which is certainly reafonable. And as their local circumftances render it next to impoffible for them to attend in England, they only afk the privilege which Britons require at home, to tax themfelves by their own reprefentatives; and if they are free men at all, and not flaves, this muft be their undoubted privilege.

In confidering the characters of nations and people, it will be difficult to find confiftency in the conduct of any that have yet exifted in this world. Our colonifts who fled from perfecution in their native country, turned tyrants to fome of their brethern, when once they got power into their own hands. The Anabaptifts and Quakers were the objects of their higheft averfion; they perfecuted them with unrelenting rigour, even unto death; and becaufe they could not believe the fame creed with them, they denied them the privileges of men and citizens. This was perverting religion to the worft of purpofes, and making the mild and merciful dictates of our Saviour, the ground-work of malice, tyranny, and perfecution. This is fuch a blot in the character of the firft fettlers, that nothing can wipe away the reproach from their fucceffors but a total renunciation of both the principles and practices which their progenitors purfued.

Liberty

Liberty, the noble privilege of all honest men, can never be consistently maintained, without allowing others as much as we take to ourselves, while they do not hold practical principles, destructive of the rights of all other people. It has been too often the disposition of religious societies, to blend the ideas of civil and religious things, and to make a certain form of religion, a *sine qua non*, of men's right to enjoy the liberty of free citizens. This at once makes the kingdom of our Lord, a kingdom of this world, and renders every form of godliness a tool of private interest, selfishness, and pride. How far the colonists have reformed their practices in this point, will appear in the sequel of this history; where they shall be set in that light they deserve, as far as their actions point them out. Free from partiality to friends or foes, we shall endeavour to steer our course, and keep truth in view, as the unerring compass of all true and impartial history. But we shall now return to the more immediate causes of the present war, and the chief object of this history.

The satisfaction which the repeal of the stamp-act gave the colonists, did not remove their apprehensions concerning the designs of the ministry to oppress them; and the future proceedings of the English parliament, in giving sanction to the requisitions of the executive power, did fully confirm their apprehensions. The laws that were passed this year, for the purpose of raising a revenue in the colonies, by the laying of duties on the importation of glass and paper, and other commodities from Britain, and the consequent establishment of custom-houses in their ports, alarmed them greatly. These caused dreadful convulsions in the colonies, and produced consequences highly prejudicial to the commercial interests

of

of the mother country. It will at least appear unfortunate, if not altogether impolitic, after the recent examples of the mischief that attended the stamp-act, and the consequent repeal thereof, from a conviction of those evils, a measure of a like tendency should have been so speedily adopted, before the chagrin on account of the former irritation was worn off the minds of the colonists. Much the same arguments have been used in the defence of those measures that were made in support of the stamp-act, which shall be taken notice of, after we have considered the opposition that was made to the new statutes of this year.

The first visible instance of opposition shewn to these statutes, happened at Boston, October 27th, 1767, where the inhabitants, at a general meeting, formed, and agreed to several resolutions, for the encouragement of manufactures, promoting frugality, and œconomy, and for lessening and restraining of all superfluities. These resolutions, which were all of them in the first instance prejudicial to the commerce of Britain, contained an enumeration of articles, which it was determined not to use at all, or in as low a degree as possible. At the same time, a subscription was opened, and a committee appointed for the encouragement of their own former manufactures, and the establishment of new ones. Among these, it was agreed to give particular encouragement to the making of paper and glass, and the other commodities that were liable to the payment of new duties upon importation. It was also resolved to restrain the expences of funerals, and to reduce dress to a degree of primitive simplicity and plainness, and in general, not to purchase from the mother country any thing that could be procured in the colonies. These resolutions were adopted, or similar ones agreed

greed upon by all the old colonies on the continent. The government of Britain might have by this time perceived that a people of such a Spartan taste were not to be easily frightened into compliance with suspicious, or arbitrary acts of a legislature, where they had none to represent them. A people that have as much public virtue as to become unfashionable, for the sake of preserving the rights of the community, and can restrain their passions and appetites for the sake of their country, are not easily to be driven to a compliance with acts they conceive to be unreasonable. Whatever may be the errors or mistakes in the conduct of the colonists, and however far they may have acted wrong in some particulars; yet they have shewn a steadiness of principle and practice, that has at least the appearance of virtue, and which their enemies must admire, though their pride will not suffer them to acknowledge it.

What had lately irritated both parties in this dispute, was the proceedings of the assembly at New-York, and the act of the British parliament, made in consequence thereof. It had been appointed by parliament in the last session, that the people of New-York should provide for the King's troops, according to a method expressed in the act; which the assembly, instead of observing, pursued a measure of their own, without paying any regard to the prescription of parliament. Whether they shewed this opposition out of mere wilfulness, or claimed it as a principal of right, to observe their own way in providing for the troops, I will not affirm; but this was so offensive to the legislature of Britain, that they passed an act, June 15th, whereby the governor, council, and assembly of New-York, are prohibited from passing any act of assembly whatsoever, till they had complied with the terms

terms of the act of parliament in every particular. This was designed as a lesson to the other colonies, to teach them more reverence to acts of the British legislature; but it did not produce the intended effect; for the colonists who had begun to question the right of the parliament to make laws for them, were not disposed to obey a statute that was specially designed to point out that they were in a state of vassalage. By such opposition of conduct, the leading actors on both sides grew more and more warm in their disposition, and scarcely could restrain themselves within the bounds of decency and temper. The speeches of each party were often uncharitable, and recriminating, and expressed more the spirit of party, than liberality of sentiment, becoming contenders for liberty and the rights of mankind.

We are now approaching to the beginning of an year that is crowded with incidents, and teems with transactions of the greatest importance. The spirits of the colonies were now agitated to a degree of enthusiasm for their liberties, and they considered every new act of parliament as a fresh attack upon their freedom, and an insult to their understanding. Upon the eleventh of February, 1768, the assembly of Massachusetts bay sent a circular letter, signed by their speaker to all the other colonies in North America*. The design of this letter, was to shew the dangerous tendency of the late acts of parliament, to represent them

*CIRCULAR LETTER.

Gentlemen, *Boston, Sept. 14.* Your are already too well acquainted with the melancholy and very alarming circumstances to which this province, as well as America in general, is now reduced. Taxes, equally detrimental to the commercial interests of the parent country and her colonies, are imposed upon the people, without their consent; taxes designed for the support of the civil government in the colonies, in a manner clearly unconstitutional, and contrary to that in which, till of late, government has been supported, by the free gift of the people in the American assemblies or parliaments; as

them as unconstitutional, and to propose a common union among the colonies in the pursuit of all legal measures to prevent their effect, on an harmony in their applications to government, to obtain a repeal of them. It also largely sets forth their constitutional rights as English subjects; all of which they affirm were infringed by these new laws.

At this period, and for some years before, the assembly of Massachusetts-bay and their governor had almost differed in their opinion upon every subject, which

also for the maintenance of a large standing army; not for the defence of the newly-acquired territories, but for the old colonies, and in time of peace. The decent, humble, and truly loyal applications and petitions from the representatives of this province, for the redress of these heavy and very threatening grievances, have hitherto been ineffectual, being assured from authentic intelligence that they have not yet reached the royal ear: the only effect of transmitting these applications hitherto perceivable, has been a mandate from one of his Majesty's secretaries of state to the governor of this province, to dissolve the general assembly, merely because the late house of representatives refused to rescind a resolution of a former house, which implied nothing more than a right in the American subjects to unite in humble and dutiful petitions to their gracious sovereign, when they found themselves aggrieved: this is a right naturally inherent in every man, and expressly recognized at the glorious Revolution as the birth-right of an Englishman.

This dissolution you are sensible has taken place; the governor has publickly and repeatedly declared that he cannot call another assembly; and the secretary of state for the American department, in one of his letters communicated to the late house, has been pleased to say, 'proper care will be taken for the support of the dignity of government;' the meaning of which is too plain to be misunderstood.

The concern and perplexity into which these things have thrown the people, has been greatly aggravated by a late declaration of his excellency Governor Bernard, that one or more regiments may soon be expected in this province.

The design of these troops is every one's apprehension; nothing short of enforcing by military power the execution of acts of parliament, in the forming of which the colonies have not, and cannot have, any constitutional influence. This is one of the greatest distresses to which a free people can be reduced.

The town which we have the honour to serve, have taken these things at their late meeting into their most serious consideration: And as there is in the minds of many a prevailing apprehension of an approaching war with France, they have passed the several votes, which we transmit to you, desiring that they may be immediately laid before the town whose prudentials are in your care, at a legal meeting

which had been the occasion of continual altercation. This altercation was carried on with great asperity on both sides, and both parties seemed more attentive to keeness of expression, and severity in their replies, than to the propriety of measures, or the advantages of civil government. These disputes so soured the tempers of the parties, that it was not easy for them to pursue measures in connection, without shewing a temper inconsistent with mutual confidence. Governor Bernard was considered as a person who was looking up to the sovereign for a dignity which his pride suggested to him he deserved, and for that reason, was more careful to please the ministry, than to study the real advantage of the colony. He had shewn an imperious stiffness in his behaviour, which did not suit the temper of a people that were exceeding jealous of their liberty. His answers to their petitions and requests were formal, arbitrary, and willfully disobliging*; and instead of endeavouring to

soften

ing, for their candid and particular attention.

Deprived of the councils of a general assembly in this dark and difficult season, the loyal people of this province will, we are persuaded, immediately perceive the propriety and utility of the proposed committee of convention: and the sound and wholesome advice that may be expected from a number of gentlemen chosen by themselves, and in whom they may repose the greatest confidence; must tend to the real service of our gracious sovereign, and the welfare of his subjects in this province, and may happily prevent any sudden and unconnected measures, which in their present anxiety, and even

agony of mind, they may be in danger of falling into.

As it is of importance that the convention should meet as soon as may be, so early a day as the 22d of this instant September has been proposed for that purpose—and it is hoped the remotest towns will by that time, or as soon after as conveniently may be, return their respective committees.

Not doubting but that you are equally concerned with us, and our fellow citizens, for the preservation of our invaluable rights, and for the general happiness of our country, and that you are disposed with equal ardour to exert yourselves in every constitutional way for so glorious a purpose.

Signed by the select-men.

* To the Gentlemen Assembled at Faneuil-hall under the name of a Committee of Convention.

As I have lately received from his majesty strict orders to support his constitutional authority within this government, I cannot sit still, and

see

soften the tempers of the assembly already sufficiently rankled and over heated, he added fuel to the flame, by talking of prerogative, and the determination of the sovereign to support his dignity. It was strongly suspected that the royal determination depended much upon the representation that he had given of the colonists, and that the ministerial vengeance proceeded in a great measure from those partial accounts of the temper of the people represented in his letters to the ministers of state.

A letter which the governors received from the Earl of Shelburne, one of the principal secretaries of state, and which contained some severe strictures on the behaviour of the colonies, and the conduct of the Massachusetts assembly, was, by the order of the governor, and according to its original design, read to that body by their secretary. This produced great debates in the assembly, when several severe things were said, with very little temper, and observations made

fee so notorious a violation of it, as the calling an assembly of the people by private persons only. For a meeting of the deputies of the towns is an assembly of the representatives of the people to all intents and purposes; and it is not the calling it a committee of convention that will alter the nature of the thing.

I am willing to believe that the gentlemen who so hastily issued the summons for this meeting; were not aware of the high nature of the offence they were committing; and they who have obeyed them have not well considered of the penalties which they will incur if they should persist in continuing their session and doing business therein. At present, ignorance of law may excuse what is past: a step farther will take away that plea.

It is therefore my duty to interpose, at this instant, before it is too late. I do therefore earnestly admonish you, that instantly, and before you do any business, you break up this assembly, and separate yourselves. I speak to you now as a friend to the province, and a well-wisher to the individuals of it.

But if you should pay no regard to the admonition, I must as a governor assert the prerogative of the crown in a more public manner. For assure yourselves (I speak from instruction), the king is determined to maintain his entire sovereignty over this province; and whoever shall persist in usurping any of the rights of it, will repent of his rashness.

FRA. BERNARD.
Province-House,
Sept. 22, 1768.

made, not quite confistent with the dignity of such a meeting. It was alledged in those debates, that Lord Shelburne's letter proceeded upon topics which the governor's representation of the colonies had suggested; and that the severity of the secretary's letter took its rise from a misrepresentation of facts, given by the governor in his dispatches to the ministry. A committee was appointed to wait upon him, to desire a copy of Lord Shelburne's letter, as well as those that he had written himself, with relation to the assembly, and to which the charges in his Lordship's letter must refer. These copies being refused, the assembly wrote a letter to the secretary of state, in which, they recite the circumstances of the whole transaction, and endeavour to vindicate themselves, and their conduct, at the expence of the governor, whom they charge with misrepresenting them, and being the occasion of the ill opinion which the secretary had concerning them. They also wrote letters to the Lords of the treasury, and several other great officers of state, wherein, together with professions of their loyalty, they remonstrated against the operations of the late acts of parliament; which they hinted, were contrary to the constitution, and totally subversive of their rights and liberties.

Such a firm opposition was by no means agreeable to the temper of the governor, who probably had given assurances to the secretaries of state, that a sharp rebuke from those in power in England, would make them return to their duty and obedience. He found himself deceived, as well as found that they had endeavoured to expose him as neither a friend to the King nor to the colonies; so when he found himself disappointed in all his other schemes, he adjourned the assembly. In the speech which he delivered on this

this occasion, he made many animadversions upon their conduct, especially with regard to Lord Shelburne's letter; and he complained greatly of some turbulent and factious members, who, under false pretences of patriotism, had unhappily procured too great influence in the assembly, and among the people, who sacrificed their country to the gratification of their passions, and to the support of an importance, which could have no existence but in times of trouble and confusion. It is a common thing for all men that are grasping at power and domination, to charge all people with the crime of factiousness, that oppose their measures; the whole struggles for liberty, in all ages of the world, have been accounted factious operations, of restless persons, who had no other intention than to disturb good and peaceable governors, who never deserved to be resisted. The famous patriots who brought about the glorious revolution, were, by the Tories of those times, accounted a faction, and charged with the worst of crimes, for saving the nation from Popery and tyranny.

While these disturbances in America were gaining ground by ministerial incapacity and opposition, a new secretary of state was appointed at home, to the department of the colonies. Much was hoped from this new institution and arrangement; but though the institution itself was good, the advantages arising therefrom, depended upon the manner of discharging the office. The first who was settled in this new department of state, was Lord Hillsborough, who did not by any lenient or softening measures, attempt to soften the tempers of the colonies. Whether his orders were express to observe the conduct which he pursued, or that he made use of the royal authority to awe the colonists into a compliance with the mandates

dates of government, I will not pretend to affirm; but in his circular letters to the governors of the colonies, which had received the circular letter from the assembly of Boston, he expresses his Majesty's dislike of that letter in very strong terms. It was declared in Lord Hillsborough's letter, that his Majesty considered the conduct of the assembly of Boston as of the most dangerous and factious tendency, calculated to inflame the minds of the people, to promote an unwarrantable combination; to excite an open opposition to, and denial of the authority of parliament, and to subvert the true principles of the constitution; and that his Majesty expected, from the known affection of the respective assemblies, that they would defeat this flagitious attempt to disturb the public peace, and treat it with the contempt it deserved, by taking no notice of it.

Another letter of the same date was sent to Governor Bernard, in which the same exceptions are made to the circular letter. It is there affirmed, that the measure had been carried in a thin house, at the end of the session, and in which the assembly departed from that spirit of prudence and respect to the constitution, which seemed to have influenced the majority of its members in a full house and at the beginning of the session: from hence his Majesty could not but consider it as a very unfair proceeding, and to have been carried by surprise through the house of representatives. It was then required in his Majesty's name that the new assembly would rescind the resolution which gave existence to the circular letter, and declare their disapprobation of, and dissent to so rash and hasty a proceeding: That as his Majesty had the fullest reliance on the affections of his subjects of Massachusets bay, he had the better ground to hope,

that

that the attempts made by a desperate faction, to disturb the public tranquility, would be discountenanced, and that the execution of the measure recommended would not meet with any difficulty. Both the ministry and the governor were mistaken in this conjecture. On the 21st of June, this part of the letter was laid before the new assembly by the governor, with a message, in which he earnestly requested their compliance; but observed, that in case of a contrary behaviour, he had received his Majesty's instructions how to act, and must do his duty. This produced a message from the assembly, in which they desired a copy of the instructions which the governor alluded to, as well as of some letters and papers he had laid before the council. The governor sent a copy of the remainder of Lord Hillsborough's letter, in which the instructions were contained, to the assembly, by which he was directed, in case of their refusing to comply with his Majesty's reasonable expectations, to dissolve them immediately, and to transmit a copy of their proceedings upon it, to be laid before the parliament. The whole of those requisitions, made by the government of Britain upon this colony, were considered by the colonists as the effects of the misrepresentations of their own governor, who, as he wanted to rule over them with an arbitrary power, was provoked at their opposition, and therefore represented them to the King and the ministry as a perverse and factious set of people that would be ruled by no law, and despised all government.

The assembly gave no answer to the governor's request, till his patience was almost worn out, and he was obliged to send a message to them, to urge their compliance with the King's demands. In answer to this message, they applied for a recess, that they might have an opportunity to confult, and advife with their conftituents upon the occafion. This was what the governor knew would be of no fervice to his fcheme, but would rather add fuel to the fire that was already kindled; he therefore refufed their requeft. Upon which they put the queftion, for refcinding the refolution of the laft affembly, which paffed in the negative, by a divifion of ninety two to feventeen. This fhews how badly the fecretary had been informed concerning the temper of the majority, when he affirmed, that the meafure had been carried in a thin meeting, contrary to the opinion of the majority, who were abfent. It appears to be a common infirmity prevailing with men of all ranks to believe, at leaft on occafions to affirm, what is moft agreeable to their own inclinations and interefts, however little evidence they have for their conduct.

The affembly then refolved to write a letter to Lord Hillfborough, and an anfwer to the Governor. In both thefe letters they endeavour to vindicate the conduct of the laft affembly, as well as the prefent, and deny the charges brought againft them, of carrying the refolution by furprife in a thin meeting of the affembly, and affirm on the contrary, that the refolution for the circular letter was paffed in a full feffion, and by a great majority. They alfo defended the legality of that meafure, and affirmed that it was the inherent right of all fubjects to petition the King, either jointly or feparately, for a redrefs of grievances. In regard to the refcinding the refolution, it was obferved, that to fpeak in the ftile of the common law, it was not now *executory*, but to all intents and purpofes *executed*: That the circular letters had been fent, and many of them anfwered: That both had appeared in the public papers, and that they could now as well rescind the letters as the resolves on which they were founded, and that both would be equally fruitless. In the letter to the secretary of state, they made several strictures with great freedom on the nature of the requisition, and alleged that it was unconstitutional, and without a precedent, to command a free assembly, on pain of its existence, to rescind any resolution, much less that of a former house. They complained greatly of the base and wicked representations that must have been made to his Majesty, to cause him to consider a measure perfectly legal and constitutional, and which only tended to lay the grievances of the subjects before the throne, as of an inflammatory nature, tending to create unwarrantable combinations, and to excite an opposition to the authority of parliament, which are the terms in which it is described in the letter. They concluded with the warmest expressions of loyalty, and the strongest remonstrances against the late laws. They were at the same time preparing a petition to the King for removal of their governor, in which they bring many heavy charges against him, that were urged with great vehemency, and expressed in very strong terms. But before they had finished this petition, the governor took care to dissolve the assembly. The assemblies in America were now become something like the English parliaments in the reign of Charles the first, by no means tractable to the call of the court and sovereign; for which reason they were continually dissolved. But they were still as similar in their cases, the new assemblies were as tenacious of their rights as the old ones, and took up the grievances where the former assemblies left them, and began with new remonstrances; while these matters were warmly pursued in the colonies, and their assemblies continually dissolved, the grand assembly of Britain continued unshaken by the whole force of petitions and remonstrances that were levelled against it. The commons of Britain and the ministry understood one another, so that the whole forces of national petitions, and remonstrances could not procure a dissolution of parliament.

The circular letters which had been written by the secretary of state to the other colonies, were attended with as little success as that which was sent to Boston. The assemblies of the other colonies wrote answers to that of Massachusett's-Bay, which were received by the late speaker, in which they express the highest and warmest approbation of their conduct, and a firm resolution to concur with their measures. Some of the colonies also addressed the secretary of state, and justified the measures taken by the assembly at Boston, and also animadverted with great freedom upon several passages in the requisition contained in his letter. In the mean time, several of them entered into resolutions, not to import or purchase any English goods, except what were already ordered for the ensuing fall, or such articles as they could not want, until the late acts were repealed.

On the 10th of June, 1768, a little before the dissolution of the assembly, a great tumult happened at Boston. The board of customs had made a seizure of a sloop belonging to one of the principal merchants of that town. That sloop had been discharged of a cargo of wine, and in part re-loaded with a quantity of oil, which is said to have been done under pretence of converting it into a store, without any great attention being paid to the new laws, or to the custom-house regulations. Upon the seizure being made, the officers made a signal to the Romney man of war, and her boats were sent manned and armed, who cut away the masts of the sloop, and conveyed her under the protection of the man of war. The people, having assembled in great multitudes upon this occasion, pelted the commissioners of the customs with stones, broke one of their swords, and treated them in other respects with great outrage; after which, they attacked their houses, broke the windows, and hauled the collector's boat to the common, and burnt it to ashes. The officers of the customs upon this outrage, took shelter aboard the man of war, from whence they removed to castle William, where they resumed the functions of their office. This transaction occasioned several town meetings, in which a remonstrance was presented to the governor, wherein they claimed rights directly opposite to the new laws of the British legislature, and demanded that the governor would issue an order for the departure of his Majesty's ships out of the harbour. The minds of the people were now greatly irritated; they perceived that the new laws would be enforced by every exertion of the king and parliament, and as they disputed the right of the British legislature to impose such laws upon them, when they had no share therein, they looked upon themselves as oppressed by an unwarrantable authority. Their spirits were now wrought up to a degree of enthusiasm, which led them to those acts of outrage which men are ready to fall into, when they are bereaved of what they believe to be their natural rights. There is no question but the leaders in the opposition neglected no arts that they thought necessary to inflame the minds of the people; which when once they were wrought to a very high pitch, could not even be restrained by the authority of those who had inflamed them. In the fervour of controversy, it is difficult for men to restrain their passions, or to

observe a proper decency in expressing them. The writer of the historical part of the *Annual Register* observes, that " their public writers, as well as speakers, were ge-
" nerally very intemperate, and a certain stile and man-
" ner was introduced, which seemed peculiar to them-
" selves, and too ridiculous for serious composition."
It is easy for such as do not immediately feel the pain which others suffer, to account their behaviour ridiculous in the paroxism of their distemper; but provided they were in their situation, their behaviour would probably be as ridiculous. There is a warmth of zeal that appears in their composition, as will happen in all cases when men are in earnest, but at the same time, a due respect to the characters they are addressing, and unless men's eyes are blinded through a selfish prejudice, they must be obliged to confess, that so far as the pen has been employed in this controversy, the colonists have made no contemptible figure. There is an inconsistency that has been urged against some of their publications, " that when on one hand,
" they seem to forget their dependency as colonies,
" and assume the tone of distinct and original states;
" on the other hand, they claim all the benefits of the
" English constitution, and the highest rights of Eng-
" lishmen, but forget that it is their dependence which
" can entitle them to any share of those rights and
" benefits." In this there does not appear so great inconsistency as some do imagine. As members of the empire, and subjects of the same sovereign, they are mutually dependent, as other subjects are upon government and the constitution; but then they certainly are entitled to some share with their brethern in the legislature, otherwise they differ nothing from slaves. We shall see afterwards what they say for themselves, and what their most sanguine opposers

have

have said against them, when the reader shall be left to judge for himself concerning the conclusions necessary to be drawn.

A report that that petition to the King had not been delivered by the secretary of state, exasperated them greatly. It was said that the petition was refused to be received at London, because the agent had not proper authority, and because the governor had not signed it. The dissolution of their assembly had encreased their suspicions, and the affair of the seizing the sloop had confirmed them. They were therefore now in a very ill temper, and shewed their indignation without much restraint. It is no wonder, in such an agitation of temper, that many outrages were committed. When the excise was at first put in execution in Scotland, there were as great tumults at Glasgow as there were on this occasion at Boston. When the passions of men are over-heated, it is not easy to make them listen to cool reasoning.

While matters were in this unhappy situation, two regiments were ordered from Ireland, and some detachments from Halifax in Nova Scotia, to support the civil government. This threw the whole town of Boston into consternation, and raised great commotions: it was considered in the light of an invasion, and animadverted upon in the severest terms. A meeting of the inhabitants was called to assemble at Faneuil-hall to consider what was to be done in that extremity, when they chose one of their late popular representatives as moderator. They then appointed a committee to wait on the governor, to know what reasons he had for some late intimations he had given, that some regiments of his Majesty's forces were expected in that town, and to present a petition, to desire that he would issue precepts to convene and assemble

semble with the greatest speed; to both which an immediate answer was required. The governor answered, that his information was of a private nature, and that he could do nothing as to the calling of another assembly for this year, until he received his Majesty's instructions under whose consideration it now was. A committee had also been appointed to consider the present state of their affairs, which gave in their report, a long declaration and recital of their rights, and the violation of them, which they conceived had been lately made; and passed several sudden resolutions, particularly with respect to the legality of raising or keeping up a standing army among them, without their consent. This resolution they founded upon an act of the first of King William, which declares it to be contrary to law to keep an army in the kingdom in the time of peace without the consent of parliament. This report and the resolutions were unanimously agreed to by the assembly, and a general resolution passed, which was also founded upon a clause in the same law, which recommends the frequent holding of parliaments. Upon this a convention was called to assemble at Boston. In pursuance of this resolution, the four members who had represented the town in the late assembly, were now appointed a committee to act for it in the convention; and the select-men were ordered to write to all the other towns in the province, to propose their appointing committees for the same purpose. These proceedings of the colonists were considered as illegal and unlawful assemblies, and according to the ideas of the governor, they undoubtedly were such. It would appear that both Governor Bernard and the ministry at home, did not consider the colonists as having the same benefit of the laws as the people in the mother

ther country, though they reckoned them bound by them in their fulleſt extent. For if they had conſidered the coloniſts as having the privilege of other ſubjects, they would not have quartered troops upon them in the time of peace, without an act of legiſlature in which they were repreſented. But they ſeem to have had in idea, a diſtinction between a Britiſh freeman and a coloniſt, which the latter did not admit.

The coloniſts judged, that from the law made in the reign of King William, they had a right to their aſſemblies, which they conſidered as their parliaments, and without their conſent, it was illegal to keep up a ſtanding army among them: the miniſtry conſidered them as emigrants that had left their country, but were bound by its laws, without enjoying the privileges that aroſe from them, and unleſs they had this idea, their conduct will appear ridiculous: but all the advocates for the mother country's ſupremacy, have founded their arguments upon the diſtinction between a free Briton and a coloniſt. Whether this diſtinction is founded in nature and reaſon, I ſhall leave to the reader to determine as he thinks beſt.

There is one piece of duplicity in the conduct of this town meeting, which cannot be vindicated, which ſhews their addreſs more than their honeſty, and it is this: they made a requiſition to the inhabitants, that as there was a prevailing apprehenſion in the minds of many, of a war with France, they ſhould accordingly be provided with arms, ammunition, and other accoutrements, ſo as to be prepared in caſe of ſudden danger. After this, a day of public prayer and faſting was appointed, and the meeting diſſolved. It is manifeſt that a war with France, was a mere pretence, to carry forward a ſcheme, to have the inhabitants provided againſt another evil than a French war.

Though

Though the assembly at Boston might have good reasons for desiring the inhabitants to have arms in readiness, they ought not to have assigned false ones before the appointing of a fast: for this was certainly an act of vile hypocrisy, which no good man can approve.

The circular letter of the select-men, was written in the same stile, and with the same temper as their acts and resolutions, which were inclosed, and on which it was founded. In this time of general commotion, ninety-six towns appointed committees to attend the convention; but the town of Hatfield refused to comply with the measure, and gave their reasons for their refusing to join with the rest. It is plain from this answer, that they either had different ideas from the rest of their brethren, or were lukewarm in the cause of liberty[*]. When the convention met, the first thing they did, was to send a message to the governor, wherein they disclaim all authoritative or governmental acts: that they were chosen by several towns, and came freely and voluntarily, at the earnest desire of the people, to consult and advise such measures as may promote peace and good order in their present situation.

They

---

[*] We have fully considered your proposal of a convention, and the reasons you are pleased to assign for it, and hereby take the liberty to express our sentiments. We are not sensible that the state of America is so alarming, or the state of this province so materially different from what they were a few months since, as to render the measure you propose either salutary or necessary. The act of parliament, for raising a revenue, so much complained of, has been in being and carrying into execution for a considerable time past, and proper steps taken by several governments on this continent to obtain redress of that grievance; and humble petitions by them, ordered to be presented to his Majesty, we trust, have already, or soon will reach the royal ear, be graciously received, and favourably answered; and the petition from the house of representatives of this province the last year among the rest: if it should not, for want of an agent from this province, at the court

They then repeat the present grievances, complain that they are grossly misrepresented in Great Britain, and press the governor in the most earnest manner to call an assembly, as the only means to guard against those alarming dangers that threatened the total destruction of the colony. The governor admonished them, as a friend to the province, and a well-wisher to the individuals of it, to break up their assembly instantly, and to separate before they did any business: that he was willing to believe that the gentlemen who issued

court of Great Britain to present it, we presume you very well know if it be an impolitic and imprudent omission, where to lay the blame, and we apprehend that nothing that can or will be done by your proposed convention can or will aid the petition.

And here we beg leave to say, that we judge that it would be much for the interest of this province to have an agent at this critical day: a person that would have served us faithfully, we make no doubt, might have been found; but the reasons given, and the methods we hear have been taking, to prevent it, are dissatisfactory, and give us much uneasiness. We are further informed, that all matters of a public and private nature lying before the last general court were fully considered and acted upon, and all then proposed to be done, and finished before the adjournment, except the impeachment of his Majesty's representative which perhaps might not have been agreed to, had they sat longer, or not been afterwards dissolved. We are sorry for that circumstance that occasioned so early a dissolution of the general court; though we must own that the governor, by charter, is vested with that power; yet we wish, if he had judged it consistent with his duty to the King, it had been

as usual; however, we hope another will be soon called, or at farthest, on the last Wednesday in May next,—and that in the mean time, the public affairs of the province will not greatly suffer.

And here we propose to your consideration, whether the circular letter, which gave such umbrage, containing these expressions, or others of the like import, 'that the King and parliament, by the late revenue act, had infringed the rights of the colonies, imposed an inequitable tax, and things yet worse might be expected from the independence and unlimited appointments of crown officers therein mentioned,' was so perfectly innocent, and entirely consistent with that duty and loyalty professed by the house of representatives the last year, in their petition to his Majesty and whether the last house might not have complied with his Majesty's requisition, with a full saving of all their rights and privileges, and thereby prevented our being destitute of a general court at this day. We cannot comprehend what pretence there can be of a proposed convention, unless the probability for a considerable number of regular troops being sent in to this province, and an apprehension of their being quartered, part in your town, and part at the castle.

—And

sued the summons for this meeting, were not aware of the nature of the high offences they were committing; and that those who had obeyed them, had not considered the penalties they should incur, if they persisted to continue their session. At present, ignorance of law, says he, may excuse what is past; a step farther will take away that plea. That a meeting of the deputies of the towns, is an assembly of the representatives of the people to all intents and purposes; and that calling it a committee of convention, will not alter

*—And here we would observe, that it was a matter of doubt and uncertainty, whether any were coming or not; if otherwise for what purpose the King was sending them, whether for your defence, in case of a French war (as you tell us there is in the minds of many a prevailing apprehension of one approaching) and, if we don't misunderstand your letter, induced them to pass the votes transmitted to us) or whether they are destined for the protection of the new-acquired territories, is altogether uncertain: that they are to be a standing army in time of peace, you give us no evidence; and if your apprehensions are well grounded, it is not even supposeable they are intended as such,—and if your town meant sincerely, we can't see the need they had of interposing in military matters, in an unprecedented way, requesting their inhabitants to be provided with arms, &c. (a matter till now always supposed to belong to another department), especially as they must know such a number of troops would be a much better defence, in case of war, than they had heretofore been favoured with: To suppose what you surmize they may be intended for, is to mistrust the King's paternal care and goodness:—if, by any sudden excursions or insurrections of some inconsiderate people, the King has been induced to think them a necessary check upon you, we hope you will, by your loyalty and quiet behaviour, soon convince his Majesty, and the world, they are not longer necessary for that purpose, that thereupon they will be withdrawn, and your town and the province saved any farther trouble and expence from that quarter. We are sensible the colonies labour under many difficulties, and we greatly fear what the consequence of the disputes with our mother country will prove, however, we are far from thinking the measures you are pursuing have any tendency to deliver the good people of this province, but on the contrary, immerge them in greater;—after all, we should hope, (were it not for your present attempt, attended with a bad complexion), we might soon have deliverance from our present troubles, and things restored as at the first. The governments have, in our opinion consulted, and are pursuing, the propresst methods to obtain redress of their grievances; our duty is to wait with patience the event, unless we are determined to take the alternative. How far passion and disappointment and private resentment may influence any to hurry their neighbours into such mad and

ter the nature of the thing. He added, that if they did not regard his admonition, he must, as governor, assert the prerogatives of the crown in a more public manner: that they may assure themselves, he spoke from instruction, the King was determined to maintain his entire sovereignty over that province, and whosoever should persist in usurping any of the rights of it, would repent of his rashness. This answer produced another message, wherein they justified this meeting, as being only an assemblage of private persons, and desired explanations as to the criminality with which their proceedings were charged. The governor refused to receive that or any other message from them, as it would be admitting them to be a legal assembly, which he would not by any means allow. The convention then appointed a committee, who drew up a report, in terms of great moderation, which was approved by the assembly. In this they assign the causes of their meeting, and disclaim all pretence to any authority whatsoever, and advise and recommend it to the people, to pay the greatest deference to government, and to wait with patience the result of his Majesty's wisdom and clemency for a redress of their grievances. They at the same time declare for themselves

and desperate measures, we don't know, but pray God prevent. Suffer us to observe, that in our opinion, the measures the town of Boston are pursuing, and proposing to us and the people of this province to unite in, are unconstitutional, illegal, and wholly unjustifiable, and what will give the enemies of our constitution the greatest joy subversive of government, destructive of that peace and good order which is the cement of society, and have a direct tendency to rivet our chains, and deprive us of transmitted to our latest posterity. Thus we have freely expressed our sentiments, having an equal right with others, though a lesser part of the community, and take this first opportunity to protest against the proposed convention,— and hereby declared our loyalty to his present Majesty, and fidelity to our country; and that it is our firm resolution, to the utmost of our power to maintain and defend our rights in every prudent and reasonable way as far as is consistent with our duty to God and

selves, that they will, in their several stations, yield every possible assistance to the civil magistrate, for the preservation of peace and order, and the suppression of riots and tumults. After they had prepared a representation of their conduct, and a detail of the late transactions to be transmitted to their agent at London, they broke up. It appears plain from the whole of these proceedings, that Governor Bernard was at more pains to provoke the people, than to quiet their discontents; for had he behaved with more mildness, and shewed less authority, he would have had more reverence paid him. His opinion concerning the legality of their meeting seems frivolous and unsatisfactory; for though the convention was chosen by the people, yet as they attempted to perform no public act, but met for advice, they could be considered in no other light, the representatives of the people, than as their commissioners, to meet with their friends, to consult what was for their common good. They determined nothing, nor proceeded to any acts of authority, and could be considered as no more than a club met to advise with one another. The governor's threatenings were therefore puerile and whimsical, rather shewing what he was disposed to do, than what he could lawfully do. If the one half of the members of the House of Commons were to meet in an assembly, to advise with one another, without proceeding to any acts of power, they certainly could not come under any legal censure. Till once there be a statute against all clubs and meetings of gentlemen, it is impossible that the governor's opinion can be well founded. But the truth of the matter seems to have been, the governor and the assembly were at variance, and they had no confidence in one another. It is highly probable, had there been a popular governor in Massachusetts

sachusetts Bay, and in some other colonies, the ruinous war that has exhausted the empire had been yet to begin. When jealousies are once raised, it is impossible to know where they may end. On September 29th, the very day that the convention broke up, the fleet from Halifax with two regiments, and a detachment of artillery, arrived in the harbour. There were some disputes at first concerning quartering the soldiers; the council refused to quarter them in the town, as the barracks of Castle William were sufficient to receive them; this was at last got over, by providing quarters, which were then to be considered as barracks, and the council upon that footing, allowed them barrack provision. Soon after General Gage arrived, as did the two regiments from Ireland. A tolerable harmony subsisted for some time between the people and the troops, and both the town and province continued for a season very quiet.

There was at this time two things which greatly alarmed the friends of liberty and of the constitution; the restraining bill, which confined the East India Company in making dividends to a certain sum; and a revival of the *nullum tempus* law, in the case of the Duke of Portland. Both these proceedings had such an arbitrary appearance in the view of the people at home, that many concluded that the maxims of oppression, practised in the reign of the Stewarts, were going to be revived. These, together with the proceedings concerning the colonies, created a jealousy in the nation, that their representatives, who were trusted with their principal concerns, were going to betray their interests into the hands of the ministry. The zealous debates upon the East India restraining bill had warmed the parties in parliament to an unusual degree; and the controversy in the nation concerning

cerning Mr Wilkes, and his election as member for the county of Middlesex, added much to the irritation of parties. The misfortune which happened in St George's Fields contributed much to inflame the minds of the people. The proceedings at law against the persons who were charged with the crime of murder, were rather offensive than satisfactory; and the escape of one of the offenders, who was charged with the crime, added to the offence. It was alledged that he had made his escape by connivance, if not by command; and that the acquittal of another had happened, in consequence of his escape, and by a management very unfair and disingenuous. The parties at home were on this occasion much in the same temper with the Americans and Governor Bernard; instead of making allowances for one another's infirmities, they did all in their power to add to their vexation. The ministry, instead of striving to soften the people, by kind or smooth words, took every step, as if by design, to disoblige them, and heighten their resentment. One of the secretaries of state, in a letter recommended, in the strongest terms to the magistrates, an early use of military power, and the secretary at war thanked the soldiers for their service in St George's fields, and promised them protection. This promise was attended with pecuniary rewards given publicly, which greatly incensed the populace, and raised their indignation to a degree of fury and madness. This conduct of the ministry was considered as a wanton violation of the people's liberties, and a cruel insult over their distress, for the loss of their friends, who had been killed by the soldiers. And indeed the secretary might have behaved more prudently, provided he meant to conciliate the affections of the people to the government. There appeared something of wantonness

ness and severity in the stile of those letters, which good policy and a proper degree of prudence, might have restrained; for though the rioters were foolish and outrageous, they were yet his Majesty's political children, and when they were killed, it made the number of his subjects less, which, instead of being matter of exultation, was rather matter of sorrow and concern.

The tempers of the people, which by proper lenient measures, might have subsided, was kept up by many inflammatory publications and discourses, which though they contained several truths, and just argument, were written without temper or charity. Every part of that late transaction was represented in the strongest colours, and placed in the most dreadful attitudes; and it was represented as if the military power that was kept up for the defence of the people, had been perverted to their destruction; and an enraged soldiery already flushed in the slaughter of their countrymen, was to be encouraged by rewards to further bloodshed, and to be freed from every terror of the law.

The ministry did all in their power to stem this popular torrent, by painting in the most striking colours, the licentiousness of the people; and that contempt of all government which rendered it necessary to apply violent remedies to a violent distemper. They stated the unhappy disposition of the people to be such, that juries, under the general infatuation, could hardly be obtained to do justice to soldiers under prosecution, unless government interposed in the most effectual manner, in the protection of those who had acted under their command. They said that such was the insolence of the populace, and the danger of the contagion becoming by degrees prevalent, even among

mong the soldiers, that it was necessary to keep them steady to their duty, by new and unusual rewards. These reasons had but little weight with the public, who were well persuaded that those who made the greatest outcry against licentiousness, had themselves set the example, and were in those departments of life in which they acted, as licentious as that rabble which they had painted in the blackest colours. The vulgar, though they have not such a taste for refinement in speculations as people bred about courts, yet have as much common sense as to understand, that such as want to restrain licentiousness, ought themselves to observe the moral law. There is no manner of question that the arguments of the ministry were very just; for in no age have the people been more loose and dissolute than the present, but these arguments, like a dilemma, look more ways than one; they turn upwards as well as downwards, and may be applied to persons in high rank, as well as to the rabble. The best method for the ruling powers to restrain vice, immorality, and licentiousness, is to shew a good example, and promote the best laws for good education: that the rudiments of virtue may be early planted in the minds of men, and tutored to the best advantage. People in the low walks of life in general look up to those above them, by whose example they are very much influenced; and it will be impossible to have the common people virtuous till they be led by imitations of those above them. When men, whom they know to be as vicious as themselves, punish and correct them, they will consider the exercise of that power, to proceed, not from a regard to the law, but from desire of dominion.

Whatever force might be in the arguments, made use of in defence of the ministry, one thing is certain, they grew more and more unpopular every day, and some political incidents happened about this time, which leſſened them ſtill more in the opinion of the public. Among theſe, was the removal of General Amherſt from the government of Virginia. The government of that province had for half a century been conſidered as a ſinecure, and the buſineſs done by a deputy, and was avowedly beſtowed upon the general in that ſenſe, as a reward of his former ſervices, and a teſtimony of approbation of his particular good conduct in America. The removal of a perſon who had done ſuch ſervices for the public, became a ſubject of general diſcuſſion, and was cenſured with great ſeverity; nor did the arguments that were uſed in ſupport of that meaſure remove, but confirm the prejudices of the people. Under a load of popular odium, and many juſt cenſures, the miniſtry ſtill kept their ſtations, contrary to the expectation of almoſt the whole nation.

Lord Chatham, who was regarded as the projector and founder of this miniſtry, being almoſt continually abſent through bodily infirmity, loſt his influence in the cabinet, which was not perceived till his friend Sir Jeffrey Amherſt was removed from his government. Then it was perceived that the meaſures of the miniſtry were not directed by his advice. Soon after the removal of the general, Lord Shelburne reſigned his office of ſecretary of ſtate, and was ſucceeded by Lord Weymouth, for the northern department, and about the ſame time Lord Chatham reſigned his place as keeper of the privy ſeal, and was ſucceeded by the Earl of Briſtol, to the great ſurpriſe of the whole nation. The Earl was an intimate friend of Lord Chatham, which made this change appear ſomewhat extraordinary. This change happened in the month of

October, and the parliament assembled November the eight.

When the national senate met, the nation was full of expectation that measures would be fallen upon to quiet the minds of the people, consistent with the dignity of the crown, and the laws of the land. The speech from the throne soon disappointed these hopes and expectations: Instead of any lenient measures to settle the disquieted minds of the nation, the speech contained severe reflections against the colonists, particularly the people of Boston were declared to be in a state of disobedience to all law and government, and to have proceeded to measures subversive of the constitution, and attended with circumstances that manifested a disposition to throw off their dependence on Great Britain. The address to the sovereign for this speech, plainly shewed what the colonies had to expect from both the King and parliament. They declared, that though they were ready to redress the grievances of the colonies, and to hear their complaints, they were nevertheless determined to support the supremacy of the British legislature over every part of the British empire. In this situation were matters when the parliament met.

Chap. IV.

The Parliament assembles—a Committee appointed to consider American affairs—the proceedings thereof—various debates in Parliament concerning the Colonies—both Houses of Parliament bent upon humbling the Colonists—the Duke of Grafton resigns—Lord North succeeds him.

THE hopes of the nation were now anxiously fixed upon the new parliament, and it was earnestly expected that some healing measures would be pursued to settle the disturbances in the colonies, and quiet the minds of the people at home. These earnest hopes of the nation were considerably damped by the speech from the throne, which rather breathed sentiments of severity, than that mildness and clemency, which was thought necessary to heal the present distempers. The friends of peace and humanity did not however despair, but that the great council of the nation, when assembled, would in some period of this session, so moderate matters, that the effects of the severe speech from the throne would be mitigated by the wise counsels of parliament. From the censures passed upon some of the colonies in the King's speech, it was easy to perceive what were the intentions of the ministry, and what measures would be pursued, provided a majority in parliament gave sanction to their designs. The whole British empire was deeply interested in the issue of this business, and waited with eager expectation, the result of parliamentary determination. There were at this time two parties who were equally agitated with concern for the issue of this business; and these were such as wanted to have the supreme authority of parliament exerted to its utmost extent; who were highly displeased at the behaviour of the Massachusett's colony, and thought that a severe check ought to be given to the licentiousness of that province. The others who were equally anxious in this affair, were those who were lovers of constitutional liberty, as well, naturally disposed to moderation and lenient measures; these were greatly alarmed, at the signatures of vigour, they perceived in the speech, and the danger that would follow in case of carrying matters to extremity.

A committee of the whole house had been formed early in the sessions, for the purpose of an enquiry into American affairs. This was a measure that the different parties in parliament were equally anxious in pursuing: but the motives by which they were influenced were very different, and the methods of pursuing their enquiry very opposite to each other. The party on the side of the ministry confined their views to those recent transactions which were most offensive, and seemed more immediately to call for interposing the authority of parliament; which were judged by the most sanguine, highly worthy of a severe censure, as a violation of all order and government. On the other side, it was proposed to enquire into the sources and springs of those disorders, and to take a retrospective view of the conduct of government towards the colonies for several years past, and if possible, to cure the distemper, by removing the causes thereof. This was a work not so easily performed, when those who

were

were judged the original causes of those evils, continued to operate against all enquiries, by which their own conduct might have been lain open.

Before the Christmas recess, an unsuccessful attempt had been made, to have copies of all the royal letters patent, charters, and commissions, now subsisting, and in force, relative to any of the American colonies, with copies of all instructions which had been given by, or in the name of his present Majesty, to any officer, civil or military, laid before the House. These papers, it is supposed, would not only have led to a discussion of the rights of the colonies, but also to a close enquiry in the conduct of some governors, and other officers of the crown, as well as into the propriety of the orders that had at different times been sent to them from home. Nothing could be more reasonable than a request of this sort; it could injure none, except such as deserved censure, which could not be accounted injury but justice, and it would have been the most effectual method to have prevented governors at a great distance from the centre of power, abusing their authority, in provoking the subjects to outrage by an arbitrary behaviour. The granting of this request would also have removed all suspicions concerning government, and would have also confirmed the national confidence towards the ministry. Administration had at this time adopted other measures than what were agreeable to the nation, and were not disposed to give any satisfaction concerning their own conduct; they therefore opposed this motion, and prevented its success. They imagined that the dignity of government might suffer from such an enquiry, and were disposed to support imaginary honor, at the expence of general utility. A vast number of other papers, were however laid before the committee, comittee, and several resolutions formed thereon, together with an address upon the same subject, which came from the House of Lords, but after long debate, the ministry carried their point and the enquiry came to nothing. In this, as in several other things, this new parliament disappointed the hopes of the nation.

Upon January the 25th, 1769, while these debates were going on, a petition, in the name of the majority of the council of Massachusett's bay, signed by Mr Danforth, as president of the council, was presented to the Commons. It appeared that this petition wanted some formalities, necessary for procuring it admission into the House. It was said that it had not passed in a legal assembly of the council, and of consequence, no person could be authorised to sign it as president. It was rejected under that title, and ordered to be brought in only as the petition of Samuel Danforth, in behalf of the several individuals, members of the council, at whose request it had been signed. It was evident from this proceeding of the Commons, that the majority were disposed to come to no terms with the colonists, and that government intended to make them submit to the absolute authority of the mother country. This petition was so far from being written in an offensive stile, that no petition could have been expressed in milder terms, nor written with more moderation. It prayed for a repeal of the late revenue acts, and enlarged upon the chartered immunities, and privileges of the colonies. The general rights of the colonists, as English subjects, were set forth, without mentioning the supremacy of the British legislature, or calling it in question, although this was also touched in a gentle manner, by asserting that their rights had been violated, and requesting

that

that in time coming they might be secured. The inability of the colony to address the House in their legislative capacity, was regretted, and a particular detail of the difficulties, hardships, and dangers which their ancestors endured; who, for preserving their civil and religious liberties, had made settlements in a wilderness, where they were exposed to the rage of the most cruel and savage enemies; where, from the nature of the climate, and the infertility of the soil, no advantage to their temporal interests was even to be hoped for; and the utmost that could be expected, was only a scanty subsistence, in consequence of the most unremitted labour. From these premises, it was inferred, that they not only dearly purchased their settlements, but acquired an additional title, besides their common claim, as men and as British subjects, to the immunities and privileges which they asserted had been granted to them by charter. Many arguments were used by their friends in behalf of the petition. Their ready and willing services at their own expence in our wars; the old colonies having been all established without any expence to the mother country; the great advantages she derives from them; the share they virtually bear in our taxes, by the consumption of our manufactures; their inability to pay the duties, and the bad consequencs resulting from the late laws, not only to them, but to the mother country, were brought as arguments to solicit the repeal, and to shew the title they had, not only to a security of their rights, but even to favour.

Administration finding that they had a majority in parliament, was determined effectually to humble the refractory colonies. These house of Lords, upon the 8th of February, passed some resolutions, and an address to his Majesty, which were sent down to the
Commons,

Commons, and approved, and so became the act of both Houses, wherein the late acts of the House of representatives of Massachusett's-Bay, which called in question the authority of the supreme legislature to make laws to bind the colonies in all cases whatever, were rescinded, and declared illegal, unconstitutional, and derogatory of the rights of the crown and parliament of Great Britain. The circular letters written by the same assembly to the other colonies, requiring them to join in petitions, and stating the late laws as infringments of the rights of the people in the colonies, were declared to be proceedings of a most unwarrantable and dangerous nature, circulated to inflame the minds of the people in the colonies, and tending to create unlawful combinations, repugnant to the laws of Great Britain, and subversive of the constitution. The town of Boston was declared in a state of great disorder and confusion, disturbed by riots and tumults of a dangerous nature, in which the officers of the revenue had been obstructed by violence in the execution of the laws, and their lives endangered: that neither the council of the province, nor the civil magistrates, had exerted their authority in suppressing the said riots and tumults: that in these circumstances of the province of Massachusett's-bay, and of the town of Boston, the preservation of the public peace, and the due execution of the laws, became impracticable, without the aid of a military force, to support and protect the civil magistrate, and the officers of his Majesty's revenue. That the resolutions, and proceedings in the town meetings at Boston, on the 14th of June, and the 12th of September, 1769, were illegal and unconstitutional, and calculated to excite sedition and insurrection: that the appointment of the town meeting upon the 12th of September, of a convention to be held in the town of Boston, on the 22d of that month, to consist of deputies from the several towns and districts in the province, and the writing of a letter by the select men in each of the towns, and distincts, for the election of such deputies were proceedings subversive of government, and evidently manifesting a design in the inhabitants of Boston, to set up a new unconstitutional authority, independent of the crown. These resolutions were founded upon an interpretation of the meaning of the proceedings at Boston, which the people of that province denied that they ever intended; they declared the design of their meeting was, to advise with one another in petitioning the King and parliament for the redress of grievances, but to perform no governmental acts; and they also promised to assist the civil magistrate in the execution of the laws, as far as it was in their power. The resolutions of the two Houses at this time appear to have been formed upon the information of Governor Bernard, between whom and the province there was no good understanding, and who by this time had wrought each other to a degree of uncommon opposition and enmity. Those who have no other object in view except truth, will easily perceive, that the ambition and pride of the governor had as great an influence in those disorders, as the licentiousness of the people. According to the history of the people of that colony, given by many that now accuse them of licentiousness, they are, when compared with the people of this country, remarkably sober: they observed divine ordinance, and kept the Sabbath-day with a strictness, not to be found in Old England. And it has also been observed by their enemies, that unless among those who come from Britain to perform revenue duty, and are servants of the crown, the vices that are common at home in England, are seldom to be seen in that colony.—And indeed it seldom happens, that a licentious and diffipated people will run any hazards for their rights and liberties: but in a controverfy there is always fomething to be faid on both fides.

The addrefs that follows the above refolutions, breathed the fame fpirit, and run much in the fame ftile. It expreffed the greateft fatisfaction with the meafures that had been purfued, to fupport the conftitution, and to induce, in the colony of Maffachufetts bay, a due obedience to the authority of the mother country. A promife and refolution was alfo made to concur effectually in fuch farther meafures as might be judged neceffary to maintain the civil magiftrates in a proper execution of the laws; and it was given as a matter of opinion, that nothing would fo effectually preferve royal authority in that province, as to bring the authors of the late unfortunate diforders to examplary punifhment. Upon this perfuafion, it was earneftly requefted, that Governor Bernard would tranfmit the fulleft information he could obtain of all treafons, or mifprifion of treafon committed within his government, fince the 30th of December 1767, together with the names of the perfons who were moft active in the committing of fuch offences: that his Majefty might iffue a fpecial proclamation for enquiring into, hearing and determining upon the guilt of the offenders within this realm, according to the provifions of a ftatute made in the 30th year of Henry the eight, in cafe his Majefty, upon Governor Bernard's report fhould fee fufficient ground for fuch a proceeding. This was an opinion very unfavourable to the colonies; it expofed them to two evils of the moft fevere kind: there character was to be taken from the report of one man, who was their enemy, and they were to be tried in a strange country, where they might have neither friends nor connections, and where they could not have the benefit of exculpatory evidence, unless at an expence, that very few people can afford, without reducing themselves to misery and distress.

Though these resolutions and the address were carried by a powerful majority, they were opposed with great firmness, and force of argument, by the friends of the colonists, and there had been few subjects for many years more ably discussed, than this was through the whole of the debate. Both the right and propriety of taxing the colonists, were warmly disputed, and the arguments made use of, were much the same with those that have been already mentioned in the case of repealing the stamp act, which, on this occasion, shall not be repeated. Many new reflections were made on this occasion, which may be of some service to consider. It was observed that the new revenue laws did not answer the end proposed, but tended to irritate the colonists, without being of any real service to government: that as the act for securing the obedience of the colonies, answered all the purposes they could propose by any new measure, it was absurd to multiply statutes, without sufficient cause and reasons for so doing: that by the measures they were pursuing, they would lay a tax upon the mother country: that the laying of duties upon British commodities and manufactures landed in the colonies, was in effect granting premiums, to excite the Americans to industry, and to put them upon raising the one, and rivalling Britain in the other. What appeared remarkable on this occasion, the Rockingham and Grenville parties, who were supposed to be irreconcileable, upon on this subject, entirely united and joined their interests, and made use of the same arguments. A reflection was made by the opposition, which, though it was very severe, was at the same time very just; namely, that it was now become the fashion with those who had been the original cause of all the disturbances in America, to represent the people in that country as in a state of rebellion, and by that stratagem to make the cause of administration the national cause, and to persuade us that the people aggrieved by a series of blunders and mismanagement, and emboldened by the weakness and inconsistency of government, had committed some rash actions, that they wanted also to throw off the authority of the mother country. This was a most severe, but a true reflection; for from all accounts of the proceedings of the colonists, it appears manifest that mild treatment, and a little soft management would have settled all the disturbances that have happened. It was urged that a number of duties had been laid upon the colonies, which derived their consequence only from their odiousness, and the mischief they produced, and an army of custom-house officers were sent, as much to create as to raise new taxes, as they could scarcely answer any other end, and were themselves as odious as the taxes they were sent to collect on account of their novelty, and some other circumstances that attended them. Another reflection which bore hard upon the majority, was that some of them who had a hand in imposing these new duties, and were become the zealous supporters of the present measures, were at the head of that opinion which denied totally the right of the legislature to tax America: that their names had been held up in the colonies as objects of the highest veneration, and their arguments were made the foundation

dation, of what ever was understood to be constitutional writing or speaking; was it then to be a matter of wonder, that the Americans, with such authorities, to support their opinions, which were in the highest degree flattering to their importance, should, in the warmth of their imagination, and the heat of their passions, commit extravagances, upon observing an immediate violation of what they had been taught to consider as their most undoubted and unalienable rights? Or was their any reason to be surprised, that such strange and unaccountable contradictions, between language and behaviour, should produce the unhappy consequences which had now happened. This was *argumentum ad hominem*, and could not be answered by those to whom it was applied, without shame and repentance.

That part of the address which related to the statute of Henry the eight was more warmly disputed, and such arguments were used as the friends of administration could not oppose with arguments of equal force. To bring delinquents from the province of Massachusett's-bay, to be tried at a tribunal in England, for crimes supposed to be committed in that country, was considered in the first instance, contrary to the spirit of the English constitution. It was said that a man charged with a crime is, by the laws of England, usually tried in the county where the offence is committed, that the circumstances of the crime may more clearly be considered and examined; and that the knowledge which the jury thereby receive of his general character, and of the credibility of the witnesses' might assist them in pronouncing, with a greater degree of certainty, upon his innocence or guilt. That as the constitution form a conviction of its utility, had secured that form justice, can he be deprived of it, by going to America? Is a man's life, fortune, and happiness, or his character of less esteem in the eye of the law, there, than in this country? or are we to mete our different portions of justice to British subjects which are to lessen in degree, in proportion to their distance from the capital? It was alledged, that if an American had transgressed the laws by committing a crime there, he ought to be tried there for the offence; but cannot justly be torn above 3000 miles from his family and his friends, his business, and connections; from every comfort and countenance, necessary to support a man under such trying and unhappy circumstances to be tried by a jury that are not his peers, who are probably prejudiced against him, and may think themselves some way interested in finding him guilty.

It was further urged, that it would be difficult, if not impossible, for the accused person to bring over the necessary evidence for his vindication, though he was entirely innocent: that it would require a man to be rich, and to have great substance to bring all the witnesses that might be necessary from Boston to London, and that after all, some might be overlooked that might be of great service, which could not be brought till the trial was over. That on the other side the witnesses against him, supported by the countenance and protection of Government, maintained at the national expence, and sure of a compensation for their loss of time, and perhaps having the hope of future reward and provision, would not only be easily collected, but that it was to be feared too many would think it good employment and become eager candidates for the service. That in this situation the case of the accused would be very hard; charged with a

the judges who are to determine his fate, are the people against whom he is supposed to have transgressed, those who have construed the act with which he is charged into a crime, whose passions might be heated and who are at the same time parties, accusers, and judges. The act upon which this trial was to proceed, it was affirmed was framed in an arbitrary and tyrannical reign, and had justly lain buried in oblivion, till now brought forth to answer a temporary and an arbitrary purpose. Many of these arguments were never answered, nor was any reply made, except by a vote, which is the most powerful answer. The ministry were on this occasion unusually languid in the support of their resolutions, and the address which they made for reviving the statute of Henry the VIII. for when they were asked which of them would own himself the adviser of that measure, they all declined to adopt it. It would appear that either their consciences condemned them, or that they felt the force of their opponent's arguments too powerful to be resisted. The arguments that were used in behalf of the measures that were now pursuing are but short, and have but little force in them, but the reader in justice shall have them as they are.

It was affirmed that the repeal of the stamp act had not produced the effects that might have been expected; that the colonists instead of gratitude for the tenderness shewn to their supposed distresses, had obstinately pursued the same course as before, and shewed the same disrespect to government; that such was their licentious opposition to all measures of the legislature, that it became highly necessary to establish some mark of their dependence upon the mother country. That the late duties so much complained of, on account of the smallness of their produce, were

chosen

chosen to answer the abovementioned purpose, at the same time that they were the least oppressive that could be advised, and that the whole produce was to support their own civil establishments. That the inhabitants of the province of Massachuset's Bay were people of republican principles, and licentious in their dispositions, and being stirred up by factious and designing men, had broken out into daring acts of outrage, and insolence, which sufficiently shewed the original necessity of making them sensible of their dependence on the British legislature; that by their words and writings they seemed rather to consider themselves as members of an independent state than as a colony and province belonging to this country. That from the ill formed system upon which the government of that colony had been originally established; the council was appointed by the assembly, and the grand juries are elected by the townships; so that these factious men having got a lead in the assembly, and being themselves leaders of the popular phrenzy, guided and directed the whole civil government as they pleased; so that all justice and order was at an end, wherever their interests or passions were concerned. That in these circumstances the populace freed from all legal restraints by these circumstances, those that should have been the conservators of the public peace, set themselves the first examples of all kinds of disorders, and proceeded at length to the commission of such acts, as if not now deemed downright rebellion, would in other times have been judged and punished as such; and which in any construction of the term could be considered but very little short of it. That it was now high time for government to interfere, and effectually to curb disorders, which if suffered to proceed farther, could no longer be considered

red by that name. That the example set by the town of Boston, and the rash and daring measure adopted by their assembly of sending circular letters to the other colonies, had already produced a great effect; and if not checked was likely to set the whole continent in a flame, and for that reason some ships of war and troops had been sent to Boston, who without bloodshed or coming to any violent measures, had restored order and quiet. That nothing but the most vigorous measures could bring the colonists to a proper sense of their duty, and of their dependence upon the supreme legislature. That the spirit which prevailed at Boston was so totally subversive of all order and civil government, and the conduct of the magistrates had left so little room for hope of their properly fulfilling ther duty during the continuance of the present ferment, that it became absolutely necessary to revive and put in execution the law of Henry the VIII. by which the king is empowered to appoint a commission in England for the trial there, of any of the subjects in all parts of the world. That unless that measure was adopted, the most flagrant acts of treason and rebellion might be committed openly in the provinces with impunity, as the civil power was neither disposed, nor could take cognizance of them. That the persons who were guilty of those crimes, and who had already caused so much trouble and confusion, were no objects of compassion, for any particular circumstances of expence or trouble that might attend this mode of bringing them to justice, which was only to be considered as a small part of the punishment due to their crimes: that it was ungenerous to suppose that government would make an improper use of this law by harrassing of innocent persons; and that there was no reason to question the integrity of

Lord
GEORGE GERMAINE.

our juries.... And they observed that it was unlikely that the act would ever be put in execution, as they were in hopes that such a seasonable shew of so much vigour and lenity would operate to bring the colonies to a sense of their duty, and to make them give over their seditious practices. These are the arguments upon the other side, which as they have little force in themselves, have hitherto in the execution produced none of those effects which the authors promised.

Administration seem to have expected more confidence from the public, than their conduct for some years past entitled them to, when they say it was ungenerous to suppose that they would make an improper use of their power in harrassing innocent persons, for their past conduct gave all the reason in the world to suppose that mercy and clemency were none of their characteristic virtues. And as they had refused to admit an enquiry into the original causes of the disorders in the colonies, there was good reason to conclude that impartiality would not be observed in prosecuting those who were the objects of their resentment. The colonists had for some time been in a state of disorder, and many irregularities had been committed, but there was a jealousy and suspicion that some mismanagement in government had been the cause thereof; it was therefore unreasonable to seek to punish the petty delinquents, without taking notice of those who had been the cause of all these evils. The constitution of the government of the Massachusett's colony, in granting that privilege to the townships, the privilege of electing juries, and to the assembly, the liberty of appointing the council, had never produced any ill consequences, till ambitious governors wanted to dictate to both councils and assemblies; and then they found that the constitution of the colony was a check upon their power, and restrained it within a certain limit. Those who formerly had no other object in view than to rule for the good of the community, never considered this part of the constitution of the colony as any hardship: they supported their own legal dignity, and never wanted to encroach upon the privileges of the people. But some late governors assumed a power which their office did not give them, and when they could not rule the colony according to their arbitrary pleasure, because the government of the province did not allow them so to do, they began to complain both of the form of government, and the conduct of the people, who did no more than it allowed them. It would have been no more than fair, to have made an enquiry into the conduct of government, that it might have appeared, whether the disturbances had arisen from mal-administration in the officers of the crown, or from the licentiousness and restlessness of the people. Had it appeared that the ministry and governors had done their duty, it would have united all ranks in this kingdom against the colonists, and added a strength to administration which would have enable them to have pursued their measures with more ease and satisfaction. But when they refused to submit to an enquiry, it confirmed the suspicions of the public, that there was something done that could not bear a trial. The allusion to the times of the Stuarts, in the reasoning of the majority, and their keenness for the revival of the statute of Henry the eight, encreased the jealousy of the colonists, and aggravated the opposition at home. Precedents taken from arbitrary reigns, and tyrannical princes, had but an ill appearance, and were not reckoned suitable to the principles of the revolution, and the government of a prince of the Brunswick line. The colonists irritated already, by what was past,

considered

considered these new measures, as contrivances of state to enslave them; and they began to apprehend that government would proceed from one thing to another, till they reduced them to the state they were in before the revolution. What gave rise to these apprehensions, was the similarity of proceedings, and the influence that the friends of the ancient family were supposed to have in the court of Britain; these ideas were confirmed by the essays of party-writers in England, who, without confining themselves always to truth, had for some years past, in the most positive manner affirmed, that all the springs of government were moved and managed by an invisible agent, whose influence turned the puppets which way he pleased. Though it cannot be reasonably supposed that any one man possessed such influence as was supposed, yet the measures of the ministry were frequently so suspicious and inconsistent, that they gave reason for such surmises. It is not strange that the colonists should have believed what was published with so much confidence in the mother country; especially when we consider that their minds by this time were warped by prejudice, and their imaginations heated with opposition and resentment. They had petitioned without success, and remonstrated in vain; they acknowledged the supremacy of the sovereign, and the authority of parliament to direct their trade and navigation, but nothing would please administration but absolute dominion over their all. This they accounted contrary to their natural rights as Englishmen, and a breach of their charters; and the new proceedings of parliament they considered as so many chains to enslave them. Thus like a stream that is fed by constant supplies, their opposition encreased, till, like a torrent, it overflowed all bounds.

Both

Both houses of parliament were so bent upon humbling the colony of Massachusett's bay, that they had proceeded, on the 13th of February, to address his Majesty, for calling all the offenders in that colony to an account before the judicatories of this nation. This declared how earnest the majority in parliament were in exercising the authority of the mother country over the colonies. Their address is expressed in the strongest terms of loyalty to the King, and severity to the offenders in the colony*. His Majesty in his answer to the address of both houses of parliament enters warmly into the spirit of the measures they

---

* THE ADDRESS.

Most Gracious Sovereign,

We, your Majesty's most dutiful and loyal subjects, the Lords spiritual and temporal, and Commons in Parliament assembled, return your Majesty our most humble thanks, for the communication your Majesty has been graciously pleased to make to your parliament, of several papers relative to public transactions in your Majesty's province of Massachusett's Bay.

We beg leave to express to your Majesty our sincere satisfaction in the measures which your Majesty has pursued, for supporting the constitution, and for inducing a due obedience to the authority of the legislature, and to give your Majesty the strongest assurances, that we will effectually stand by and support your Majesty, In such further measures as may be found necessary to maintain the civil magistrates in the due execution of the laws, within your Majesty's province of Massachusett's bay. And we conceive nothing can be immediately necessary either for the maintaining of your Majesty's authority in the said province, or for guarding your Majesty's subjects therein from being further deluded by the arts of wicked and designing men, than to proceed in the most speedy and effectual manner for bringing to condign punishment the chief authors and instigators of the late disorders. We must humbly beseech your Majesty, that you will be graciously pleased to direct, your Majesty's Governor of Massachusett's bay to take the most effectual methods for procuring the fullest information that can be obtained, touching all treasons, misprision of treason committed within his government since the 30th of December, 1767; and to transmit the same, together with the names of the persons who were most active in the commission of such offences, to one of your Majesty's principal secretaries of state in order that your Majesty may issue a special commission for enquiring of hearing, and determining the said offences within the realm, pursuant to the provisions of the statute of the 35th year of the reign of King Henry the eight, in case your Majesty shall, upon receiving the said information, see sufficient ground for such a proceeding.

To this Address, his Majesty gave the following most gracious Answer.

My Lords and Gentlemen,

The sincere satisfaction you express in the measures I have already

they recommend, and breathes the spirit of vengeance against some leading persons in the colony of Massachusett's bay. It was now manifest that nothing could bring matters to a proper temper, except an unconditional submission on the part of the colonists; for both king and parliament were determined to humble them. At this time it appeared to almost all ranks of people, an easy matter to have settled the difference. Moderation in the government, equal to the submission of the colonists might have settled all the commotions; but it was now determined to make use of the most rigorous measures, and to bring the colonists to the feet of the minister. Wise men began to perceive the absurdity of the measures of the ministry, and publicly shewed their dislike of their proceedings, and on that account were considered as disloyal and disaffected to the government. The most wretched and despicable tools of administration, over all the nation, were, on all occasions, ready to insult every person that hinted the smallest dislike of the violent measures that were now proposed. Petitions and remonstrances were considered as seditious libels, and the petitioners and remonstrators accounted factious and disloyal persons. The very Jacobites and Papists, who, it is well known never were well affected to the revolution settlement, nor the Hanoverian succession, became now the accusers of the King's most loyal subjects, and were not ashamed openly to charge the revolution with rebellion. The great numbers of those who had been concerned in the rebellion in the year 1745

being

dy taken, and the strong assurances you give of supporting me in those which may be still necessary to maintain the just legislative authority, and the due execution of the laws in my province of Massachu-

I will not fail to give those orders which you recommend as the most effectual method of bringing the authors of the late unhappy disorders in that province to condign punishment.

being restored to their fortunes and estates, as well as preferred in the army and navy, gave suspicion to those who were friends of the constitution, that some dark schemes were operating to bring the empire under a more arbitrary government. What added to these suspicions was, that ever since, 1745, it had been the constant conversation of the Jacobites in their private assemblies, that they would walk more surely, and play a more certain game in their future proceedings, than they and their fathers had done since the revolution; that it would be a work of more time, to worm themselves into places of power and trust, by a specious behaviour, but would operate with more certainty, than proceeding to acts of violence. These secret manoeuvres were not kept so close, as to be totally concealed; they had, upon occasions, admitted some into their meetings who were unknown to them, not of their principles. These made no secret of what they had heard, but told them to others, and they at last circulated so wide as to spread over the whole nation. These hints moved the friends of the revolution, and made them publish their suspicions to the nation. The friends of the ministry declared that all this was slander, proceeding from malice and disappointment: that the people in opposition had nothing in view except to embarrass government, and to have the management, and the perquisites belonging thereto, into their own hands. This assertion was not unplausible; for it oftentimes happens that the clamour against the ministry proceeds more from a love of their places, than from any dislike of their measures. The ministry on this occasion, as on many occasions since, were but badly served by those whom they employed to defend their measures, to the public. The writers upon their side, were not equal in abilities to those in the opposition; and though they had been equal to it, it indeed is impossible for hirelings to write with so much spirit and freedom as those who write from principle, and from the heart.

What irritated the colonists to the highest degree, was an act passed in 1767, for granting certain duties in the British colonies and plantations in America. This law contains a vast number of articles which the colonists thought heavy and grievous, and which were judged inconsistent with those ideas implied in the law repealing the stamp act. But that the reader may judge for himself, I have given this law, together with the declaratory act, in the notes below*. In no year since his Majesty's accession to the throne, were there greater commotions

---

* For every hundred weight avoirdupois of crown, plate, flint, and white glass, four shillings and eight pence.

For every hundred weight avoirdupois of Green glass, one shilling and two pence.

For every hundred weight avoirdupois of red lead, two shillings.

For every hundred weight avoirdupois of white lead, two shillings.

For every hundred weight avoirdupois of painters colours, two shillings.

For every pound weight avoirdupois of tea, three pence.

For every ream of paper, usually called or known by the name of atlas fine, twelve shillings.

For every ream of paper called atlas ordinary, six shillings.

For every ream of paper called ballard, or double copy, one shilling and six pence.

For every single ream of blue paper for sugar bakers, two pence halfpenny.

For every ream of paper called blue royal, one shilling and six pence.

For every bundle of brown paper containing forty quires, not made in Great Britain, six pence.

For every ream of paper called brown cap, not made in Great Britain, nine pence.

For every ream of paper called brown large cap, made in Great Britain, four pence halfpenny.

For every ream of paper called small ordinary brown, made in Great Britain, three pence.

For every bundle, containing forty quires of paper called white brown, made in Great Britain, four pence halfpenny.

For every ream of cartridge paper, one shilling and one penny halfpenny.

For every ream of paper called chancery double, one shilling and six pence.

For every ream of paper called Genoa crown fine, one shilling and one penny halfpenny.

For every ream of paper called Genoa crown second, nine pence.

For every ream of paper called German crown, nine pence.

For every ream of paper called fine printing crown, nine pence.

For every ream of paper called second

commotions and debates in the empire than in this. Not only were the colonies in a state of commotion, but the nation at home was in a continual bustle. Addresses on one side, and petitions on the other, were presented in great numbers to the throne. The principles upon which they proceeded were so opposite, and contrary to each other, that one would conclude, by comparing them, that the human mind must have, in some people, different faculties, from what others are possessed of, and that right and wrong are not the same

second ordinary printing crown, six pence three farthings.

For every ream of paper called crown fine, made in Great Britain, nine pence.

For every ream of paper called crown second, made in great Great Britain, six pence three farthings.

For every ream of paper called demy fine, not made in Great Britain, three shillings.

For every ream of paper called demy second, not made in Great Britain, one shilling and four pence halfpenny.

For every ream of paper called demy fine made in Great Britain, one shilling and one penny halfpenny.

For every ream of paper called demy second, made in Great Britain, nine pence.

For every ream of paper called demy printing, one shilling and three pence.

For every ream of paper called Genoa demy fine, one shilling and six pence.

For every ream of paper called Genoa demy second, one shilling and one penny halfpenny.

For every ream of paper called German demy, one shilling and one penny halfpenny.

For every ream of paper called elephant fine, six shillings.

For every ream of paper called elephant ordinary, two shillings and five pence farthing.

For every ream of paper called Genoa fools cap fine, one shilling and one penny halfpenny.

For every ream of paper called Genoa fools cap second, nine pence.

For every ream of paper called German fools cap, nine pence.

For every ream of paper called fine printing fools cap, nine pence.

For every ream of paper called second ordinary printing fools cap, six pence three farthings.

For every ream of any other paper called fools cap fine, not made in Great Britain, one shilling and ten pence halfpenny.

For every ream of any other paper called fools cap fine, second, not made in Great Britain, one shilling and six pence.

For every ream of paper called fools cap fine, made in Great Britain, nine pence.

For every ream of paper called fools cap second, made in Great Britain, six pence three farthings.

For every ream of paper called imperial fine, twelve shillings.

For every ream of paper called second writing imperial, eight shillings and three pence.

For every ream of paper called German lombard, nine pence.

For every ream of paper called

same to all mankind. The address and petitions are so essentially different in their nature, that by the one you would determine the nation to be in the most flourishing condition, and in a state of the greatest happiness, and by the other you would be led to believe, that it was upon the verge of utter ruin, and on the very brink of destruction. Perhaps neither the cases, as stated in the one or the other are strictly true, nor is it possible that they could be both true; but one thing is certain, that neither the one nor the other were

medium fine, four shillings and six pence.

For every ream of paper called Genoa medium, one shilling and ten pence halfpenny.

For every ream of paper called second writing medium, three shillings.

For every ream of painted paper not made in Great Britain, six shillings.

For every ream of paper called fine large post, one shilling and ten pence halfpenny.

For every ream of paper called small post, one shilling and one penny halfpenny.

For every ream of paper called fine Genoa pot, six pence three farthings.

For every ream of paper called second Genoa pot, six pence three farthings.

For every ream of paper called superfine pot, not made in Great Britain, one shilling and six pence.

For every ream of other paper called second fine pot, not made in Great Britain, one shilling and one penny halfpenny.

For every ream of paper called ordinary pot, not made in Great Britain, six pence three farthings.

For every ream of paper called fine pot, made in Great Britain, nine pence.

For every ream of paper called second pot, made in Great Britain, four pence halfpenny.

For every ream of paper called super royal fine, nine shillings.

For every ream of paper called royal fine, six shillings.

For every ream of paper called fine Holland royal, two shillings and five pence farthing.

For every ream of paper called fine Holland second, one shilling and six pence.

For every ream of paper called second fine Holland royal, one shilling and six pence.

For every ream of paper called ordinary royal, nine pence.

For every ream of paper called Genoa royal, two shillings and five pence farthing.

For every ream of paper called second writing royal, four shillings and one penny halfpenny.

For every ream of paper called second writing super royal, six shillings.

For every hundred weight avoirdupois of paste-boards, mill-boards, and scale-boards, not made in Great Britain, three shillings and nine pence.

For every hundred weight avoirdupois of paste-boards, mill-boards, and scale-boards, made in Great Britain, two shillings and three pence.

And for and upon all paper which shall

were really the voice of the nation. For as the ministry and the court party used their utmost efforts to procure addressers, so leading men in the opposition did all they could to procure petitioners, who knew as little about the grievances, as the addressers did about the happiness of the nation. Both were the occasion of great noise and confusion; people were taken off their business, and idle disposed men went rioting for several days together, without doing any thing except drinking and making noise in the streets of towns and cities. The number of petitioners was by far the greatest, and shewed that among those who pretended

shall be printed, painted, or stained, in Great Britain, to serve for hangings or other uses, three farthings for every yard square, over and above the duties payable for such paper by this act, if the same had not been printed, painted, or stained; and after the rate respectively for any greater or less quantity.

DECLARATORY ACT.

'Whereas several of the houses of Representatives in his Majesty's colonies and plantations in America, have of late, against law, claimed to themselves, or to the general assemblies of the same, the sole and exclusive right of imposing duties and taxes upon his Majesty's subjects in the said colonies and plantations; and have, in pursuance of such claim, passed certain votes, resolutions, and orders, derogatory to the legislative authority of parliament, and inconsistent with the dependency of the said colonies and plantations upon the crown of Great Britain;' May it therefore please your most excellent Majesty, that it may be declared, and be it declared by the King's most excellent Majesty, by and with the advice and consent of the Lords Spiritual and Temporal, and Commons, in this present parliament assembled, and by the authority of the same, That the said colonies and plantations in America have been, are, and of right ought to be, subordinate unto, and dependent upon, the imperial crown and parliament of Great Britain; and that the King's Majesty, by and with the advice and consent of the Lords Spiritual and Temporal, and Commons of Great Britain, in parliament assembled, had, hath, and of right ought to have, full power and authority to make laws and statutes of sufficient force and validity to bind the colonies and people of America, subjects of the crown of Great Britain, in all cases whatsoever.

II. And be it further declared and enacted by the authority aforesaid, That all resolutions, votes, orders, and proceedings, in any of the said colonies or plantations, whereby the power and authority of the parliament of Great Britain, to make laws and statutes as aforesaid, is denied or drawn into question, are, and are hereby declared to be, utterly null and void, to all intents and purposes whatsoever.

pretended to have a right to intermeddle in those matters, the majority was on the side of the opposition. The great number of petitions that were sent to the throne, gave great offence to the ministry, and they were treated with the utmost contempt. This provoked the petitioners to the highest degree, and made many of them both speak and write many severe things against the ministry. Thus the parties irritated one another, that charity and love among men became a very rare thing. Those on the side of the court being in general the more wealthy and substantial part of the nation, looked with contempt upon the other side, and despised them, as not worthy of being consulted in any affairs of government; while the others considered them as oppressors and enemies of their country. The debates both in and out of parliament run high. The court party cried out for severe measures, They said the authority of parliament had been trampled upon, t e sovereign had been insulted on the throne, by the most absurd and provoking proceedings and insolent petitions. A dissolution of parliament was requested, for no other reason than because they had complied with the King's ministers, whom the King himself had appointed. How could the King expect to be obeyed in such critical emergencies, that must occur in any plan for aggrandizing the crown; when the ministers who formed such plans were given up, and the parliament, who had acted under their influence was disolved? This kind of reasoning was, by the other side, considered as partial, selfish, and inconclusive; they looked upon such arguments as the shifts of guilty persons to cover their iniquities, rather than the reasoning of true and good politicians. To threaten the nation for petitioning the sovereign, which was a right that belonged to every

every individual, was looked upon as an infolence which none but defperate men would have been guilty of. The arguments on this occasion went much against the ministry, which did not a little provoke them; and as usually happens in the time of controversy, many indecent reflections were thrown forth against individuals, which were a difgrace to the caufe they were fupporting. Magistrates, however many errors they may be guilty of, as long as they continue in office, perfons in oppofing their mifconduct, ought always to obferve decency. It adds no luftre to any caufe to fupport it with fcandal and perfonal reflections. A fpecies of writing was now become fafhionable, wherein all the private foibles of men's lives were drawn into the argument, and their private infirmities painted with the moft uncharitable colourings. This wantonnefs of the prefs provoked the court and the miniftry exceedingly, fo that they were determined to make examples of offenders as foon as they could have a proper opportunity. This was a very weak refolution; for the offence was mutual, and neither fide could plead innocent. The writers on the fide of the court were often as illiberal as thofe on the fide of the oppofition; but where men of power are irritated, it requires much wifdom to make them reftrain their power within the bounds of right reafon and juftice. The miniftry were fadly galled, and felt the ridicule of their opponents, which was often very fcurrilous.

When the parliament met this year, upon the 9th of January, the nation was in great expectations concerning the manner how the ftate of public affairs would be introduced in the fpeech from the throne; when, to the amazement of all, the chief contents thereof, were filled up with a diftemper among the

horned

horned cattle! It was expected that notice would have been taken of the domestic commotions in the nation at home, and of the disturbances in America, but with regard to all these there was a perfect silence. The speech became an object of ridicule over all the nation, as the distemper it referred to was scarcely known to have any existence, and had not become an object of serious reflection among the people who were more immediately concerned.

The cold reserve in the speech from the throne, was not imitated by those in opposition to the measures of the ministry. When the address was read, a motion was made for an amendment, in the following terms: that they would immediately enquire into the causes of the prevailing discontents throughout his Majesty's dominion. This introduced some long debates, that were carried on with great heat and acrimony of expression, unknown before in parliament, and in which many severe animadversions were made upon the several parts of the speech from the throne. The affair concerning the petitions was agitated with great violence, and the grievances of the nation painted in the strongest colours by the opposition,—while the other side openly denied their existence, and seemed to threaten those who set them forth. There was a party on the side of the ministry that were more moderate; these admitted the existence of the grievances alledged, but affirmed they were exaggerated beyond all bounds. They acknowledged the discontents in the nation, and declared themselves willing to consider them at a proper season, as well as to reconsider the election of Middlesex, which was now a great bone of contention; they said they were willing to listen to methods of redress soberly proposed, and at a time when they had leisure; but they objected to the motion, as it would fix a crime upon themselves, to assure his Majesty that by an abuse of power, they had been the cause of all the prevailing discontents, and would be joining in a prayer for their own dissolution. The majority upon this side pursued another method of argument; they allowed the discontents, but charged them and the petitions, to the gentlemen in the opposition, through whose influence the people were persuaded to imagine the one, and subscribe the other.

And it was boldly affirmed, that the only cause of both, was the hatred of their leaders to those in administration. It was insisted that the majority of gentlemen of large fortunes, and the magistrates throughout the nation, together with the clergy in several counties, had not joined in the petitions, and that a majority of counties had not petitioned at all: that the inferior class of freeholders were not capable of understanding what they subscribed; that the farmers and manufacturers throughout the nation could neither know nor take any interest in the present disputes, provided they had not been stirred up by factious and seditious persons, who were hunting after grievances, and continually fabricating petitions.—That by men of that character, meetings had been advertised, where the people were harangued with inflammatory speeches, and writings published and scattered through the kingdom, in which government had been reproached and vilified, the parliament abused, and the minds of the people inflamed. All this was done, it was alledged, to distress government; but it was added, that although the majority of such freeholders had signed the petitions without any influence or solicitation, they were only to be considered as the acts of a rabble, and of an ignorant multitude, incapable of

judging,

judging. This kind of ſtile, as it was in its own nature opprobrious, ſo it was alſo not true in fact, becauſe thoſe whom the court party called a rabble, behaved with as much wiſdom and diſcretion, as even the beſt of the friends of the miniſtry. It is a ſort of lunacy which often prevails among ſelfiſh politicians, to imagine that the people in the lower walks of life are deſtitute of all penetration and diſcernment; and that they are not qualified to judge concerning their own affairs. Nothing but mere ignorance of their characters, or a wilful intention to miſrepreſent them, could diſpoſe men of ſenſe and underſtanding to judge in ſuch a manner. Among thoſe whom vain and high minded courtiers denominate the rabble, and the ſcum of the earth, are to be found as much common ſenſe, and prudence, as among thoſe of the higheſt ranks in the nation, if we take them in equal proportion. By taking a ſurvey of the hiſtory of bankruptcies, failures, and delinquencies, it will appear that there is a good proportion of theſe to be found among thoſe who are not accounted the ſcum of the nation. The abuſe which many in government at this time received from the people, proceeded from leſſons they had learned from courtiers themſelves, whoſe abſurd and ridiculous ſtile the vulgar turned againſt them, and paid back with conſiderable intereſt.

The charge which thoſe in adminiſtration brought againſt the minority, or thoſe in oppoſition, namely, that they had been active in promoting the petitions, was openly acknowledged and defended by them. They ſaid they accounted themſelves bound in duty to render an account of their conduct in parliament to their conſtituents, and alſo to give them their beſt advice, and opinion, when required, in any thing that related to their intereſts, and to give them the moſt early notice of all measures that tended to subvert their rights, or were dangerous to the constitution. The charges of meeting, writing, and speaking, which had been brought against them, were ridiculous, and it was asked by what other methods people could communicate their sentiments. It was also observed that it had been insinuated that our grievances were imaginary, because the peasants or manufacturers in Devonshire and Yorkshire would not immediately feel them, nor perhaps discover them till they felt them. But it was urged that though those who were busily employed, might not find time to consider these matters immediately, till they began to feel their effects, yet this was no reason why those who saw their distant approach, should keep silent, and not warn them. Those who perceive the subversion of liberty in the cause thereof, may be few, which is generally the case; but this will not prove that there are never approaches to oppression, or remote causes of the subversion of freedom, If the few who perceive effects in their causes can open the eyes of others, they do no more than what is their duty, and perform a piece of real service to the community.

It was added on this side of the question, that though many gentlemen of large fortunes, and the clergy, had not signed the petitions, yet a great number had done it, and these of the most independent rank and character; and of those who had refused to sign, many of them were under a particular influence. That the justices of the peace were officers of the crown, and that no body of men were under greater influence than the clergy, yet that some of these had even signed the petitions. It was asked likewise if the generality of the freeholders were of no signification? if their opinion was of no weight? and it was

asserted

asserted that they were that respectable body of men who were alone superior to all threatenings, fear, and influence. It was further urged, that the petitioning counties, cities, and towns were in respect to opulence and number of inhabitants, far superior to those that had not petitioned; and that they contributed more to the land-tax, which was now a test of freehold property in this country, than the rest of the united kingdom. These, with some other similar arguments were used on this occasion on the side of the opposition.

Soon after the meeting of the parliament, a long train of resignations took place. Lord Camden resigned the seals; the Marquis of Granby, all his places except the regiment of Blues; the Duke of Beaufort his place of Master of the Horse to the Queen; the Duke of Manchester and Earl of Coventry, of Lords of the Bed-chamber; the Earl of Huntington his place of groom of the stable, and Mr James Grenville his office of one of the Vice-treasurers of Ireland, Mr Dunning, the Solicitor-general, also resigned that employment. The whole of administration seemed in a shattered condition, and such convulsions prevailed as struck a panic in the body politic; the court was, however, resolved to pursue the plan it had set out upon, and was determined to govern by men who had no popular views or connections, and to maintain its ground, notwithstanding so many of its principal managers had deserted its cause. There are certain periods of fatality in the history of nations, when men employed in the management of public affairs proceed upon the most absurd principles, contrary to all reason, and conviction, and rush headlong over the precipice of their own despotism into the gulf of anihilation. What prudence and moderation might have preserved for ages, they frequently destroy in one day, and by the rapidity of the most jarring and discordant measures, grind to pieces those springs and wheels of government, which, by the course of regular motion would have endured as long as time. The English constitution is a contrivance of wisdom, formed to last for ever, when pursued upon its own principles; when the several balances are kept in equilibrio, and every power acts in its own sphere; but if any of its powers are permitted to encroach upon the sphere of another, the frame will soon fall to pieces, and become a perfect ruin. This was the case before the revolution, when the executive power overbalanced the legislative, and reduced the community to a state of nature. In the time of the long parliament, one part of the legislature overbalanced the other, and overturned the constitution, and introduced anarchy. All this shews that the greatest care should be observed by those employed in public matters, to preserve an equilibrium in all parts of the constitution. But this can never be done, when the crown has it in its power to corrupt the legislature. Riches committed into the hands of the sovereign to oil the wheels of government, will soon make a prime minister, unless he is both wise and virtuous, like the son of Phœbus,—drive so furiously till he set the nation in a flame. Anarchy is an evil and dangerous thing, but it is not equally so bad as tyranny. The jarring parts of a broken constitution, that through popular convulsions, are thrown into confusion, may, by wisdom, be arranged and put into order, and reared up like a new creation; but when there is no power but one existing, into which all the rest are absorbed, it will be next to impossible to restore the fabric.

Upon

Upon the 22d of January, this year, Sir John Cust resigned his office of speaker of the House of Commons on account of his bad state health, and was succeeded by Sir Fletcher Norton. Sir Fletcher was proposed by the minister, and the opposition set up another against him; this brought the strength of the parties to a trial, when the ministry carried their point in a division of near two to one. The influence of the court began now to be so strong, that it carried every measure wherein it was engaged. This was truly alarming to the nation, because some points of the most unpopular, as well as of the most unreasonable nature, had been carried by that Influence.

The affair of the Middlesex election, and the disqualifying of Mr Wilkes, were carried on and supported by the influence of the minister; these proceedings were considered by the greatest part of the nation, as exertions of power, intended to crush the spirits of the people, and to shew them that their voice was of no consideration in the esteem of government, and that matters would be carried on without their consent. Those proceedings alarmed all the friends to liberty, who considered the blow given to the people of Middlesex, a stroke aimed at the freedom of the whole nation.

The citizens of London made some spirited, noble, and bold efforts to stem the tide of ministerial infatuation, and to stop the torrent of despotism, that appeared now to carry all before it. They concluded, as was natural to suppose, that his Majesty, if rightly informed of the state of the nation, and the sentiments of his people, would dismiss such servants as, by their mismanagement, had irritated the minds of his faithful subjects, and were likely, by proceeding in the same course to alienate their hearts from their just and

and lawful sovereign. They therefore, on the 24th of June, the preceding year, presented a petition to his Majesty, setting forth the many heavy grievances which the nation laboured under, through the obstinate mismanagement of the officers of the crown; which grievances are specially pointed out in the petition itself in sundry articles. Their petition, as well as that of the county of Middlesex, and many others received no answer. Upon the 14th of March, this year, they presented an address, remonstrance, and petition to his Majesty, setting forth all the former grievances in their first petition, with other new articles, and craved h t is Majesty would dissolve the parliament, as now become no longer a representation of the people, nor could be, in the sense of the constitution, considered as a legal parliament. To this address and remonstrance they received a severe answer. This did not hinder the intrepid citizens of London to present another address of remonstrance and petition to the King upon the 23d of May, wherein they assert their right of petitioning, and express their astonishment at the awful censure passed upon them in his Majesty's late answer from the throne. To this remonstrance they received much the same answer as before; shorter indeed in its size, but equally severe in its contents. It was on this occasion that Mr Alderman Beckford, a person intrepid and zealous for the cause of liberty, and that of the citizens of London, delivered a speech to his Majesty, which stands recorded in the journals of the court of common-council, as a perpetual memorial of his greatness of mind, integrity, and resolution. The austere beams of majesty could not damp his spirits, nor the splendor of royalty in frowns, intimidate him, when the freedom and liberty of England and London seemed to be

in

in danger. His speech was worthy of a great citizen to deliver, and worthy of the greatest monarch to hear. It seems to have been dictated by wisdom, and delivered with true zeal; the contents are important, the stile elegant and manly; and the whole is a master-piece in its kind. The petition and remonstrances the reader will see in the notes, with the royal reply, and this speech of Mr Beckford subjoined*. There was another address and remonstrance presented upon the 21st of November, this year,

---

* *To the King's most Excellent Majesty.*

The humble Petition of the Livery of the City of London, in Common-Hall assembled.

Most gracious Sovereign,

We, your Majesty's dutiful and loyal subjects, the Livery of the City of London, with all the humility which is due from free subjects to their lawful Sovereign, but with all the anxiety which the sense of the present oppressions, and the just dread of future mischiefs produce in our minds, beg leave to lay before your Majesty some of those intolerable grievances, which your people have suffered from the evil conduct of those who have been entrusted with the administration of your Majesty's government, and from the secret unremitting influence of the worst of counsellors.

We should be wanting in our duty to your Majesty, as well as to ourselves and our posterity, should we forbear to represent to the throne the desperate attempts which have been, and are too successfully made, to destroy the constitution, to the spirit of which we owe the relation which subsists between your Majesty and the subjects of these realms, and to subvert those sacred laws which our ancestors have sealed with their blood.

Your ministers, from corrupt principles, and in violation of every duty, have, by various enumerated means, invaded our invaluable and unalienable right of trial by jury.

They have, with impunity, issued general warrants, and violently seized persons and private papers.

They have rendered the laws non-effective to our security, by evading the *Habeas Corpus.*

They have caused punishments, and even perpetual imprisonment to be inflicted without trial, conviction, or sentence.

They have brought into dispute the civil magistracy, by the appointment of persons who are, in many respects, unqualified for that important trust, and have thereby purposely furnished a pretence for calling in the aid of a military power.

They avow and endeavour to establish a maxim, absolutely inconsistent with our constitution, "that an occasion for effectually employing a military force, always presents itself, when the civil power is trifled with or insulted." And by a fatal and false application of this maxim, they have wantonly and wickedly sacrificed the lives of many of your Majesty's innocent subject's, and have prostituted your Majesty's sacred name and authority, to justify, applaud, and recommend

year, which set forth much the same grievances, and prayed for the same redress; but as they contain very little new, I have passed them over.

About six days after the resignations which have been mentioned above, the Duke of Grafton resigned his place and office of first Lord of the Treasury, and was succeeded by Lord North, who was already Chancellor of the Exchequer. Various reasons were assigned for his grace's resignation, though perhaps none of them the true ones: Some imputed his conduct

countenance their own illegal and bloody actions.

They have screened more than one murderer from punishment, and in its place have unnaturally substituted reward.

They have established numberless unconstitutional regulations and taxations in our colonies; they have caused a revenue to be raised in some of them by prerogative; they have appointed civil law judges to try revenue causes, and to be paid from out of the condemnation money.

After having insulted and defeated the law on different occasions, and by different contrivances, both at home and abroad, they have at length completed their design, by violently wresting from the people the last sacred right we had left, the right of election, by the unprecedented seating of a candidate, notoriously set up and chosen only by themselves; they have thereby taken from your subjects all hopes of parliamentary redress, and have left us no resource, under GOD, but in your Majesty.

All this they have been able to effect by corruption; by a scandalous misapplication and embezzlement of the public treasure, and a shameful prostitution of public honours and employments; procuring deficiencies of the civil list to be made good without examination, and instead of punishing, conferring honours on a pay-master, the public defaulter of unaccounted millions.

From an unfeigned sense of the duty we owe to your Majesty, and to our country, we have ventured thus humbly to lay before the throne these great and important truths, which it has been the business of your ministers to conceal. We most earnestly beseech your Majesty to grant us redress; it is for the purpose of redress alone, and for such occasions as the present, that those great and extensive powers are entrusted to the Crown, by the wisdom of that constitution, which your Majesty's Illustrious family was chosen to defend, and which, we trust in GOD, it will for ever continue to support.

To the King's most Excellent Majesty.

The humble Address, Remonstrance, and Petition, of the Lord Mayor, Aldermen, and Livery of the City of London, in Common-Hall assembled.

May it please your Majesty,

We have already in our petition dutifully represented to your Majesty, the chief injuries we have sustained. We are unwilling to believe

duct, to fear of being responsible for measures which he was not allowed to conduct according to his own judgement, and others to some certain disgust which they could not account for. Whatever was the cause, both parties reproached him, and the friends of the court, though he still supported their measures, complained of him for deserting them. Lord North now catched hold of the helm, where, we will find him steering the vessel of state through the greatest part of this history; with what success, the period of his political career

have that your Majesty can slight the desires of your people, or be regardless of their affliction, and deaf to their complaints. Yet their complaints remain unanswered; their injuries are confirmed; and the only judge removeable at the pleasure of the crown, has been dismissed from his high office, for defending in parliament, the law and the constitution.

We, therefore, venture once more to address ourselves to your Majesty, as to the father of your people; as to him who must be both able and willing to redress our grievances; and we repeat our application with the greater propriety, because we see the instruments of our wrongs, who have carried into execution the measures of which we complain, more particularly distinguished by your Majesty's royal bounty and favour.

Under the same secret and malign influence, which through each successive administration has defeated every good, and suggested every bad intention, the majority of the House of Commons have deprived your people of their dearest rights.

They have done a deed more ruinous in its consequences than the levying of ship money by Charles the first, or the dispensing power assumed by James the second. A deed, which must vitiate all the future proceedings of this parliament; for the acts of the legislature itself can no more be valid without a legal House of Commons, than without a legal prince upon the throne.

Representatives of the people are essential to the making of laws, and there is a time when it is morally demonstrable, that men cease to be representatives; that time is now arrived: The present House of Commons do not represent the people.

We owe to your Majesty, an obedience under the restrictions of the laws for the calling and duration of parliaments; and your Majesty owes to us, that our representation, free from the force of arms or corruption, should be preferred to us in parliament. It was for this we successfully struggled under James the second; for this we seated, and have faithfully supported your Majesty's family on the throne; The people have been invariably uniform in their object, though the different mode of attack has called for a different defence.

Under James the second, they complained that the sitting of parliament was interrupted, because it

career, and the matters of fact will declare. The debates concerning domestic affairs had been so warmly agitated, that American affairs which had been recommended in his Majesty's speech, had hitherto been overlooked. It was not now to be expected, considering the temper of the ministry with regard to affairs at home, that the colonists who were insisting upon the same privileges, would find much favour.

Upon the 5th of March, the minister, however, thought proper to bring in a bill for a repeal of so much

It was not corruptly subservient to his design: We complain now, that the sitting of this parliament is not interrupted, because it is corruptedly subservient to the designs of your Majesty's ministers. Had the parliament under James the second, been as submissive to his commands, as the parliament is at this day to the dictates of a minister, instead of clamours for its meeting, the nation would have rung, as now, with outcries for its dissolution.

The forms of the constitution, like those of religion, were not established for the form's sake, but for the substance we call; and GOD and men to witness, that as we do not owe our liberty to those nice and subtle distinctions, which places and pensions, and lucrative employments have invented, so neither will we be deprived of it by them; but as it was gained by the stern virtue of our ancestors, by the virtue of their descendants it shall be preserved.

Since, therefore, the misdeeds of your Majesty's ministers, in violating the freedom of election, and depraving the noble constitution of parliaments are notorious, as well as subversive of the fundamental laws and liberties of this realm; and since your Majesty, both in honour and justice, is obliged inviolably to preserve them according to the oath made to GOD and your subjects at your coronation; We your Majesty's remonstrants assure ourselves, that your Majesty will restore the constitutional government and quiet of your people, by dissolving this parliament, and removing those evil ministers for ever from your councils.

His Majesty's Answer, delivered the 14th of March, 1770.

I shall always be ready to receive the requests, and to listen to the complaints of my subjects; but it gives me great concern, to find that any of them should have been so far misled as to offer me an address and remonstrance, the contents of which I cannot but consider as disrespectful to me, injurious to my parliament, and irreconcileable to the principles of the constitution.

I have ever made the law of the land the rule of my conduct, esteeming it my chief glory to reign over a free people. With this view, I have always been careful, as well to execute faithfully the trust reposed in me, as to avoid even the appearance of invading any of those powers which the constitution has placed in other hands. It is only by persevering in such conduct, that I can rather discharge my own duty, or secure to my subjects the free

FREDERICK lord NORTH.

much of the late act passed in the seventh of the present reign, as related, to the imposing of a duty upon paper, painters colours, and glass; the tax upon tea which was laid on by the same act, being still to be continued. The reasons given for this repeal were, that the act had been the occasion of dangerous combinations on the other side of the Atlantic, and had created discontents at home among the merchants trading to those parts, which made the repealing of the act a matter of serious consideration. This said little for the wisdom of the legislature, in passing a law, which in its own nature could not but give general discontent and commotion among the subjects. It would appear that the minister did not intend to pursue the principles of consistency when he repealed only part of that act, and condemned the whole of it, as inconsistent with true wisdom, and the character of the British legislature. The colonists had as great an objection

BECKFORD's Speech.

Most Gracious Sovereign,

Will your majesty be pleased so far to condescend as to permit the Mayor of your loyal city of London, to declare in your royal presence, on behalf of his fellow citizens, how much the bare apprehension of your Majesty's displeasure would at all times affect their minds. The declaration of that displeasure, has already filled them with inexpressible anxiety, and with the deepest affliction. Permit me, Sire, to assure your Majesty, that your Majesty has not in all your dominions any subjects more faithful, more dutiful, or more affectionate to your Majesty's person and family, or more ready to sacrifice their lives and fortunes in the maintenance of the true honour and dignity of your crown.

We do, therefore, with the greatest humility and submission, most earnestly supplicate your Majesty, that you will not dismiss us from your presence, without expressing a more favourable opinion of your faithful citizens, and without some prospect, at least of redress.

Permit me, Sire, farther to observe, that whoever has already dared, or shall hereafter endeavour, by false insinuations and suggestions, to alienate your Majesty's affections from your loyal subjects in general, and from the city of London in particular, and to withdraw your confidence in, and regard for your people, is an enemy to your Majesty's person and family, a violator of the public peace, and a betrayer of our happy constitution, as it was established at the glorious revolution.

objection to the authority that had laid a duty on teas, as that which laid a duty upon paper and glass. They considered the authority, imposing such duties upon them without their consent, as illegal and oppressive, and were not willing to admit a claim of the English legislature, that denied them the common rights of other subjects. They inferred, if this claim was admitted or complied with, that a parliament which lay at such a distance from them, where in a great measure ignorant of their strength, and whose interest it was to ease themselves by oppressing of them, would never come to an end in their requisitions, as long as they could find any thing to tax in the colonies. They therefore considered the partial repeal of the act as no favour, while the parliament insisted upon their taxing them when they pleased. Those in the opposition reasoned much upon the same principles; but also added that it would be a real injury to Great Britain, and prevent the colonists from buying our manufactures, which would bring on distress at home, as well as on the other side the Atlantic. They gave instances how much the exports to America had fallen short in the space of two years; that in 1768 they had exceeded 1769 no less than the prodigious sum of 744,000l. they amounting in the former to 2,378,000l. and in the latter to 1,634,000. This was a convincing proof of the operation of those new laws that had given rise to the disturbances in the colonies. The ministry seemed to think light of all this, and endeavoured to account for this difference upon a plan of their own, which they could not but see was salacious and absurd. They said the difference was accounted for, by supposing that the non-importation which ensued was foreseen by the importers, and that they had laid in a double quantity of goods. This

was

was speaking at random, without any certainty, and the true account might have been discovered, by examining the exports before the contest began, which would have led them to have made a better estimate. The opposition, argued against the tea act, from the inutility thereof; they affirmed that it would produce little advantage to this nation, and would be a source of perpetual discontent to the colonies: that by the keeping up the establishment of custom-houses for that trifling tax, we would oppress the Americans without any real advantage: that these voracious officers and their dependants would eat up the whole revenue that arose from the duty, and where then would be the profit?—That the tea duty would not pay the charge of collecting it. It is manifest that this act could have no other object except dominion; for instead of being any advantage to government or this country, it was a real disadvantage. It was heaping charges upon the mother country, to collect from the colonies what would not pay the collectors on which account the people at home would have that deficiency to make up. There could no political end be answered by it, except one, and that is to provoke the colonies to rebellion, with an intention to seize upon their possessions. If men are not infatuated with the strongest partiality, they can find no other reason for continuing this part of the act, after they had repealed the other parts of it. Supremacy seems to have been the leading idea with the ministry, which of itself is so mean and foolish, that even folly itself would be ashamed of it, when there is no moral or political end to be answered thereby. For one country to claim dominion over another at so great a distance, would require the legislature born to be omniscient and omnipotent. It was certainly sufficient

for

for Britain to live in friendship with their brethren under the same sovereign, and suffer each other to be their own legiflators, walking according to the principles of their firft conftitution. But fuch manoeuvres of government have not been uncommon in the world; nations often ftretch their power and authority, till by proceeding too far their government is defpifed.

The government was now pofitively bent upon purfuing the principles of dominion and fupremacy, and determined to fupport the tea act at all events. The colonifts who were well informed of all the proceedings of our parliament, which they confidered as the real deeds of the court, and the miniftry, grew more and more obftinate in their oppofition, and were determined not to comply with ftatutes, which they confidered as directly contrary to their natural rights and the pofitive laws of the Britifh empire. The whole American continent was in a ftate of the utmoft agitation, and nothing was to be feen but deep concern, commotion, and forrow throughout the colonies.

Upon the 12th of March, a moft dreadful fray happened between the foldiers of the twenty-ninth regiment and the inhabitants of Bofton, in which feveral people loft their lives, and the whole city was thrown into the utmoft confufion. The reports concerning this dreadful riot have been fo various and contradictory, that it is difficult to difcover the truth from fuch difcordant reprefentations. The military who had been fent to Bofton by the authority of government, to enforce the new laws, arrived in that city with the ftrongeft impreffions of their being fent there to quell an actual rebellion. They therefore began to ufe freedoms inconfiftent with the rules of peace, and the tranquility of that city. Their behaviour gave great offence to the citizens, who were

not

not a little prejudiced againſt them, from the conſideration that they were ſent there, to be a check upon their liberties. It was not that the officers were guilty of any diſreſpect to the inhabitants, but did all that was in their power to promote a good underſtanding between the ſoldiers and the townſmen. But thoſe who know the compoſition of Britiſh regiments in theſe modern times, will eaſily perceive that it is no eaſy taſk to reſtrain them from outrage when they have the ſmalleſt occaſion to exert their powers. A collection of men gathered, not only from the loweſt but the baſeſt of the people, who have nothing to reſtrain them but military diſcipline, and who always conſider themſelves in an enemy's country, where ever they are, will always be ready upon the ſmalleſt relaxation of command, to fall into extravagances. By comparing the accounts given by Captain Preſton and that from Boſton, it appears that the ſoldiers had not behaved orderly, nor the townſmen very diſcreetly. The private quarrels of individuals ſoon grew to open outrage, and the colliſion of oppoſite parties, kindled a flame that was not eaſily quenched. The ſoldiers paraded the ſtreets with drawn cutlaſſes and bayonets, and the people provoked them with inſults, and opprobrious ſpeeches. The ſoldiers conſidered the people to be rebels, and behaved to them accordingly, and the citizens looked upon them as a banditti of oppreſſors, ſent by government to enſlave them. It was no wonder that people inſpired with ſuch different ſentiments ſhould not agree.

When once matters are carried ſo far as to iſſue in ſhedding of blood, it is not an eaſy taſk to reconcile the contending parties. Though the lieutenant-governor the magiſtrates, and other officers did all that was in their power to ſatisfy the people; yet the remembrance

brance of their slaughtered friends put them into such a state of agitation, that it was impossible to reconcile their minds to the military. They interpreted this transaction as only a prelude to the enforcing of laws by military execution, when once the government had perfected their measures; and the rest of the colonies pretended to see their own fate in what had now happened at Boston. This unhappy commotion was the occasion of more evils, both to the government and the colonies; for as the representation of the facts were coloured on both sides in the strongest manner, it left impressions upon the minds of the partizans, which were not easily effaced. The controversy at home concerning the same subjects, added additional fuel to the flame of contention, and the secret manœuvres of government, to disappoint the efforts of those that were struggling for liberty, being sometimes discovered, encreased the violence of opposition. The house of assembly of South Carolina had voted the sum of 1500l. sterling to the society of the bill of rights, which was opposed by the lieutenant-governor, in consequence of instructions from the ministry in England. Copies of the letters from England were demanded by the assembly, but were refused by the lieutenant-governor, which created great disgust in the province. Provoked with this interference of the crown; they were determined to shew their opposition more openly; and agreed to stop all commercial intercourse with New York, on account of that province breaking the non-importation agreement. This and other public deeds of legislative bodies, animated those who were more cool in the opposition, and by degrees made all the colonies unite in one common cause. It is difficult to ascertain what is the whole truth in this controversy,

but

but the reader will judge for himself when he reads the accounts of both parties, which shall be left to his confideration.

A Letter from Boston sets this matter in a true light.

On the evening of Monday, being the 5th of March, several soldiers of the 29th regiment were seen parading the streets with their drawn cutlasses and bayonets, abusing and wounding numbers of the inhabitants.

A few minutes after nine o'clock, four youths, named Edward Archbald, William Merchant, Francis Archbald, and John Leech, jun. came down Cornhill together, and separating at Dr Loring's corner, the two former, in passing a narrow alley, where a soldier was brandishing a broad sword, of an uncommon size, against the walls, out of which he struck fire plentifully, and a person of a mean countenance, armed with a large cudgel, by him, Edward Archbald bid Mr Merchant take care of the sword, on which the soldier turned round, struck Archbald on the arm, and then pushed at Merchant. Merchant then struck the soldier with a short stick, and the other person ran to the barrack, and brought with him two soldiers, one armed with a pair of tongs, the other with a shovel; he with the tongs pursued Archbald through the alley, collared and laid him over the head with the tongs. The noise brought people together, and John Hicks, a young lad, coming up, knocked the soldier down, but let him up again; and more lads gathering, drove them back to the barrack, where the boys stood some time as it were to keep them in. In less than a minute ten or twelve soldiers came out, with drawn cutlasses, clubs, and bayonets, and set upon the unarmed boys, who, finding the inequality of their equipment, difperfed. On hearing the noife, one Samuel Atwood came up to fee what was the matter, and met the foldiers aforefaid rufhing down the alley, and afked them if they intended to murder people? they anfwered, Yes, by G—d, root and branch! with that one of them ftruck Mr Atwood with a club, which was repeated by another, and, being unarmed, he turned to go off, and received a wound on the left fhoulder, which reached the bone. Retreating a few fteps, Mr Atwood met two officers, and faid, Gentlemen, what is the matter? they anfwered, you'll fee by and by. Immediately after, thefe heroes appeared in the fquare, afking where were the boogers? where were the cowards? Thirty or forty perfons, moftly lads, being by this means gathered in King-ftreet, Captain Prefton, with a party of men with charged bayonets, came from the main-guard, and taking their ftations by the cuftom-houfe, began to pufh and drive the people off, pricking fome, and threatening others; on which the people grew clamorous, and, it is faid, threw fnowballs. On this the captain commanded his men to fire, and more fnow-balls coming, he again faid, d—n you, fire, be the confequence what it will! – One foldier then fired, and a townfman, with a cudgel ftruck him over the hands with fuch force that he dropt his firelock, and, rufhing forward, aimed a blow at the captain's head, which grazed his hat, and fell pretty heavy upon his arm, however, the foldiers continued the fire, fucceffively, till feven or eight, or, as fome fay, eleven guns were difcharged.

By this fatal manœuvre, feveral were laid dead on the fpot, and fome lay ftruggling for life; but what fhewed a degree of cruelty unknown to Britifh troops, at leaft fince the houfe of Hanover has directed their operations,

operations, was an attempt to fire upon, or stab with their bayonets, the persons who undertook to remove the slain and wounded! At length,

Mr Benjamin Leigh, of the Delph Manufactory, came up, and after some conversation with Captain Preston, relative to his conduct, advised him to draw off his men; with which he complied.

The dead are Mr Samuel Gray, killed on the spot, the ball entering his head and beating off a large portion of his skull.

A mulatto man, named Crispus Attucks, born in Framingham, who was here in order to go for North Carolina, also killed instantly: two balls entering his breast, one of them in special goring the right lobe of the lungs, and a great part of the liver most horribly.

Mr James Caldwell, mate of Captain Morton's vessel, in like manner killed by two balls entering his back.

Mr Samuel Maverick, a promising youth of seventeen years of age, son of the widow Maverick, mortally wounded; a ball went through his belly, and was cut out at his back: he died the next morning.

A lad, named Christopher Monk, about seventeen years of age, apprentice to Mr Walker, shipwright, wounded; a ball entered his back about four inches above the left kidney, near the spine, and was cut out of the breast on the same side; apprehended he will die.

A lad named John Clark, about seventeen years of age, whose parents live at Medford, wounded; a ball entered just below his groin and came out at his hip, on the opposite side; apprehended he will die.

Mr Edward Payne, of this town, merchant, standing at his entry door, received a ball in his arm, which shattered some of the bones.

Mr John Green, taylor, coming up Leverett's-lane, received a ball juſt under his hip, and lodged in the under part of his thigh, which was extracted.

Mr Robert Patterſon, a ſea-faring man, wounded; a ball went through his right arm, and he ſuffered great loſs of blood.

Mr Patrick Carr, about thirty years of age, who worked with Mr Field, leather breeches maker, in Queen-ſtreet, wounded; a ball entered near his hip and went out at his ſide.

A lad named David Parker, an apprentice to Mr Eddy the wheelwright, wounded; a ball entered his thigh.

The people were immediately alarmed with report of this horrid maſſacre, the bells were ſet a ringing, and great numbers ſoon aſſembled at the place where this tragical ſcene had been acted; their feelings may be better conceived than expreſſed; and while ſome were taking care of the dead and wounded, the reſt were in conſultation what to do in thoſe dreadful circumſtances. But ſo little intimidated were they, notwithſtanding their being within a few yards of the main-guard, and ſeeing the 29th regiment under arms, and drawn up in King-ſtreet, that they kept their ſtation, and appeared, as an officer of rank expreſſed it, ready to run upon the very muzzles of their muſkets. The lieutenant-governor ſoon came into the town-houſe, and there met ſome of his Majeſty's council, and a number of civil magiſtrates; a conſiderable body of the people immediately entered the council-chamber, and expreſſed themſelves to his honour with a freedom and warmth becoming the occaſion. He uſed his utmoſt endeavours to pacify them, requeſting that they would let the matter ſubſide for the night, and promiſing to do all in his power that juſtice ſhould be done, and the law have its courſe: men of influence and weight with the people were not wanting on their part to procure their compliance, by representing the horrible consequence of a promiscuous and rash engagement in the night. The inhabitants attended to these suggestions, and the regiment under arms being ordered to their barracks, they separated, and returned to their dwellings by one o'clock. At three o'clock Captain Preston was committed to prison, as were the soldiers who fired, a few hours after him.

Tuesday morning presented a most shocking scene, the blood of our fellow-citizens running like water through King-street, and the merchants Exchange, the principal spot of the military parade for about 18 months past. Our blood might also be tracked up to the head of Long Lane, and through divers other streets and passages.

At eleven o'clock the inhabitants met at Faneuil-hall, and after some animated speeches, they chose a committee of fifteen respectable gentlemen to wait upon the lieutenant-governor in council, to request of him to issue his order for the immediate removal of the troops.

Their message was,

"That it is the unanimous opinion of this meeting, that the inhabitants and soldiery can no longer live together in safety; that nothing can rationally be expected to restore the peace of the town, and prevent further blood and carnage, but the immediate removal of the troops; and that we therefore most fervently pray his honour that his power and influence may be exerted for their instant removal."

The Governor replied:

"I am extremely sorry for the unhappy differences between the inhabitants and troops, and especially for the action of the last evening, and I have exerted myself upon that occasion that a due enquiry may be made, and that the law may have its course. I have in council consulted with the commanding officers of the two regiments who are in town. They have their orders from the general at New-York. It is not in my power to countermand those orders. The council have desired that the two regiments may be removed to the castle. From the particular concern which the 29th regiment has had in your differences, Colonel Dalrymple, who is the commanding officer of the troops, has signified that that regiment shall, without delay, be placed in the barracks at the castle, until he can send to the general, and receive his further orders concerning both the regiments; and that the mainguard shall be removed, and the 14th regiment so disposed and laid under such restraint, that all occasion of future disturbances may be prevented."

The foregoing reply having been read and fully considered—the question was put, Whether the report be satisfactory? It passed in the negative (only one dissentient) out of upwards of 4000 voters;

It was then moved that John Hancock, Esq; Mr Samuel Adams, Mr William Molyneux, William Phillips, Esq; Dr Joseph Warren; Joshua Henshaw, Esq; and Samuel Pemberton, Esq; be a committee to wait on his honour the lieutenant-governor, and inform him, that the reply made to the vote of the inhabitants is by no means satisfactory; and that nothing less will satisfy them, than a total and immediate removal of all the troops.

The committee having waited upon the lieutenant-governor, his honour laid before the board a vote of the town of Boston, passed this afternoon, and then addressed the board as follows:

"I lay

"I lay before you a vote of the town of Boston, which I have just now received from them, and I now ask your advice, what you judge necessary to be done upon it."

The council thereupon expressed themselves to be *unanimously* of opinion, "that it was absolutely necessary for his Majesty's service, the good order of the town, and the peace of the province, that the troops should be immediately removed out of the town of Boston; with which opinion Colonel Dalrymple gave his word of honour that he would acquiesce."

Upon the above report, the inhabitants expressed the highest satisfaction; and after measures were taken for the security of the town, the meeting was dissolved.

A most solemn procession was made through Boston at the funeral of the four murdered youths. On this occasion all the shops were shut up, all the bells in the town were ordered to toll, as were those in the neighbouring towns, and the bodies that moved from different quarters of the town, met at the fatal place of action, and were carried together through the main streets, followed by the greatest concourse of people ever known, all testifying the most sensible grief, to a vault provided for them in the middle of the great burying-ground.

From the time of this fatal tragedy, a military guard of town militia has been constantly kept in the town-house and town-prison, at which some of the most respectable citizens have done duty as common soldiers.

In consequence of this affair, the inhabitants of Roxburgh petitioned the Lieutenant-governor Hutchinson infon to remove the troops from Bofton; and received for anfwer, *That he had no authority to order the King's troops from any place where they are pofted by his Majefty's order;* at the fame time he acquainted them with what had been done with the concurrence of the commanding officer.

Captain Prefton's own account will fet this matter in its full light.

It is matter of too great notoriety to need any proofs, that the arrival of his Majefty's troops in Bofton was extremely obnoxious to its inhabitants. They have ever ufed all means in their power to weaken the regiments, and to bring them into contempt, by promoting and aiding defertions, and with impunity, even where there has been the cleareft evidence of the fact, and by grofsly and falfely propogating untruths concerning them. On the arrival of the 64th and 65th their ardour feemingly began to abate; it being too extenfive to buy off fo many; and attempts of that kind rendered too dangerous from the numbers. But the fame fpirit revived immediately on its being known that thofe regiments were ordered for Hallifax, and hath ever fince their departure been breaking out with greater violence. After their embarkation, one of their juftices, thoroughly acquainted with the people and their intentions, on the trial of the 14th regiment, openly and publicly, in the hearing of great numbers of people, and from the feat of juftice declared, "that the foldiers muft now take care of themfelves, *nor truft too much to their arms,* for they were but a handful; that the inhabitants carried weapons concealed under their cloaths, and would deftroy them in a moment, *if they pleafed.*" This, confidering the malicious temper of the people, was an alarming circumftance to the foldiery. Since which
feveral

several disputes have happened between the towns-people and the soldiers of both regiments, the former being encouraged thereto by the countenance of even some of the magistrates, and by the protection of all the party against government. In general such disputes have been kept too secret from the officers. On the 2d of March, two of the 29th going through one Gray's rope-walk, the rope-makers insultingly asked them if they would empty a vault. This unfortunately had the desired effect, by provoking the soldiers, and from words they went to blows. Both parties suffered in this affray, and finally the soldiers retired to their quarters. The officers, on the first knowledge of this transaction, took every precaution in their power to prevent any ill consequences. Notwithstanding which, single quarrels could not be prevented; the inhabitants constantly provoking and abusing the soldiery. The insolence, as well as utter hatred of the inhabitants to the troops, increased daily; insomuch, that Monday and Tuesday, the 5th and 6th instant, were privately agreed on for a general engagement; in consequence of which several of the militia came from the country, armed, to join their friends, menacing to destroy any who should oppose them. This plan has since been discovered.

On Monday night, about eight o'clock, two soldiers were attacked and beat. But the party of the towns-people, in order to carry matters to the utmost length, broke into two meeting-houses, and rang the alarm bells, which I supposed was for fire, as usual, but was soon undeceived. About nine, some of the guard came to and informed me, that the town inhabitants were assembling to attack the troops, and that the bells were ringing as the signal for that purpose, and not for fire, and the beacon intended to be fired to bring in the distant people of the country. This, as I was captain of the day, occasioned my repairing immediately to the main-guard. In my way there I saw the people in great commotion, and heard them use the most cruel and horrid threats against the troops. In a few minutes after I reached the guard, about an hundred people passed it, and went towards the Custom-house, where the King's money is lodged. They immediately surrounded the centinel posted there, and with clubs and other weapons threatened to execute their vengeance on him. I was soon informed by a townsman, their intention was to carry off the soldier from his post, and probably murder him. On which I desired him to return for further intelligence; and he soon came back and assured me he heard the mob declare they would murder him. This I feared might be a prelude to their plundering the King's chest. I immediately sent a non-commissioned officer and twelve men to protect both the centinel and the king's money, and very soon followed myself, to prevent (if possible) all disorders; fearing lest the officer and soldiery by the insults and provocations of the rioters should be thrown off their guard and commit some rash act. They soon rushed through the people, and, by charging their bayonets in half circle, kept them at a little distance. Nay, so far was I from intending the death of any person, that I suffered the troops to go to the spot where the unhappy affair took place, without any loading in their pieces, nor did I ever give orders for loading them. This remiss conduct in me perhaps merits censure; yet it is evidence, resulting from the nature of things, which is the best and surest that can be offered, that my intention was not to act offensively, but the contrary part, and that not without compulsion. The mob still increased, and were more outrages, striking their clubs or bludgeons one against another, and calling out, 'Come on, you Rascals, you bloody Backs, you Lobster Scoundrels; fire if you dare, G— damn you, fire and be damn'd; we know you dare not;' and much more such language was used. At this time I was between the soldiers and the mob, parleying with and endeavouring all in my power to persuade them to retire peaceably; but to no purpose. They advanced to the point of the bayonets, struck some of them, and even the muzzles of the pieces, and seemed to be endeavouring to close with the soldiers. On which some well-behaved persons asked me if the guns were charged; I replied, yes. They then asked me if I intended to order the men to fire; I answered no, by no means; observing to them, that I was advanced before the muzzles of the men's pieces, and must fall a sacrifice if they fired; and that the soldiers were upon the halfcock and charged bayonets, and my giving the word fire, in those circumstances, would prove me no officer. While I was thus speaking, one of the soldiers, having received a severe blow with a stick, stepped a little on one side, and instantly fired; on which turning to, and asking him why he fired without orders, I was struck with a club on my arm, which for some time deprived me of the use of it; which blow, had it been placed on my head, most probably would have destroyed me. On this a general attack was made on the men by a great number of heavy clubs, and snow-balls being thrown at them, by which all our lives were in imminent danger; some persons at the same time from behind calling out, 'Damn your bloods, why do not you fire?' Instantly three or four of the soldiers fired, one after another, and directly after three more in the same confusion and hurry.

G g   The

The mob then ran away, except three unhappy men who instantly expired, in which number was Mr Gray, at whose rope-walk the prior quarrel took place; one more is since dead, three others are dangerously, and four slightly wounded. The whole of this melancholy affair was transacted in almost twenty minutes. On my asking the soldiers why they fired without orders, they said they heard the word, 'Fire,' and supposed it came from me. This might be the case, as many of the mob called out, ' Fire, fire,' but I assured the men that I give no such order, that my words were 'Don't fire, stop your firing:' In short, it was scarce possible for the soldiers to know who said fire, or don't fire, or stop your firing. On the people's assembling again to take away the dead bodies, the soldiers, supposing them coming to attack them, were making ready to fire again, which I prevented by striking up their firelocks with my hand. Immediately after a townsman came and told me, that 4 or 5000 people were assembled in the next street, and had sworn to take my life with every man's with me; on which I judged it unsafe to remain there any longer, and therefore sent the party and centry to the main-guard, and when they arrived there, telling them off into street-firings, divided and planted them at each end of the street to secure their rear, momently expecting an attack, as there was a constant cry of the inhabitants, 'To arms, to arms—turn out with your guns ;' and the town drums beating to arms. I ordered my drum to beat to arms, and being soon after joined by the different companies of the 29th regiment, I formed them as the guard into street firings. The 14th regiment also got under arms, but remained at their barracks. I immediately sent a serjeant with a party to Colonel Dalrymple, the commanding officer,

officer, to acquaint him with every particular. Several officers going to join their regiment were knocked down by the mob, one very much wounded, and his sword taken from him. The lieutenant-governor and Colonel Carr, were soon after met at the head of the 29th regiment, and agreed that the regiment should retire to their barracks, and the people to their houses; but I kept the piquet to strengthen the guard. It was with great difficulty that the lieutenant-governor prevailed on the people to be quiet and retire: at last they all went off, excepting about a hundred.

A council was immediately called, on the breaking up of which, three justices met, and issued a warrant to apprehend me and eight soldiers. On hearing of this procedure, I instantly went to the sheriff, and surrendered myself, though for the space of four hours I had it in my power to have made my escape, which I most undoubtedly should have attempted, and could easily have executed, had I been the least conscious of any guilt. On the examination before the justices, two witnesses swore that I gave the men orders to fire; the one testified he was within two feet of me; the other, that I swore at the men for not firing at the first word. Others swore they heard me use the word, fire; but whether do or do not fire, they could not say; others, that they heard the word fire, but could not say if it came from me. The next day they got five or six more to swear I gave the word to fire. So bitter and inveterate are many of the malecontents here, that they are industriously using every method to fish out evidence to prove it was a concerted scheme to murder the inhabitants. Others are infusing the utmost malice and revenge into the minds of the people, who are to be my jurors, by false publications,

blications, votes of towns, and all other artifices. That so, from a settled rancour against the officers and troops in general, and the suddenness of my trial after the affair, while the people's minds are greatly inflamed, I am, though perfectly innocent, under most unhappy circumstances, having nothing in reason to expect, but the loss of life in a very ignominious manner, without the interposition of his Majesty's justice and goodness.

Here ends Captain Preston's account, to which may be added his trial, which began on Wednesday the 24th of October, and was continued from day to day, Sunday excepted, till Tuesday the 30th. The witnesses who were examined on both sides amounted to about 50. The lawyers for the crown were Mr Barne and Mr Samuel Quincy; for the prisoner, Mr Auchmuty and Mr John Adams. Each of them spoke three hours at least. About Monday noon the judges began their charge. Judge Trowbridge, who spoke first, entered largely into the contradictory accounts, given by the witnesses, and declared, that it did not appear that the prisoner gave orders, to fire; but if the jury should think otherwise, and find it proved that he did give such orders, the question then would naturally be, What crime is he guilty of?, They surely could not call it murder.—Here he explained the crime of murder in a very distinct manner, and gave it as his opinion, that by law the prisoner was not guilty of murder; observing, that the King had a right to send his troops here; that the commanding officer of these troops had a right to place a centinel at the custom-house: that the centinel placed there on the night of the 5th of March was in the King's peace; that he durst not quit his post; that if he was insulted or attacked, the captain of the guard had a right to
protect

protect him;' that the prisoner and his party, who came there for that purpose, were in the King's peace; that while they were at the custom-house, for the purpose of protecting the centinel, it was plainly proved that they had been assaulted by a great number of people; that the people assembled there were not in the King's peace, but were by law considered as a riotous mob, as they attacked the prisoner and his party with pieces of ice, sticks, and clubs; and that even one of the witnesses against him confessed he was armed with a highland broad-sword; that the rioters had knocked down one of the soldiers of the party, laid hold of several of their muskets, and that, before the soldiers fired, the cry was, Knock them down! Kill them! Kill them! That all this was sworn to by the witnesses, and if the jury believed them, the prisoner could not be found guilty of murder. He then proceeded to explain what the law considered as man-slaughter, and observed, as before, that if they gave credit to the witnesses, who testified the assaults made on the prisoner and his party, they could not find him guilty of man-slaughter; and concluded with saying, that if he was guilty of any offence, it could only be excusable homicide; that this was only founded on the supposition of the prisoner's having given orders to fire, for if this was not proved, they must acquit him.

"Judge Oliver, who spoke next, began with representing, in a very nervous and pathetic manner, the insults and outrages which he, and the court, through him, had received on a former occasion, (meaning the trial of Richardson) for giving his opinion in a point of law, that, notwithstanding, he was resolved to do his duty to his God, his King, and his country; that he despised both insults and threats, and that he would

not

not forego a moment's peace of confcience for the applaufe of millions. He agreed in fentiment with the former judge, that the prifoner was not guilty.

Judge Cufhing fpoke next, and agreed entirely with the other two, with regard to the prifoner's cafe.

Judge Lyndex concluded. He fpoke a confiderable time, and was of the fame opinion with the other judges. Towards the clofe of his fpeech, he faid, "Happy I am to find, that, after fuch ftrict examination, the conduct of the prifoner appears in fo fair a light; yea I feel myfelf, at the fame time, deeply affected, that this affair turns out fo much to the difgrace of every perfon concerned againft him, and fo much to the fhame of the town in general." The jury then returned their verdict, *Not Guilty*. He was immediately difcharged, and is now in the caftle. Great numbers attended during the trial, which was carried on with a folemn decency.

As one evil generally introduces another, during the time of thefe commotions on the continent of America, a fet of lawlefs ruffians in Orange county, Carolina, broke out into open violence, and fet all law and government at defiance. They called themfelves Regulators, and committed many wicked and cruel outrages. Their principal averfion was directed againft courts of juftice, and gentlemen of the law, to whom they fhewed all manner of defpite and contempt. When Judge Henderfon and feveral lawyers were returning from Salifbury circuit to Hillfborough to hold the court there, they lay in wait for them, with rifle guns to difpatch them; but the Judge receiving intelligence of their defign, went another way, and by that means preferved his own life, and that of his attendants. They ftill threatened to meet him at Hillfborough,

Hillsborough, and to execute their vengeance on him and his company there. They put their threatenings in execution, and in a most merciless and cruel manner treated Colonel Fanning, Mr Hooper, and some others. They desired the judge to proceed, but according as they directed him, and put a stop to all proceedings of justice. The judge escaped with difficulty, by secretly withdrawing, which put them into a great rage, and provoked them to such a degree, that they plundered and destroyed all the furniture in Colonel Fanning's house, seized all his papers and books, and scattered them in the wind; they also carried off all his money and plate, drank plentifully of his liquors, and set the rest a-running in the streets. They next broke the church bell in pieces, and were going to pull down the church, but in this they did not agree. To finish their tragedy, they took a negro that was hanging in chains, and placed him in the judge's chair, to shew their entire contempt of all justice. Such is the dangerous tendency of commotions in government; under the shadow and pretence of pursuing their own privileges, mischievous and wicked men often despise all legal government, and plunder their fellow subjects. The reports concerning the riot at Boston had now reached England, which made it necessary for parliament to enquire into the causes and reasons of that unfortunate affair. The minister appeared shy on this occasion, for though two regiments were shut up in Castle William, without any order from government, which was no small affront to the minister and the court, yet they were afraid to enter upon an enquiry, for fear of the opposition insisting upon an enquiry concerning the whole affair. It was thought that government imagined, by suffering the matter to hang in suspence, that the colonists would divide and fall out among themselves, and so make the business of the ministry more easy. In this they were, however, mistaken.

A motion was made upon the 8th of May, for an address to the throne, setting forth the disputes that had arisen among the several governors and commanders, in almost all the colonies since the appointment of a commander in chief; that the colonies have been for some time, and still are, from this and other causes, in a state of great disorder and confusion; that the people of America complain of the establishment of an army there, as setting up a military government over the civil; and therefore praying that all these matters may be considered, and such measures taken as would replace things upon a constitutional footing. This motion was introduced by observing, that in the present critical situation of affairs, they were expressly called upon to enquire, how the ministers here, no less than their officers there, have managed so unfortunately, as to kindle the present flame of dissention between the mother country and the colonies. That in fulfilling this duty, they must not only consider the matter of fact, but the right of things: not only the turbulence of the Americans, but the cause of that turbulence: and not only the power of the crown, but the equity with which that power has been exercised. This was a motion which was not likely to be carried in a house where the minister had a powerful majority. It met with the fate of many others of the like nature, and had a negative put upon it. Upon reflections, one cannot help thinking it strange, that men who are employed in business, and manage it fairly, should have such an aversion to having their conduct examined. A refusal of this sort always implies, either some defect

fect in management, or an arbitrary despotism in those employed in public affairs; both of which are inconsistent with the true exercise of good government.

In the debates on this occasion, the ministerialists made a poor figure; after ages, when tamely reading the debates in this session of parliament, will be filled with astonishment to find, that in a matter of so much consequence, there should have been any occasion for debate at all; and it will equally amaze them, unless they are equally corrupted, to view the defences of administration, of a cause, which none, except men of corrupt minds, and destitute of all sense of honour, shame, and humanity, would attempt to maintain. The ministry on this occasion were charged with tergiversation, and want of system. It was affirmed that they had sent contradictory orders to the governors in the colonies, and made their servants blunder like themselves, for want of a settled plan of operation; that they had imposed taxes, and repealed them, imposed them, and repealed them again; dissolved assemblies, and called them again; and suffered them to sit and proceed to business, without disavowing or discountenancing the measures that had procured their dissolution. Promises had been made to the assemblies, that certain duties should be taken off, and repealed, which were unwarrantable, of dangerous consequence, and an high breach of privilege; and that it was equally derogatory from the honour of the crown, and freedom of parliamentary deliberations, to have its faith pledged to perform such promises. Troops had been sent, driven out with disgrace, and violence and submission had alternately succeeded one another; that treasons had been charged and adopted by parliament, which were neither proved, nor attempted to be proved: or if they existed, were

they

they attempted to be detected and punished, which was an high reflection upon the dignity of parliament. This sort of reasoning had no influence; the ministry with a sort of stoical indifference, bore all with patience, without attempting even to make their usual defence. A few reflections, for the sake of form, were thrown out against the colonists, as turbulent, disloyal, and disaffected to the government of this country, and people that wanted to be independent of Great Britain. It was asserted that the crown had a right to send troops to any part of the empire, and station them there according to pleasure; and that there was a necessity of employing them at that time, for supporting the progress of the laws, against a people that were nearly in a state of rebellion. These reflections were only thrown out as hints, without any particular discussion, rather to get clear of the debate for the present, than as arguments intended to convince the opposite party of the propriety of the reasoning. Those that are guided by the dictates of common sense, and plain arguments must not expect them from the ministry at this time. Even their champions, who undertook to defend their measures in long laboured dissertations upon government, and the rights of supreme powers to rule over all their dominions with absolute sway, were in great distress to find principles and conclusions which plain men could understand. Many dark and dismal productions teemed from the press, stuffed with arbitrary conclusions, void of all possibility of demonstration. These were echoed by the hirelings of the ministry as unanswerable productions, though those who trumpeted their fame most, did not understand a word that was in them. They were intended to throw a mist in the eyes of the public, to cover

designs

designs that could not be decently avowed openly, and this was all that the authors could propose, except their pensions, which they greatly expected." After all the dusts of the schoolmen and casuists had been swept together, and thrown in the eyes of the people, the majority still preserved their sight, and perceived the designs of the ministry. It would be the greatest insult to truth and common sense, to affirm that the arguments on both sides were of equal force. There were many absurd things said on both sides, as will often happen in the course of disputation, but in forming an estimate of the force of the arguments, a man of very plain understanding will be at no loss, (setting aside private interest and prejudice), which way to determine. Those who attempt to defend the proceedings of either party in all particulars, will find it a task not easily to be performed; and it will shew more of partiality than good sense, to affirm that there were not errors on both sides.——It is a part of our natural infelicity which has prevailed for some time past, that parties in opposition have been for defending their own proceedings, when they have totally given up the principles by which they only could be defended; and by departing from the true principles of charity, have made no allowances for the prejudices and weakness of their opponents. What has much aggravated this evil is, that in the various disputes upon this subject, the moral side of the question has been but little considered. Systems of policy, or of government, without morality, are like a body without a spirit, only dead and beggarly elements, generated by corruption, and supported by obstinacy. Moral privileges are by the laws of nature as much the right of rational creatures, as those that come under the notion of political; and human policy, with-not being built upon moral principles, will in the end become like a baseless fabric of a vision, vanish and not leave a wreck behind it. The best foundation of government and policy, is truth; without this they will always turn to oppression.

This year the ministry were so busily employed in prosecuting the printers and booksellers for publishing libels, and the magistrates of the city of London for refusing to execute the orders of the Commons, that very little of American affairs came before parliament. It may not be unprofitable in this chasm of modern affairs in the American history, to fill the blank with a few particulars of the ancient history of the colonies. And as this history is principally intended to record the wars in the western part of the world, we shall take a short view of some of the first wars with the Indians, which was carried on by the English in those parts.

CHAP.

CHAP. V.

A view of the first War between the Colonists and the Natives—The taking of Acadia—An attempt upon Quebec, &c.

WE are scarcely sufficiently informed by the annals of those times concerning the true causes and springs of the first Indian war. The war itself is sufficiently described, though the causes still in a great measure lie hid. Two things seem to have given rise to those bloody and cruel measures; the covetousness of the colonists, and the treachery of the French. The new colonists frequently in the extending their territories, did not strictly observe the lines which bounded their new acquired possessions, and frequently were found making encroachments upon the possessions of the original natives, which though they were very inconsiderable, were magnified by the French emissaries, who were scattered among the Indians, as the most atrocious acts of injustice and iniquity. These emissaries stirred up the Indians, who were not ill to irritate against a people for whom they had but little regard, and against whom their own private interest inclined them to believe the smallest accusations. What added much to the disgust the natives had against the colonists, and created in their minds a very strong antipathy against them, was the practice of some occasional traders, who came upon their coasts without design of settling. These, upon occasions, committed depredations and enticed some of the Indians aboard their ships, and carried them to Europe, and sold them for slaves. The natives who considered those free-booters as friends and connections of the colonists, mutually engaged in the same designs of plunder and depredation, were determined to extirpate this new race of people, as enemies to all their common and natural rights. Their minds could not suggest any other reason why they came to settle among them, except to invade their rights, and seize their possessions.—Being ignorant of their language, and uncapable of understanding on a sudden their signs and signatures of expression, they interpreted the whole as tokens of hostility, or signs of dissimulation.

The writers of the history of New England have drawn the characters of the Indians of those times in the most frightful and forboding colours.———They have represented them as worshippers of the devil, and as true subjects of the prince of the power of the air.— Cruel, barbarous, unmerciful, and unrelenting. Among the various tribes of these infidel savages, none were more powerful, warlike, and formidable than the nation of the *Pequots*, which lay between the *Naragansets* and the *Moghenas*. This tribe had now become a terror not only to the new settlers, but to the other tribes of Indians in their neighbourhood, on account of their power, cruelty, and oppression. Their arms were almost irresistible, and their power intolerable; and the late thefts and pillagings of the English free-booters had encreased their rage to the highest degree of revenge and resentment. It was no wonder that the colonists, when they fell in their way,

way, felt the effects of their unbridled fury and revenge.

In the year 1634, an open rupture began between these fierce natives and the colonists. A party of Indians attacked Captain Stone and Captain Norton, when they were sailing up the river Connecticut, and killed them, with six men who were in company, and sunk the vessel in the river. Historians do not inform us whether these gentlemen were sailing within the boundaries of the colony, or were for the sake of fishing, or for some other reasons, beyond the line of agreement. It was a practice so frequently pursued by the colonists, to proceed beyond the bounds of their purchase, that the natives often complained of the encroachments which they made upon their possessions. Whatever was the cause of these hostilities, the truth is, that the Indians began now to take a most severe revenge. These savages attacked the crew of a vessel that were cast upon Long-Island, and killed several of the men; and in 1636, they boarded a ship near Block Island, killed the captain, and committed several more outrages. The colonists finding that this Indian war turned more serious than they expected, began to consider upon some suitable methods of defence, as well as offensive projects, to annoy those cruel and barbarous assailants. The governor and council of Boston sent an hundred and twenty men, under the command of the Captains Endicot, Underhill, and Turner;—who boldly attacked the Indians, who left their huts, and retired to the swamps and woods for their safety and preservation. Before this army proceeded any further, they sent a message to the Pequots, desiring them to deliver up the murderers, who were the occasion of the war; that the innocent might not be involved

with

with the guilty in the calamity of war. These fierce and furious people either confidered their caufe to be juft, or were determined, at all events, to fupport their brethren in the caufe they were now engaged in. They would liften to no propofals of accommodation, but were determined to carry on the war. Their refufal brought on a fkirmifh, in which the natives were defeated, and all their huts in that part of the country, and their corn were deftroyed. Thefe fkirmifhes were only prefaces to a more bloody war that now followed, which was carried on with great fury and barbarity on the fide of the natives. The prifoners which fell into their hands, were tortured in the moft fhocking and inhuman manner, and put to all the extremities of pain that wanton barbarity could devife. Maids and children were roafted alive, and the barbarous favages all the while mocking their pains, and ridiculing their geftures and expreffions of agony.

This nation of Pequots joined policy and craft to their barbarity and cruelty; they at this time devifed a fcheme, which had it taken place, muft have totally deftroyed all the infant colonies. They fent Talks to all the various tribes of Indians of their acquaintance, fetting forth the neceffity of an affociation among themfelves, to extirpate this new race of people, which might be eafily done, by a confederacy of the various tribes, before the colonifts were provided for a defence, or were grown ftrong by an increafe of their numbers; that by one decifive blow, they had it now in their power to free themfelves of neighbours, who, if they were not at this time fubdued, would in a fhort time become their mafters, and deprive them of all their poffeffions. This was a moft judicious and political fcheme, and would have proved

proved the total ruin of the New England colonies. This scheme was however frustrated, by providence, through the antipathy of the rest of the tribes to these Pequots. The other Indian nations had suffered so severely at the hands of these oppressors, that they were determined to leave them to themselves, and the event of the war which they were engaged in. They took pleasure in seeing a people crushed, that had behaved so tyrannically to the rest of their brethren; and instead of affording them assistance, indulged a secret pleasure at their ruin and destruction.

The English colonists knowing both the power and enmity of these savages, raised forces with all expedition for their own defence, with a design, if possible, to put an end to the war, by extirpating that revengeful tribe of Indians. With an army of about 700 men, of which 500 were Indians of the Naraganset tribes, the rest were colonists, they advanced to the enemy's country. Their commanders were Israel Stoughton, Captain Underhill, and Captain John Mason Underhill and Mason marched before the other troops could join them, and advanced in search of Saffacus, the grand Sachem of the Pequots, who had retired with his men into what he thought an impregnable fortress. The Naraganset Indians, upon hearing of the name of Saffacus, fell a trembling, and would not advance; they said he was a god, and no man could kill him: They were therefore of no use in this expedition. The officers with their small handful of troops, under the direction of an Indian spy, which they had sent to search for the Pequots, came upon them by surprise, and entered their fort sword in hand; after making prodigious slaughter among the savages, they set fire to the fort, and totally destroyed

stroyed it. On this occasion, six hundred Indians of the tribe of Pequots were slain, and only two men of the colonists. Of the whole forces in this fort only eight escaped to carry the tidings of the disaster to their friends. The heat of the action, and the want of provision had now greatly exhausted the strength of the colonists, which would have proved fatal to them, had not some vessels arrived with provisions in Pequot harbour in the very time of need, and in the midst of their distress. This supply refreshed their spirits, and prepared them for another sharp encounter which soon happened. There was another Indian fort at some distance, whither the news had been carried of the defeat of their troops, and the destruction of their fort: In this sort of fortress, there were upwards of three hundred savages of the best troops of the Pequots. These advanced with all expedition to revenge the death of their friends, and attacked the colonists with great fury. But they met with such a warm reception, that they betook themselves to a swamp, after leaving a great number dead upon the spot. The former defeat of their friends, and the repulse they now met with, in a great measure damped their courage, they expressed their chagrin and disappointment with most piniful howling and cries, according to the manner of their country. By this time the Captains Patrick and Stoughton came up with the forces of the Massachusets bay, which was a seasonable reinforcement to the Connecticut forces, which were now both much fatigued, and many of them wounded in the two foregoing skirmishes. There were still a great number of the Pequot savages scattered in different parties, concealed in swamps and thickets, lying ready to take the first opportunity of revenge; but when they perceived this new reinforcement

ment of the colonists, they fled to the fort where Saffacus had taken refuge, and upbraided him as the cause of the late disasters, and of their total ruin. Several hundreds of these miserable creatures were taken by Captain Stoughton; the women were carried captives, and the men put aboard of a ship of one Skipper Geelop, where they all perished, by what accident historians do not inform us. During this war, thirteen of their Sachems, or little kings, were slain, and Saffacus was betrayed, and at last put to death by the Maqua Indians, a tribe of savage Cannibals, to whom he had fled for safety. How far the necessity of the case might justify the conduct of the colonists in this war, I will not pretend to say, but it appears to have been carried on with a vigour which approached very near to an excess of severity. This war was soon ended, and the whole tribe of Pequots extirpated. From the beginning to the finishing thereof, three years were not fully elapsed.

In the year 1638, another Indian war had well nigh broke out, on account of some English vagabonds having murdered an Indian in the woods. This savage belonged to the tribe of the Naragansets, which on this occasion began to rise, but the war was prevented by the punishment of the murderers, and proper satisfaction was given to the injured party. What most struck the Indians on this occasion was, that all the three men who had been concerned in the murder, were executed, which they considered as an excess of justice. Although there were many jealousies and suspicions between the colonists and the natives, yet from this time, till 1674, there was no open war. Matters were always settled in such a manner, that the general tranquility was preserved. In 1674, one John Saufman, an Indian preacher, who had been

sent

sent to preach the Gospel among the Indians, informed the governor of Plymouth, that Philip, an Indian king, near mount Hope, with several other tribes, had formed a plot to extirpate the English throughout the country. Soon after this, Sausman was murdered, and his body found in a pond, and his hat and gun upon the ice. Upon enquiry, it was found that one Tobias, a counsellor of Philip, had murdered him, and thrown him into the pond, to prevent a discovery. The murderer was punished, as he deserved, but Philip continued to carry on his plot; and in the month of June, this year, began the hostilities, by plundering the plantations near *Mount Hope*. The governor, to prevent the further pillagings of the Indians, sent out a small army to protect the plantation, and to defend it against the designs of Philip. As every thing had the appearance of a war, and hostilities were begun, the colony of Plymouth appointed a day of fasting and humiliation, to ask the Divine aid and assistance against their cruel and savage enemies. On this occasion they had given no offence to these new foes, and therefore could with confidence appeal to heaven concerning the justness of their cause. But as the best of men, and the most righteous cause are liable to particular misfortunes in the course of providence, so these colonists upon the very day of their humble devotion were assaulted by their enemies. The inhabitants of Sirnazey, in returning from prayers, were attacked by some lurking Indians, when some were killed, and several wounded. This both alarmed and roused the colonists, who now thought that their safety and preservation depended upon their activity, and the vigour of the measures which they pursued. Upon the 26th of June, a company of horse, under the command of Captain Thomas Prentice,

tice, and another of foot, under the command of Captain Daniel Henchman, marched from Boston to Mount Hope. They were afterwards joined by a company of volunteers, under Captain Mosley, and another company of foot from Swansey, under Captain Cudworth. Upon the 28th, they sent out a scout of twelve men to see if they could discover the enemy, who were soon acquainted with their situation, by a discharge of musquetry from a thicket, with which one was killed and another wounded. The remaining ten, instead of retreating to their main body, pushed boldly forward and attacked the Indians, and put them to flight, though their numbers were ten times more than this small reconoitering party. The main body of the colonists next morning charged the Indians in their quarters, routed them, and put them to flight; upon which their whole country was left open to this victorious army. In the quarters of this enemy were found the mangled bodies of several Englishmen, whose heads were stuck upon poles, and Bibles torn in pieces, in contempt of their religion. In the wigwams of the enemy were found all the signatures of hurry and a precipitate retreat. Philip now fled from these parts, but was the occasion of several more bloody conflicts, which in the issue ruined his cause, and was the reason of many Indians losing their lives.

It is really amazing in the history of this war what remarkable defeats were given to large bodies of Indians, by mere handfuls of colonists, though they were armed in the same manner, and fought with the same weapons. In an open field, a very small party of English would often defeat ten times their own number, and the enemy leave a third part of their forces dead in the field of battle. Were I to mention the several particular engagements in which fifteen have routed an hundred and forty-five, I should certainly, in this sceptical age, be accused of a great degree of credulity. This war, which was principally carried on in the way of bush-fighting, was exceeding bloody both to the colonists and the Indians. Many of the new built towns were burnt, and the plantations laid waste, the inhabitants were often instantly put to death, or carried captive, and reserved for the most lingering and excruciating torture; and considering the infant state of those plantations, it was next to a miracle that they were not totally extirpated by such numerous and powerful enemies, who were formidable of themselves, and sometimes assisted by the French.

Philip, who had been the original cause of this bloody war, fled from one tribe to another, as the chance of war and the various accidents of his fortune obliged him; and such was his inveterate and unrelenting enmity against the colonists, that in all parts whither he fled, he endeavoured to make the people parties in the war against the English. As his revenge was excessive, the schemes of his policy were deep, and often concerted with a sagacity which more civilized and enlighted politicians would have marked with the epithets of wisdom.—But as he paid no regard to the moral principles of government, when he pursued the dictates of his fury and revenge, he at last laid a snare in which he himself was entangled, and which proved the ruin of his cause. To provoke the Maquas, a neighbouring tribe, against the colonists, he set upon some of their people in the woods and killed them, and then published that the English had done it; but as such daring wickedness seldom passes unpunished, providence laid open his schemes, and exposed

posed the whole of his designs. One of the Maquas people, whom Philip thought had been killed, was only dangerously wounded, who informed his nation of the real actor in that tragedy. This excited the revenge of the whole tribe, who fell upon Philip, and destroyed many of his people, and would have dispatched himself, had he not fled, and taken shelter in Mount Hope, from whence, in a short time he was also forced to flee. This desperate Indian was as superstitious as he was revengeful; he believed in all the prognostications of his *magicians* and *powwaws*, and from an assurance of one of their prophecies, was persuaded that no Englishman could kill him. He was at last shot through the body by an Indian in the service of the colonies, and expired soon after in the very place where he had first concerted the scheme of extirpating the colonists, and his head was carried to Plymouth. The people of New England at this time made an observation with regard to the state of their affairs, which perhaps will hold in general with regard to all countries in the same situation. They took notice, that till once they began to reform their manners, and observe the institutions of the Gospel with more exactness, that they never prospered in pursuing this war; but after they began in earnest to reform abuses, and observe the moral institutions of God in sincerity, their affairs took quite a different turn, and they prospered in their undertakings. It may be necessary to observe here, how all parties in all nations are ready to declare others in a state of rebellion, that oppose the measures they are fond of pursuing.

Cotton Mather in his History of New England observes, that on September the 6th, 1676, four hundred Indians were surprised in Quechebo, of which,

one

one half had been acceſſary to the *late rebellion*, and for that reaſon were ſold for ſlaves. As theſe natives were not the ſubjects of England, nor of the colonifts, it was impoſſible that they could be rebels in the common acceptation of that word. If the coloniſts claimed all that country as their own, their claim was unjuſt, and the reſiſtance of the natives was lawful defence againſt invaders: or if the Indians attacked the Engliſh unjuſtly, it was an unlawful invaſion, but not a rebellion of ſubjects againſt lawful government.

One of the moſt remarkable actions in this war, was an attack upon a fort in the country of the Naraganſets, which lies eaſt of Connecticut river, and ſouth of Patuſet. The coloniſts of New England finding themſelves harraſſed by thoſe tribes in that neighbourhood, reſolved upon giving them an effectual overthrow, that in time coming they might behave with more civility to their neighbours. Having muſtered an army of fifteen hundred men, they marched in the middle of winter into their enemies country, in the midſt of froſt and ſnow, and came upon one of their principal forts by ſurpriſe, which they carried, after much ſlaughter on both ſides. This fort was ſituated upon an iſland of about ſix acres, in the middle of a ſwamp, to which there was only acceſs one way, which was by paſſing along a ſingle tree, where only one perſon could paſs, with difficulty.

An Indian, whoſe name was Peter, who had taken ſome diſguſt at his tribe, was guide to the New England forces, and led them to this fortreſs. This deſerter ſhewed them a certain place in the foreſt, where, by throwing four or five trees, about a foot from the ground, over the ſwamp, they might attack the garriſon with good hopes of ſucceeding. This was the only place where it appeared vulnerable,

though

though over against this passage there was a block-house, which rendered the attempt exceedingly dangerous. The colonists began the attack at one o'clock, which was led on by Captain Mosley and Captain Davenport, who rushed into the fort, when a bloody conflict began. Six of the principal officers were killed in the first assault, and a great many of their private men; but they at last carried the fortress, and slew above seven hundred Indians in arms. The rest fled, and betook themselves to a cedar swamp, at some distance, whither the colonists did not pursue them. This expedition was commanded by Josiah Winslow, Esq; who had under him many brave and intrepid officers, who behaved with a gallantry that would have done honour to a Roman legion. The Indians in this short siege had seven hundred men killed, and three hundred mortally wounded, besides old men, women, and children that were pressed to death in the midst of the encounter. Of the New England forces, eighty-five were slain, and an hundred and fifty wounded. The other exploits during this war consisted chiefly in the burning of towns, and laying waste of villages, on the part of the Indians, and of defeating small parties of the enemy, on the part of the colonists. On these occasions, many desperate actions were performed; which those that are accustomed to the method of carrying on war in Europe, would scarcely be able to give credit to, were it not that they are too well authenticated to be called in question. In those encounters with the Indians, the colonists shewed an uncommon bravery, and were never afraid to engage three times their own number in the open field, at the same weapons. Nor in general can it be affirmed, that they coveted war merely for the sake of dominion. The only error that they appear to have fallen into in carrying

rying on their wars, seems to have been, a desire to enlarge the dominion of Great Britain, and of making conquests for their mother country, which they delivered up to the disposal of her government.

In the month of April, 1690, a naval force, with seven hundred troops, under the command of Sir William Phipps, sailed from Nantasket, in New England, with orders to seize the French settlements in Nova Scotia, then called Acadia, which they attacked, and had them delivered up to King William, whom the colonists in those parts had acknowledged as their sovereign. The reason of this expedition, seems to have been to distress the French, who at this time stirred up the Indians against the colonists, under the pretence that they were rebels against their sovereign, and furnished them with arms and ammunition; with which they did great damage to the planters. The colonists considered this method as the most effectual to put an end to the war; for, provided they could once subdue the French, or drive them from their settlements, they knew that the Indians would soon be overcome. Sir William Phipps, with a fleet of thirty sail of ships, sailed from New England to Quebec, but did not arrive till the 7th of October, when the frost was setting in. This expedition was intended to support an army of land forces that were to march from New York, of some colonists and Christian Indians. After some bold efforts, this attempt miscarried; but who was to blame, is not easily learned from the history of those times. It is well known, that although this expedition miscarried, the French were in great terror, and expected nothing less than to be driven out of Canada. This shews what the colonists were then able to attempt, without any assistance from the mother country.

Besides

Besides the agency of the French, there were other reasons which the Indians gave for this war with the colonists. They alledged that the English refused to pay the yearly tribute of corn, agreed upon at the conclusion of the peace—that they hindered them from catching fish in Sago river, by the nets, which hindered the fish from coming where they were wont to come. They said, though the colonists had got their lands, they imagined the fishes in the rivers had been still their privilege. But the greatest grievance of all, was the giving patents for lands which belonged to them; this incensed them greatly. And it must be allowed that neither the people of Old or New England had any right to give any persons patents to the lands of the Indians without their consent. It is a strange method of reasoning, that is used by many selfish politicians, that European sovereigns, because some of their subjects take possession of some parts of a continent, that therefore they may portion out the whole to their friends, according to their good will and pleasure. Yet this is the force of all the arguments of either the French or the English for their right of possession of many parts of the world.

What gave the first and most considerable influence to the Indian war, was the behaviour of the French in Canada.—These ambitious Gauls had no sooner made a settlement in those parts of the western world, than they began to make conquests, and endeavoured to subject the Indians to the French dominion. When these natives found themselves in a situation to resist the power of France, they defended their own rights, and made reprisals upon the enemy; and frequently were so successful, that notwithstanding the French having the advantage of fire arms, they were defeated by the Indians, with great loss, and put in

fear

fear of losing their own dominions. The five nations as they are called, of Sinekas, Cayugas, Onoidos, Onadagues, and Mohawks, which lie south east of the lake Ontorio, and north west from New York and Albany, were zealous opposers of the French dominion. These tribes were united among themselves upon the most liberal principles of freedom and liberty, and abhorred all sorts of slavery to such a degree, that they would not even enslave a captive. Such were their ideas of liberty and justice, that when a certain man broke the jail of New York and fled to the five nations, that they paid his debt, but would not deliver up his person, but adopted him into their tribes, and made him free. Lacedemon, in the very height of its glory, did not excel the five nations in their ideas of liberty. It was no wonder that a people so zealous for freedom should have had an hearty aversion to a nation which, for many ages, attempted to make slaves of all the world.

The Dutch who settled at New York, 1609, about six years after the French came to Canada, made no attempts of conquest, but lived peaceably with the five nations, and carried on trade: between the Dutch and these Indians, there was a perfect friendship. The English, who succeeded to the Dutch in the settlement of New York, observed nearly the same plan, between whom and the five nations, there continued a good understanding for many years; though it must be granted that the English did not support the principles of friendship with the same ardour and zeal that the five nations supported it, yet the alliance which the English entered into with the five nations was never broken on their part for the space of sixty years. This may plainly teach us, that had the European Christians been as honest and faithful as the Indians

of

of the five nations, there would have been no occasion for such horrid wars, as have often happened in those parts of the world.

The colonists of New England, after many bloody skirmishes with the French and eastern Indians, wherein many lives were lost on both sides, entered into a treaty with the five nations at Albany, in the year 1689. The reason of this treaty, upon the part of the New England colonists was, that they were informed that the eastern Indians, by the means of the French, were soliciting a confederation with the five nations, which they very wisely conjectured, would not be for the interest of the English, nor be consistent with their safety. The five nations had been formidable to the French, even before they were in possession of fire arms, and now that they were supplied with these, should they be engaged against the English, they would be very dangerous enemies. For this reason it was considered as a piece of needful policy, to have them, if possible, united in one interest with New England, against the French, and the Indians in the French interest. The agents on the part of New England were Colonel John Pynchon, Major John Savage, and Captain John Bull, and on the side of the five nations was, Tahajadoris, a Mohawk Sachem. After the usual formalities on such occasions, Tahajadoris addressed the agents in the following manner:

" Brethren, you are welcome to this house, which is appointed for our treaties, and public business with the Christians: We thank you for renewing the covenant chain. It is now no longer of iron, and subject to rust as formerly, but of pure silver, and includes in it all the King's subjects, from the Senakas country, eastward, as far as any of the great King's subjects live,

live, and southward from New England to Virginia. Here he gave a beaver.

"We are glad to hear of the good success our great King has had over the French by sea, in taking and sinking so many of their men of war. You tell us in your proposals that we are one people; let us then go hand in hand together, to ruin and destroy the French, our common enemy. Gives another beaver. The covenant-chain between us is ancient, as you tell us, and of long standing, and it has been kept inviolably by us. When you had wars sometime ago with the Indians, you desired us to help you; we did it readily, and to the purpose, for we pursued them very closely; by which we prevented the effusion of much blood. This was a sign that we loved truly and sincerely, and from our hearts—Gives a belt.

"You advise us to pursue our enemies, the French, vigorously. This we assure you we are resolved to do to the utmost of our power; but since the French are your enemies likewise, we desire our brethren of the three colonies to send us an hundred men for the security of this place, which is ill provided, in case of an attack from the French—The Christians have victuals enough for their entertainment. Gives one belt.

"We patiently bore many injuries from the French, from one year to another, before we took up the axe against them. Our patience made the governor of Canada think that we were afraid of him, and durst not resent the injuries we had long suffered; but now he is undeceived. We assure you that we are resolved never to drop the axe; the French shall never see our faces in peace; we shall never be reconciled as long as one Frenchman is alive: we shall never make peace, though our nation should be ruined by it, and every

every one of us cut in pieces. Our brethren of the three colonies may depend on this—Gives a beaver.

"As to what you told us of the *Orvaiagungas* and *Uragees*, we anſwer: that we were never ſo proud and haughty as to begin a war without provocation. You tell us that they are treacherous rogues. We believe it; and that they will undoubtedly aſſiſt the French. If they ſhall do this, or ſhall join with any of our enemies, either French or Indians, then we will kill and deſtroy them."—Gives a beaver.

Then the Mohawks offered five of their men to guard the agents home againſt any of their Indian enemies, who they were afraid might be lying in wait for the agents, and gave a belt. Then the ſpeaker proceeded, and ſaid, "We have ſpoke what we had to ſay of the war, we now come to the affairs of peace: we promiſe to preſerve the chain inviolably, and wiſh that the ſun may always ſhine in peace over our heads, that are comprehended in this chain. We give two belts, one for the ſun, the other for his beams. We make faſt the roots of the tree of peace and tranquillity, which is planted in this place. Its roots extend as far as the outmoſt of your colonies. If the French ſhould come to ſhake this tree, we would feel it by the motion of its roots, which extend into our country. But we truſt it will not be in the governor of Canada's power to ſhake this tree, which has been ſo firmly and ſo long planted with us."—Gives two beavers.

Laſtly, he deſired the Magiſtrates of Albany to remember what he had ſaid, and gave them a beaver. The New England agents were not fully ſatisfied with all that the Sachem had ſaid; for the chief thing they wanted, was to know their diſpoſition concerning this point. The five nations anſwered, "We cannot

cannot declare war againſt the eaſtern Indians, for they have done no harm; neverthelefs our brethren of New England may be aſſured, that we will live and die in friendſhip with them. When we took up arms againſt the French and their confederates, we did not make war with them at the perſuaſions of our brethren here; for they did not ſo much as know our intention till fourteen days after our army had begun to march."

Theſe Indians whom we call ſavages, appear in many inſtances to have better notions of juſtice than the polite and civilized Chriſtians in Europe: they conſider war as unrighteous, without men receive injury, and do not account it a ſufficient reaſon to engage in war even in behalf of their friends, till once they know the grounds of the controverſy.

Among all the Indian tribes, none were ſuch enemies to the Engliſh coloniſts as thoſe who were called the French praying Indians. Theſe being perverted by Jeſuit miſſionaries, who not only poiſoned their minds with all the abſurdities of Popery, but inſtilled into them the greateſt antipathy againſt the Engliſh by lyes and falſe repreſentations. Theſe tribes were ſo fully under the French influence, that they took every opportunity to harraſs and diſtreſs all their neighbours that were inclined to favour the Engliſh. They had loſt their former honeſty which they had while they were Heathens, and were become ſuch conſummate diſſemblers, that there was no depending upon any thing they ſaid.—And what rendered them ſtill more dangerous and abominable, they were more barbarous and cruel than when they were profeſſed Infidels. The French prieſts had inſtructed them in none of thoſe principles of religion and humanity which ſoften the heart, and ſooth the rugged paſſions

of

of the foul: they had still concealed from them the Scriptures, and the pure doctrines of morality which they contain, and only taught them concerning the infallibility of the Pope, and the omnipotence of the French king. These missionaries of Rome in the first instance taught them that all the English were heretics, and in a state of damnation; and that it was meritorious to destroy as many of them as they were able; and that cheating them with lyes and false promises, was so far from being a crime, that it was the greatest virtue, and would meet with an ample reward in the other world. Under the influence of such tutorage, it was no wonder that a barbarous and savage people turned worse than they were before.

One thing which often rendered the colonists unsuccessful in their attempts against the French and Indians was, the neglect or incapacity of their governors, which were then sent from Great Britain. As it frequently happened that those gentlemen who were appointed to these offices were more intent in pursuing their own interest, than looking after the welfare of the colonies, they often neglected the proper measures necessary for obtaining their welfare. The colonists who were not allowed by government to interfere in that department which belonged to the crown, but who at the same time suffered by the misconduct of its servants, were ready, in their hearts, to despise men, whom they found take upon them posts of importance they were not qualified to fulfil. Governors appointed by authority, at so great a distance, and not connected with the inhabitants, by the common ties of mutual interest, unless they are both men of good sense and great virtue, will seldom answer the purposes of good legislature. When a government intends the general welfare of the community, it should lay aside all partiality in the appointment

ment of men to offices of state, and always chuse the wisest and best, and such as are fittest for the department assigned. A particular acquaintance with the people where the magistrates are to reside and rule, as well as common interests joined together with theirs, will always be found necessary to make men acceptable in that character. It has been much owing to the English government not being careful in this particular, that such discord has arisen between Great Britain and her once flourishing colonies.

Before we return to the regular course of the history of the present war, it will be necessary to take a view of the constitution of the several colonies in America, that, by examining their fundamental rights and privileges, we may be able to judge concerning the cause of the bloody contest that is now carrying on.

CHAP.

CHAP. VI.

The government and constitution of the Colonies,—of Rhode Island,—Connecticut,—Virginia,—Pensylvania,—Maryland,—Georgia, &c.

WE have already taken a view of the constitution of the colony of Massachusets bay, their original charter of privileges, and the tenure by which they hold their right of possession of their lands in those parts. It was not long after the first colonists settled in America, before they differed concerning some points of religion, and carried their contentions so far as to persecute those who could not, or would not conform to their articles of faith. This barbarous and inhuman disposition proceeded so far as not only to make them deny the Dissenters, from their creed, the privileges of citizens, but also to banish them out of the country, with threatenings of severe punishment provided they should return. This violent and intolerant practice, though it is a severe reflection upon the character of the colonists, in the course of providence, turned out for good to those who were persecuted, and made them seek to provide for themselves in other parts of the country, which they would not have thought of in an ordinary course of affairs. It was for the reasons just now mentioned, that some of the persecuted colonists, in the year 1639, began a settlement in Rhode

Rhode Island. This is one of the smallest provinces, of which New England is composed. It lies off Mount Hope, and consists of a small island of that name, and is the old plantation of Providence. This Island, from whom the Province has its name, lies in Naraganset bay, and is about fifteen or sixteen miles in length, and four or five in breadth. This island is one of the most beautiful and pleasant parts in New England. On account of the fruitfulness of the soil, and temperateness of the climate, it is called by some the Paradise of New England; for though it does not lie above 60 miles south of Boston, it is much warmer in winter, being surrounded by the sea, and not so affected by land breezes as the neighbouring parts on the continent. There was a very considerable trade carried on before the war in this island with the sugar colonies, with butter and cheese, horses, sheep, beef, pork, timber, and frames for houses. The freeness of the situation in process of time invited so many planters to this island, that it was soon overstocked, and some of them purchased land, and built the towns of Providence and Warwick. What contributed much to the population of this colony was, the free unlimited toleration that was granted in it, to all sorts of religious professions. This practice of toleration will always have a great influence, both upon the encrease of the inhabitants of colonies, and the government of all nations; for though it is affirmed by some that toleration of sectaries is the occasion of divisions, and contentions in nations, yet the very contrary is matter of fact. For it is by laying unnecessary restraints upon men's consciences that creates sectaries, which if they were permitted to take their own way, would seldom give any trouble. Government ought therefore to tolerate all forms of religion, except

such

such as will not give liberty to others. Rhode Island was formed into a distinct government by a charter granted in the fifteenth of King Charles the second. This charter gives to the inhabitants of this colony free liberty for the exercise of their religion, and makes Rhode Island a corporation politic, in name and fact, by the name of the governor, and company of the English colony of Rhode Island and Providence plantations, in New England, in America; and that by the same name they and their successors shall and may have perpetual succession, and shall and may be persons capable in law to sue and plead for all their just privileges *. The governor and company were

to

* RHODE ISLAND CHARTER.—Charles the second, by the grace of God, &c. To all to whom these presents shall come, greeting. Whereas we have been informed by the humble petition of our trusty and well beloved subjects, John Clarke, on the behalf of Benjamin Arnold, William Brenton, William Codington, Nicholas Easton, William Boulston, John Porter, John Smith, Samuel Gorton, John Weekes, Roger Williams, Thomas Olney, Gregory Dexter, John Coggeshall, Joseph Clarke, Randall Haulden, John Greene, John Roome, Samuel Wildbore, William Field, James Barker, Richard Tew, Thomas Harris, and William Dyre, and the rest of the purchasers, and free inhabitants of our island called Rhode Island, and the rest of the colony of Providence Plantations, in the Naraganset bay, in New England in America, That they, pursuing with peace and loyal minds, their sober, serious, and religious intentions, of godly edifying themselves, and one another in the holy Christian faith and worship as they were persuaded, together with the gaining over and conversion of the poor ignorant Indian natives, in those parts of America, to the sincere profession and obedience of the same faith and worship, did not only by the consent and good encouragement of our royal progenitors, transport themselves out of this kingdom of England into America; but also since their arrival there, after their first settlement amongst other our subjects in those parts, for avoiding of discord, and those many evils which were likely to ensue upon those our subjects, not being able to bear in those remote parts their different apprehensions in religious concernments; and in pursuance of the aforesaid ends, did once again leave their desirable stations and habitations, and with excessive labour and travel, hazard and charge, did transplant themselves into the midst of the Indian natives who, as we are informed, are the most potent princes and people of all that country; whereby the good providence of God (from whom the plantations have taken their name) upon their labour and industry, they have not only been preserved to admiration, but have increased and prospered, and are seized and possessed, by purchase and consent of the said natives, to their full content, of such lands, islands, rivers, harbours, and roads as are very convenient both for plantations,

to have a common seal, and the governor might assemble the company as often as he pleased. The governor, by the charter, was to be elected annually by the general assembly in the month of May, and every accidental vacancy, by death, or otherwise, was to be filled up by the assembly. The governor and deputy-governor were to take an oath for the due and faithful performance of their duty, and all other inferior officers were to govern the colony, according to the laws that were then in being and in use, as far as they were

and also for building of ships, supply of pipestaves, and other merchandize, and which lies very commodious in many respects for commerce, and to accommodate our southern plantations, and may much advance the trade of this our realm, and greatly enlarge the the territories thereof, they having, by near neighbourhood to, and friendly society with, the great body of the Narraganset Indians, given them encouragement, of their own accord, to subject themselves, their people and lands, unto us; whereby (as is hoped) there may, in time, by the blessing of God upon their endeavours, be laid a sure foundation of happiness to all America. And whereas, in their humble address, they have freely declared, That it is much on their hearts (if they be permitted) to hold forth a lively experiment, that a most flourishing civil state may stand, and best be maintained, and that among our English subjects, with a full liberty in religious concernments, and that true piety, rightly grounded upon gospel principles, will give the best and greatest security to sovereignty, and will lay in the hearts of men the strongest obligations to true loyalty: now know ye, That we being willing to encourage the hopeful undertaking of our said loyal and loving subjects, and to secure them in the free exercise and enjoyment of all their civil and religious rights appertaining to them as our loving subjects; and to preserve unto them that liberty in the true Christian faith and worship of God, which they have sought with so much travel, and with peaceable minds and loyal subjection to our royal progenitors, and ourselves, to enjoy: and because some of the people and inhabitants of the same colony cannot, in their private opinion, according to the liturgy, form, and ceremonies of the church of England, or take or subscribe the oaths and articles made and established in that behalf; and for that the same, by reason of the remote distances of those places, will, as we hope, be no breach of the unity and uniformity established in this nation, have therefore thought fit, and do hereby publish, grant, ordain, and declare, that our royal will and pleasure is, That no person within the said colony, at any time hereafter, shall be any-wise molested, punished, disquieted, or called in question, for any differences in opinion in matters of religion, and do not actually disturb the civil peace of our said colony; but that all and every person and persons may, from time to time, and at all times hereafter, freely and fully have

were not contrary to the laws of England. When the assembly was not sitting to arm the people, and lead them forth to war against any enemy that came against them. The right to the soil is held in the same manner as that of Massachusetts bay, and upon the same tenure, as is manifest from the charter. In case of doubtful or perplexed controversies, an appeal was to be made to the King as the dernier resort.

The reader will judge for himself, whether the legislature of Britain has any right to make laws for this

have and enjoy his and their own judgments and consciences, in matters of religious concernments, throughout the tract of land hereafter mentioned, they behaving themselves peaceably and quietly, and not using this liberty to licentiousness and profaneness, not to the civil injury or outward disturbance of others, any law, statute or clause therein contained, or to be contained, usage or custom of this realm, to the contrary hereof, in any wise notwithstanding. And that they may be in the better capacity to defend themselves in their just rights and liberties against all the enemies of the Christian faith, and others, in all respects, we have further thought fit, and at the humble petition of the persons aforesaid, are graciously pleased to declare, That they shall have and enjoy the benefit of our late act of indemnity, and free pardon, as the rest of our subjects in other our dominions and territories have; and to create and make them a body politic or corporate, with the powers or privileges herein after mentioned; and accordingly, our will and pleasure is, and our especial grace, certain knowledge, and mere motion, we have ordained, constituted, and declared, and by these presents, for us, our heirs and successors, do ordain, constitute, and declare, That they the said William Brenton, William Codington, Nicholas Easton, Benedict Arnold, William Boulston, John Porter, Samuel Gorton, John Smith, John Weekes, Roger Williams, Thomas Olney, Gregory Dexte, John Cogeshall, Joseph Clarke, Randall Houlden, John Greene, John Roome, William Dyre, Samuel Wildbore, Richard Tew, William Field, Thomas Harris, James Barker, ―― Rainsborrow, ―――― Williams, and John Nickson, and all such others as are now, or hereafter shall be admitted, free of the company and society of our colony of Providence Plantations, in the Narraganset bay, in New England, shall be, from time to time, and for ever hereafter, a body corporate and politic, in fact and name, by the name of the Governour and company of the English colony of Rhode Island, and Providence Plantations, in New England, in America; and that by the same name they and their successors shall and may have perpetual succession, and shall and may be persons able and capable in the law to sue and be sued, to plead and be impleaded, to answer and to be answered unto, to defend and to be defended, in all and singular this colony, according to the language of their charter; or whether at that time it was understood that the sovereign had as good a right to make that people free, as he has to make free men in England. If the right to the foil was in the King, then undoubtedly it was given away upon the condition of that charter. If he had no such right, then the right of the colony is good for nothing. But this was not the idea of either the King or parliament, or the colonists at the time the charter was granted.

The gular suits, causes, quarrels, matters, actions, and things of what kind or nature soever; and also to have, take, possess, acquire, and purchase lands, tenements, or hereditaments, or any goods or chattels, and the same to lease, grant, demise, alien, bargain, sell and dispose of, at their own will and pleasure, as other our liege people of this our realm of England, or any corporation or body politic within the same, may lawfully do; and further, That they the said Governor and Company, and their successors, shall and may, for ever hereafter, have a common seal, to serve and use for all matters, causes, things, and affairs whatsoever, of them and their successors, and the same seal to alter, change, break, and make new from time to time, at their will and pleasure, as they shall think fit. And further, we will and ordain, and by these presents, for us, our heirs and successors, do declare and appoint, That for the better ordering and managing of the affairs and business of the said company and their successors, there shall be one governor, one deputy governor, and ten assistants, to be from time to time constituted, elected, and chosen out of the freemen of the said company, for the time being, in such manner and form as is hereafter in these presents expressed; which said officers shall apply themselves to take care for the best disposing and ordering of the general business and affairs of and concerning the lands and hereditaments herein after mentioned to be granted, and the plantation thereof, and the government of the people there. And for the better execution of our royal pleasure herein, we do for us, our heirs and successors, assign, name, constitute, and appoint, the aforesaid Benedict Arnold to be the first and present governor, of the said company and the said William Boulston, John Porter, Roger Williams, Thomas Olney, John Smith, John Greene, John Coggeshall, James Barker, William Field, and Joseph Clarke, to be the ten present assistants of the said company, to continue in the said several offices respectively, until the first Wednesday which shall be in the month of May now next coming. And further, we will, and by these presents, for us, our heirs and successors, do ordain and grant, That the governor of the said company, for the time being, or in his absence, by occasion of sickness, or otherwise, by his leave or permission, the deputy-governor, for the time being, shall and may, from time to time, upon all occasions, give order for the assembling of the said

The colony of Connecticut, comprehending New Haven

said company, and calling them together to consult and advise of the business and affairs of the said company; and that for ever hereafter, twice in every year, that is to say, on every first Wednesday in the month of May, and on every last Wednesday in October, or oftener, in case it shall be requisite, the assistants, and such of the freemen of the said company, not exceeding six persons for Newport, four persons for each of the respective towns of Providence, Portsmouth, and Warwick, and two persons for each other place, town, or city, who shall be from time to time thereunto elected or deputed by the major part of the freemen of the respective places, towns, or places for which they shall be so elected or deputed, shall have a general meeting or assembly, then, and there to consult, advise and determine, in and about the affairs and business of the said company and plantations. And further, we do of our especial grace, certain knowledge, and mere motion, give and grant unto the said governor and company of the English colony of Rhode Island and Providence plantations, in New England, in America, and their successors; That the governor, or in his absence, or by his permission, the deputy-governor of the said company, for the time being, the assistants, and such of the freemen of the said company as shall be so aforesaid elected or deputed, or so many of them as shall be present at such meeting or assembly, as aforesaid, shall be called the General Assembly; and that they, or the greatest part of them present, whereof the governor, and six of the assistants, at least, to be seven, shall have, and have hereby given and granted unto them, full power and authority, from time to time, and at all times hereafter, to appoint, alter, and change such days, times, and places of meeting, and general assembly, as they shall think fit, and to chuse, nominate, and appoint, such and so many persons as they think fit, and shall be willing to accept the same, to be free of the said company and body politic, and them into the same to admit, and to elect, and constitute such officers and officers, and to grant such needful commissions as they shall think fit and requisite, for ordering, managing, and dispatching of the affairs of the said governor and company, and their successors; and, from time to time, to make, ordain, constitute, or repeal, such laws, statutes, orders and ordinances, forms and ceremonies of government and magistracy, as to them shall seem meet, for the good and welfare of the said company, and for the government and ordering of the lands and hereditaments herein after mentioned to be granted, and of the people that do, or at any time hereafter shall inhabit, or be within the same; so as such laws, ordinances, and constitutions, so made, be not contrary and repugnant unto, but, as near as may, be agreeable to the laws of this our realm of England, considering the nature and constitution of the place and people there; and also, to appoint, order, and direct, erect and settle such places and courts of jurisdiction, for hearing and determining of all actions, cases, matters and things, happening within the said colony and plantation, and which shall be in dispute, and depending there, as they shall think fit; and also to distinguish and set

forth

Haven received a charter the year before, from the same

forth the several names and titles, duties, powers and limits, of each court, office and officer, superior and inferior; and also, to contrive and appoint such forms of oaths and attestations, not repugnant, but as near as may be agreeable as aforesaid to the laws and statutes of this our realm, as are convenient and requisite, with respect to the due administration of justice, and due execution and discharge of all offices and places of trust, by the persons that shall be therein concerned; and also to regulate and order the way and manner of all elections to offices, and places of trust, and to prescribe, limit, and distinguish the number and bounds herein-after-mentioned, and not of all places, towns, and cities, with the limits and bounds, herein particularly named, who have or shall have the power of electing and sending of freemen to the said general assembly; and also to order, direct, and authorise the imposing of lawful and reasonable fines, mulcts, imprisonments, and executing other punishments, pecuniary and corporal, upon offenders and delinquents, according to the course of other corporations, within this our kingdom of England; and again, to alter, revoke, annul or pardon, under their common-seal, or otherwise, such fines, mulcts, imprisonments, sentences, judgments and condemnations, as shall be thought fit; and to direct, rule, order and dispose of all other matters and things, and particularly that which relates to the making of purchases of the native Indians, as to them shall seem meet: whereby our said people and inhabitants in the said plantations, may be so religiously, peaceably, and civilly governed, as that by their good life, and orderly conversation, they may win and invite the native Indians of the country to the knowledge and obedience of the only true God and Saviour of mankind; willing, commanding, and requiring, and by these presents, for us, our heirs and successors, ordaining and appointing, that all such laws, statutes, orders, and ordinances, instructions, impositions, and directions, as shall be so made by the governor, deputy, assistants, and freemen, or such number of them as aforesaid, and published in writing under the common-seal, shall be carefully and duly observed, kept, performed, and put in execution, according to the true intent and meaning of the same. And these our letters patent, or the duplicate or exemplification thereof, shall be to all and every such officers, superior, or inferior, from time to time, for the putting of the same orders, laws, statutes, ordinances, instructions and directions, in due execution against us, our heirs and successors, a sufficient warrant and discharge. And further, our will and pleasure is, and we do hereby for us, our heirs and successors, establish and ordain, That yearly, once in the year for ever hereafter, namely, the aforesaid Wednesday in May, and at the town of Newport, or elsewhere, if urgent occasion do require, the governor, deputy-governor, and assistants of the said company, and other officers of the said company, or such of them as the General Assembly shall think fit, shall be in the said general court or assembly, to be held from that day or time, newly chosen for the year ensuing, by greater part of the said company for the time being, as shall be then and there present. And if it shall happen that the present governor, deputy-governor,

and

same authority, and much in the same stile, and upon the

and assistants, by these presents appointed, or any such as shall hereafter be newly chosen into their rooms, or any of them, or any other the officers of the said company shall die, or be removed from his or their several offices or places, before the said general day of election, (whom we do hereby declare for any misdemeanor or default, to be removable by the governor, assistants and company, or such greater part of them, in any of the said public courts to be assembled, as aforesaid) that then, and in every such case, it shall and may be lawful to and for the said governor, deputy-governor, assistants, and company aforesaid, or such greater part of them, so to be assembled, as is aforesaid, in any of their assemblies, to proceed to a new election of one or more of their company, in the room or place, rooms or places, of such officer or officers, so dying or removed, according to their directions. And immediately upon and after such election or elections made of such governor, deputy-governor, assistant or assistants, or any other officer of the said company, in manner and form aforesaid, the authority, office, and power, before given to the former governor, deputy-governor, and other officer and officers so removed, in whose stead and place new shall be chosen, shall, as to him and them, and every of them respectively, cease and determine: provided always, and our will and pleasure is, That as well such as are by these presents appointed to be the present governor, deputy-governor, and assistants of the said company, as those which shall succeed them, and all other officers to be appointed and chosen as aforesaid, shall before the undertaking the execution of the said offices and places respectively, give their solemn engagement by oath or otherwise, for the due and faithful performance of their duties in their several offices and places, before such person or persons as are by these presents hereafter appointed to take and receive the same; (that is to say) the said Benedict Arnold, who is herein before nominated and appointed the present governor of the said company, shall give the aforesaid engagement before William Brenton, or any two of the said assistants of the said company, unto whom we do, by these presents, give full power and authority to require and receive the same; and the said William Brenton, who is hereby before nominated and appointed the present deputy-governor of the said company, shall give the aforesaid engagement before the said Benedict Arnold, or any two of the assistants of the said company, unto whom we do, by these presents, give full power and authority to require and receive the same; and the said William Poulston, John Porter, Roger Williams, Thomas Olney, John Smith, John Greene, John Coggeshall, James Barker, William Field, and Joseph Clarke, who are herein nominated and appointed the present assistants of the company, shall give the said engagement to their offices and places respectively belonging, before the said Benedict Arnold and William Brenton, or one of them, to whom respectively we do hereby give full power and authority to require, administer, or receive the same. And further, our will and pleasure is, that all and every other future governor, or deputy-governor, to be elected and chosen by virtue of these presents, shall give the said engagement before two or more of the said assistants

the same principles. This Colony is by its charter empowered

of the said company for the time being, unto whom we do by these presents, give full power and authority to require, administer, or receive the same; and the said assistants, and every of them, and all and every other officer or officers, to be hereafter elected and chosen by virtue of these presents, from time to time, shall give the like engagement to their offices and places respectively belonging, before the governor, or deputy-governor, for the time being; unto which said governor, or deputy-governor, we do by these presents give full power and authority to require, administer, or receive the same accordingly. And we do likewise, for us, our heirs, and successors, give and grant unto the said governor and company, and their successors, by these presents, that for the more peaceable and orderly government of the said plantations, it shall and may be lawful to the governor, deputy governor, assistants, and all other officers and ministers of the said company, in the administration of justice, and exercise of government, in the said plantations, to use, exercise, and put in execution, such methods, rules, orders, and directions, not being contrary and repugnant to the laws and statutes of this our realm, as has been heretofore given, used, and accustomed in such cases respectively, to be put in practice, until at the next, or some other general assembly, especial provision shall be made and ordained in the cases aforesaid. And we do further, for us, our heirs and successors give and grant unto the said governor and company, and their successors, by these presents, that it shall and may be lawful to and for the said governor, or in his absence the deputy-governor, and major part of the said assistants for the time being, at any time when the said general assembly is not sitting, to nominate, appoint, and constitute such and so many commanders, governors, and military officers, as to them shall seem requisite, for the leading, conducting and training up the inhabitants of the said plantations in martial affairs, and for the defence and safe-guard of the said plantations; and that it shall and may be lawful to and for all and every such commander, governor, and military officer, that shall be so as aforesaid, or by the governor, or in his absence the deputy-governor, and six of the assistants, and major part of the freemen of the said county, present at any general assemblies, nominated, appointed and constituted, according to the tenor of his and their respective commissions and directions, to assemble, exercise in arms, marshal, array, and put in warlike posture, the inhabitants of the said colony, for their especial defence and safety, and to lead and conduct the said inhabitants, and to encounter, repulse, and resist by force of arms, as well by sea as by land, and also to kill, slay and destroy, by all fitting ways, enterprizes, and means whatsoever, all and every such person or persons, as shall at any time hereafter attempt or enterprize the destruction, invasion, detriment, or annoyance of the said inhabitants or plantations; and to use and exercise the law martial, in such cases only as occasion shall necessarily require: and to take and surprise, by all ways and means whatsoever, all and every such person and persons, with their ship or ships, armour, ammunition, or other goods of such persons as shall in hostile manner invade or attempt the defeating of the

powered to chuse its own governor, and to hold two assemblies

the said plantation, or the hurt of the said company and inhabitants; and upon just causes to invade and destroy the natives, Indians, or other enemies of the said colony. Nevertheless, our will and pleasure is, and we do hereby declare to the rest of our colonies in New-England, that it shall not be lawful for this our said colony of Rhode Island, and Providence plantations in New-England, in America, to invade the natives inhabiting within the bounds and limits of their said colonies, without the knowledge and consent of the said other colonies. And it is hereby declared, that it shall not be lawful to or for the rest of the colonies to invade or molest the native Indians, or any other inhabitants inhabiting within the bounds or limits hereafter mentioned, (they having subjected themselves unto us, and being by us taken into our special protection) without the knowledge and consent of the governor and company of our colony of Rhode Island and Providence plantation. Also our will and pleasure is, and we do hereby declare unto all Christian Kings, Princes and States, that if any person, which shall hereafter be of the said company or plantation, or any other by appointment of the said governor and company, for the time being, shall at any time or times hereafter rob or spoil by sea or land or do any hurt or unlawful hostility, to any of the subjects of us, our heirs and successors, or any of the subjects of any prince or state, being then in a league with us, our heirs and successors; upon complaint of such injury done to any such prince or state, or their subjects, we, our heirs, and successors, will make open proclamation, within any parts of our realm of England, fit for that purpose, that the person or persons committing any such robbery or spoil, shall within the time limited by such proclamation, make full restitution or satisfaction of all such injuries done or committed, so as the said prince, or others so complaining, may be fully satisfied and contented; and if the said person or persons, who shall commit any such robbery or spoil, shall not make satisfaction accordingly, within such time so to be limited, and then we, our heirs and successors, will put such person or persons out of our allegiance and protection; and that then it shall and may be lawful and free for all princes or others, to prosecute with hostility such offenders, and every of them, their and every of their procurers, aiders, abbettors, and counsellors, in that behalf. Provided also, and our express will and pleasure is, and we do by these presents, for us, our heirs and successors, ordain and appoint, that these presents shall not in any manner hinder any of our loving subjects whatsoever, from using and exercising the trade of fishing upon the coast of New-England, in America, but that they, and every or any of them, shall have full and free power and liberty to continue and use the trade of fishing upon the said coast, in any of the seas thereunto adjoining, or any arms of the sea, or salt-water, rivers and creeks, where they have been accustomed to fish, and to build and set upon the waste land belonging to the said colony and plantations, such wharfs, stages, and work-houses as shall be necessary for the salting, drying and keeping of their fish, to be taken or gotten upon that coast. And further, for the encouragement of the inhabitants of our said colony of Providence plantation, to set up

assemblies in the year, in the months of May and October,

on the business of taking whales, it shall be lawful for them, or any of them having struck a whale, dubertus, or other great fish, it or them to pursue unto that coast, and into any bay, river, cove, creek or shore, belonging thereto, and it or them, upon the said coast, or in the said bay, river, cove, creek or shore, belonging thereto, to kill and order for the best advantage without molestation, they making no wilful waste or spoil; any thing in these presents contained, or any other matter or thing to the contrary notwithstanding. And further also we are graciously pleased, and do hereby declare, that if any of the inhabitants of our said colony do set upon the planting of vineyards, (the soil and climate both seeming naturally to concur to the production of wines) or be industrious in the discovery of fishing-banks, in or about the said colony, we will, from time to time, give and allow all due and fitting encouragement therein, as to others in cases of like nature. And further of our more ample grace, certain knowledge, and mere motion, we have give and granted, and by these presents, for us, our heirs and successors, do give and grant, unto the said governor and company of the English colony of Rhode Island and Providence plantation in the Narraganfett bay in New-England, in America, and to every inhabitant there, and to every person and persons trading thither, and to every such person or persons as are or shall be free of the said colony. full, power and authority, from time to time, and at all times hereafter, to take, ship, transport, and carry away, out of any of our realms and dominions, for and towards the plantation and defence of the said colony, such and so many of our loving subjects and strangers, as shall or will willingly accompany them in and to their said colony and plantation, except such person or persons as are or shall be therein reftrained by us, our heirs and successors, or any law or statute of this realm; and also to ship and transport all and all manner of goods, chattels, merchandize, and other things whatsoever, that are or shall be useful or necessary for the said plantations, and defence thereof, and usually transported, and not prohibited by any law or statute of this our realm; yeilding and paying unto us, our heirs and successors, such the duties, customs and subsidies, as are or ought to be paid or payable for the same. And further, our will and pleasure is, and we do, for us, our heirs and successors, ordain, declare, and grant unto the said governor and company, and their successors, which are already planted and settled within our said colony of Providence plantations, or which shall hereafter go to inhabit within the said colony, and all and every of their children, which have been born there, or going thither or returning from thence, shall have and enjoy all liberties and immunities of free and natural subjects, within any the dominions of us, our heirs or successors, to all intents, constructions, and purposes whatsoever, as if they and every of them were born within the realm of England. And further know ye, that we, of our more abundant grace, certain knowledge, and mere motion, have given, granted and confirmed, and by these presents, for us, our heirs and successors, do give, grant and confirm, unto the said governor and company, and their successors, all that part of our dominions, in New England, in America, containing the Nahantick and Nanhygansett, alias Naraganfett

tober. The charter of this province is as compleat as

fett bay and countries and parts adjacent, bounded on the west, or westerly, to the middle or channel of a river there, commonly called and known by the name of Pawcatuck alias Pawcawtuck river, and so along the said river, as the greater or middle stream thereof reacheth or lies up into the north country, northward unto the head thereof, and from thence by a strait line drawn due north, until it meet with the south line of the Massachusetts colony, and on the north or northerly, by the aforesaid south or southerly line of the Massachusetts colony or plantation, and extending towards the east or eastwardly three English miles, to the east and north-east of the most eastern and north-eastern parts of the aforesaid Narraganfett bay, as the said bay lieth or extendeth itself from the ocean on the south or southwardly unto the mouth of the river which runneth towards the town of Providence, and from thence along the eastwardly side or bank of the said river (higher called by the name of Seacunk river) up to the falls called Patucket falls, being the most westwardly line of Plymouth colony; and so from the said falls, in a strait line due north, until it meet with the aforesaid line of the Massachusetts colony, and bounded on the south by the ocean, and in particular the lands belonging to the town of Providence, Patuxet, Warwick, Misquammacock alias Pawcatuck, and the rest upon the main land, in the tract aforesaid, together with Rhode-Island, Block-Island, and all the rest of the islands and banks in the Narraganfett bay, and bordering upon the coast of the tract aforesaid, (Fisher's-Island only excepted) together with all firm lands, soils, grounds, havens, ports, rivers, waters, fishings, mines

royal, and all other mines, minerals, precious stones, quarries, woods, wood-grounds, rocks, slates, and all and singular other commodities, jurisdictions, royalties, privileges, franchises, preeminences and hereditaments whatsoever, within the said tract, bounds, lands and islands aforesaid, to them or any of them belonging, or in any-wise appertaining. To have and to hold the same, unto the said governor and company, and their successors for ever, upon trust, for the use and benefit of themselves, and their associates, freemen of the said colony, their heirs and assigns. To be holden of us, our heirs and successors as of the manor of East-Greenwich, in our county of Kent, in free and common socage, and not in capite, nor by Knight's service. Yielding and paying therefore to us, our heirs and successors, only the fifth part of all the ore of gold and silver, which from time to time, and at all times hereafter, shall be there gotten, had or obtained, in lieu and satisfaction of all services, duties, fines, forfeitures made or to be made, claims and demands whatsoever, to be to us, our heirs or successors, therefore or thereout rendered, made or paid: any grant or clause in a late grant to the governor and company of Connecticut colony in America, to the contrary thereof in any wife notwithstanding: the aforesaid Pawcatuck river having been yielded after much debate, for the fixed and certain bounds between these our said colonies, by the agents thereof, who have also agreed, that the said Pawcatuck river shall be also called alias Narragancett or Narraganfett river, and to prevent future disputes that otherwise might arise thereby; for ever hereafter, shall be construed, deemed and taken to be the Narragancett river, in our late grant

to

as it is possible for any royal charter to be, and if the sovereigns of England had ever any power to grant franchises of that sort, this is undoubtedly as good a security for the liberties of that province, as reason would desire*.

In reading the annals of nations, men who have no other object in view except truth, would be ready to conclude from this and the following charter, that these two provinces were to all intents and purposes as free as any of the freeholders in Great Britain, and had as good a right to be their own legislatures, as either the freemen of counties or towns in England. But casuists who have a mind to dispute every thing, and can, for particular ends and reasons, affirm what no man of common sense is able to give his assent to, think no shame to deny the very immediate signification

to Connecticut colony, mentioned as the easterly bounds of that colony. And further, our will and pleasure is, that in all matters of public controversies, which may fall out between our colony of Providence plantation, to make their appeal therein to us, our heirs and successors, for redress in such cases, within this our realm of England; and that it shall be lawful to and for the inhabitants of the said colony of Providence plantation, without lett or molestation, to pass and repass with freedom into and through the rest of the English colonies, upon their lawful and civil occasions, and to converse, and hold commerce, and trade with such of the inhabitants of our other English colonies as shall be willing to admit them thereunto, they behaving themselves peaceably among them;

any act, clause or sentence, in any of the said colonies provided, or that shall be provided, to the contrary in any wise notwithstanding. And lastly, we do for us, our heirs and successors ordain and grant unto the said governor and company, and their successors, by these presents, that these our letters patents shall be firm, good, effectual and available, in all things in the law, to all intents, constructions and purposes whatsoever, according to our true intent and meaning herein before declared; and shall be construed, reputed and adjudged, in all cases, most favourably, on the behalf, and for the best benefit and behoof of the said governor and company, any their successors, although express mention, &c. In witness, &c. witness, &c.

Per ipsum Regem

*CONNECTICUT CHARTER.

Charles the Second, by the grace of God, &c. to all to whom these presents shall come, greeting. Whereas by the several navigations, discoveries,

tion of this charter. As if words either had no meaning, or were liable to change their signification at the nod of politicians, they boldly affirm that these colonies never had a right to be their own legislature.

It would be accounted a very hard case in England, for no just reason, to take away the charters of all corporations in the nation, many of which have no other security than the grants of princes, and the prescription of time. If these societies were refused the privilege of representation, according to the laws of the land,

discoveries, and successful plantations of divers of our loving subjects of this our realm of England, several lands, islands, places, colonies and plantations, have been ordained and settled in that part of the continent of America called New-England, and thereby the trade and commerce there hath been of late years much increased; and whereas we have been informed by the humble petition of our trusty and well-beloved John Winthrop, John Mason, Samuel Wills, Henry Clarke, Matthew Allen, John Tappan, Nathan Gould, Richard Treate, Richard Lord, Henry Woolcot, John Talcott, Daniel Clarke, John Ogden, Thomas Wells, Obadiah Brewton, John Clarke, Anthony Hawkins, John Deming, and Matthew Camfield, being persons principally interested in our colony or plantations of Connecticut in New-England, that the same colony, or the greatest part thereof, was purchased and obtained for great and valuable considerations, and some other part thereof gained by conquest and with much difficulty, and at the only endeavours, expence and charge of them and their associates, and those under whom they claim, subdued and improved, and thereby become a considerable enlargement and addition of our dominions and interest there: now know ye, that in consideration thereof, and in regard the said colony is remote from other of the English plantations in the places aforesaid, and to the end the affairs and business, which shall from time to time happen or arise concerning the same, may be duly ordered and managed, we have thought fit, at the humble petition of the persons aforesaid, and are graciously pleased to create and make them a body politic and corporate, with the powers and privileges herein after mentioned; and according our will and pleasure is, and of our especial grace, certain knowledge, and mere motion, we have ordained, constituted and declared, and by these presents, for us, our heir and successors, do ordain, constitute and declare, that they the said John Winthorp, John Mason Samuel Willis, Henry Clerke Matthew Allen, Thos. Tapen, Nathan Gould, Richard Treate, Richard Lord, Henry Woolcot. John Talcott, Daniel Clarke, John Ogden, Thomas Wells, Obadiah Brewton, John Clarke, Antony Hawkins, John Deming, and Mathew Camfield, and all such others, as now are or hereafter shall be admitted and made free of the company and society of our colony of Connecticut, in America, shall, from time to time

land, they could not be juftly obliged to pay any revenue to the government. If the cafe of the colonifts be different from this, they are only flaves, and not free fubjects of the Britifh empire.

Virginia, which firft had a very large fignification, though granted to a company then refident in London, is held by much the fame tenure as the other colonies, with this difference, that the council has, by the charter, a power to make laws for the good of the colony, according to their own difcretion; whereas

time, and for ever hereafter be one body corporate politic, in fact and name, by the name of Governor and company of the Englifh colony of Connecticut in New-England in America; and that by the fame name they, and their fucceffors fhall and may have perpetual fucceffion, and fhall and may be perfons able and capable in the law to plead and be impleaded, to anfwer and to be anfwered unto, to defend and be defended in all and fingular fuits, caufes, quarrels, matters, actions and things of what kind or nature foever; and alfo to have, take poffefs, acquire, and purchafe lands, tenements, or hereditaments, or any goods or chattels, and the fame to leafe, grant, demife, alien, bargain, fell, and difpofe of, as our other liege people of this our realm of England, or any other corporation or body politic within the fame may lawfully do. And further, That the faid governor and company and their fucceffors fhall and may for ever hereafter, have a common feal to ferve and ufe for all caufes, matters, things, and affairs whatfoever, of them and their fucceffors, and the fame feal to alter, change, break, and make new from time to time, at their wills and pleafures, as they fhall think fit. And further we will and ordain and by thefe prefents for us our heirs and fucceffors, do declare and appoint, That for the better ordering and managing of the affairs and bufinefs of the faid company and their fucceffors, there fhall be one governor, one deputy-governor, and twelve affiftants to be from time to time, contructed, elected, and chofen out of the freemen of the faid company for the time being, in fuch manner and form as hereafter, in thefe prefents is expreffed; which faid officers fhall apply themfelves to take care for the beft difpofing and ordering of the general bufinefs and affairs of and concerning the lands and hereditaments herein after-mentioned to be granted, and the plantation thereof and the government of the people thereof. And for the better execution of our royal pleafure, herein we do for us, our heirs and fucceffors affign, name, conftitute, and appoint the aforefaid John Winthrop to be the firft and prefent governor of the faid company, and the faid John Mafon to be the deputy-governor and the faid Samuel Willis, Matthew Allen, Nathan Gould, Henry Clarke, Richard Treate, John Ogden, Thomas Tappen, John Talcutt, Thomas Wells, Henry Woolcot, Richard Lord, and Daniel Clarke, whereas the other colonists are bound to confine all new laws to the spirit of the constitution of Great Britain. This is a power granted to persons living within England, to rule British subjects at discretion, which is not consistent with either the character of Englishmen, nor the constitution of England. There are three charters which were granted at different times by King James the first, to the Virginia company, one to Sir Thomas Gates, Sir George Somers, and others, April 10, 1606, and two to the treasurer and company

Clerke, to be the twelve present assistants of the said company, to continue in the said several offices respectively until the second Thursday, which shall be in the month of October, now next coming. And further, we will, and by these presents, for us, our heirs, and successors, do ordain and grant, That the governor of the said company, for the time being, or in his absence, by occasion of sickness or otherwise, by his leave or permission, the deputy-governor for the time being shall and may, from time to time upon all occasions, give order for the assembling of the said company, and calling them together, to consult and advise of the business and affairs of the said company, and that for ever hereafter, twice in every year that is to say, on every second Thursday in October, and on every second Thursday in May, or oftener, in case it shall be requisite, the assistants and freemen of the said company, or such of them not exceeding two persons from each place, town, or city, who shall be from time to time, thereunto elected or deputed by the major part of the freemen of the respective towns, cities, and places, for which they shall be so elected or deputed, shall have a general meeting or assembly, then and there to consult and advise in and about the affairs and business of the said company; and that the governor, or in his absence the deputy-governor of the said company for the time being, and such of the assistants and freemen of the said company as shall be so elected or deputed, and be present at such meeting or assembly, or the greatest number of them, whereof the governor or deputy-governor, and six of the assistants at least to be seven, shall be called the general assembly, and shall have full power and authority to alter and change their days and times of meeting or general assemblies, for the electing the governor, deputy-governor, and assistants, or other officers, or any other courts, assemblies, or meetings, and to chuse, nominate, and appoint such, and so many other persons as they shall think fit, and shall be willing to accept the same, to be free of the said company and body politic, and them into the same to admit, and to elect and constitute such officers as they shall think fit and requisite for the ordering, managing, and disposing of the affairs of the said governor and company, and their successors. And we do hereby for us, our heirs and successors, establish and ordain, That once in the year, for ever hereafter, namely

pany for Virginia, the one dated March 23, 1609, and the other March 12, 1611-12. These being exceedingly long and tedious, shall be given at the end of this volum.

Pennsylvania, which is a proprietory colony, was granted to the proprietor, William Penn, much in the same manner as the others are granted to the proprietors and possessors thereof. The charter gives Sir William power to make laws, raise money by the consent of the freemen or their deputies, to appoint judges and

namely, the said second Thursday in May, the governor, deputy-governor, and assistants, of the said company, and other officers of the said company, or such of them as the said general assembly shall think fit, shall be in the said general court and assembly, to be held from that day or time newly chosen for the year ensuing, by such greater part of the said company for the time being, then and there present.

And if the governor, deputy-governor and assistants, by these presents appointed, or such as hereafter be newly chosen into their rooms, or any of them, or any other the officers to be appointed for the said company shall die, or be removed from his or their several offices or places before the said general day of election, (whom we do hereby declare, for any misdemeanour or default, to be removeable by the governor, assistants, and company, or such greater part of them so to be assembled, as is aforesaid) that then, and in every such case, it shall and may be lawful to and for the governor, deputy-governor, and assistants, and company aforesaid, or such greater part of them so to be assembled, as is aforesaid in any of their assemblies, to proceed to a new election of one or more of their company, in the room or place, rooms or places, of such governor, deputy-governor, assistant, or other officer or officers so dying, or removed, according to their discretions. And immediately upon, and after such election, or elections, made of such governor, deputy-governor, assistant or assistants, or any other officer of the said company, in manner and form aforesaid, the authority, office, and power before given to the former governor, deputy-governor, or other officer and officers so removed, in whose stead and place new shall be chosen, shall, as to him and them and every of them respectively, cease and determine. Provided also, and our will and pleasure is, That as well such as are by these presents appointed to be the present governor, deputy-governor, and assistants of the said company, as those that shall succeed them, and all other officers to be appointed and chosen as aforesaid, shall, before they undertake the execution of their said offices and places respectively, take their several and respective corporeal oaths; for the due and faithful performance of their duties to the several offices and places, before such person or persons as are, by these presents, hereafter appointed to take and receive

and officers necessary for the probates of wills, a power to pardons crimes, except murder and high treason, and in these to grant reprieves. Also to make any laws not repugnant to the laws of England. But in doubtful cases, the subjects were allowed to appeal to the King. In this charter there is a particular reserve concerning the British parliament with regard to taxation; this power of parliament is expressed in the charter; for it is said no taxes shall be laid upon the inhabitants but by act of assembly or act of parliament.

Such

receive the same; that is to say, The said John Winthrop, who is herein before nominated and appointed the present governor of the said company, shall take the said oath before one or more of the masters of our court of chancery, for the time being; unto which master of chancery we do, by these presents, give full power and authority to administer the said oath to the said John Winthrop accordingly; and the said John Mason, who is herein before nominated and appointed the present deputy-governor of the said company, shall take the said oath before the said John Wintrop, or any two of the assistants of the said company; unto whom we do, by these presents, give full power and authority to administer the said oath to the said John Mason accordingly; and the said Samuel Willis, Henry Clarke, Matthew Allen, Thomas Tappen, Nathaniel Gould, Richard Treate, Richard Lord, Henry Woolcot, John Talcott, Daniel Clarke, John Ugden, and Thomas Wells, who are herein before nominated and appointed the present assistants of the said company, shall take the oath before the said John Winthrop, and John Mason, or one of them; to whom we do hereby give full power and authority to administer the same accordingly. And our further will and pleasure is, That all and every governor, or deputy-governor, to be elected and chosen, by virtue of these presents, shall take the said oath before two or more of the assistants of the said company, for the time being; unto whom we do, by these presents, give full power and authority to give and administer the said oath accordingly. And the said assistants, and every of them, and all or every other officer or officers to be hereafter chosen, from time to time, to take the said oath before the governor or deputy-governor, for the time being; unto which said governor, we do, by these presents give full power and authority to administer the same accordingly. And further, ofour more ample grace, certain knowledge, and mere motion, we have given and granted, and by these presents, for us, our heirs and successors, do give and grant unto the said governor and company of the English colony of Connecticut, in New-England, in America, and to every inhabitant there, and to every person and persons trading thither, and to every such person and persons as are or shall be free of the said colony, full power and authority, from time to time and at all times hereafter to take ship, transport, and carry away, for and towards the plantation and defence of the said colony, such of our lov-

HISTORY OF A.D. 1771.

Such as have accepted of this charter ought not to complain of parliamentary taxation, unless they understood that they were both to have a representation in their own assemblies, and in the parliament of Britain; which it is manifest they never dreamed of. This shews us that the far greater part of those patent privileges are imperfect, and that many arguments taken from grants are in the natural right.

Mr Penn, according to this charter, framed a system of government for the ruling the province of Pensylvania,

ing subjects and strangers as shall or will willingly accompany them, in and to their said colony and plantation, except such person or persons as are or shall be therein restrained by us, our heirs and successors; and also to ship and transport all, and all manner of goods, chattels, merchandizes, and other things whatsoever, that are or shall be useful or necessary for the inhabitants of the said colony, and may lawfully be transported thither; nevertheless not to be discharged of payment to us, our heirs and successors, of the duties, customs and subsidies, which are or ought to be paid or payable for the same. And further, our will and pleasure is and we do for us our heirs and successors ordain, declare, and grant unto the said governor and company, and their successors, that all and every the subjects of us, our heirs and successors, which shall go to inhabit within the said colony, and every of their children which shall happen to be born there, or on the sea in going thither or returning from thence, shall have and enjoy all liberties, and immunities of free and natural subjects within any of the dominions of us, our heirs or successors to all intents, constructions and purposes whatsoever, as if they and every of them were born within the realm of England. And we do authorize and empower the governor, or in his absence the deputy-governor for the time being, to appoint two or more of the said assistants, at any of their courts or assemblies to be held as aforesaid, to have power and authority to administer the oath of supremacy and obedience to all and every person and persons, which shall at any time or times, hereafter go or pass into the said colony of Connecticut; unto which said assistants, so to be appointed as aforesaid, we do by these presents give full power and authority to administer the said oath accordingly. And we further, of our especial grace, certain knowledge, and mere motion, give and grant unto the said governor and company of the English colony of Connecticut, in New-England in America, and their successors, that it shall and may be lawful to and for the governor, or deputy-governor, and such of the assistants of the said company for the time being, as shall be assembled in any of the general courts aforesaid, or in any courts to be especially summoned or assembled for that purpose, or the

nia, consisting of forty articles, which both shew his wisdom and justice, as proprietor of that province. The preface to the frame, and the form itself, are expressed as follows:

"For particular Frames and Models, it will become me to say little; and comparatively I will say nothing. My reasons are: First, That the age is too nice and difficult for it; there being nothing the wits of men are more busy and divided upon. 'Tis true, they seem to agree in the end, to wit, Happiness; but in the greater part of them, whereof the governor, or deputy-governor, and six of the assistants, to be always seven, to erect and make such judicatories for the hearing and determining of all actions, causes, matters, and things happening within the said colony or plantation, and which shall be in dispute and depending there, as they shall think fit and convenient; and also, from time to time, to make, ordain, and establish, all manner of wholesome and reasonable laws, statutes, ordinances, directions, and instructions, not contrary to the laws of England, as well for settling the forms and ceremonies of government and magistracy, fit and necessary for the said plantation, and the inhabitants there, as for naming and stiling all sorts of officers, both superior and inferior, which they shall find needful for the government and plantation of the said colony, and the distinguishing and setting forth of the several duties, powers and limits of every such office and place, and the forms of such oaths, not being contrary to the laws and statutes of this our realm of England, to be administered for the execution of the said several offices and places: as also for the disposing and ordering of the election of such of the said officers as are to be annually chosen, and of such others as shall succeed, in case of death or removal, and administering the said oath to the new elected officers, and granting necessary commissions, and for imposition of lawful fines, mulcts, imprisonments, or other punishments upon offenders and delinquents, according to the course of other corporations within this our kingdom of England; and the same laws, fines, mulcts, and executions, to alter, change, revoke, annul, release or pardon, under their common seal, as by the said general assembly, or major part of them, shall be thought fit; and for the directing, ruling and disposing of all other matters and things, whereby our said people, inhabitants there, may be so religiously, peaceably, and civilly governed, as their good life, and orderly conversation, may win and invite the natives of the country to the knowledge and obedience of the only true God and Saviour of mankind, and the Christian faith; which in our royal intentions, and the adventurers free profession, is the only and principal end of this plantation; willing, commanding, and requiring, and by these presents, for us, our heirs and successors, ordaining, and appointing, that all such laws, statues, and ordinances, instructions, impositions and directions, as shall be so ma 'e

by

the means they differ, as to divine, so also to this human felicity; and the cause is much the same, not always want of light and knowledge, but want of using them rightly. Men side with their passions against their reason, and their sinister interests have so strong a bias upon their minds, that they lean to them against the good of the things they know.

"Secondly, I do not find a model in the world, that time, place, and some singular emergencies have not necessarily altered; nor is it easy to frame a civil government that shall serve all places alike.

"Thirdly,

by the governor, deputy-governor and assistants, as aforesaid, and published in writing under their common-seal, shall carefully and duly be observed, kept, performed and put in execution, according to the true intent and meaning of the same; and these our letters patents, or the duplicate or exemplification thereof, shall be, to all and every such officers, superiors and inferiors, from time to time, for the putting of the same orders, laws, statutes, ordinances, instructions and directions in due execution, against us, our heirs and successors a sufficient warrant and discharge. And we do further, for us, our heirs and successors, give and grant unto the said governor and company and their successors, by these presents, that it shall and may be lawful to and for the chief commanders, governors and officers of the said company for the time being, who shall be resident in the parts of New England hereafter mentioned, and others inhabiting there, by their leave, admittance, appointment, or direction, from time to time, and all times hereafter, for their special defence and safety, to assemble, martial array, and put in warlike posture, the inhabitants of the said colony, and to commissionate, empower and authorize such person or persons as they shall think fit, to lead and conduct the said inhabitants, and to encounter, expulse, repel, and resist by force of arms, as well by sea as by land, and also to kill, slay and destroy, by all fitting ways, enterprizes and means whatsoever all and every such person and persons as shall at any time hereafter attempt or enterprize the destruction, invasion, detriment or annoyance of the said inhabitants and plantations, and to use and exercise the law martial in such cases only as occasion shall require, and to take or surprize, by all ways and means whatsoever, all and every such person or persons, with their ships, armour, ammunition, and other goods, as such as shall, in such hostile manner, invade or attempt the defeating of the said plantation, or the hurt of the said company and inhabitants, and, upon just causes, to invade or destroy the natives or other enemies of the said colony. Nevertheless our will and pleasure is, and we do hereby declare unto all Christian kings, princes and states, and if any persons, which shall hereafter be of the said company or plantation, or any other, by appointment of the said governor and company, for the time being, shall at any time or times hereafter

Thirdly, I know what is said by the several admirers of monarchy, aristocracy, and democracy, which are the rule of one, a few, and many; and are the three common ideas of government, when men discourse on that subject. But I chuse to solve the controversy with this small distinction, and it belongs to all three: Any government is free to the people under it (whatever be the frame) where the laws rule, and the people are a party to those laws; and more than this is tyranny, oligarchy, or confusion.

O o But

after rob or spoil, by sea or by land, and do any hurt, violence, or unlawful hostility, to any of the subjects of us, our heirs or successours, or any of the subjects of any prince or state, being then in league with us, our heirs or successours, upon complaint of such injury done to any such prince or state, or their subjects, we, our heirs and successours, will make open proclamation within any parts of our realme of England, fit for that purpose, that the person or persons committing any such robbery or spoil shall, within the time limited by such proclamation, make full restitution or satisfaction of all such injuries done or committed; so as the said prince or others so complaining may be fully satisfied and contented: And if the said person or persons, who shall commit any such robbery or spoil, shall not make satisfaction accordingly, within such time so to be limited, that then it shall and may be lawful for us, our heirs and successours, to put such person or persons out of our allegiance and protection; and that it shall and may be lawful and free for all princes and others to prosecute with hostilities such offenders, and every of them, and every of their procurers, aiders, abettors, and counsellors in that behalf. Provided also, and our express will

and pleasure is, and We do, by these presents for us, our heirs and successors, ordain and appoint, that these presents shall not, in any manner, hinder any of our loving subjects whatsoever to use and exercise the trade of fishing, upon the coast of New England in America, but they, and every or any of them shall have full and free power and liberty to continue and use the said trade of fishing upon the said coast, in any of the seas thereunto adjoining, or any arms of the seas, or salt-water rivers, where they have been accustomed to fish; and to build and set upon the waste lands belonging to the said colony of Connecticut, such wharfs, stages, and work-houses, as shall be necessary for the salting, drying, and keeping of their fish, to be taken or gotten upon that coast; any thing in these presents contained to the contrary notwithstanding. And know ye further, that wee, of our more abundant grace, certain knowledge, and meere motion, have given, granted and confirmed, and by these presents, for us, our heirs and successours, do give, grant and confirm, unto the said Governour and Company, and their successours, all that part of our dominions in New England in America, bounded on the East by the Narragansett river, commonly

But lastly, when all is said, there is hardly one frame of government in the world so ill designed by its first founders, that in good hands would not do well enough; and story tells us, the best in ill ones can do nothing that is great or good; witness the Jewish and Roman states. Governments, like clocks, go from the motion men give them; and as governments are made and moved by men, so by them they are ruined too. Wherefore governments rather depend upon men, than men upon governments. Let men be good and the government can't be bad; if it be ill, they will cure it. But if men be bad, let the government be

commonly called Narraganset bay, where the said river falleth into the sea, and on the north by the line of the Massachusets plantation, and on the south by the sea, and in longitude, as the line of Massachusets colony running from east to west (that is to say) from the said Narragansett bay, on the east, to the South Sea, on the west part, with the islands thereunto adjoining together with all the firm lands, soils, grounds, havens, ports, rivers, waters, fishings, mines, minerals, precious stones, quarries, and all and singular commodities, jurisdictions, royalties, privileges, franchises, pre-eminences, and hereditaments whatsoever, within the said tract, bounds, lands, and islands aforesaid, or to them, or any of them belonging. To have and to hold the same, unto the said governor and company, their successor, and assigns, for ever, upon trust and for the use and benefit of themselves, and their associates, freemen of the said colony, their heirs and assigns; to be holden of us, our heirs and successors, as of our manor of East Greenwich, in free and common soccage, and not in capite, nor by knights service; yielding and paying therefore to us, our heirs and successors, only the fifth part of all the are of gold and silver, which from time to time and at all times hereafter, shall be there gotten, had or obtained. In lieu of all services, duties and demands whatsoever, to be to us, our heirs or successors, therefore or thereout rendered, made, or paid. And lastly, we do for us, our heirs and successors, grant to the said governor and company and their successor, by these presents, that these our letters patents shall be firm, good, and effectual in the law, to all intents, constructions and purposes whatsoever, according to our true intent and meaning herein before declared, as shall be construed, reputed, and adjudged most favourable on the behalf, and for the best benefit and behoof of the said governor and company, and their successors, although express mention, &c. In witness, &c. Witness the King, at Westminster, the three and twentieth day of April,

Par Breve de Private Sigillo

be never so good, they will endeavour to warp and spoil it to their turn.

I know some say, Let us have good laws, and no matter for the men that execute them: But let them consider, That though good laws do well, good men do better: For good laws may want good men, and be abolished or evaded by ill men; but good men, will never want good laws, nor suffer ill ones. 'Tis true, good laws have some awe upon ill ministers, but that is where they have no power to escape or abolish them, and the people are generally wise and good: But a loose and depraved people (which is to the question) love laws and an administration like themselves. That therefore which makes a constitution, must keep it, viz. Men of wisdom and virtue, qualities, that because they descend not with worldy inheritances, must be carefully propagated by a virtuous education of youth; for which after ages will owe more to the care and prudence of founders and the successive magistracy, than to their parents for their private patrimonies.

These considerations of the weight of government, and the nice and various opinions about it, made it uneasy to me to think of publishing the ensuing frame and conditional laws, forseeing, both the censures they will meet with from men of different humours and engagements, and the occasion they may give of discourse beyond my design.

But next to the power of necessity, (which is a solicitor that will take no denial), this induced me to a compliance, that we have (with reverence to God and good conscience to men) to the best of our skill, contrived and composed the *Frame* and *Laws* of this government, to the great end of all government, viz. To support power in reverence with the people, and to

secure

secure the people from the abuse of power; that they may be free by their just obedience, and the magistrates honourable for their just administration: For liberty without obedience is confusion, and obedience without liberty is slavery. To carry this evenness is partly owing to the constitution, and partly to the magistracy: Where either of these fail, government will be subject to convulsions; but where both are wanting, it must be totally subverted: Then where both meet, the government is like to endure. Which I humbly pray, and hope GOD will please to make the lot of this of Pensilvania. Amen.

WILLIAM PENN.

The FRAME, &c.

"To all people to whom these presents shall come. Whereas King Charles the second, by his letters patents, under the great seal of England, for the consideration therein mentioned, hath been graciously pleased to give and grant unto me William Penn (by the name of William Penn, Esq; son and heir of Sir William Penn deceased) and to my heirs and assigns forever, all that tract of land, or province, called Pensylvania, in America, with divers great powers, preeminences, royalties, jurisdictions, and authorities, necessary for the well-being and government thereof: Now know ye, That for the well-being and government of the said province, and for the encouragement of all the freemen and planters that may be therein concerned, in pursuance of the powers afore-mentioned, I the said William Penn have declared, granted, and confirmed, and by these presents, for me, my heirs and assigns, do declare, grant and confirm unto all the freemen, planters and adventurers, of, in and to the said province, these liberties, franchises, and properties,

properties, to be held, enjoyed and kept by the freemen, planters and inhabitants of the said province of Pensylvania for ever.

Imprimis. That the government of this province shall, according to the powers of the patent, consist of the governor and freemen of the said province, in form of a provincial council and general assembly, by whom all laws shall be made, officers chosen, and public affairs transacted, as is hereafter respectively declared. That is to say,

II. That the freemen of the said province shall on the twentieth day of the twelfth month, which shall be in this present year one thousand six hundred eighty and two, meet and assemble in some fit place, of which timely notice shall be beforehand given by the governor or his deputy, and then and there shall chuse out of themselves, seventy-two persons of most note for their wisdom, virtue, and ability, who shall meet on the tenth day of the first month next ensuing, and always be called and act as the provincial council of the said province.

III. That at the first choice of such provincial council, one third part of the said provincial council shall be chosen to serve for three years then next ensuing, one third part for two years then next ensuing, and one third part for one year then next following such election, and no longer; and that the said third part shall go out accordingly ; and on the twentieth day of the twelfth month as aforesaid, yearly forever afterward, the freemen in the said province shall in like manner meet and assemble together, and then chuse twenty-four persons, being one third of the said number, to serve in provincial council for three years: It being intended, that one third part of the whole provincial council (always consisting, and to consist of

sevent-

seventy-two persons, as aforesaid) falling off yearly, it shall be yearly supplied by such new yearly elections, as aforesaid ; and that no one person shall continue therein longer than three years ; and in case any member shall decease before the last election during his time, that then at the next election ensuing his decease, another shall be chosen to supply his place for the remaining time he was to have served, and no longer.

IV. That after the first seven years, every one of the said third parts that goeth yearly off, shall be incapable of being chosen again for one whole year following: That so all may be fitted for government, and have experience of the care and burden of it.

V. That the provincial council in all cases and matters of moment, as their arguing upon bills to be past into laws, erecting courts of justice, giving judgment upon criminals impeached, and choice of officers, in such manner as is herein after mentioned ; nor less than two-thirds of the whole provincial council shall make a quorum: and that the consent and approbation of two-thirds of such quorum shall be had in all such cases and matters of moment. And moreover, that in all cases and matters of lesser moment, twenty four members of the said provincial council shall make a quorum, the majority of which twenty-four shall and may always determine in such case and causes of lesser moment.

VI. That in this provincial council the governor, or his deputy, shall or may always preside, and have a treble voice ; and the said provincial council shall always continue and sit upon its own adjournments and committees.

VII. That the governor and provincial council shall prepare and propose to the general assembly hereafter mentioned,

mentioned, all bills, which they shall at any time think fit to be passed into laws within the said province; which bills shall be published and affixed to the most noted places in the inhabited parts thereof, thirty days before the meeting of the general assembly, in order to the passing them into laws, or rejecting of them, as the general assembly shall see meet.

VIII. That the governor and provincial council shall take care, that all laws, statutes and ordinances, which shall at any time be made within the said province, be duly and diligently executed.

IX. That the governor and provincial council shall at all times have the care of the peace and safety of the province, and that nothing be by any person attempted to the subversion of this frame of government.

X. That the governor and provincial council shall at all times settle and order the situation of all cities, ports, and market-towns in every county, modelling therein all public buildings, streets, and market-places, and shall appoint all necessary roads and highways in the province.

XI. That the governor and provincial council shall at all times have power to inspect the management of the public treasury, and punish those who shall convert any part thereof to any other use, than what hath been agreed upon by the governor, provincial council, and general assembly.

XII. That the governor and provincial council shall erect and order all public schools, and encourage and reward the authors of useful sciences and laudable inventions in the said province.

XIII. That for the better management of the powers and trust aforesaid, the provincial council shall from time to time divide itself into four distinct and proper committees.

committees, for the more easy administration of the affairs of the province, which divides the seventy-two into four eighteens, every one of which eighteens shall consist of six out of each of the three orders or yearly elections, each of which shall have a distinct portion of business, as followeth: First, a committee of plantations, to situate and settle cities, ports, and market-towns, and highways, and to hear and decide all suits and controversies relating to plantations. Secondly, a committee of justice and safety, to secure the peace of the province, and punish the mal-administration, of those who subvert justice to the prejudice of the public or private interest. Thirdly, a committee of trade and treasury, who shall regulate all trade and commerce according to law, encourage manufacture and country-growth, and defray the public charge of the province. And fourthly, a committee of manners, education, and arts, that all wicked and scandalous lying may be prevented, and that youth may be successively trained up in virtue and useful knowledge and arts: The quorum of each of which committees being six, that is, two out of each of the three orders or yearly elections, as aforesaid, make a constant and standing council of twenty-four which will have the power of the provincial council, being the quorum of it, in all cases not excepted in the fifth article; and in the said committee and standing council of the province, the governor or his deputy shall or may preside as aforesaid; and in the absence of the governor or his deputy, if no one is by either of them appointed, the said committees or council shall appoint a president for that time, and not otherwise; and what shall be resolved at such committees, shall be reported to the said council of the province, and shall be by them resolved and confirmed

before

before the same shall be put in execution; and that these respective committees shall not sit at one and the same time, except in cases of necessity.

XIV. And to the end that all laws prepared by the governor and provincial council aforesaid, may yet have the more full concurrence of the freemen of the province, it is declared, granted, and confirmed, That at the time and place or places for the choice of a provincial council as aforesaid, the said freemen shall yearly chuse members to serve in a general assembly as their representatives, not exceeding two hundred persons, who shall yearly meet from the twentieth day of the second month, which shall be in the year one thousand six hundred eighty and three following, in the capital town or city of the said province, where during eight days the several members may freely confer with one another; and, if any of them see meet, with a committee of the provincial council (consisting of three out of each of the four committees aforesaid, being twelve in all) which shall be at that time, purposely appointed to receive from any of them proposals for the alteration or amendment of any of the said proposed and promulgated bills: And on the ninth day from their so meeting, the said general assembly, after reading over the proposed bills by the clerk of the provincial council, and the occasions and motives for them being opened by the governor or his deputy, shall give their affirmative or negative, which to them seemeth best, in such manner as herein after is expressed. But not less than two-thirds shall make a quorum in the passing of laws, and choice of such officers as are by them to be chosen.

XV. That the laws so prepared and proposed as aforesaid, that are assented to by the general assembly shall be enrolled as the laws of the province, with this stile;

stile: By the governor, with the consent and approbation of the freemen in provincial council and general assembly.

XVI. That, for the better establishment of the government and laws of this province, and to the end there may be an universal satisfaction in the laying of the fundamentals thereof; the general assembly shall, or may for the first year, consist of all the freemen of and in the said province, and ever after it shall be yearly chosen as aforesaid; which number of two hundred shall be enlarged as the country shall encrease in people, so as it do not exceed five hundred at any time: The appointment and proportioning of which, as also the laying and methodizing of the choice of the provincial council and general assembly in future times, most equally to the divisions of the hundreds and counties, which the country shall hereafter be divided into, shall be in the power of the provincial council to propose, and the general assembly to resolve.

XVII. That the governor and the provincial council shall erect from time to time standing courts of justice, in such places and number as they shall judge convenient for the good government of the said province. And that the provincial council shall on the thirteenth day of the first month yearly, elect and present to the governor or his deputy, a double number of persons, to serve for judges, treasurers, masters of rolls, within the said province for the year next ensuing; and the freemen of the said province in the county-courts, when they shall be erected, and till then in the general assembly, shall on the three and twentieth day of the second month yearly elect and present to the governor or his deputy, a double number of persons to serve for sheriffs, justices of the peace, and coroners, for the year next ensuing; out of of which respective elections and presentments, the governor or his deputy shall nominate and commissionate the proper number for each office the third day after the said presentments; or else the first named in such presentment for each office, shall stand and serve for that office the year ensuing.

XVIII. But forasmuch as the present condition of the province requires some immediate settlement, and admits not of so quick a revolution of officers; and to the end the said province may, with all convenient speed, be well ordered and settled, I William Penn do therefore think fit to nominate and appoint such persons for judges, treasurers, masters of the rolls, sheriffs, justices of the peace, and coroners, as are most fitly qualified for those employments; to whom I shall make and grant commissions for the said officers, respectively, to hold to them to whom the same shall be granted, for so long time as every such person shall well behave himself in the office or place to him respectively, granted, and no longer. And upon the decease or displacing of any of the said officers, the succeeding officer or officers shall be chosen as aforesaid.

XIX. That the general assembly shall continue so long as may be needful to impeach criminals fit to be there impeached, to pass bills into laws, that they shall think fit to pass into laws, and till such time as the governor and provincial council shall declare that they have nothing further to propose unto them for their assent and approbation: and that declaration shall be a dismiss to the general assembly for that time; which general assembly shall be notwithstanding capable of assembling together upon the summons of the provincial council, at any time during that year, if the said provincial council shall see occasion for their so assembling.

XX. That all the elections of members or representatives of the people to serve in provincial council and general assembly, and all questions to be determined by both or either of them, that relate to passing of bills into laws, to the choice of officers, to impeachments made by the general assembly, and judgment of criminals upon such impeachments by the provincial council, and to all other cases by them respectively judged of importance, shall be resolved and determined by the ballot; and unless on sudden and indispensible occasions, on business in provincial council, or its respective committees, shall be finally determined the same day that it is moved.

XXI. That at all times, when, and so often as it shall happen that the governor shall or may be an infant under the age of one and twenty years, and no guardians or commissioners are appointed in writing by the father of the said infant, or that such guardians or commissioners shall be deceased; that during such minority, the provincial council shall from time to time, as they shall see meet, constitute and appoint guardians or commissioners, not exceeding three; one of which three shall preside as deputy and chief guardian, during such minority, and shall have, and execute, with the consent of the other two, all the power of a governor, in all the public affairs and concerns of the said province.

XXII. That as often as any day of the month mentioned in any article of this charter, shall fall upon the first day of the week, commonly called the Lord's day, the business appointed for that day shall be deferred till the next day, unless in case of emergency.

XXIII. That no act, law, or ordinance whatsoever, shall at any time hereafter be made or done by the governor of this province, his heirs or assigns, or by the

freemen

freemen in the provincial council, or the general assembly, to alter, change or diminish the form or effect of this charter, or any part or clause thereof, without the consent of the governor, his heirs or assigns, and six parts of seven of the said freemen in provincial council and general assembly.

XXIV. And lastly, that I the said William Penn, for myself, my heirs and assigns, have solemnly declared, granted, and confirmed, and do hereby solemnly declare, grant, and confirm, That neither I, my heirs nor assigns, shall procure or do any thing or things, whereby the liberties in this charter contained and expressed shall be infringed or broken; and if any thing be procured by any person or persons contrary to these premisses, it shall be held of no force or effect. In witness, whereof, I the said William Penn have unto this present charter of liberties set my hand and broad seal, this five and twentieth day of the second month, vulgarly called April, in the year of our Lord one thousand six hundred and eighty-two.

WILLIAM PENN.

The following *Laws* were agreed upon in England, &c.

I. That the charter of liberties, declared, granted, and confirmed the five and twentieth day of the second month called April, 1682, before divers witnesses, by William Penn, governor and chief proprietor of Pensylvania, to all the freemen and planters of the said province; is hereby declared and approved, and shall be for ever held for fundamental in the government thereof, according to the limitations mentioned in the said charter.

II. That every inhabitant in the said province, that is or shall be a purchaser of one hundred acres of land, or upwards, his heirs and assigns, and every person
who

who shall have paid his passage, and taken up one hundred acres of land at one penny an acre, and have cultivated ten acres thereof; and every person that hath been a servant or bondsman, and is free by his service, that shall have taken up his fifty acres of land, and cultivated twenty thereof; and every inhabitant, artificer, or other resident in the said province: And pays scot and lot to the government, shall be deemed and accounted a freeman of the said province: And every such person shall and may be capable of electing, or being elected representatives of the people in provincial council or general assembly in the said province.

III. That all elections of members, or representatives of the people and freemen of the province of Pensylvania, to serve in provincial council or general assembly to be held within the said province, shall be free and voluntary: And that the elector, that shall receive any reward or gift, in meat, drink, monies, or otherwise, shall forefeit his right to elect; and such person as shall directly or indirectly, give, promise, or bestow any such reward as aforesaid, to be elected, shall forefeit his election, and be thereby incapable to serve as aforesaid; and the provincial council and general assembly shall be the sole judges of the regularity or irregularity of the elections of their own respective members.

IV. That no money or goods shall be raised upon or paid by any of the people of this province by way of public tax, custom, or contribution, but by a law for that purpose made; and whosoever shall levy, collect, or pay any money or goods contrary thereunto, shall be held a public enemy to the province, and a betrayer of the liberties of the people thereof

V. That

V. That all courts shall be open, and justice shall neither be sold, denied, nor delayed.

VI. That in all courts, all persons of all persuasions may freely appear in their own way, and according to their own manner, and there personally plead their own cause themselves; or if unable, by their friend: And the first process shall be the exhibition of the complaint in court, fourteen days before the trial; and that the party complained against may be fitted for the same, he or she shall be summoned, no less than ten days before, and a copy of the complaint delivered him or her, at his or her dwelling-house. But before the complaint of any person be received, he shall solemnly declare in court, that he believes in his concience his cause is just.

VII. That all pleadings, processes, and records in court shall be short, and in English, and in an ordinary and plain character, that they may be understood, and justice speedily administered.

VIII. That all trials shall be by twelve men, and as near as may be, peers or equals, and of the neighbourhood, and men without just exception; in cases of life there shall be first twenty-four returned by the sheriffs for a grand inquest, of whom twelve at least shall find the complaint to be true; and then the twelve men, or peers, to be likewise returned by the sheriff, shall have the final judgment. But reasonable challenges shall always be admitted against the twelve men, or any of them.

IX. That all fees in all cases shall be moderate, and settled by the provincial council and general assembly, and be hung up in a table in every respective court; and whosoever shall be convicted of taking more, shall pay two-fold, and be dismissed his employment, one moiety of which shall go to the party wronged.

X. That

X. That all prisons shall be work-houses for fellons, vagrants, and loose and idle persons; whereof one shall be in every county.

XI. That all prisoners shall be bailable by sufficient sureties, unless for capital offences, where the proof is evident, or the presumption great.

XII. That all persons wrongfully imprisoned or prosecuted at law, shall have double damages against the informer or prosecuter.

XIII. That all prisons shall be free as to fees, food, and lodging.

XIV. That all lands and goods shall be liable to pay debts, except where there is legal issue, and then all the goods, and one third of the land only.

XV. That all wills in writing attested by two witnesses, shall be of the same force, as to lands, as other conveyances, being legally proved within forty days, either within or without the said province.

XVI. That seven years quiet possession shall give an unquestionable right, except in cases of infants, lunaticks, married women, or persons beyond seas.

XVII. That all briberies and extortions whatsoever, shall be severely punished.

XVIII. That all fines shall be moderate, and saving men's contentments, merchandise, or wainage.

XIX. That all mariages (not forbidden by the law of God, as to nearness of blood and affinity by marriage) shall be encouraged; but the parents or guardians shall be first consulted, and the marriage shall be published before it be solemnized; and it shall be solemnized by taking one another as husband and wife, before credible witnesses, and a certificate of the whole, under the hands of parties and witnesses shall be brought to the proper register of that county, and shall be registered in his office.

XX

XX. And to prevent frauds and vexatious suits within the said province, that all charters, gifts, grants, and conveyances of land, (except leases for a year or under) and all bills, bonds, and specialties above five pounds, and not under three months, made in the said province, shall be enrolled or registered in the public enrollment-office of the said province, within the space of two months next after the making thereof, else to be void in law. And all deeds, grants, and conveyances of land (except as aforesaid) within the said province, and made out of the said province, shall be enrolled or registered as aforesaid, within six months next after the making thereof, and settling and constituting an enrollment office or registry within the said province, else to be void in law against all persons whatsoever.

XXI. That all defacers or corrupters of charters, gifts, grants, bonds, bills, wills, contracts, and conveyances, or that shall deface or falsify any enrolment, registry or record within this province, shall make double satisfaction for the same; half whereof shall go to the party wronged, and they shall be dismissed of all places of trust, and be publicly disgraced as false men.

XXII. That there shall be a register for births, marriages, burials, wills, and letters of administration, distinct from the other registry.

XXIII. That there shall be a register for all servants, where their names, time, wages, and days of payment shall be registered.

XXIV. That all lands and goods of felons shall be liable to make satisfaction to the party wronged twice the value; and for want of lands or goods, the felons shall be bondmen to work in the common prison or workhouse, or otherwise, till the party be satisfied.

XXV.

XXV. That the estates of capital offenders, as traitors and murderers, shall go one third to the next of kin to the sufferer, and the remainder to the next of kin to the criminal.

XXVI. That all witnesses, coming or called to testify their knowledge in or to any matter or thing in any court, or before any lawful authority within the said province, shall there give or deliver in their evidence or testimony by solemnly promising to speak the truth, the whole truth, and nothing but the truth, to the matter or thing in question. And in case any person so called to evidence, shall be convicted of wilful falsehood, such person shall suffer or undergo such damage or penalty, as the person or persons against whom he or she bore witness, did or should undergo; and shall also make satisfaction to the party wronged, and be publicly exposed as a false witness, never to be credited in any court, or before any magistrate in the said province.

XXVII. And to the end that all officers chosen to serve within this province, may with more care and diligence answer the trust reposed in them, it is agreed, that no such person shall enjoy more than one public office at one time.

XXVIII. That all children within this province of the age of twelve years, shall be taught some useful trade or skill, to the end none may be idle, but the poor may work to live, and the rich, if they become poor, may not want.

XXIX. That servants be not kept longer than their time, and such as are careful, be both justly and kindly used in their service, and put in fitting equipage at the expiration thereof, according to custom.

XXX. That all scandalous and malicious reporters, backbiters, defamers, and spreaders of false news, whether against magistrates or private persons, shall he accordingly severely punished, as enemies to the peace and concord of this province.

XXXI. That for the encouragement of the planters and traders in this province, who are incorporated into a society, the patent granted to them by William Penn, governor of the said province, is hereby ratified and confirmed.

XXXII. — ⸺ ⸺ ⸺
— — — — — —
— — — —

XXXIII. That all factors or correspondents in the said province, wronging their employers, shall make satisfaction and one third over, to their said employers: And in case of the death of any such factor or correspondent, the committee of trade shall take care to secure so much of the deceased party's estate, as belongs to his said respective employers.

XXXIV. That all treasurers, judges, masters of the rolls, sheriffs, justices of the peace, and other officers and persons whatsoever, relating to courts or trials of causes, or any other service in the government; and all members elected to serve in provincial council and general assembly, and all that have a right to elect such members, shall be such as profess faith in Jesus Christ, and that are not convicted of ill fame, or unsober and dishonest conversation, and that are of *twenty-one* years of age at least; and that all such so qualified, shall be capable of the said several employments and privileges as aforesaid.

XXXV. That all persons living in this province, who profess and acknowlege the one Almighty and eternal God, to be the Creator, Upholder, and Ruler of the world; and that hold themselves obliged in conscience to live peaceably and justly in civil society, shall in no ways be molested or prejudiced for their religious

ligious perſuaſion or practice in matters of faith and
worſhip, nor ſhall they be compelled at any time to
frequent or maintain any religious worſhip, place or
miniſtry whatever.

XXXVI. That according to the good example of
the primitive Chriſtians, and the eaſe of the creation
every *firſt* day of the week, called the Lord's day,
people ſhall abſtain from their common daily labour,
that they may the better diſpoſe themſelves to worſhip
God according to their underſtandings.

XXXVII. That as a careleſs and corrupt adminiſtration of juſtice draws the wrath of God upon magiſtrates, ſo the wildneſs and looſeneſs of the people
provokes the indignation of God againſt a country:
Therefore, That all offences againſt God, as ſwearing,
curſing, lying, prophane talking, drunkenneſs, drinking of healths, obſcene words, inceſt, ſodomy, rapes,
whoredom, fornication, and other uncleanneſs, (not to
be repeated) all treaſons, miſpriſions, murders, duels,
felony, ſedition, maims, forcible entries, and other
violences, to the perſons and eſtates of the inhabitants
within this province; all prizes, ſtage-plays, cards,
dice, May-games, gameſters, maſques, revels, bull-
baitings, cock-fightings, bear-baitings, and the like,
which excite the people to rudeneſs, cruelty, looſeneſs and irreligion, ſhall be reſpectively diſcouraged,
and ſeverely puniſhed, according to the appointment
of the governor and freemen in provincial council and
general aſſembly; as alſo all proceedings contrary to
theſe laws, that are not here expreſly made penal.

XXXVIII. That a copy of theſe laws ſhall be hung
up in the provincial council, and in public courts of
juſtice: And that they ſhall be read yearly at the opening of every provincial council and general aſſembly,
and

and court of justice; and their assent shall be testified, by their standing up after the reading thereof.

XXXIX. That there shall be at no time any alteration of any of these laws, without the consent of the governor, his heirs or assigns, and six parts of seven of the freemen, met in provincial council and general assembly.

XL. That all other matters and things not herein provided for, which shall and may concern the public justice, peace or safety of the said province; and the raising and imposing taxes, customs, duties, or other charges whatsoever, shall be, and are hereby referred to the order, prudence and determination of the governor and freemen in provincial council and general assembly, to be held from time to time in the said province.

Signed and sealed by the governor and freemen aforesaid, the fifth day of the third month, called May, one thousand six hundred and eighty-two.

The boundaries granted by the charter of King Charles to William Penn and his heirs, are all that tract or part of land in America, with the islands therein contained, as the same is bounded on the east by the river Delawar, from twelve miles distance northwards of Newcastle town, unto the three and fortieth degree of northern latitude, but if the river shall not extend so far northward, then by the said river, so far as it doth extend, and from the head of the said river, the eastern bounds are to be determined by the Meridian line to be drawn from the head of the said river, unto the forty-third degree. The said land to extend westward five degrees in longitude, to be computed from the said eastern bounds, and the said lands to be bounded on the north by the beginning of the three and fortieth degree of northern latitude, and on the south by a circle drawn at twelve miles distance from Newcastle, northward and westward, unto the beginning of the fortieth degree of northern latitude, and then by a strait line westward, to the limits above mentioned.

It appears somewhat strange in considering this as well as the other charters, how any sovereign or parliament in Europe could pretend to parcel out the lands of other people, by charters and patents, to their own subjects, without first purchasing them of the original proprietors, or asking their consent. William Penn seems to have been sensible of this absurdity when he received his charter, because he first purchased the lands of the natives before he claimed any right of possession. Had Penn considered his charter as giving an undoubted title to the possession of Pennsylvania, he had no occasion to carry a price in his hands to the natives to pay them for a right of possession. His paying a small price to the Indians, though it had the appearance of justice, did not come up to that measure of rectitude which the spirit of equity requires. It gave Mr Penn the character of an honest man without being deserving of it; for he ought first to have made his purchase from those who had the lands to dispose of, and then as a subject of Great Britain solicited a charter of protection for such considerations as he could have agreed for with the government. By receiving a charter before-hand, he undoubtedly supposed that the king was engaged to make good the contents of his patent; and if the natives had sold the possession to some other persons belonging to some other power before the arrival of Penn, it would have probably been the occasion of war and desolation in the country. It cannot be doubted but that the natives had a right to dispose of their possessions to those

who

who would give them most; and suppose they had sold them to the French or any other nation, it would have been no just reason for the government of Britain to have insisted to make good their promise to Mr Penn, or any other patentee.—But in cases of this kind, justice and equity are seldom strictly pursued. Maryland is a proprietory colony, granted to Lord Baltimore, his heirs and successors, saving the allegiance of the inhabitants, and the sovereign dominion of the country. It is held by the same tenure as the castle of Windsor in the county of Berks, in free soccage, by fealty only. The proprietor has power to make laws, by the advice, and with the consent of the freemen and their deputies, and power to execute the said laws, provided that they are agreeable to reason, and not reguguant to the laws of England. The proprietor has the power of life and limb, freeholds, goods and chattels, without an assembly of the freemen; to make free all settlers in the said province, both for the present and to come; to grant the said settlers a liberty to trade, and to confer honours upon the inhabitants, with proper titles. In a word, this proprietor has almost all the power of a sovereign, and in one sense he is superior to the king; for it is granted that no taxes shall be imposed by the kings of England upon the inhabitants of this province. Maryland was at first settled with about 200 Roman Catholics, most of them of good families; but the proprietory, with great wisdom, introduced a general toleration for Christians of all persuasions, a measure which tended much to the flourishing state of the colony. This colony, as well as Pensylvania, for a long time, had the honour of being untainted with the disgrace of religions persecution; and, as well as the other, free from the calamities of war, offensive or defensive, with their neighbours the Indians, with whom they lived in the moſt exemplary harmony. It happened once through miſtake in a war with the Indians, carried on againſt Virginia, that they made an incurſion into the territories of Maryland, but were ſoon ſenſible of their miſtake. The laſt war changed matters greatly, and the Indians, through the falſe inſinuations of the French, were inſtructed to laugh at their ancient alliances. The people of Maryland are of the ſame eſtabliſhed religion as thoſe in Virginia, that is of the church of England; but the clergy here are provided for in a much more liberal manner. The principal buſineſs of the people of Maryland, before the preſent war, was like thoſe of Virginia to cultivate tobacco, and the planters live in farms ſcattered up and down the country, and have their goods carried from them when ready, by ſhips which come to Cheſapeak bay, and the navigable rivers which run into it. The tobacco of this country is called Oroonoko, which is accounted ſtronger than that of Virginia, and is greatly demanded in the eaſtern and northern parts of Europe, where it is even preferred to the ſweet ſcented tobacco of James and York river in Virginia. About 40,000 hogſheads has been ſhipped in one year. In this colony, in the time of the laſt war, there were ſuppoſed to be 40,000 white inhabitants, and 60,000 negroes. The profits ariſing from this colony and Virginia, to Great Britain were immenſe, and the government received great revenues therefrom. The provinces of Virginia and Maryland are ſuppoſed, in tobacco only, to have exported in 1763, to the annual value of 768,000l. into Britain. This, at 8 l. per hogſhead, makes the number of hogſheads amount to 96,000. Of theſe it is computed that above 13,500 hogſheads are conſumed in Britain, the duty on which, at 26l. 1s. per hogshead, comes to 351,675l. the remaining 82,500 hogsheads are exported by our merchants to the other countries of Europe, and their value returned to Britain. The value of this trade appears from the very recital thereof.—And it may be added, that this single branch employs 330 sail of ships, and 3960 seamen. This trade not only encreased our wealth, but braced the sinews of our strength, and ought to have been carefully nourished for the good and advantage of the mother country, as well as that of the colonies.

Carolina is a colony which was granted to some English noblemen in 1663. These were Edward Earl of Clarendon, then Lord High Chancellor of England; George Duke of Albemarle; William Lord Craven; John Lord Berkley; Anthony Lord Ashley; Sir George Carteret; Sir William Berkely; and Sir John Colliton; who, according to the stile of the charter, being excited with a laudable and pious zeal for the propagation of the gospel, begged a certain country in the parts of America, not yet cultivated and planted, and only inhabited by barbarous people, who had no knowledge of God. Wherefore, the king granted them all that territory in his dominions in America, from the north end of the Island called Luke-Island, which lies in the southern Virginian sea, and within thirty-six degrees of north latitude; and to the west as far as the south sea; and so far southerly as the river Matheo, which borders on the coast of Florida, and is within thirty-one degrees of north latitude; and so west in a direct line, as far as the south seas aforesaid. This patent was accompanied with the usual investitures of fisheries, mines, power of life and limb, and other requisites for territorial property. The state of England at this time happened to be exceeding favourable

able for a settlement of this sort. The dissenters had undergone some severe hardships, episcopacy was now restored, and many sober and well meaning Englishmen were far from being satisfied with the designs of the court. Some of the proprietaries themselves were at best but very moderate favourers of the act of uniformity; and they very wisely obtained a clause of toleration in their charter, by which the king granted the proprietaries full and free license, liberty, and authority, by such legal ways and means as they should think proper to give unto such person and persons, inhabiting and being within the said province, or any part thereof, who really in their judgements, and for conscience sake, cannot conform to the liturgy, form and ceremonies of the church of England, and take and subscribe the oaths and articles, made and established in that behalf, or any of them, such indulgences and dispensations in that behalf, for, and during such time and times, and with such limitations and restrictions as they shall think fit.

The original constitutions, of which there were an hundred and twenty, proceeded upon the same plan of toleration, and are thought to be suggested by Lord Ashley, afterwards Earl of Shaftsbury, and penned by the great Mr Locke, an intimate friend of that nobleman. By several of these fundamental articles and constitutions, it is provided,[*] " That since the natives of that place, who will be concerned in our plantations, are utterly strangers to Christianity, whose idolatry, ignorance, or mistake, give us no right to expell or use them ill; and that those who remove from other parts to plant there, will unavoidably be of different opinions concerning matters of religion, the liberty whereof they will expect to have allowed them; and that

[*] Article 96, 101, 102, 106.

that it will not be reasonable for us, on that account, to keep them out.—Therefore, that sure peace may be maintained, amidst the diversity of opinions, and our agreement and compact with all men may be duly and faithfully observed, the violation whereof, upon whatever pretence, cannot be without great offence to Almighty God, and scandal to the true religion which we profess: and also, the Jews, heathens, and other dissenters from the purity of the Christian religion, may not be scared and kept at a distance from it; but by having an opportunity of acquainting themselves with the truth and reasonableness of its doctrines, and the peaceableness and inoffensiveness of its professors, may, by good usage and persuasion, and all those convincing methods of gentleness and meekness, suitable to the rules and designs of the gospel, be won over to embrace, and unfeignedly receive the truth. Therefore, the said constitutions provided for their liberty; but declared that no person above seventeen years of age, should have any benefit or protection of law, which is not a member of some church profession, having his name recorded in some one religious register." These articles, which were signed by the proprietaries, are declared by the last article, to be the sacred and unalterable form and rule of government in Carolina for ever. So far did the religious constitution of this colony proceed.

As to the articles concerning the civil government of the colony, the first provides, that a palatine be chosen out of the proprietaries, who shall continue during life, and be succeeded by the eldest of the other proprietaries. This palatine acted as a president of a court, composed of himself, and three other proprietaries, and who were vested with the execution of all the powers of the charter; and it is called the palatine's tine's court. Each member had a power of nominating a deputy, who acted for him in Carolina, but according to his directions. The fundamental constitutions require that there should be three great hereditary landholders in every county one called the landgrave, and the other called by the Indian name caciques. Their great assembly, or what has been called their parliament, was to consist of the governor, the proprietaries and their deputies, and the commons; in imitation of the king, lords, and commons of Great Britain. The commoners were to be elective, like those in England, by the freeholders of every county; and this assembly was to sit in one house, once in every two years, and oftener, if need required; and the votes of the members were to be of equal weight. This government appears to have been too unweildy, and scarcely practicable for an infant colony to observe. It was overcharged with so many courts and forms, in one body politic, that the execution appears to have been impracticable. It was upon the whole a sort of foeudal government, with some few exceptions. One thing in which it approached very near to the foeudal system was, that the inhabitants from sixteen to sixty years of age, if called upon by the sovereign power there, which was the great council, were obliged to take the field with proper arms. Every planter, if he did not buy it off, was also to pay annually to his proprietary, one penny an acre of quit rent; and each county had one sheriff, and four justices of the peace.

The settling this colony cost the proprietaries at first large sums of money; 44,000l. were expended in transporting inhabitants and cattle thither, and it was long before the proprietaries received any return from their estates. All free persons who came over were

to

to have fifty acres of land for themselves; fifty for each man servant, and as many for each woman servant that was marriageable; and every servant after his or her servitude was expired, was deemed to be free, and to have fifty acres, paying the quit rent of one penny an acre. But the proprietaries were careful where any of the colonists bought their quit rents, to except the mines and minerals, and quarries of precious stones. In the year 1670, Colonel William Sayle was appointed governor of Carolina by the proprietaries. At this time, the lands about Albemarle and Port-Royal Rivers as being most convenient for trade, were most frequented; but experience soon taught the colonists, that pasturage and tillage were necessary for their establishment, so that Ashly and Cooper rivers drew hitherto such numbers, that their neighbourhood soon became the best inhabited part of the country. In 1661, Captain Halstead arrived with a supply of provisions of all kinds from the proprietaries in England, who created James Carteret, Sir John Yeoman, and John Locke, Esq; landgraves and caciques. At this time also some deviations were made from the original constitutions. It was discovered that the number of landgraves and caciques, required by the original constitution, were not to be found, and therefore a governor was named by the palatine. The council was to consist of seven deputies of proprietaries, as many chosen by the assembly, or as it was called, the parliament, and as many of the landgraves and caciques. To those were added all of them nominated by the proprietaries; an admiral, a chamberlain, chancellor, chief justice, secretary, surveyor, treasurer, high steward, high constable, register of births and burials and marriages, register of writings, and marshal of the admiralty. The quorum of the council

cil was to confift of the governor and fix of the members, three of whom were to be proprietary deputies; and an aſſembly was compoſed of the governor, the deputies of the proprietaries, ten members to be choſen by the freeholders of Berkley county, and ten by thoſe of Colliton county; this number was to be encreaſed according to the encreaſe of the colony.

The firſt palatine of this colony was the Duke of Albemarle, who was ſucceeded by the Earl of Craven, in 1671. At this time the proprietaries had conceived very ſanguine hopes of their colony: for they ordered Captain Halſtead to ſail up Aſhley river to make diſcoveries; and the model of a very magnificent town was ſent over with him, to be built as the metropolis of the province. At this time the majority of the coloniſts were diſſenters; but the promiſſing appearance of the colony invited over to it many of the old cavilier character, and others, whoſe irregular and libertine conduct and behaviour gave great ſcandal to the original planters, which in time produced a ſchiſm, or rather, a civil war in the colony. Sir John Yeoman ſucceeded Colonel Sayle as governor; but the diſorders of the colony encreaſed ſo much, that the Indians were abuſed, and though at that time very numerous in Carolina, were provoked to a war, in which much blood was ſhed, and many lives loſt on both ſides. Theſe imprudent proceedings would have proved fatal to the colony, had it not been for the wiſdom and prudence of the proprietaries; for their party, and that of the planters beſides, having the natives on their ſides, came often to blows; and one of the name of Culpepper was ſent over priſoner to England, where he was tried for high treaſon in Weſtminſter hall, for raiſing a rebellion in Carolina, but acquitted. Theſe unruly proceedings plainly ſhew

that

that nothing contributes more to the peace and happiness of a people than the practical principles of pure and undefiled liberty. The Tory principles of cavaliers, which always will incline their votaries to aim at dominion, will ever be inimical to the peace and tranquility of society; whereas, just ideas of liberty make men grant as much freedom to others as they take to themselves, and by that means they are not ready to quarrel and fall out.

To put a period to these disorders, or at least to provide some remedy, the proprietaries chose one Col. West to be their governor, and from his character and behaviour he appears to have been a man of wisdom, sagacity, and courage. He found great licentiousness prevailing in the colony when he came to the government, parties risen to a great height, and the Indian war not extinguished. This new governor, by taking the popular side, in a great measure cured the public divisions so much, that the parties united in repelling the Westoes, an Indian nation who were very troublesome to the inhabitants. In 1682 he held a parliament at Charlestown, where several good laws passed; and particularly an act for highways, for suppressing drunkenness and profane swearing, for observation of the Lord's day, and for settling the militia. Those, and some other popular acts were displeasing to the proprietaries; and West, in 1685, was removed from his government, and was succeeded by Joseph Moreton, Esq.

The wisdom of the proprietaries did not appear in this change of a governor, nor in the commission which they sent to appoint and determine differences between the English and the Indians of Carolina. The commissioners that were appointed for the purpose above mentioned were, Morice Matthews, William

Fuller, Jonathan Fitz, and John Boon, Esqrs. Those gentlemen were accused of unfair practices in their decisions, and were soon dissolved. Though there were many discouraging circumstances attended the colony at this time, yet it still prospered; and Charles-town was built and fortified in a very fine and inviting situation, upon a rock between Ashley and Cooper rivers. Three counties, those of Berkley, Craven, and Colliton, were laid out and divided into squares of 12000 acres, proportioned to the shares held in them by the proprietaries, landgraves, and caciques. The colonists at this time carried on a trade with the Indians, which the proprietaries did not at all approve of; for they wanted to engross this trade into their own hands, which rendered their authority less respectable in the esteem of the inhabitants. To answer their several purposes they frequently changed their governors, with little advantage to themselves, and with little satisfaction to the colonists. Men who reside in England, and are engaged in forming Utopian schemes of wealth and riches, are ready to imagine, before they try experiments, that there is nothing to stand in the way of their imaginations and form their schemes of government, according to what they wish to happen, rather than according to principles of certainty or real probability. Mr West, who was again restored to his government, did not long continue; he became popular by doing good, and was envied by the proprietaries. He was succeeded by James Colliton, Esq; a Barbadoes gentleman, who was exceedingly unpopular. He and his friends attempted to alter the fundamental constitutions of the colony, and to substitute other articles under the title of standing laws, and temporary laws. This proceeding pleased none of the principal parties concerned, but was disagreeable to both the proprietaries and the planters; so that Mr Colliton was not only deprived of his office, but driven out of the colony. Upon the expulsion of Colliton, some of the most considerable gentlemen had the management of affairs, till a new governor was appointed. Four governors succeeded one another in a short period; the last of whom sent notice to the proprietaries, that unless some of themselves, or one in the character of proprietary, came among them with full power to settle all grievances, matters would never be put to rights. Upon this the Lord Ashley, eldest son to the Earl of Shaftsbury, was chosen by the proprietaries to be governor. This was the famous author of the Characteristics, a book, though condemned by many who never were able to understand it, contains some as just and good reasonings as is to be met with in most modern compositions. Lord Ashley's constitution not being suited to such active scenes of life, he declined accepting of the government. It was at this time conferred upon Mr Archdale, who published an account of Carolina, to which the public is indebted for the principal things we know of that colony at that time.

Mr Archdale soon found that he had more to do than he expected, and that he had a very difficult task to perform; but he behaved so well, and managed with so much prudence, discretion, and patience, that the assembly voted him an address of thanks. There was at this time a good understanding between the government of Spain, and that of Great Britain; but it was a common practice for the people of Jamaica and Barbadoes to buy Spanish Indians for slaves, who had been taken prisoners by other Indian savages. The Tammasees were a nation under the protection of the English, though they had been formerly under that of the Spaniards. They had taken some prisoners from an Indian belonging to Spain. Mr Archdale, when he heard of this, imediately ordered the king of the Tammasees to repair to Charlestown with his prisoners, which he did, when Archdale commanded him to march to St Augustine, where he was to present them, with a letter to the Spanish governor. All which the Indian prince most punctually obeyed; and Mr Archdale received a very polite letter from the governor in return. This act of justice was the beginning of mutual good offices between the two nations; for the Spaniards soon after made the like return to the English governor of Carolina.

The Earl of Bath came at last to be palatine, who was an enthusiastic zealot for the church of England; his great ambition was to establish that worship in Carolina, exclusive of all others; the same doctrine being inforced in England by the bill against occasional conformity. One Moor was at this time governor, a man tractable to the views of the palatine. His character in the history of that time is far from being amiable; he was possessed of a persecuting spirit, which will, on all occasions, tarnish a man's character even suppose it had no other blots upon it. Though it never happens that a man truely good will ever persecute others for conscience sake. Moor seems to have been a man void of all principle, as his after behaviour testified; for upon the breaking out of the war with Spain, he carried on a slave trade, which disgraced both the proprietaries and himself. He sold the Spanish Indians to the British Islands, at a lower price than they could purchase African slaves, and by that means made a considerable advantage to himself. But his violence and injustice had almost proved the ruin of the colony.

Moor was succeeded by Johnston, a man of the same principles and temper, and carried on matters with great violence; under his government a bill was brought in to exclude all persons from being chose members of the commons house, who did not conform to the religious worship of the church of England. This was expresly contrary to the constitutions of the colony. By this law all dissenters were disqualified, though legally elected, from sitting in the assembly, and the candidate who had the greatest number of votes, after the disqualified dissenter was set a side, was admitted. The dissenters were now sadly harrassed, by a set of tyrannical managers, and left without all redress, and many foolish and oppressive things were done, inconsistent with the spirit of all good government. Such was the madness of the Tories in that colony, that they proceeded from one thing to another till they broke their charter, and were obliged to surrender it into the hands of the queen in 1705. It is somewhat strange, that in all governments where a tyranny is carried on, they work its dissolution in the end; and where liberty is supported, that the weakest governments encrease, and at last flourish. From the many examples of this, in the history of mankind, one would think that sovereigns and rulers would learn to support liberty for their own sake, and that of their successors, because they have so many instances of the fall of empires and governments, when once they began to introduce oppression. One thing which the oppression of the palatine and governors produced was, a rising of the Indians, whom they proceeded to oppress as well as the colonists. The power of the proprietaries was now sunk to nothing, and so weak was their administration, that the colonists in Carolina were obliged to apply to the crown to

take

take them under its protection; which the government of England pretended implied a resumption of their charter. The proprietaries found that they were not able to carry on the war against the Indians upon their own bottom, they therefore resolved to surrender their charter, which they accordingly did to a number of persons in trust for the crown.

It is plain that the arbitrary principles of the proprietaries and their managers, almost ruined the colony, and lost them their charter. There is something of infatuation, for the most part, that attends people that grasp at unreasonable dominion, for they never can tell when they have enough, and stretch their power so far that they over reach themselves. The desire of dominion over others is sweet to the most part of mankind, but there is nothing in nature more unreasonable, nor any thing that argues more a weakness of understanding than the desire thereof. In proceeding through the history of the smallest colonies, we may see their ruin inseperably connected with arbitrary government; and that whenever the ideas of liberty are lost, prosperity ends, and confusion begins. It is of no signification whether a few or many exercise tyranny, the effects will be the same, and will always follow their cause. Civil and religious liberty are essential to all good government; for there is in fact no government without them; they are the springs of both rational rule and obedience. Without these two springs all forms of government will be tyrannical, and all professions of obedience hypocrisy and dissimulation. Unless men suppose themselves free, they will never obey from the heart, and legislators have but a poor hold of mankind, when they rule them only by principles of fear. This may restrain some from acts of violence, but it will never stimulate to great and noble actions. There is not a great action recorded in the whole history of slavery, since the creation of the world.

Although in this and the two preceding years, very little was done in parliament concerning American affairs, yet the progress of the ministry, and the court party in parliament, became more and more alarming to the friends of liberty in the British empire. The most sacred rights of private property, which had been secured by royal patent, confirmed by the sanction of parliament, were now confirmed by a junto of ministerial puppets, who acted at the nod of the political commander in chief. The East India company, whom experience had convinced of the infidelity of their servants in the eastern parts of the world, had determined to send out some friends whom they could confide in, in the character of supervisors, to rectify past abuses, and to direct the affairs of the company in time coming, till things were put into such order as the intention of their institution required.

Though the company had been taken in some measure into the hands of administration, and their affairs came under the cognizance of parliament, as early as the year 1767, yet nothing had been done all this time towards their regulation and settlement, except the restricting of their dividends, rescinding their acts, and the obtaining from them, without any visible equivalent, immense sums of money, which were far beyond their abilities. No order was taken suited to the change in their condition and circumstances, for the regulation and government of their new acquisitions; nor any new powers lodged in their hands to counterbalance the vast trusts which they were now under a necessity of reposing in their servants; nor to restrain or prevent those evils which ordinarily attend the sudden transition from the direction of a counting house, to the government of an extensive territory.

These disorders had been visible for some time past and if government had merely intended the welfare of the company, they would have applied the benevolent influence of their power, as soon as they perceived the rise and progress of that evil, which they now considered to be so imminent, and of such a dangerous nature. It was alledged that government had voluntarily permitted these disorders to go on, that by suffering the company to render themselves odious and ridiculous, through the misconduct of their servants, an handle might be made thereof, to shew its incapacity of governing such large possessions, and to prepare the nation for the changes that were intended to succeed. Whether this allegation was true or false, it is certain that the bad administration in India, with all its consequences, were suffered to pass unnoticed; and it is manifest in the transactions of the year 1772, that though the affairs of the company were alluded to, at the opening of the sessions, in the speech from the throne, they were notwithstanding suffered to lie over till near the close thereof, when a bill was brought in by the deputy chairman, for enlarging the controuling powers of the company, with respect to their servants, in the eastern parts of the world. This bill however came to nothing. But a member in the king's service, not indeed connected with the ministry, whether with or without their advice, at length roused their attention to this object. This gave rise to a select committee, which was armed with full powers for all purposes of enquiry, concerning the officers of the company.

The whole company were now greatly alarmed, and not only dreaded the rigour of an enquiry, but
from

from late experience were too sensible of the inefficacy of charters for their protection, in a dispute wherein government found it for the service of their purposes of power, to set them aside. In a senate where the majority are under the influence of an omnipotent ministry, no former rights and privileges are safe and secure; for yes or no, will, in such an assembly, set aside the very constitutional rights of an empire. Charters granted to incorporated bodies of people, confirmed by the legislature, are certainly as legal tenures for holding rights and possessions, as any deeds that can be devised, and cannot justly be infringed by public authority, unless the possessors are guilty of such crimes, as legally deprive them of the rights of other subjects. But when it is admitted to be a maxim of government, that future parliaments may reverse the constitutional deeds of former legislatures, for reasons of state or conveniency, there are no rights which any subjects can possess, but what are merely precarious and uncertain.

The East India company foresaw the storm that was gathering fast, and would, unless provided against, at last burst upon their heads. They therefore endeavoured to prevent its effects by the best measures and methods they could devise. It was proposed, during the recess of parliament, to send out a new commission of supervision, with full powers to regulate all the company's affairs abroad. This was a subject that took up much time, it being not less difficult to agree upon the persons who were to be appointed to an office of so great importance, than upon the extent of the powers with which they were to be intrusted. They at last agreed upon sending six gentlemen for the purpose intended, and a general officer of high rank and character, who had commanded with great honour in
the

the American war. All these consented to go out at the head of the supervision.—But before matters could be fully adjusted and brought into execution, the meeting of parliament put an end to the design. A select committee, as well as a committe of secrecy, was appointed for examining the company's affairs, which were careful to state them in such a point of view as greatly exposed both the company and its servants, and excited a general indignation against them. Those enquiries, and the proceedings of parliament in consequence thereof, were upon the whole arbitrary and illegal, as the East India company was restrained from the management and direction of its own properties, without any just reason assigned for applying such an incapacitating authority. What appeared exceedingly unreasonable was, that though the ministry acknowledged that the company's affairs were in a very confused situation in Bengal, yet they wanted to restrain them from sending out supervisors to rectify those errors and abuses, which were so much complained of. This was considered as an high degree of oppression, and viewed in the light of a design to make the company subservient to the ends of government, to all intents and purposes. The arguments that were used on this occasion in parliament, will speak best for themselves, and they shall be given nearly in the same words as they were delivered.

" The plea of distress was examined, and alledged to be only temporary, by a deficiency of present cash; but it was insisted, that in point of solvency, the company was in the highest degree of credit. That the minister himself had admitted this fact. That the gross abuses committed in India, had rendered it necessary, to appoint a set of gentlemen, in whom the confidence of the company, whose interest was at stake,

stake, was placed to reform those abuses and regulate their affairs; by whose interposition, notwithstanding the expence, vast sums might be, and probably would be saved to the company; that it was a new system of conduct, as well as a new mode of argument, that because people were distressed, they should not be permitted to take proper measures to retrieve their affairs; that this was a proposal for an *ex post facto* law, and was to restrain the company from doing what was already legally done; that the report was founded upon a false principle, the alledged motive being to preserve the company from a farther embarassment in the present state of their affairs, by their running into an extraordinary expence; whereas the expences of the supervision, were to be paid, and paid only, out of the savings which it might be productive of in India, and could have no possible effect on their present distresses at home. That the company, notwithstanding the full powers with which they were legally furnished, for the management of their internal affairs, and the appointment of their servants, had shewn so great an attention and deference to parliament, that though the supervisors were appointed, and the gentlemen in readiness to depart, they had already suspended the commission, only upon hearing that the house had begun an enquiry into their affairs, and were determined it should not take place, till the issue of that enquiry. That the report strikes at the very charter and constitution of the company; was unprecedented, and unparliamentary; and it was hoped would be dismissed, in such a manner as should vindicate the honour of the house, and prevent such attempts for the future.

In answer to these arguments the minister declared,

against the company; that it was the intention of parliament, and the great wish of administration, to render it a great and glorious company, and to settle it upon the most permanent foundation; but that they were entering into a very expensive commission, at a time, that from their former misconduct, their distresses were so great, as to put them under the necessity of applying to the public for a loan of money, and that they, owed considerable arrears to government; that it was undoubtedly the duty of parliament to preserve them from ruin; that the committee which had been appointed by the house to inspect the affairs of the company, have judged it expedient that a restraint should be laid upon them in respect to that measure, and that as no restraint could possibly be laid but by act of parliament, it was necessary to bring in a bill for that purpose. Doubts were also raised in the debate (though no more than doubts) whether the company could legally issue such a commission. If they could, it was asserted, that the company could not give their commissioners proper and effectual authority without the aid of parliament; nor were they, under whose government all those abuses had arisen, in the least equal to the correction of them.

In order to elude the present temper, and to prevent the establishment of a precedent so fatal to their rights, two gentlemen who were directors of the India company, and then in their places as members, offered to pledge themselves to the house, that the suspension should not be taken off, nor the supervisor suffered to depart, until such a progress was made in the present enquiry, as should afford full satisfaction, both with respect to the state of their affairs, and the propriety of the measure.

This

This proposal was rejected. It was said, that though the company might for the present have resolved to suspend the departure of the supervisors, nothing but an act of parliament could make that resolution effectual; that they might rescind on one day, their own resolutions or measures of the preceding; that the opinion or promises of the whole court of directors, could afford no security in this respect, as the direction was inferior to the general courts, where their acts were liable to be over-ruled by the proprietors; and that an advantage might be taken during the Christmas recess, of sending the supervisors far out of the reach of parliament. That this bill was no invasion of any charter, it was only an act to prevent a possible evil; to prevent the company from crowning all their former extravagance, by entering into an unnecessary and ruinous expence, when they were just upon the brink of bankruptcy.

On the other side, the whole measure, as well as the unconstitutional nature of the committee from which it originated, were condemned in the most severe and pointed terms. It was said to be neither more nor less, than a bill to suspend the laws of the land; that it was subversive of rights, which the company not only enjoyed by charter, but had purchased from the public, for high and valuable considerations. That it disgraced the dignity of parliament, by a wanton exertion of authority, without a motive; that too many complaints were already loudly and publicly made, that every ministerial job was adopted as soon as proposed, without regard to reason, argument, or consequences, whereby the respect, and confidence, so essential to the nature of parliament, were sunk to a degree that could scarcely be paralleled in the worst of times. That administration had found out an admirable

admirable method of rendering the company great and glorious; they began, by plundering them, under the name of an agreement, of above two millions, and now put the laſt hand to the work, by taking advantage of the diſtreſs principally cauſed by that plunder, to deprive them of their charter, and overthrow their conſtitution: firſt they tempt and terrify them into a ruinous extravagance of grants and dividends, and then as a puniſhment, deprive them of whatever this extravagance had left. That indeed the miniſter was laviſh in his declarations of his friendly intentions towards the company and theſe declarations muſt be conſidered as a full compenſation for every thing they ſuffered. It was farther ſaid, that this bill muſt be productive of the moſt fatal conſequences with reſpect to the other funds, and put an end to all confidence in the public faith; and it was aſked with great bitterneſs, what ſecurity there could be in a country, where the royal charters, repeatedly ratified and confirmed by acts of parliament, could give no permanent eſtabliſhment to property. That the argument of expence was a mere pretext to cover worſe deſigns. That it was admitted ſome ſort of ſuperviſion was neceſſary and the objection of expence was equally applicable to any ſort of ſuperviſion. As to the want of powers, it was ſaid, that if there was any defect of that ſort in the company's charter, they might be given with equal effect to the commiſſioners who are legally appointed, and without any violation of the rights or charter of the company.

To theſe and many other ſtrictures, the diſtreſſes and extravagance of the company, the neceſſity of obſerving the ſtricteſt œconomy in their affairs, together with a due regard for their welfare, which was ſo intimately connected with that of the ſtate, and a
juſt

just attention to the security of their creditors, were deemed in general sufficient answers; it was also insisted on, that this measure was no invasion of their rights; and that if it had, the legislature had an unquestioned right to interfere, to prevent their running headlong to ruin. Upon a division, the question was carried by a great majority, being supported by 114 votes, against 43 only, who opposed the bringing in of the bill.

In the farther progress of this bill, a petition, couched in the strongest terms, was presented against it by the India company; and several of their servants, consisting of the examiner of the records, the auditor of Indian accounts, the accountant general, and the superintendant of the custom-house accounts, were examined, by the company's desire, at the bar of the house of commons, in order as well to shew a true state of their affairs, as the misconduct and disobedience of their servants abroad, and the consequent necessity of the supervision. In the course of these examinations it appeared, that the exorbitances and oppressions still continued to be committed by the company's servants in India. Through their own imprudence, in asking needless or improper questions, a full share of those charges, were brought directly home, to some of those gentlemen who were then sitting in the house.

It appeared, that since the year 1765, the company's expences had encreased, from 700,000l. to the enormous sum of 1,700,000l. annually. It also appeared, that government had received by the nett duties, the indemnity upon tea, and the stippulated 400,000l. little less than two millions annually from the company. That the latter had lost by the indemnity agreement, from its first commencement, at least one million; of which 700,000l. went to government, and the remainder

der to the purchasers. It was also shewn, that government had profited, extraordinarily, by the company, within the last five years, to the vast amount of 3,395,000l. viz. by the produce of the annual stipulated sum, 2,200,000l. and by the increase of the revenue, compared on a medium with the five preceding years, 1,185,000l. That the whole of the company's receipts of dividend during the same period, scarcely amounted to 900,000l. more than six per cent upon its capital, which was the lowest trading dividend that had ever been made during the most expensive and dangerous war. It appeared upon the whole, that the company's mercantile profits during the above period, amounted on an average, to 464,000l. annually, which would have afforded a dividend of twelve and a half per cent; so that while government profited to the great amount we have mentioned the company and proprietary, instead of benefiting a single shilling, lost considerably of the dividend, which the profits on their trade, only, would have afforded. Thence they argued, that far from being delinquents, their merits with the public were unparalleled by any example. That the abuses committed by their servants, were such as they could not prevent, because they could not foresee; that when they were known, they endeavoured by reiterated orders from home to correct them; that they had prepared various commissions for that purpose; one under Lord Clive; a second, which had been unfortunately lost; and a third, which contrary to their rights, was now proposed to be rescinded. They contended, that parliament could not take this step, as being contrary to public faith. The matters of fact in the petition, were stated by the evidence with clearness and precision. I have been the more particular

lar in this detail, as it will undoubtedly excite the admiration of future ages to confider the power and opulence, which had been once in the poffeffion of a company of Englifh merchants.

A fecond report had been made during this time by the fecret committee, which contained a long ftatement of the company's affairs; of their debts, credits, and effects, both at home and abroad. It was objected that this piece was fo overloaded with figures and accounts, and fo full of intricacies, that it could afford but little information, (except what was taken for granted from the grofs fums) within the narrow time that fuch information could be neceffary, with refpect to the prefent bill. This ftate of their affairs, was confidered by the company and its friends, as a very unfavourable, if not unfair, reprefentation of them; and drew many ftrictures upon the committee, the darknefs of its proceedings, and the doubtful information that could be obtained through fuch a medium. It was again lamented, that a fair and open enquiry had not been carried on, according to the happy genius and fpirit of the Englifh conftitution, by which every gentleman would have had an opportunity, of founding his opinion upon matters as they appeared to himfelf, and of requiring fuch explanations as he thought neceffary; that the time unavoidably fpent in fuch an inveftigation, would afford leifure for cool deliberation, and for digefting, in fome degree, the feveral parts of fuch complicated matter? whereby random opinions and hafty reports, framed in a hurry, and without a poffibility of feeing all the fides of the fubject, would be precluded; and at the fame time, the parties concerned, would have an equitable opportunity of attending to their refpective interefts, the satisfaction of knowing the ground upon which measures were to be founded, in whose consequences they were so deeply affected.

On the other hand it was urged, that the committee had acquitted itself of its trust with the most distinguished fidelity, and dispatched and had gone through so complicated a business in less time than could be expected; which could not have been done, if the committee had been open, and subject to debate on the several articles. That it is no wonder, that matters of account in such a business should appear to produce different conclusions, according to the different manner of viewing and stating them. But unless direct falsification were proved, the house must necessarily abide by the statement of those whom they had chosen for the purpose.

Upon the third reading of the bill, counsel was heard in behalf of the company; after which great debates arose. It was advanced by the opposers of the bill, that as the company's legal right to the appointment of all its own servants, and to the entire management and regulation of its internal affairs, had been so clearly proved as not to admit of a question, and that the rapacity, misconduct, and disobedience, of the servants in the presidencies abroad, was so notorious as to be allowed on all hands, no reasonable objection could now lie to the exercise of that right, when its expediency, and even necessity, were so evident; and that as every delay in the present circumstances, must be ruinous in the highest degree to the company, and proportionally prejudical to the nation; it was to be hoped, that no farther opposition would be made, to the carrying of the commission of supervision into immediate execution, and that the present bill would be rejected, as founded upon false principles, and of an unconstitutional and dangerous tendency.

To this it was answered, that the evidence given at the bar, and the arguments opposed by the counsel against the bill, contained the strongest reasons that could possibly have been brought to shew the urgent necessity of its being passed. That they fully demonstrated the evils in India to be of such magnitude, that nothing less than the legislature could reform them; that no powers could be granted to the supervision, competent to the remedy of such enormities; that the commission was besides faulty in its principles, as the governors and counsels in the respective presidencies in India, were joined in power by it, with the supervisors who were intended to be sent from England; that as the number of the former was permanent, they must soon, by death or sickness, become a majority; that by this means, the capital offenders, who were the authors of all the evils complained of, would become the judges of their own crimes, and the redressers of their own oppressions; was it then by men, who had long rioted with the most unrelenting cruelty in the distresses of their miserable fellow-creatures, that justice was to be restored to her proper course, and the mischiefs which their iniquities caused were to be removed;

That the legislature had a supreme controuling power, to which all must, and ought to submit; that this power could never be applied with greater propriety, or benefit, than in the present instance, when the welfare and security of many millions, and the preservation of great countries and revenues depended upon its exertion. That laws, as well as charters, must submit to a change of times and seasons, and must be altered, modelled, or repealed, as circumstances, and the nature of things require; that it could never have been intended at the time of granting the company's charters, to give them a power of legislation over great countries, in which it was not possible to be supposed they ever could have any other footing, than a permission to trade as inmates and strangers. That India affairs were now under the consideration of parliament, and while matters were in this suspence, it would be absurd to allow the company to proceed on their own bottom, and to snatch the business out of their hand: either there was, or there was not occasion for the interposition of parliament; if there was, how could the company pretend to act independant of them, after they had applied for relief to the minister? if there was not, why did they apply?

On the other side it was observed, that parliamentary interposition had hitherto been attended with very little advantage to the company. That the last parliament had undertaken, in the year 1767, the regulation of their affairs, and after spending the greater part of the session upon that business, the result was, the extortion of a vast sum of money from the company without an equivalent, and the leaving their affairs to shift for themselves, without the smallest regulation; that their affairs had since continued open to parliament, without any thing being done, but the making or renewing of bargains for the benefit of government, without the smallest attention to that of the company; that a select committee had been appointed in the preceding session, which had continued its sittings throughout the summer, and it was not pretended that the company had reaped any advantages from them; and that a secret committee had newly started up, the benefits of which were yet to be discovered, as nothing

but

but complaints had hitherto attended its proceedings. That if the company was not armed with sufficient powers for the punishment of its servants, and the regulation of its government in India, the fault lay wholly in administration, as a bill had been brought in for that purpose in the preceding session, which was laid by, under pretence of waiting for the discoveries that were to be made by the select committee.

That the evils apprehended, from the extraordinary powers of the supervision falling into the hands of the offenders in India, were merely imaginary; the company had well foreseen, and effectually provided against those evils, in the body of the commission; no act of the supervision can be valid without the presence of the three commissioners; the first of these is to have the casting voice, and they are to be assisted by the governor, the commander in chief, and second in council only as inferior assessors; and the supervisors have power, if they see cause, to dismiss the governor and whole council, and have a power of controul in all cases.

That if the particular interests of the company were considered as matters of indifference, the great revenues, and immense benefits it afforded to the public, were not to be wantonly sported with; that as the restraint in the bill was laid for six months, and the season of the year would of necessity continue it for six more, twelve whole months, in the present critical state of their affairs, would be totally lost to the company, before any intended regulation, whether by parliament, or otherwise, could possibly take place; that this delay might be productive of the most mischievous effect to the company, as the grievances and evils, which they wanted to remedy or prevent, would have the accumulation of all that time added to

ther

their present amount; and as the design of regulation, would be so long known before-hand to the offenders, they would use such industry in their several departments, that there would not be much left for redress, by the time that it could take place.

But the great force of the arguments on this side, was principally directed, to the present unusual and extraordinary stretch of parliamentary authority; it was acknowledged that a supreme undefined power was ultimately lodged in the legislature; but it was insisted, that such an exertion of it, could only be justified by the most urgent necessity; and that as no such necessity now existed, it was a wanton violation of public faith, law, and constitution, without an equitable motive. That it was the invasion of a right, which parliament had not granted but sold; a right for which the faith of the nation was pledged, and which could not be taken away without an act of forfeiture in the company; nor even in that case without due compensation. That this violent and dangerous exertion of power, must not only destroy the credit of the India company, but also affect the bank, the South-sea, and all other public companies, none of which could have any other securities than those which are now violated; that whenever a war took place, the effects of this unjust and pernicious measure, upon the national credit in general, would be too late and too fatally experienced; and that it was not less dangerous in its principle, nor mischievous in its precedent, to the city of London, and all the other corporated bodies in the British empire.

A particular charge was also made upon administration, with regard to their motives for this suspension. It was said that they had arbitrarily and capriciously suspended the legal course of business in the court of proprietors,

proprietors, and forced this matter into parliament, only to gratify a private refentment; that the company had been officioufly informed by their chairman, and deputy-chairman, (the only medium through which they could have any communication with government) that the meafures relative to the fupervifion were approved of by adminiftration; but that as foon as it was found, that the company did not chufe to intruft their affairs in the hands of thofe who were nominated for that purpofe by the minifters, they immediately fet their faces againft the whole meafure, and now had the fortune to find the houfe fo compliant as to adopt their refentments.

It was obfervable, that many of thofe, who either in themfelves or their families, were under great obligations to the company, and particularly fuch as had obtained vaft fortunes in her fervice, now joined adminiftration in this bill. The effects of the party difputes with refpect to the appointment of fupervifors, were alfo very vifible on this occafion. Though the queftion was debated warmly and ably by the oppofition, fuch was the force of the general odium in which the company ftood, and fuch the weaknefs arifing from its internal diffentions, that the numbers againft the bill were very trifling. Befides, many of the oppofition had not then come to town. Upon a divifion late at night, and not a very thin houfe, the bill was carried by a majority of more than five to one, the numbers being 153, to 28 only.

The reftraining bill was prefented the next day to the houfe of Lords, and it being fo near the holidays, was carried through with the greateft difpatch. It did not, however, pafs without oppofition; though, as in the other houfe, the opponents were few. A noble duke, who had long been diftinguifhed in oppofition,

position, and who of late had applied himself with uncommon industry to obtain a perfect knowledge of India affairs, traversed this bill with great vigour and almost alone, for the short time in which it was passing through its several stages. As the bill was brought in on a Saturday, and a report was spread in the evening, and inserted in the news-papers, that it had been carried that day through its last reading, (a matter, however uncommon, which was readily believed) the India company had not time to go through the necessary forms, for assembling in its corporate capacity, and framing and presenting a petition, before the following Wednesday, on which it was finally passed. A petition signed by 14 proprietors was, however, received, and witnesses were examined, and counsel heard at the bar against the bill.

We shall take notice of some of the arguments that were used upon this occasion, so far as they were peculiar to the place, or may seem to throw new light upon the subject. As the house of Lords is close shut we are obliged to gather the arguments of the minority in that house from their protests; those of the ministry, we must suppose nearly the same with those used in the house of commons. It was urged against the bill, that the arbitrary taking away of legal franchises and capacities, without any legal cause of forfeiture, establishes a precedent, which leaves no sort of security to the subject for his liberties; since his exercising them, in the strictest conformity to all the rules of law, general equity, and moral conduct, is not sufficient to prevent parliament from interesting its sovereign powers to divest them of those rights; by means of which insecurity, the honourable distinction between the British, and other forms of government, is in a great measure lost; that this misfortune is greatly growing upon

upon us, through temporary, occasional, and partial acts of parliament, which, without consideration of their conformity to the general principles of our law and constitution, are adopted rashly and hastily upon every petty occasion; that though it may be difficult to fix any legal limit to the extent of legislative power; it is to be supposed, that parliament is as much bound as any individual to the observance of its own compacts; or otherwise, it is impossible to understand what public faith means, or how public credit can subsist.

That the India company might have been legally called in question, and even its charter endangered, for a neglect of exercising those necessary powers with which it is entrusted, and the use of which it is now proposed to suspend; and that it must be a government composed of deceit and violence, where men are liable to be punished if they decline, or to be restrained if they endeavour to exercise their lawful powers. That it appears by evidence, upon oath at the bar, that the company had been authoritatively informed, that the commission for regulating their affairs, would have been approved of by administration; and that their situation was peculiarly unfortunate, when driven from all confidence in public faith, and the laws of their country, they shall find no security for their charter privileges even in those very ministers, under whose sanction they had every possible reason to believe they were acting.

It was much objected to, that the bill was brought in at a season, when the house is always ill attended, and hurried through with a violent, and it was said, indecent precipitation. That a reason of fact was alledged in the preamble, stating the expence of the commission to be very considerable: and they had not before them any account or estimate of the expences actual or probable, nor were supplied with any account tending to shew the present ability or inability of the company to bear it; so that the Lords were to assert facts, and on these facts to ground a law, altering the condition, and suspending the charter rights of the company, without a possibility of knowing whether the facts be true or false; and that with a determination to continue uninformed, it had been refused to call for the evidence of the directors concerning the expence; or in a matter of such importance, both in itself and its example, to follow the ancient settled parliamentary course of desiring a conference with the commons, in order to be acquainted with the evidence which they received as the grounds of their proceeding.

It was said, that it must be a matter of astonishment to the public, who had for a long time earnestly and anxiously looked to the company, or to parliament, for redress of the grievances in India, to find at length, that the latter is only employed in preventing the former from doing its duty; that instead of correcting the abuse, they oppose themselves to the reformation; that when it was expected, that those who had wronged the company should have been brought to exemplary punishment, the suffering company itself is deprived of its right; and instead of calling delinquents to account, the persons legally empowered to correct or restrain them, are by parliament suspended from their office.

On the other side, besides many of those arguments which we have before seen stated in support of the bill, it is said, that the charge upon administration, of having at one time given a sanction to the commission for superintending the company's affairs, was positively denied, with respect to such of its members as belonged

longed to that house; and reasons were brought to shew, why it could not be well founded with respect to others. As to the dangers that were apprehended from this measure with respect to the national credit, they were represented as merely imaginary; and it was said, that it would have a totally contrary effect, as the Dutch, who had much more money in our public funds, than any other foreigners, would think themselves much safer, when they found that the India Company was under the care and protection of parliament, than if they had been abandoned to their own wild schemes of regulation and management.

That they had no evidence that this bill was contrary to the company's inclinations, any more than to their interests; that the petition they had heard at the bar, was no corporate act, and was signed only by fourteen proprietors, out of about seventeen hundred, of which the company consisted; that the vast majority by which it was carried through the other house, where the most ample information was obtained of the Company's affairs, and the very small number that had dissented to it, sufficiently shewed the justice, propriety, and expediency of the measure. Other charges or censures were answered, by the shortness of the time, and the advantage the company might take of parliament during the recess. Upon a division, the bill was carried by nearly a proportional majority, to that which had attended it in the house of commons, 26 lords having voted for it, to 6 only who opposed its passing; it was, however, followed by a remarkably pointed and severe protest."

What passed in the house of Lords upon this subject, will appear manifest from the protests of a number of noble Lords, against the regulating bill, and upon the motion made by the Duke of Richmond, for
making

making certain entries relative to the East India company, and the holding of a conference with the commons upon that subject. "Because," say they, "the preamble to this bill, stating defects in the powers of the East India company, abuses in its administration, and injuries to public and commercial credit ought to have been supported by evidence adapted to the nature of the several matters alledged. But the production of charters has been refused by the house; no witnesses have been called to ascertain the existence or quality of the supposed abuses; no enquiry has been made into the condition of public credit; and no state of the company's commercial affairs have ever been laid before us.

2dly, Because, if the defects in the charters, and abuses in the administration of the company, exist in the manner stated in the preamble, no effectual provision is made in the enacting part of the bill for supplying the one or reforming the other: on the contrary, the utmost distraction is introduced into the whole œconomy of their affairs. The nomination to the subordinate presidencies, and inferior offices in India, is left to the company; but a superior presidency is appointed by parliament to govern those inferior officers. The superior presidency is to receive orders from the court of directors; but it is left to the private will of the king how far these orders shall be obeyed. The presidency is appointed to make ordinances and regulations, but neither directors or company are to determine on their validity. The king alone is to allow or disallow those acts, as he shall chuse to signify his pleasure under his sign manual. This mode of vesting ultimately the whole management of the company's weighty political affairs, their vast revenues and their extensive commerce in the king's private direction,

without

without any provision in the bill for the intervention of any public body, (either the East-India company or the privy-council) or any responsible public minister, is, we insist, not only a high and dangerous violation of the yet unquestioned charters of the company, but a total subversion of all the principles of the law and constitution of this kingdom.

3dly, Because the election of executive officers in parliament, is plainly unconstitutional, and an example of the most pernicious kind, productive of intrigue and faction, and calculated for extending a corrupt influence in the crown. It frees ministers from responsibility, whilst it leaves them all the effect of patronage. It defeats the wise design of the constitution, which placed the nomination of all officers, either immediately or derivatively, in the crown, whilst it committed the check upon improper nominations to parliament. But this bill, by confounding those powers which the constitution meant to keep separate, has destroyed this controul, along with every wise provision of the laws to prevent the abuses in the nomination to, or exercise of office.

4thly, Because this usurpation of the company's rights in appointing the servants is loaded with the additional injustice of a compulsory payment of salaries, arbitrarily fixed and chargeable on the company's revenues, without their consent.

5thly, Because the violation of the charter is not justified by the importance of the provisions of this bill, which operates only to transfer patronage without conferring new powers, it being expresly provided by the bill, that these powers should be the same as were formerly exercised by the company's servants, under the company's authority; neither is any advantage gained with regard to the particular officers named ed in this bill, the person first in rank and importance in the new parliamentary presidency, being the very same now at the head of the company's presidency at Bengal. We mean to reflect neither upon that gentleman, nor any other, who (for any thing we know to the contrary) may be men of competent ability and good character; but we think ourselves bound to declare against the manifest contradiction and absurdity of this bill, which, stating abuses as now existing in India, for the ground of its regulations, yet appoints the very person to preside there, who, if the allegations in the bill be true, must be concerned, either by neglect, or actual commission in all the abuses complained of.

6thly, Because the appointing judges by the nomination of the crown, with large salaries, payable out of the company's revenue, without the company's consent, either to the appointment or the payment, is an act of flagrant injustice, and an outrage on all the rights of property. No necessity can be pleaded in favour of this violence, as the company did last year voluntarily propose a nomination of judges, with far better provisions for securing a proper appointment, than any contained in this bill.

7thly, Because the clause of this bill, which deprives of all share in the management of their own property, all proprietors not possessed of 1000l. capital stock, disfranchising without the assignment of any delinquency or abuse, no less than 1240 persons legally qualified, is an heinous act of injustice, oppression, and absurdity, and a gross perversion of the high powers entrusted to legislature; the part of the charter which regulates the right of voting, was made to establish exclusively that class of voters which this act has destroyed; the charter knows of no right of voting, but

the

the poffeffion of 500l. capital ftock. It excludes all title to fuperior influence from fuperior property. The feveral laws to prevent the fplitting of ftock are all in affirmance of this principle, and made to fecure this voter. But by a fyftem of contradiction, that, except in this bill, has no example, the very grievance of fplitting of ftock by which the proprietor under 1000l. has been injured, is affigned as the fole ground for depriving him of his franchife. This lower proprietor could not poffibly have been guilty of this offence, and yet he is punifhed; and the large ftockholder, who alone could be guilty of the fplitting, is indulged with new privileges, in contradiction to the fpirit of that charter, which he is fuppofed to have violated.

8thly, Becaufe the great principle upon which the bill has been fupported will, not only in this, but in all cafes, juftify every infringement of the public faith, and render parliamentary fanction the worft of all fecurities. We never can admit that a mere fpeculation of political improvement can juftify parliament in taking away rights, which it exprefly covenanted to preferve, efpecially when it has received a valuable confideration for the franchifes fo ftipulated. Nor are grants of parliament under thefe circumftances to be confidered as gratuitous, refumable merely at the pleafure of the giver; but matters of binding contract, forfeitable only on fuch delinquency or neceffity as is implied in the nature of every other bargain. With fuch matters before us that require the beft, we are denied all manner of information. A bill, the object of which has taken the commons near eight months to confider, is precipitated through this houfe in little more than eight days, without any attention to parliamentary ufage or decorum, as if the lords were the loweft of minifterial tools, who are not to be indulged

even

ven with an appearance of difcuffion, concerning the mandates they receive.

In this fituation we feel the honour of the peerage tarnifhed, and this dignity degraded. If the provifions and precedent of this bill fhould render the public faith of Great-Britain of no eftimation, the franchifes, rights and properties of Englifhmen precarious, and the peerage diftinguifhable only by a more than common meafure of indolence and fervility; if the boundlefs fund of corruption furnifhed by this bill to the fervants of the crown, fhould efface every idea of honour, public fpirit, and independence from every rank of people, after ftruggling vainly againft thefe evils, we have nothing left but the fatisfaction of recording our names to pofterity, as thofe who refifted the whole of this iniquitious fyftem, and as men who had no fhare in betraying to blind prejudices or forded intereft every thing that has hitherto been held facred in this country*".

From all which it appears plain, that the miniftry were aiming more at a defpotical power, than feeking the real good of the Eaft-India company. There is no matter of doubt but the company's fervants had been guilty of many acts of oppreffion, injuftice and tyranny, and deferved a very exemplary punifhment, but it does not appear that the parliament were fo zealous

* Abingdon.   King.
Torrington.   Milton.
Boyle.   Richmond.
Grofvenor.   Archer.
Devonfhire.   Rockingham.
Ponfonby.   Fitzwilliam.
Portland.

in purfuing juftice, as they were eager in grafping at the emoluments which tended to ftrengthen the power and dominion of the crown. It does not appear that the principal agents of iniquity in India, have, by the authority of parliament, been yet brought to juftice, or that the company have been much advantaged by the interference of government. The minifterial proceedings in parliament on this occafion, feem to have had the fame fprings with thofe that have for fome years been carried on with regard to the colonifts in America. The managers have always pretended that they meant the peace, happinefs, and profperity of the colonifts, but when their defigns were fairly divulged, their own dominion and emolument have fairly appeared to have been the fprings of their actions. A circumftance which naturally falls in the way of the hiftory of this year, confirms the above obfervations.

The inhabitants of the ifland of St. Vincent, which are called Carribs, who have been, time immemorial, in poffeffion of that ifland, and have juftly claimed the property of the foil, were offended at the Englifh furveyors who were fent from England to furvey their poffeffions. Their oppofition to this arbitrary act of the Englifh government, was foon determined to be rebellion, and meafures immediately purfued to chaftife thefe infidel rebels. By taking a fhort view of the hiftory of this people, and the behaviour of the Englifh government towards them, we will find fome of the true fprings of our modern war with our colonifts, and dependants upon the fupreme legiflature.

Hiftorians inform us that the Carribs are of two forts, different in their colour as well as in their extract and originial. They are diftinguifhed by the epithets of black and yellow Caribs; the latter being the defcendants of the original natives, and the others negroes

negroes brought from Africa aboard an English ship, which was cast away upon the coast of St. Vincent, about an hundred years ago. The negroes having recovered their liberty by this accident, were kindly received by the natives, and settled among them. It is said, that having women of their own, they still continued a distinct people, and soon became numerous. The two sorts of people were not more different in their colour, than in their temper and disposition; the Americans being timid and inoffensive, the Africans hardy, designing, and intrepid. With these qualifications, together with the accession of the negroes which run away from the neighbouring islands, they soon became superior in number and power to the natives, who melted away insensibly as the strangers increased. History does not inform us of any hostilities that these strangers committed upon the natives; and it would rather seem that by intermingling with the original inhabitants, the character of the people had changed from that of the weaker to the stronger. In this situation the Carribs continued for some time, until the French, from the neighbouring islands, by their address, insinuated themselves among them, and purchased the best of their soil for brandy and other French trinkets, which suited the taste of the Carribs. By the address and cunning peculiar to that nation, they got possession of the most fruitful vallies, that interfect the mountains on the leeward side of the island, and brought them into a state of cultivation.

The French and natives lived upon good terms for some time, and the latter embraced the language and religion of the former; yet the neighbourhood of villages and cultivation, was but ill suited to the convenience and genius of a people that subsisted

upon

upon hunting and fishing. There is something in nature which inspires men with a desire of liberty and independence, which, though they naturally love society, yet they shun crowds, and love a certain retirement, still desiring to live free and unrestrained in their actions, without observation or interference of others. The Carribs at last totally abandoned their old possessions, and retired to the windward and level side of the island. The French, it is said, once attempted to enslave these people, and that the Carribs defended their liberties so resolutely, that the French were glad to renounce their design, and were obliged to acknowledge them as a free and independent people.

The French and Carribs continued to live in friendly intercourse and correspondence, and the Carribs retained a power in their own hands of executing justice upon those who did them any real injuries; and it does not appear that ever the French had reason to complain of those natives, for any acts of rigour or injustice in their revenging injuries or affronts. The French king always treated the natives as proprietors of the island, and shewed them respect and regard upon every occasion. But what is somewhat extraordinary, upon the treaty of peace with Great Britain, the French king ceded the island of St Vincent to England, without so much as taking notice of the Carribs. This was giving up what he had always acknowledged was not his own, and the government of Great Britain accepted what they well knew did not belong of right to the king of France. It is no wonder that all nations who have any knowledge of the two empires of France and Britain, should hate both them and the Christian religion which they profess, when they commit, under the cloak of that religion, such manifest acts of injustice. We scarcely find greater violations of the rights of mankind committed among the most barbarous nations, than those which the English and French have been guilty of committing towards the inhabitants of the island of St Vincent.

It must, however, be allowed, that the Carribs, by changing masters at the treaty of peace, changed much for the worse; for, during the French government, they were independent, and were proprietors of the island, but since the English received the supremacy, they have lost their liberty, and are slaves, or to use a more *soft word*, subjects of Britain. The French, who at the time of the peace were reckoned between four or five thousand, soon after abandoned their estates, which were purchased by new adventurers from England, by which means the English soon became a considerable body, possessed of vast property. The Carribs were at this time computed to be a thousand fighting men, and upwards; and it is probable they were far more numerous, but in the treaty, they were never considered but disposed over as the property of France, to the government of Great Britain.

Though the Carribs were not mentioned in the treaty of peace, yet the court of Britain gave instructions in the year 1764, that they should not be disturbed in the possession of their estates, and the commissioners for sales were directed not to attempt any survey, without particular orders for that purpose. The new settlers, after they had time to look about them, perceived with anxiety, that the plain and fertile part of the island was in the possession of the Carribs, to whom its valuable properties rendered it of little more advantage than any equael extent of the rudest and most uncultivated country. Both their fear and their covetousness, operated strongly to make them

them desire the removal of the black inhabitants. Representations were accordingly made in the warmest manner, both by the new settlers and the commissioners of sales, to deprive the Carribs of their possessions, and to grant them such an equivalent, whether in the island or in some other part, as should be thought necessary. The arguments that were used to inforce these representations, were the immediate profits to the crown, from the sale of lands; the dangers arising to those who had already made purchases under the faith and protection of government, as well as to the island in general, from the neighbourhood of a lawless banditti who were strongly attached to the French, with whom they held a constant correspondence in the neighbouring islands, and who, from their religion and manners, were much averse to our people and government.

These representations had the intended effect upon the lords of the British treasury, who, in 1768, issued instructions for the surveying and disposing of the land possessed by the Carribs; for the parts of which that were cleared and cultivated, they were to be paid a certain price per acre in money, and were to have other lands assigned them in return, sufficient for their support, in a different part of the island. The new lands were to be granted and secured for ever to them and their posterity, and to be free from all quitrents, charges, and condition, except peaceable behaviour and obedience to government: these possessions were to descend among them, according to their own customs and usages of inheritance, and were to be for ever unalienable to any white person. Five years were given for effecting this change and transplantation. Nothing could be more unreasonable and repugnant to the principles of nature, and morality,

than

than this proposal of the British government. They were first to rob and divest the Carribs of their natural rights and possessions, and then to secure to them what they had an undoubted a right to possess, as the inhabitants of Britain have to possess the island where they reside. The king of Britain had no more right to the island of St Vincent except to those lands which belonged to the French, than the French have a right to Holland, or any other country which belongs to other people; and therefore, to lay claim to any of the possessions of the Carribs, or to assume dominion over them, was perfect tyranny and despotism. A minister that could be guilty of advising such a measure, ought to have answered for it with his head. The impartial pages of history will post up to future ages the characters of such men, as base, infamous, and detestable.

The Carribs, from many circumstances, concluded that they were now either to be extirpated, or made slaves; they therefore applied to the governor of Martinico for advice and protection. The last he absolutely refused; and as to the first, he advised them to submit to the British government. This advice had no effect upon them. Their answer to the British commissioners was noble and just, for which they deserve to be praised, and for which all true Englishmen must revere them. They said, that the whole island was originally their property; that however, as they had permitted the French to settle upon a part of it, their king might dispose of that part as he pleased; but as they were not his subjects, he had no authority over them, and consequently could not grant or dispose of the part of their country which they had reserved for themselves. They concluded, with absolutely refusing to part with their lands, or to admit

of

of any exchange. It might have been expected, that such sound reasoning would have convinced any Englishman of the iniquity of proceeding against the Carribs; but avaricious adventurers, and ministers of state, whose moral principles hang very easy upon them, seldom feel the force of arguments, when the lust of dominion, and the love of gain rule in their hearts. If the proceedings of the English government against the Carribs, can be vindicated upon any principal of sound and good reasoning, it will be easy to prove that there is now no wickedness in the universe. Selfish politicians, or the hirelings of a state, may attempt to varnish such actions of a minister, with all the false colourings of sophistry and deceit; but in spite of all the thick daubings of falsehood, and the fair strokes of flattery, the vile complexion of the men and their measures, will appear to the view of impartial observers. Ages to come will stand amazed, when they read in the annals of Britain, that in an æra of liberty, and under the government of a pious and religious sovereign, such unjust and arbitrary proceedings should have been carried on.

It may appear to some exceeding strange, that men in a Christian nation, brought up under a free government, and instructed in the principles of liberty, should be so abandoned to reason, justice, and humanity, as to have accepted a commission to survey the lands of a people against their will, and without their consent, when no act of wickedness or injustice was yet imputed to them. Yet such were found, and actually went upon the practice of surveying the lands of the Carribs. The moderation of that people, as well as their steadiness on this occasion, might have confounded the commissioners, provided covetous and interested men were capable of any generous feelings; for they

shewed

shewed an unwillingness to come to violence, and even when it was in their power, did not destroy them. They shewed, however, so much disgust at their making roads into their country, as greatly alarmed the surveyors, and it was found necessary in the beginning of May, 1769, to send an officer and forty men to the surveyors and their company. This small detachment, as if all the country had of right belonged to their masters, took post in the midst of the possessions of the Carribs, where some temporary huts were erected for their reception. But they soon found themselves surrounded, and all communication with their friends, and subsistence cut off, so that they were little better than prisoners. The prudence of the commanding officer, who considered the inequaliy of his force, and the extreme unwillingness of the Carribs, of bringing matters to the last extremity, not only saved the detachment from being cut off, but prevented the smallest violence to be offered on either side. In the mean time, the surveyors and their company were so frighted that they gave over their work, and were permitted to depart with safety; but their huts were demolished, and their new roads broke up, so far as time would permit. This fate of the detachment caused an universal alarm among the English settlers, who were as yet uncertain of the situation of their friends. They immediately took up arms, and joined the few regular forces that were in the island, and marched with speed to the aid of their brethren. Instead of enquiring concerning the justice of their cause, or the righteousness of the behaviour of the surveyors and their party, they were determined at all events to shed blood, provided they could do it with success. But as they found the detachment safe, it was considered as the most prudent step not to

proceed

proceed to violence against the Carribs till they received further instructions from England, and the matter was laid before the king and council. The Carribs agreed to this proposal, and a stop was for this time put to the survey. The Carribs were disposed to have suffered the English to enjoy what had been surrendered to them by the French, and never intended to interrupt them in the enjoyment of their own property; but the new settlers considered the island as their own, and wanted to make the natives vassals of the king of Britain. These Indians were of right, as independent in St. Vincent, as the English in Britain; it was therefore unjust in the English government to seek to deprive them of their natural rights.

When men have a favourite object in view, suited to their leading passion and interest, it is not easy to divert them from pursuing it, however inconsistent it may be with the rights and interests of others. Tho' the planters in St. Vincent were in no degree equal to the reduction of the Carribs, the number of the rivers in the country, and the richness of the soil which they had discovered in their late progress, wrought so powerfully upon their passions, that they could not refrain from expressing their concern at being prevented from bringing matters to an immediate extremity, in terms which gave no favourable opinion of their justice and humanity. False reports were industriously spread abroad, which kept the island in perpetual fear and alarm; and the most passionate complaints were sent home, representing the Carribs as a most daring and incorrigible set of rebels. It is somewhat surprizing how a people could be rebels against a government to which they never owed any allegiance, and which instead of deserving any regard from the Carribs, deserved both to be despised and resisted. This may shew us how easy it is to form a rebellion, and determine the most just and righteous people in the world, incorrigible and obstinate rebels. The Carribs were never under either the French nor English government, but were a free and independent people, and therefore owed no allegiance to the monarchs of France or Great Britain. How then could they be rebels, when they were only defending their own rights and properties against invaders, who were unjustly and violently attempting to wrest them from them? These covetous and cruel planters were so zealous for the extirpation of the Carribs, for the sake of their lands, that they proposed to have them transported to the coast of Africa, or to some desart island in that quarter. The indignation of the reader must rise at the thoughts of such a shocking proposal from British Christians, who boast of their liberties, religion, and humanity.

When the new lieutenant governor of the new islands arrived at St Vincent's, he issued a proclamation to quiet the minds of the Carribs, and to remove their fears and suspicions; nor do we find that any further violence was committed, than the destruction of the new roads, and the burning of a house which belonged to a person that was particularly obnoxious to them; and they quietly submitted to the imprisonment of one of their chiefs, who was suspected of committing this outrage; nor is there the smallest proof, that their was a drop of blood spilt in all this commotion.

The government at home seem to have been conscious of the iniquity of the proceedings against the Carribs, for notwithstanding the warm remonstrances that were made in behalf of this measure, they seemed for some time unwilling to proceed to violence against these people. In the beginning of the year 1771, the commiſſioners held another meeting with ſeveral chiefs of the Carribs, and propoſed a new partition and exchange of lands upon a narrower ſcale, and terms more favourable to them, than were contained in the plan that had been formerly propoſed; but the Carribs rejected every propoſal for parting with their lands, with the greateſt firmneſs and reſolution: And when the queſtion was put to them, whether they acknowledged themſelves ſubjects of the king of Great Britain, and would take the oath of allegiance, they boldly refuſed, and anſwered in the negative. They ſaid they were independent, and were not ſubject to either the kings of Great Britain or France. To this anſwer the commiſſioners could make no rational reply. The king of Britain had no right in juſtice to demand allegiance from a free and independent people and if any allegiance was due, it was due from the planters to the government of the iſland. It has been alledged, that the French in the neighbouring iſlands ſpirited the Carribs to this conduct, which is more than has ever been proved; and ſuppoſe they had, it was no reaſon why Britain ſhould have plundered them of their properties, and robbed them of their natural rights. This refuſal of the Carribs was determined to be contumacy, and orders were iſſued from home for an hoſtile force to be ſent againſt them. Two regiments were ordered from North America, to join as many already at St Vincent's, or what could be ſpared from the neighbouring iſlands for that ſervice, which, with his majeſty's ſhips on that ſtation, were to reduce the Carribs to a due ſubmiſſion to government, or, provided they continued obſtinate, that they might be removed from the iſland to ſuch places as ſhould be thought moſt proper for their reception; the ſtricteſt orders

orders at the same time being given that they should be furnished with ships for their transportation, plentifully provided with provisions and necessaries, and treated with all imaginable humanity in their passage. This was a strange kind of humanity and benevolence first to rob a people of their natural rights and possessions, without any fault on their part, and then discreetly set them adrift in some strange country to shift for themselves, left at the mercy of some unknown people to be slaves, or to perish as the caprice of strangers should happen to operate. Such proceedings are perhaps not to be equalled in the history of any protestant free people, upon the face of the globe. The success and event of this expedition was not known when this affair of St Vincent became a matter of debate in parliament, in December 9th, this year. The arguments on both sides of the question. will appear in the following parliamentary history.

"Soon after the opening of the session, upon the presenting of an estimate from the war office in the committee of supply, of the land service for the ensuing year, the number of troops that were stated to be in the West-India-islands, gave an opportunity to the gentlemen in opposition, to animadvert upon this expedition, and to give notice, that they would, on a future day, propose an enquiry, into its nature, justice, and propriety, together with the motives that led to so extraordinary a measure. This enquiry being agreed to by administration, the matter was afterwards frequently brought up; but still deferred, in hopes of obtaining new information, and to give an opportunity of procuring and considering the necessary papers.

It was accordingly a considerable time after the Christmas recess, before this affair was taken finally into consideration; when at length, two general officers

officers were examined, as to the latest accounts they had received of the state of their regiments, which were then employed on the service against the Carribs. One of these gentlemen read part of a letter which he had received upon the subject from St Vincent's, in which the expedition was greatly complained of, not only in respect of its having been undertaken in the rainy season, which had occasioned a great mortality among the troops, but also with regard to its injustice and cruelty, with both of which it was strongly charged by the writer; who emphatically complained, that the poor Carribs had been very ill used; and wished, with the energy characteristic of an officer, that the contrivers and promoters of the expedition, might be brought to a speedy and severe account. By the same authority it was represented, that the woods were so thick, that the Carribs killed our men, with the greatest security to themselves, and without their being able even to see the enemy that destroyed them; that at the time of writing the letter, which was on the 14th of November, the troops' had not been able to penetrate above four miles into their country.

It was not then enquired of administration, whether they had received any late accounts from the island; when to the surprize of every body, it appeared that their latest intelligence from thence, was above a month prior in date, to the letter which had been read by the general. A gentleman who had been lieutenant-governor of the New Islands, was examined as to the temper, behaviour, and disposition of the Carribs, of all which he gave a very favourable account, and represented them as a quiet inoffensive people; he was farther asked, if he had heard that the planters were envious of them for their lands, to which

which he anſwered in the affirmative; and being preſſed as to particular names, mentioned one of conſiderable rank and conſequence in the iſland, and who had a principal ſhare in all the meaſures that had been purſued for ſtripping them of their poſſeſſions.

Some officers were examined, who had ſerved, or borne command, at different times in St Vincent's; theſe gentlemen, in general, gave favourable accounts of the Carribs, and attributed entirely their late turbulent and ſuſpicious temper, to the attempts that had been made to deprive them of their lands: they all concurred in their accounts of the unhealthineſs of the iſland, and particularly in the rainy ſeaſon, when, they declared, it muſt prove fatal to any troops that were under a neceſſity of acting in it, and that the conſtitution of ſuch as eſcaped with life, would be totally ruined.

On the other ſide, one of the principal planters in the iſland, and of conſiderable rank by his office, with ſome others, were examined. They, in general, deſcribed the Carribs as a faithleſs, cruel, and treacherous, race, who were abandoned to all manner of exceſſes, particularly with reſpect to liquor, in which ſtate they were capable of the moſt barbarous actions. That while they continued on the iſland, there could be no ſecurity for the perſons or property of the inhabitants; they were charged with murders, robberies, with enticing the negro ſlaves from their maſters, and deſtroying others whom they caught in the fields; no particular proofs were, however, brought in ſupport of theſe charges. The connections and intelligence which the Carribs held with the French, and their application to the governor of Martinique for protection and aſſiſtance, were ſhewn in a very dangerous light; and no care was neglected to deſcribe

the

the fatal consequences that must attend the island, whenever a war broke out with France, with such a deadly enemy lying in its bosom. Their mortal enmity to our government and people, was also much insisted on; and it was concluded upon the whole, that there was no other alternative, but that either his majesty's natural subjects, or the Carribs, must quit the island, if the latter are permitted to continue in their present state of independence.

After several strictures upon the nature of this evidence, and on the interested views by which it was said to be apparently directed, the following motions were made, 1st, That the expedition against the Carribs in the island of St Vincent was undertaken, without sufficient provocation on the part of those unhappy people, and at the instigation of persons interested in their destruction, and appears to be intended to end in their total extirpation; 2dly, That the sending the troops, part of which were totally unprovided with camp equipage and necessaries, on that service, in the unhealthy season of the year, is not justified by any necessity of immediately increasing the military force in that island, was contrary to the voice of the governour, and must prove unnecessarily destructive to some of the best troops in the service, probably defeat the purpose for which they were sent, and bring disgrace on his majesty's arms; and, 3dly, That an humble address be presented, desiring that his majesty will be graciously pleased to acquaint the house, by whose advice the measure was undertaken, of attacking the Carribs in the island of St Vincent; and of sending the troops for that purpose in the most unhealthy season of the year; a measure equally repugnant to the known humanity of his majesty's temper, disgraceful to his arms, and dishonourable to the character of the British nation.

These motions were principally supported upon the injustice of the measure, and the dishonour it brought upon our national character, as being equally a violation of the natural rights of mankind, and contrary to his majesty's proclamation of the year 1764, in favour of the Carribs; on the extreme cruelty of attempting to transport a whole people from their native soil, and to land them defenceless on the coast of Africa, where they had no right, no property, no connection, and where they must be liable to all the dangers and enmities, to which Europeans, or any others, who were turned adrift in a strange country, would be subject; that they had been guilty of no act of forfeiture, even supposing them to be natural subjects of Great Britain, unless an opposition to a violent invasion of their rights and properties, was to be considered as such; that the only evidence of any weight against them, was himself the deviser of the projects that had been formed for their extirpation, was deeply interested in their destruction; that on the contrary, the united testimony on the other side, where there was not a possibility, of supposing the smallest bias or partiality, was uniformly in favour of the Carribs, and represented them as a quiet, peaceable, and inoffensive people, and to all appearance, well affected to our government, until they were urged by violence and injustice to a different conduct. These arguments, with such others as the state we have already represented afford, were concluded with severe strictures on the weakness of those counsels, which had blindly adopted the views of avaricious, rapacious, and merciless planters, and thereby rendering government the instrument of their iniquitous design, engaged it in cruel

cruel, unjust, and dishonourable measures, which were not more injurious to the Carribs, than destructive to ourselves, by wantonly sporting with the constitutions and lives of some of our bravest troops, whose former services merited another return, and who were now sacrificed upon an inglorious service, in which they were ashamed to draw their swords.

On the other side it was observed, that an amazing fund of tenderness and humanity had been displayed in favour of the Carribs, while the smallest degree of either was refused to our natural born subjects and countrymen, who had purchased estates at high prices from the crown under the sanction of its protection and security, and whose lives and fortunes were at stake in the event of the present expedition. That the charge of injustice was ill founded, as the yellow Carribs, who were the aborigines, and real proprietors of the island, were in no degree affected by the present measures, except only so far as they would obtain security, by the reduction or removal of a cruel and perfidious race of savages, by whom they had been nearly exterminated; that it could not be pretended, that the black Carribs had any legal or natural rights in the island, but those which they had obtained through the kindness and hospitality of the natives; and that those rights, would, in the eye of the strictest justice, have been fully cancelled, by their subsequent conduct and ingratitude.

That the charge of cruelty was equally ill founded; the removal of the black Carribs being the last resort; and only to be put in execution, in case of their proving so incorrigible, that all means would be found ineffectual for reducing them to such a state of submission to government, as was absolutely necessary, not only for the security but the preservation of the island; that

that even in that last extremity, the measure of transportation was guarded from being accompanied with any circumstances of cruelty, or even of hardship, except those which might be supposed to arise from their feelings, on quitting a country in which they had hitherto lived, and going to another, equally fit for them, but with which they were not yet acquainted; that whether they were removed to the coast of Africa, or to the island of St Mathew, care had been taken, that they were to have sufficient lands assigned them for their support, and were to be laid down, in nearly the same degrees of latitude and climate, and in a country furnished with much the same advantages as to fishing and hunting, which they had enjoyed at St Vincent's.

It was said, that government had neither adopted the views, nor been misled by the schemes of interested planters; that it had duly weighed, as well the circumstances of the island, as the representations of the governour, council, and assembly, together with those of the commissioners for the sale of lands; that as the Carribs were possessed of near two thirds of the profitable lands, and the French inhabitants of a great part of the remainder, it was evident, that we never could in that state, have a natural interest or strength in the island, sufficient for its security; that as these lands were of no particular value to the Carribs, who had neither means nor inclination to cultivate them, equitable terms had been repeatedly proposed to them for an exchange, all of which, they not only contumaciously rejected, but daringly disclaimed all allegiance to the king, and refused all obedience to government. As to the strictures that had been passed, with respect to the employment of the troops in an unhealthy climate and season, there were answered by
the

the necessity of the occasion; and the measure justified upon that principle, by the practice of all ages.

Upon a division on the separate questions, after long debates, the first motion was rejected by a majority of 206, against 88 who supported it; the majority was less upon the others, as the house grew thinner.

About the same time, the expedition which gave birth to this enquiry, was also terminated. The Carribs, notwithstanding the strength of their fastnesses, their courage, in which they were not at all deficient, and their expertness in the use of fire arms, were under many disadvantages in this war. They were surrounded by sea and land, their quarters becoming every day more contracted, were cut off from their great source of subsistence by fishing, and their bodies worn down by continual watching and fatigue. Our troops also suffered infinitely in the service. Without a considerable reinforcement, it was probable, the reduction of the enemy could not be effected. The object, either for advantage, or glory, was not worthy of so much toil and fatigue, even if the justice of such a war could be clearly defended.

These mutual sufferings, and the dispositions they gave rise to, brought on a treaty between the Carribs and Major General Dalrymple, who commanded the forces, by which the former obtained better conditions than they had reason to expect. The original object of the war, the transplantation to Africa, was wholly abandoned. The Carribs on their part acknowledged his majesty's sovereignty without reserve, agreed to take an oath of fidelity and allegiance, and to submit to the laws and government of the island, so far as relates to their intercourse, and to all transactions with the white inhabitants; but in their own districts.

diſtricts, and in all matters that relate to their intercourſe with each other, they are to retain their ancient policy, and ſtill to be governed by thoſe cuſtoms and uſages, to which they have given the force of laws. They have alſo ceded a large tract of very valuable land to the crown; but the diſtricts which they ſtill retain, are ſecured in perpetuity to them and their poſterity. There are a number of other articles, which relate to domeſtic regulation, or tend to the future tranquility and ſecurity of the iſland.

The loſs upon this expedition, though conſiderable, was not altogether ſo great as was apprehended from the nature, length, and ſeverity of the ſervice. The killed and wounded did not much exceed 150, among the former of which was a lieutenant-colonel, and ſome other officers; the lives loſt by the climate amounted to 110; but there remained 428 ſick, at the time of concluding the treaty.

After ſuch proceedings againſt an innocent and inoffenſive people, which owed no allegiance to the Britiſh government, and had given the nation no real offence, the after behaviour of the miniſtry towards the American coloniſts, will be no ſurprize to any perſon who examines the cauſes of things attentively.

CHAP.

Chap. VII.

The American Congress assembles—Forms an association—Their resolves—They address the people of Great Britain—They write to the people of Quebec—A view of their rights—Proceedings at home, &c.

FROM the beginning of the present controversy with the colonies, it was always imagined, and also affirmed at home by the ministry and their friends, that the colonists were greatly divided among themselves; that they would never unite; that they would not hang together; that they were only under a temporary ferment, created by the artifice of popular and designing men, that would soon subside when once they saw that Great Britain was in earnest to support her authority. And that notwithstanding the riotous disposition of some of the colonies, they were in general cowards, and durst not appear before the king's forces. This was the stile of the ministry and their party at home, and was echoed in all the venal pamphlets and news-papers published throughout the kingdom.

The assembly of the representatives of twelve of the colonies, which has since received the name of the congress, met at Philadelphia, on the 5th of September this year, and, after more than a month's deliberation, proceeded to several resolutions which shewed that they were in earnest, as well as unanimous in their opposition to the new statutes of the British legislature. Upon the 14th of October, the congress proceeded to business, and after reciting those laws that were particularly obnoxious, they came to several animated resolutions, which, in their then situation, were surprizing to all the world*. The association which they entered into is a bold and intrepid resolution to maintain what they consider to be their just rights and privileges, and a purpose to pursue such measures as may best support these rights against invasion, from the ministerial power of Great Britain. As this association will appear in its truest colours by itself

* Friday, *October* 14, 1774. The Congress came into the following Resolutions:——

WHEREAS, since the close of the last war, the British parliament claiming a power of right to bind the people of America by statute, in all cases whatsoever, hath in some acts expressly imposed taxes on them, and in others under various pretences, but in fact for the purpose of raising a revenue, hath imposed rates and duties payable in these colonies, established a board of commissioners with unconstitutional powers, and extended the jurisdiction of courts of admiralty, not only for collecting the said duties, but for the trial of causes merely arising within the body of a county.

And whereas in consequence of other statutes, judges, who before held only estates at will in their offices, have been made dependant on the crown alone for their salaries, and standing armies kept in time of peace. And it has lately been resolved in parliament, that by force of a statute made in the thirty-fifth year of the reign of King Henry the Eighth, colonists may be transported to England and tried there upon accusations for treasons and misprisions, or concealment of treasons committed in the colonies; and by a late statute, such trials have been directed in cases therein mentioned.

And whereas in the last session of parliament, three statutes were made; one intituled, "An act to discontinue in such manner, and for such time as are therein mentioned, the landing and discharging, lading or shipping of goods, wares and merchandize, at the town, and within the harbour of Boston, in the province of Massachusetts-Bay, in North America." Another intituled, "An act for the better regulating the government of the province of the Massachusetts-Bay, in New-England." And another intituled, "An act for the impartial administration of justice, in the cases of persons questioned for any act done by them in the execution of the law, or for the suppression of riots and tumults, in the province of the Massachusetts-Bay, in New-England." And another statute was then made, "For making more effectual provision for the government of the province of Quebec, &c." All which statutes are impolitic, unjust and cruel, as well as unconstitutional, and most dangerous and destructive of American rights.

And whereas, assemblies have been frequently dissolved, contrary to the rights of the people, when they

itself, I shall give it in the very words of the congress, and leave it to the judgment of every reader, to determine of it as he may judge proper.

WE, his majesty's most loyal subjects, the delegates of the several colonies of New-Hampshire, Massachusett's-Bay, Rhode-Island, Connecticut, New-York, New-Jersey, Pennsylvania, the Three Lower Counties

they attempted to deliberate on grievances; and their dutiful, humble, loyal and reasonable petitions to the crown for redress, have been repeatedly treated with contempt by his majesty's ministers of state.

The good people of the several colonies of New-Hampshire, Massachusett's-Bay, Rhode-Island and Providence plantations, Connecticut, New-York, New-Jersey, Pennsylvania, New-Castle, Kent and Sussex on Delaware, Maryland, Virginia, North-Carolina and South-Carolina justly alarmed at these arbitrary proceedings of parliament and administration, have severally elected constituted, and appointed deputies to meet and sit in general congress in the city of Philadelphia, in order to obtain such establishment as that their religion, laws, and liberties may not be subverted: Whereupon the deputies so appointed being now assembled in a full and free representation of these colonies, taking into their most serious consideration the best means of retaining the ends aforesaid, do in the first place, as Englishmen their ancestors in like cases have usually done, for asserting and vindicating their rights and liberties, DECLARE.

That the inhabitants of the English colonies in North-America, by the immutable laws of nature, the principles of the English constitution, and the several charters or compacts, have the following RIGHTS.——

Resolved, N. C. D. 1, That they are entitled to life, liberty, and property; and they have never ceded to any sovereign power whatever, a right to dispose of either without their consent.

Resolved, N. C. D. 2. That our ancestors, who first settled these colonies, were at the time of their emigration from the mother country, entitled to all the rights, liberties, and immunities of free and natural born subjects, within the realm of England.

Resolved, N. C. D. 3. That by such emigration they by no means forfeited, surrendered, or lost any of those rights, but that they were, and their descendants now are, entitled to the exercise and enjoyment of all such of them, as their local and other circumstances enable them to exercise and enjoy.

Resolved, 4. That the foundation of English liberty and of all free government, is a right in the people to participate in their legislative council: and as the English colonists are not represented, and from their local and other circumstances cannot properly be represented in the British parliament, they are entitled to a free and exclusive power of

ties of Newcastle, Kent, and Sussex, on Delaware, Maryland, Virginia, North-Carolina, and South-Carolina, deputed to represent them in a continental Congress, held in the city of Philadelphia, on the fifth day of September, 1774, avowing our allegiance to his majesty, our affection and regard for our fellow-subjects in Great Britain and elsewhere, affected with the deepest anxiety, and most alarming apprehensions at those grievances and distresses, with which his majesty's American subjects are oppressed, and having taken under our most serious deliberation, the state of the whole continent, find, that the present unhappy situation

of legislation in their several provincial legislatures, where their right of representation can alone be preserved, in all cases of taxation and internal polity, subject only to the negative of their sovereign, in such manner as has been heretofore accustomed: But from the necessity of the case, and a regard to the mutual interests of both countries, we chearfully consent to the operation of such acts of the British parliament as are bona fide, restrained to the regulation of our external commerce, for the purpose of securing the commercial advantages of the whole empire to the mother country, and the commercial benefits of its respective members, excluding every idea of taxation internal or external, for raising a revenue on the subjects in America without their consent.

Resolved, N. C. D. 5. That the respective colonies are entitled to the common law of England, and more especially to the great and inestimable priviledge of being tried by their peers in the vicinage, according to the course of that law.

Resolved, 6. That they are entitled to the benefit of such of the English statutes, as existed at the time of their colonization; and

which they have, by experience, respectively found to be applicable to their several local and other circumstances.

Resolved, N.C.D.7. That these his majesty's colonies, are likewise entitled to all the immunities and priviledges granted and confirmed to them by royal charters, or secured by their several codes of provincial laws.

Resolved, N. C. D. 8. That they have a right peaceably to assemble, consider of their grievances, and petition the king; and that all prosecutions, prohibitory proclamations, and commitments for the same, are illegal.

Resolved, N. C. D. 9. That the keeping a standing army in these colonies, in times of peace, without the consent of the legislature of that colony in which such army is kept, is against law.

Resolved, N. C. D. 10. It is indispensibly necessary to good government, and rendered essential by the English constitution, that the constituent branches of the legislature be independent of each other; that, therefore, the exercise of legislative power in several colonies, by a council appointed, during pleasure, by the crown, is unconstitutional, dangerous, and destructive

situation of our affairs, is occasioned by a ruinous system of colony administration adopted by the British ministry about the year 1762, evidently calculated for inslaving these colonies, and with them, the British empire. In prosecution of which system, various acts of parliament have been passed for raising a revenue in America, for depriving the American subjects, in many instances, of the constitutional trial by jury, exposing their lives to danger, by directing a new and illegal trial beyond the seas, for crimes alledged to have been committed in America: And in prosecution of the same system, several late, cruel and oppressive acts

tive to the freedom of American legislation.

All and each of which, the aforesaid deputies in behalf of themselves, and their constituents, do claim, demand, and insist on, as their indubitable rights and liberties; which cannot be legally taken from them, altered or abridged by any power whatever, without their own consent, by their representatives in their several provincial legislatures.

In the course of our inquiry, we find many infringements and violations of the foregoing rights; which, from an ardent desire that harmony and mutual intercourse of affection and interest may be restored, we pass over for the present, and proceed to state such acts and measures as have been adopted since the last war, which demonstrate a system formed to inslave America.

Resolved, N. C. D. That the following acts of parliament are infringements and violations of the rights of the colonists; and that the repeal of them is essentially necessary, in order to restore harmony between Great Britain and the American colonies, viz.

The several acts of 4 George III. ch. 15. and ch. 34.——5 Geo. III. ch. 25.——6 Geo. III. ch. 52.——7 Geo. III. ch: 41 and ch. 46.—8 Geo. III. ch. 22. which impose duties for the purpose of raising a revenue in America, extend the powers of the admiralty courts beyond their ancient limits, deprive the American subject of trial by jury, authorise the judge's certificate to indemnify the prosecuter from damages, that he might otherwise be liable to, requiring oppressive security from a claimant of ships and goods seized, before he shall be allowed to defend his property, and are subversive of American rights.

Also, 12 Geo. III. ch. 24. intituled " An act for the better securing " his majesty's dock yards, maga " zines, ships, ammunition and " stores." Which declares a new offence in America, and deprives the American subject of a constitutional trial by jury of the vicinage, by authorising the trial of any person charged with the committing of any offence described in the said act out of the realm, to be indicted and tried for the same in any shire or county within the realm.

Also the three acts passed in the last session of parliament, for stopping the port and blocking up the harbour of Boston, for altering the charter

acts have been passed respecting the town of Boston and the Massachusett's-Bay, and also an act for extending the province of Quebec, so as to border on the western frontiers of these colonies, establishing an arbitrary government therein, and discouraging the settlement of British subjects in that wide extended country; thus by the influence of civil principles and ancient prejudices to dispose the inhabitants to act with hostility against the free protestant colonies, whenever a wicked ministry shall chuse so to direct them.

To obtain redress of these grievances, which threaten destruction to the lives, liberty, and property of his charter and government of Massachusetts-Bay, and that which is intituled, "An act for the better administration of justice, &c."

Also the act passed in the same session for establishing the Roman catholic religion in the province of Quebec, abolishing the equitable system of English laws, and erecting a tyranny there, to the great danger, from so total a dissimilarity of religion, law and government to the neighbouring British colonies, by the assistance of whose blood and treasure the said country was conquered from France.

Also the act passed in the same session for the better providing suitable quarters for officers and soldiers in his majesty's service in North America.

Also, that the keeping a standing army in several of these colonies, in time of peace, without the consent of the legislature of the colony in which such army is kept, is against law.

The Congress, from time to time, passed the following Resolves:

Resolved, That this Congress do approve of the opposition made by the inhabitants of the Massachusett's-Bay, to the execution of the late acts of parliament; and if the same shall be attempted to be carried into execution by force, in such case, all America ought to support them in their opposition.

Resolved, That it is the opinion of this body, that the removal of the people of Boston into the country, would be, not only extremely difficult in the execution, but so important in its consequences, as to require the utmost deliberation before it is adopted. But in case the provincial meeting of that colony shall judge it *absolutely* necessary, it is the opinion of this Congress, that all America ought to contribute towards recompensing them for the injury they may thereby sustain; and it will be recommended accordingly.

Resolved, That this Congress do recommend to the inhabitants of the colony of the Massachusett's-Bay, to submit to a suspension of the administration of justice, where it cannot be procured in a legal and peaceable manner, under the rules of the charter, and the laws founded thereon, until the effects of our application for a repeal of the acts, by which their charter rights are infringed, is known.

Resolved,

his majesty's subjects in North-America, we were of opinion, that a non-importation, non-consumption, and non-exportation agreement, faithfully adhered to, will prove the most speedy, effectual, and peaceable measure; And therefore we do, for ourselves and the inhabitants of the several colonies, whom we represent, firmly agree and associate under the sacred ties of virtue, honour, and love of our country as follows,

First, That from and after the first day of December next, we will not import into British America,

Bbb from

Resolved unanimously, That every person or persons whomsoever, who shall take, accept, or act under any commission or authority, in any wise derived from the act passed in the last session of parliament, changing the form of government, and violating the charter of the province of Massachusett's-Bay, ought to be held in detestation and abhorrence by all good men, and considered as the wicked tools of that despotism, which is preparing to destroy those rights, which God, nature, and compact hath given to America.

Resolved unanimously, That the people of Boston and the Massachusett's-Bay, be advised still to conduct themselves peaceably towards his excellency General Gage, and his majesty's troops now stationed in the town of Boston, as far as can possibly consist with their immediate safety and the security of the town; avoiding and discountenancing every violation of his majesty's property, or any insult to his troops; and that they peaceably and firmly persevere in the line in which they are now conducting themselves on the defensive.

Resolved, That the seizing, or attempting to seize, any person in America, in order to transport such person beyond the sea, for trial of offences committed within the body of a county in America, being against law, will justify, and ought to meet with resistance and reprisal.

Saturday, *October* 22.

Resolved, As the opinion of the congress, that it will be necessary, that a congress should be held on the 10th day of May next, unless the redress of grievances, which we have desired, be obtained before that time.—And we recommend, that the same be held at the city of Philadelphia, and that all the colonies in North America chuse deputies as soon as possible, to attend such congress.

Tuesday, *October* 25.

Resolved, That the congress in their own names, and in behalf of all those whom they represent, do present their grateful acknowledgements to those truly noble, honourable, and patriotic advocates of civil and religious liberty, who have so generously and powerfully, though unsuccessfully, espoused and defended the cause of America, both in and out of parliament.

from Great Britain or Ireland, any goods wares or merchandize whatsoever, or from any other place any such goods, wares or merchandize, as shall have been exported from Great Britain or Ireland; nor will we, after that day, import any East-India tea from any part of the world; nor any molasses, syrups, paneles, coffee or piemento, from the British plantations, or from Dominica; nor wines from Maderia, or the Western Islands; nor foreign indigo.

Second, That we will neither import, nor purchase any slave imported, after the first day of December next; after which time, we will wholly discontinue the slave trade, and will neither be concerned in it ourselves, nor will we hire our vessels, nor sell our commodities or manufactures to those who are concerned in it.

Third, As a non-consumption agreement, strictly adhered to, will be an effectual security for the observation of the non-importation, we, as above solemnly agree and associate, that, from this day, we will not purchase or use any tea imported on account of the East-India company, or any on which a duty hath been or shall be paid; and from and after the first day of March next, we will not purchase or use any of East India tea nor will we nor shall any person for or under us, purchase or use, any of those goods, wares or merchandize, we have agreed not to import, which we shall know or have cause to suspect, were imported after the first day of December except such as come under the rules and directions of the tenth article hereafter mentioned.

Fourth, The earnest desire we have, not to injure our fellow subjects in Great Britain, Ireland, or the West-Indies, induces us to suspend a non-exportation, until the tenth day of September 1775; at which time, if the said acts and parts of acts of the British parliament, herein after mentioned, are not repealed, we will not, directly or indirectly, export any merchandize or commodity whatsoever to Great Britain, Ireland, or the West-Indies, except rice to Europe.

Fifth, Such as are merchants, and use the British and Irish trade, will give orders, as soon as possible, to their factors, agents, and correspondents, in Great Britain and Ireland, not to ship any goods to them, on any pretence whatsoever, as they cannot be received in America; and if any merchant, residing in Great Britain or Ireland, shall directly or indirectly ship any goods, wares, or merchandize, for America, in order to break the said non-importation agreement, or in any manner contravene the same, on such unworthy conduct being well attested, it ought to be made public; and, on the same being so done, we will not from thenceforth have any commercial connection with such merchant.

Sixth, That such as are owners of vessels will give positive orders to their captains or masters, not to receive on board their vessels any goods prohibited by the said non-importation agreement, on pain of immediate dismission from their service.

Seventh, We will use our utmost endeavours to improve the breed of Sheep and increase their number to the greatest extent, and to that end, we will kill them as sparingly as may be, especially those of the most profitable kind; nor will we export any to the West-Indies or elsewhere; and those of us who are or may become over-stocked with, or can conveniently spare any sheep, will dispose of them to our neighbours, especially to the poorer sort, on moderate terms.

Eighth, That we will in our several stations encourage frugality, œconomy, and industry; and promote agriculture, arts and the manufactures of this country, discourage every species of extravagance and dissipation, especially all horse-racing, and all kinds of gaming, cock-fighting, exhibitions of shews, plays, and on the death of any relation or friend, none of us, or any of our families, will go into any further mourning dress, than a black crape or ribbon on the arm or hat for gentlemen, and a black ribbon or necklace for ladies, and we will discontinue the giving of gloves and scarfs at funerals.

Ninth, That such as are venders of goods or merchandize, will not take advantage of the scarcity of goods that may be occasioned by this association, but will sell the same at the rates we have been respectively accustomed to do, for twelve months last past.— And if any vender of goods or merchandize, shall sell any such goods on higher terms, or shall in any manner, or by any device whatsoever, violate or depart from this agreement, no person, ought, nor will any of us deal with any such person, or his, or her factor or agent, at any time thereafter, for any commodity whatever.

Tenth, In case any merchant, trader, or other persons shall export any goods or merchandize after the first day of December, and before the first day of February next, the same ought forthwith at the election of the owner, to be either re-shipped or delivered up to the committee of the county or town wherein they shall be imported, to be stored at the risque of the importer, until the non-importation agreement shall cease, or be sold under the direction of the committee aforesaid; and in the last mentioned case, the owner or owners of such goods, shall be reimbursed (out of the saels) the first cost and charges, the profit, if any, to be applied towards relieving and employing such

such poor inhabitants of the town of Boston, as are immediate sufferers by the Boston port bill; and a particular account of all goods so returned, stored, or sold, to be inserted in the public papers; and if any goods or merchandizes shall be imported after the first day of February, the some ought forthwith to be sent back again, without breaking any of the packages thereof.

Eleventh, That a committee be chosen in every county, city and town, by those who are qualified to vote for representatives in the legislature, whose business it shall be, attentively to observe the conduct of all persons touching the association; and when it shall be made to appear to the satisfaction of a majority of any such committee, that any person within the limits of their appointment has violated this association, that such majority do forthwith cause the truth of the case to be published in the gazette, to the end, that all such foes to the rights of British America may be publicly known, and universally contemned as the enemies of American liberty; and thenceforth we respectively will break of all dealings with him or her.

Twelfth, That the committee of correspondence in the respective colonies do frequently inspect the entries of their custom-houses, and inform each other from time to time of the true state thereof, and of every other material circumstance that may occur relative to this association.

Thirteenth, That all manufactures of this country be sold at reasonable prices, so that no undue advantage be taken of a future scarcity of goods.

Fourteenth, And we do further agree and resolve, that we will have no trade, commerce, dealings or intercourse whatsoever, with any colony or province in North America, which shall not accede to, or which shall hereafter violate this association, but will hold them as unworthy of the rights of freemen, and as inimical to the liberties of their country.

And we do solemnly bind ourselves and our constituents, under the ties aforesaid, to adhere to this association until such parts of the several acts of parliament passed since the close of last war, as impose or continue duties on tea, wine, molasses, syrups, pancies, coffee, sugar, piemento, indigo, foreign paper, glass and painters colours, imported into America, and extend the powers of the admiralty courts beyond their ancient limits, deprive the American subject of trial by jury, authorise the judge's certificate to indemnify the prosecutor from damages, that he might otherwise be liable to, from a trial by his peers, require oppressive security from a claimant of ships or goods seized before he shall be allowed to defend his property, are repealed.—And until that part of the act of the 12. Geo. 3. ch. 24. intituled, " An act for the better securing his majesty's dock-yards, magazines, ships, ammunition, and stores," by which, any persons charged with committing any of the crimes therein described, in America, may be tried in any shire or county within the realm, is repealed.—And until the four acts passed in the last session of parliament, viz. that for stopping the port and blocking up the harbour of Boston,—That for altering the charter and goverment of the Massachusett's-Bay.—And that which is intituled, " An act for the better administration of justice, &c." are repealed. And we recommend it to the provincial conventions, and to the committees in the respective colonies, to establish such farther regulations as they may think proper, for carrying into execution this association.

The

The foregoing association determined upon by the Congress, was ordered to be subscribed by the several members thereof; to which they set their names*.

In their address to the people of Great Britain they insist upon their right of British subjects, and affirm that no power on earth has a right to take away their property without their consent; and they claim all the rights secured to subjects by the English constitution, especially that invaluable one of trial by jury. The

---

* In Congress, Philadelphia, Oct. 20, 1774, signed,
PEYTON RANDOLPH, President.
New-Hampshire.
John Sullivan,
Nathaniel Folsom.
Massachusett's-Bay.
Thomas Cushing,
Samuel Adams,
John Adams,
Robert Treat Paine.
Rhode-Island.
Stephen Hopkins,
Samuel Ward.
Connecticut.
Eliphalet Dyer,
Roger Sherman,
Silas Deane.
New-York.
Isaac Low,
John Alsop,
John Jay,
James Duane,
William Floyd,
Henry Wisner,
S. Boerum.
New-Jersey.
James Kinsey,
William Livingston,
Stephen Crane,
Richard Smith.
Pennsylvania.
Joseph Galloway,

John Dickinson,
Charles Humphreys,
Thomas Mifflin,
Edward Biddle,
John Morton,
George Ross.
New-Castle, &c.
Cæsar Rodney,
Thomas M'Kean,
George Read.
Maryland.
Matthew Tilghman,
Thomas Johnson,
William Paca,
Samuel Chase.
Virginia.
Richard Henry Lee,
George Washington,
P. Henry, Jun.
Richard Bland,
Benjamin Harrison,
Edmund Pendleton.
North-Carolina.
William Hooper,
Joseph Hewes,
R. Caswell.
South-Carolina.
Henry Middleton,
Thomas Lynch,
Christopher Gadsden,
John Rutledge,
Edward Rutledge.

They consider it essential to English liberty that no man be condemned unheard, or punished for supposed offences, without having an opportunity of making his defence. They gave it as their opinion that the legislature of Great Britain is not authorised by the constitution to establish a religion fraught with sanguinary and impious tenets, or to erect an arbitrary form of government in any quarter of the globe. They consider the proprietors of the soil in America as much masters of their own property, as those of Great Britain are, and affirm that they are not bound to submit to any parliament not of their own election. They insist that the intervention of the sea which divides America from Britain, can make no disparity in rights; nor can the distance of three thousand miles from the royal palace, make the rights of subjects less than the distance of three hundred miles. Reason, they declare, looks with indignation on such distinctions, and free subjects can never perceive their propriety. They express their amazement at the pretensions of the British parliament to bind them in all cases whatsoever without exception, without their consent, and to take and use their property when and in what manner they please: and to make the colonists pensioners on their bounty, and that they can hold it no longer than they vouchsafe to permit. Such declarations they consider as heresies in English politics, which can no more operate to deprive them of their property, than the interdicts of the Pope can divest kings of their sceptres, which the laws of the land, and the voice of the people, have placed in their hands.

They attribute the plan for enslaving them to that minister and his associates, who made the late inglorious peace, and declare that ever since that time, that scheme

scheme of oppression has been pertinaciously carrying into execution. In this address they next appeal to the mother country, how patiently they have suffered the restraint upon their trade in every way that could conduce to the emolument of Britain. Say they, you have exercised unbounded authority over the the sea; you have named the ports and nations to which alone our merchandize should be carried, and with whom alone we should trade; and though some of these restrictions were grievous, we nevertheless did not complain; we looked up to you as our parent state to which we were bound by the strongest ties, and were happy in being instrumental to your prosperity and grandeur. They warmly call upon the inhabitants of Britain to bear witness to their loyalty, and attachment of the common interests of the whole empire, and appeal to them, if they did not, in the last war, add all the strength of the American continent to the force which repelled the common enemy. Did we not, say they, leave our native shores, and meet disease and death to promote the success of the British arms in foreign climates? And did not you thank us for our zeal, and even reimburse us large sums of money, which you confessed we had advanced beyond our proportion, and far beyond our abilities. To what causes then, are we to attribute this sudden change of treatment, and that system of slavery which was prepared for us at the restoration of the peace?

They add, before we had recovered from the distresses, which ever attend war, an attempt was made to drain our country of money by the oppressive stamp act. Painted glass, and other commodities, which you would not permit us to purchase of other nations, were taxed: Nay, though no wine is made in any country subject to the British state, you prohibited us

Ccc

from

from procuring it of foreigners, without paying a tax imposed by your parliament on all we imported. These, say they, and many other impositions, were laid upon us unjustly and unconstitutionally, for the express purpose of raising a revenue. In order to silence complaint, it was indeed provided that this revenue should be expended in America for its protection and defence. But, say they, these exactions, however, can receive no justification from a pretended necessity of defending us. They are lavishly squandered, on court favourites and ministerial dependents, generally avowed enemies to America, and employing themselves by partial representations, to traduce and embroil the colonies. For the necessary support of government here, say the colonists, we ever were, and ever shall be ready to provide. And whenever the exigencies of the state may require it, we shall, as we have hitherto done, chearfully contribute our full proportion of men and money. To inforce this unconstitutional and unjust scheme of taxation, every fence that the wisdom of our British ancestors had carefully made against arbitrary power, has been violently thrown down in America, and the inestimable right of trial by jury taken away, in cases that touch both life and property. It has been ordained that whenever offences should be committed in the colonies against particular acts, imposing various duties and restrictions upon trade, the prosecutor might bring his action for the penalties in the court of the admiralty; by which means the subject lost the advantage of being tried by an honest and uninfluenced jury of the vicinage, and was subject to the sad necessity of being judged by a creature of the crown, and according to the course of law which exempts the prosecutor from the trouble of proving his accusation, and obliges the

defendant

defendant either to evince his innocence or suffer. To give this new judicatory the greater importance, and as if with a design to protect false accusers, it is further provided that the judge's certificate of their having being probable causes of seizure and prosecution, shall protect the prosecutor from actions at common law, for recovery of damages.

In this address it is also represented, that although justice is impartially administered in all the colonies, yet by the construction of some, and the direction of other acts of parliament, offenders are to be taken by force, together with all such persons as may be pointed out as witnesses, and carried to England there to be tried in a distant land by a jury of strangers, and subject to all the disadvantages that result from want of friends, want of witnesses, and want of money. The colonists in this address do not forget to take notice of the tea act, with a design to raise a revenue in America; and it must be allowed they represent this affair both warmly and judiciously. They observe, that when the design of raising a revenue from the duties upon tea, imported into America, was in a great measure rendered abortive by their ceasing to import that commodity, a scheme was concerted by the ministry with the East India company, and an act passed enabling and encouraging them to transport and vend their tea in the colonies. Aware of the danger of giving success to this insiduous manœuvre, and of permitting a precedent of taxation thus to be established among us, say they, various methods were tried to elude the stroke. The people of Boston, then ruled by a governour, whom, as well as his predecessor, Sir Francis Bernards, all America considers as her enemy, were extremely embarassed. The ships which had arrived with the tea were, by his management, prevented from returning. The duties would have been paid; the cargoes landed and exposed to sale; a governour's influence would have procured and protected many purchasers. While the town was suspended by deliberations on this subject, the tea was destroyed. But supposing, say the colonists, a trespass was committed, and the proprietors of the tea entitled to damages; the courts of law were open, and judges appointed by the crown presided in them. The East India company, however, did not think proper to commence any suits, nor did they even demand satisfaction either from individuals, or from the community in general. The ministry officiously made the case their own, and the great council of the nation descended to intermeddle with private property. Divers papers, letters, and other unauthenticated ex parte evidence, were laid before them; neither the persons who destroyed the tea, nor the people of Boston, were called upon to answer the complaints. The ministry being incensed in being disappointed in a favourite scheme, were determined to recur from the little arts of finesse, to open force and unmanly violence. The port of Boston was blocked up by a fleet, and an army placed in the town. Their trade was to be suspended, and thousands reduced to the necessity of gaining subsistance from charity, till they should submit to pass under the yoke, and consent to become slaves, by confessing the omnipotence of parliament, and acquiescing in whatever disposition they might think proper to make of their own lives and properties.

Having represented this state of facts, they then warmly exclaim, Let justice and humanity cease to be the boast of your nation! Consult your history, examine your records of former transactions; nay, turn the annals of the many arbitrary states and kingdoms that surround you, and shew us a single instance of men being condemned to suffer for imputed crimes, unheard, unquestioned, and without even the specious formality of a trial; and too, by a law made expressly for the purpose, and had no existence at the time that the fact was committed. If it be difficult to reconcile these proceedings to the genius and temper of your laws and constitution, the task will become more arduous when we call upon our ministerial enemies, to justify condemning men untried, and by hear-say, but involving the innocent in one common punishment with the guilty, and for the act of thirty or forty, to bring poverty, distress, and calamity on thirty thousand souls, and those not your enemies, but your friends, brethren, and fellow citizens. They make use of several other arguments and topics, which they urge home with all the force of language and warm zeal, and the impartial world in some ages hence, when the mist of prejudice is removed from their eyes, will be obliged to confess that there is much reason in what they say. What has greatly darkened this controversy between Great Britain and the colonies, is the difference of political reasoning on different sides of the question. The advocates for the dominion of parliament, draw their arguments from mystical subtleties, grounded upon obsolete laws that were never constitutional, and which few, unless men learned in the law, can understand. From these they draw positive conclusions, as if their first principles were self-evident, and conclude that nothing except obstinacy, or real want of understanding, can hinder all others from perceiving the justness of their arguments. The colonies and their friends establish their arguments upon common sense; and the constitutional laws of the empire, which, as they are plain and self-evident, are calculated to affect all minds that are not warped by prejudice, or biassed by private interest.

There is no question but men's prejudices and interests are concerned on both sides, but the extreme appears to be more on the one side than the other, provided we confine our views to the evidence upon the face of the arguments. The rights of mankind are not mysteries to be lodged in the hands of a few, as articles of faith are in some countries, but like the common salvation, are exposed to the view of every individual person, and the privilege of all to know, as well as to enjoy. When doctrines of state are so deep, as to be beyond the reach of men of common understanding, they are not fit to be put in practice. Whatsoever men are bound to obey ought first to be made a plain object of their understanding, otherwise obedience is not a reasonable service. All honest men will ever desire to have those designs they profess to be for the good of society, made as manifest to the members thereof as possible, and will never want to impose their authority, except under the divine light of reason and truth.

But it will be necessary to take a view of the management at home, which gave rise to this spirited and violent opposition of the colonies. This will naturally lead us to take a view of the arguments made use of by the parties at home in support of the different sides of the question in which they were engaged. It has often been affirmed by people at home, that the colonists deduced their arguments from speeches made in the parliament of Britain, and from writings sent from this country to America. Upon this supposition, the patriots as they are called in derision,

are

are principally blamed for the opposition and resistance which the colonists have made. But such as consider their petitions, resolves, and apologies impartially, will soon perceive that they needed no assistance from the mother country, in any matter of argument. There is a clearness and precision in their writings, united with a warm zeal for truth and liberty, that is not to be met with in any of these venal performances which have been published against them. In some future period of time, when men read this controversy with calm impartiality, they will give judgment freely on the side of the colonists, and stand in amazement that there should have been the smallest dispute in a case so clear and obvious.

The state of parties were this year much the same as before, except that the general strength of the opposition was much declined. The Rockingham party continued unbroken, and consistently pursued its first original line of public conduct. Though it was often overpowered by numbers, it notwithstanding continued formidable, and gave some severe checks to the prevailing influence of the court. The same difference of opinion and affections, and the same occasional union among others, took place between them and that party which was attached to the Earl of Chatham. This appearance of the want of true union, very much enfeebled the opposition.

While matters were in this situation at home, an incident took place which kindled into a violent flame of discontent and rage in the colonies. The insignificant duty of threepence the pound on tea, which had been singly left behind in the year 1770, when all other articles enumerated in the same bill, for the purpose of raising a revenue, had been repealed, was now determined to be made the fatal bane of contention

tion between the mother country and her colonies. It had been foretold by those who struggled hard for the repeal of the whole, and who always declared against every notion of an internal taxation of America; that the leaving of one duty, and the discharging of the others, could answer no other purpose than the lessening of that scanty revenue, which was scarcely sufficient, in its whole amount, to answer the expence of the collection; that by this means, instead of profit, a new charge to supply the deficiency would be thrown upon the state at home, while all the other evils, which were then acknowledged as the motives of a partial repeal, would be continued in their utmost extent.

These political predictions in the end proved to have a real foundation, and were but too well verified by after events. The discontents of the colonies encreased from the measures of government, and an universal spirit of opposition to the tea act prevailed among them all. The measures of the ministry, and the prevailing party in parliament, so irritated the colonists, that they formed the association which has been already mentioned, and passed the spirited resolutions which have been taken notice of, to shew the ministry that they were not ready to comply with such unreasonable demands. In this state of affairs there was one thing which greatly increased the division between the mother country and the colonists; the governours of most of the colonies and the people, were in a continual state of warfare; and such was the opposition between them, that what the one proposed the others were always determined to contradict. It has been generally believed that this evil had its rise at home in the mother country, and that the governours had their instructions how to behave from the ministry, which they servilely executed, without considering

sidering either the reasonableness of the commands, or the temper of the colonists. It is, however, manifest, and sad experience has proved, that the governours have not understood, or they have willfully perverted the state of the colonies in their accounts thereof to the ministry; for it is hardly possible that government would have proceeded so far as they have done, provided they had not received false information from their servants. The variances between the governours and the people put an end to all regular proceedings; the assemblies were repeatedly called, and suddenly dissolved. When they were sitting they were employed in repeating grievances, and framing remonstrances, and in the midst of their disputes new matters sprung up, besides the duty on tea and the custom-house, which encreased the general discontent. A measure which had been lately adopted of rendering the governours and judges dependent on the crown, by having their salaries paid by government, and to be removed at the pleasure of the sovereign, gave the colonies great offence. They considered this measure as an attempt of the crown to render all offices of government subservient to arbitrary purposes, that they might employ them at their pleasure to suppress the liberties of the people. Whether this was the design of government or not, it was certainly the opinion of the colonists concerning this measure. In an ordinary course of affairs it would probably have been over looked, but in such a violent collision of parties it was the mean of kindling a most violent flame of opposition and resentment.

It is not to be expected in such a state of agitation, when the laws were in a great measure suspended, and men left to pursue the dictates of their passions and resentment, that every thing would proceed in an orderly

orderly courfe, confiftent with right reafon and true juftice. The Gafpee, an armed fchooner, had been ftationed at Rhode-Ifland to prevent fmuggling, for which that place had been remarkable; the vigilance of the officer who commanded the veffel fo enraged the people, that they boarded her at midnight to the amount of two hundred armed men, and after wounding the commander, and forcing him and his people to go afhore, fet fire to the fchooner. This greatly incenfed the government, and a reward of 500 l. together with a pardon if claimed by an accomplice, was offered for difcovering and apprehending any of the perfons concerned in this atrocious act. But no effectual difcovery was made. This daring act of fome fmugglers was, by the courtiers, imputed to the whole colony, though fome as daring adventures have been performed in the mother country, without being confidered as the act and deed of a whole province. It has been obferved in this hiftory, that many of the captains of veffels, that were fent upon this office of preventing fmuggling, were often ignorant of their duty, and exceedingly arbitrary in their behaviour, which tended much to irritate the people, and to ftir them up to actions which, in ordinary cafes, were far from their thoughts. And it is probable that there was fomething of this fort that gave occafion to this outrage.

Before matters came to fuch a crifis as they did afterwards, a very ftrange and extraordinary accident happened, which revived with double force all the ill temper and animofity that had fubfifted between the government and the people, in the province of Maffachufetts-Bay. This was a difcovery and publication of fome confidential letters, which had been written during the courfe of the unhappy difputes with the mother country, by the then governour, and deputy governour, to the miniſtry of England. Theſe letters contained a very unfavourable repreſentation of the ſtate of affairs, the temper and diſpoſition of the people, and the views of the leaders in that province; and tended to ſhew, not only the neceſſity of the moſt coercive meaſures, but that even a very conſiderable change of the conſtitution, and ſyſtem of government was neceſſary, to inforce the obedience of the colony. Theſe letters had been ſent by Governor Hutchinſon privately and in confidence; but the people of the colony inſiſted, that they were evidently intended to influence government, and ought therefore to be ſhown to ſuch perſons as had an intereſt in preſerving their privileges. Upon the death of a gentleman, in whoſe poſſeſſion theſe letters happened to be lodged, they, by ſome means which are not yet known, fell into the hands of the agent to the colony of Maſſachuſett's-Bay, who immediately transferred them to the aſſembly of that province, which was then ſitting at Boſton.

The indignation and rage which thoſe letters excited on the one ſide, and the confuſion on the other, neither need, nor can admit of deſcription. The people found themſelves miſrepreſented and betrayed, by one whom they imagined bound in duty to ſupport their intereſt, and perceived that the late meaſures of government had proceeded from falſe information, that had been given by their governour, and lieutenant governour.

In the frenzy of rage and reſentment which theſe letters occaſioned, the houſe of repreſentatives paſſed many violent reſolutions. The letters were preſented to the council, under the ſtricteſt injunctions from the repreſentatives, that the perſons who were to ſhew them, ſhould not by any means ſuffer them, even for a moment, out of their own immediate hands. This affront to the governour was adopted by the council; and upon his requiring to examine the letters that were attributed to him, thereby to acknowledge them if they were genuine, or disapprove them if they were spurious, that board, under the pretence of this restriction, refused to deliver them into his hands, but sent a committee to open them before him, that he might examine the hand writing. To this indignity he was obliged to submit, as well as to the mortification of acknowledging the signature that was affixed to them.

The colony of Massachusetts-Bay was sufficiently irritated before, and needed no new fuel to encrease the flame of their resentment.—These letters pushed them on to measures of the most spirited nature; the house of assembly passed a petition and remonstrance to his majesty, in which they charged the governour, and lieutenant-governour, with being betrayers of their trusts, and of the people they governed; of giving private, partial, and false information; declared them enemies to the colony, and prayed for justice against them; and for their speedy removal from their places. Such were the discontent, and so weak were the powers of government in that assembly, that those charges, with many others, were carried by a majority of 82 to 12.

The time of the arrival of the ships with the execrated tea approaching, when the new plan of taxation was to have been put in execution, the people assembled in different parts in great bodies, and proceeded to take such measures as seemed most effectual to prevent the landing of the cargoes. The consignees, who had been appointed by the East-India company to receive the tea, were obliged in most

places

places to give up their appointment, and to enter into public engagements not to act in that capacity. Committees were appointed by the people in different towns and provinces, whom they invested with such powers as they supposed themselves authorized to give. They were impowered to inspect the books of merchants, to propose tests, to punish those they considered to be contumacious, by the dangerous prescription of declaring them enemies to their country, and to assemble the people when they thought it necessary. Their power was, in one word, as indefinite as the authority under which they acted. The assemblies which were held on these occasions, were frequently violent and hasty in their resolutions; their passions were warm, and they did not wait long to deliberate what they were to do. The greatest part of their resolutions were exceedingly derogatory to the supreme legislature; government had now lost their affection and they paid the governours no honour nor regard. This will always be the case when rulers themselves transgress the laws, by substituting power in the place of justice, without regarding the natural and fundamental statutes of the compact between the governours, and the governed. When the people, by the tyranny and mismanagement of governours, are driven back to a state of nature, rulers must expect that they will use their natural powers, in such a manner as best suits their inclination or advantage. The same reason that makes princes keep standing armies in the time of peace, makes the people use their natural powers on particular occasions. Both are intended for the support of rights which each party lays claim to, and which they consider it just to maintain.

The

The colonists were at this time greatly inflamed, as they had been for some time past, not only by the treatment of government, but by inflammatory writings, which were published by some zealous persons in the opposition. From the time that the riot happened at Rhode-Island, till the passing of the Boston Port-bill, almost all things tended to bring matters to a crisis. The public news papers were made vehicles of conveyance, to transmit to different parties the sentiments of those on their side, and were frequently filled with as much rancour as argument. In the peaceful colony of Philadelphia, long celebrated for the excellency of its police, and the temperate and placid manners of its inhabitants, printed papers were dispersed, warning the pilots on the Delaware not to conduct any of the tea ships that were expected into the harbour, which were only sent out for the purpose of enslaving and poisoning all America; at the same time, giving them plainly to understand it was expected, that they would apply their knowledge of the river, under the colour of their profession, in such a manner as would effectually secure their country from the danger with which it was threatened. A similar publication made its appearance at New-York, wherein the tea ships were represented as loaded with setters, forged in Britain, to bind the colonists in slavery; and vengeance was denounced against all persons who should dare, in any manner, to introduce those chains. All the colonies seemed instantly to have united in this point.

The town of Boston, which had been so long obnoxious to government, was the scene of the first outrage. What rendered the people of that town more violent in opposition to landing the tea, it was consigned to a son of Governour Hutchison, whose letters

letters had misrepresented them, and enraged the government against them. They perceived a monopoly formed in favour of very obnoxious persons, and with a design of confirming a most odious tax. When three ships laden with tea arrived in that port, the masters were frightened into a concession, that if the persons to whom the tea was consigned, the board of customs, and the Fort of Castle William, would permit, they would return with their cargoes to England. But they could not fulfil their promise, for the consignees refused to discharge the captains from the obligations under which they were chartered for the delivery of their cargoes; the custom-house refused them a clearance, and the governour to grant them a passport for clearing the fort. The people of the town easily perceived, that as the ships lay so near, it would be impossible to hinder the tea from being landed by degrees, notwithstanding any guard they could keep, or measures they could take to prevent it; and they understood, that if once it was landed, nothing could prevent its being disposed of, and thereby the purpose of establishing a monopoly, and raising a revenue would be accomplished. To prevent this consequence, which the people considered as the most dangerous, a number of armed men, under the disguise of Mohawk Indians, boarded the ships, and in a short time, discharged their cargoes of tea into the sea, without doing any other damage, or offering any injury to the captains or their crews. It appears somewhat strange, that the government, civil and military, the Fort of Castle William, and armed ships in the harbour, were totally inactive on this occasion. Some smaller quantities of tea were thrown into the sea at Boston and Carolina; but in general the commissioners for the sale of that commodity, were obliged to give up their employment, and none durst receive the cargoes that were configned to them. The masters of vessels, from these circumstances, as well from the knowledge of their danger, and the determined resolution of the people, readily complied with the terms that were prescribed, of returning to England, without entangling themselves with any entry at the custom-houses. There was some tea landed at New-York, under the cannon of a man of war; but the government were obliged to consent to its being locked up from use, and the consignees durst not expose it to sale. Such was the issue of this tea scheme, which was foolish in its contrivance, and unsuccessful in its execution; a scheme which no wise man would have begun, and no good man would have chosen to execute. Ages to come will look upon the history of this transaction in the light of fable, and will scarcely be able to believe, that in an age renowned for knowledge in arts and policy, such instances of folly and madness could have existed. The destroying of this tea, was undoubtedly an unwarrantable act of outrage, for which the actors are much to be blamed, and deserved to have been punished; but it is scarcely chargeable with as much folly, as the act which appointed the tea to be sent to Boston, and the other parts of America. It is plain that it could neither bring a revenue to the government, nor ready money to the proprietors; and seems only to have been sent to provoke the outrage which happened, that government might have some plausible reason of falling out with the colonies, and for sending an armed force to curb the spirit of liberty which prevailed among them. In times of corruption, when bad men are in possession of power, it almost always happens that a spirit of freedom is an eye-sore to

tlers, which they interpret into the signification of faction, and in process of time, work up into the form of rebellion, that they may have some handle to proceed against it, and if possible, to crush what they so heartily abhor. But in the history of nations it does not once appear that ever the spirit of liberty, attended with virtue, was subdued or overcome. Licentiousness will always end in ruin, and will never fail to bring nations to destruction; but while righteousness prevails, it will be impossible to ruin them, for thereby they will be exalted. It would be of service to politicians to consider attentively the progress of society, and the means by which empires have risen and fallen; it would help them to form their schemes with more discretion, and prevent them falling into dangerous extremes.

When the parliament assembled upon the 13th of January, it was expected that some notice would have been taken of the disturbances in America, but concerning that subject there was a perfect silence. Nothing was done in parliament with regard to American affairs till the 7th of March, when dispatches arrived with an account of destroying the tea at Boston. This information arrived a few days after the question on the Grenville bill was carried. The minister being defeated in that question felt his spirits in a state of agitation, which were far from being soothed by the news from Boston. This disagreeable intelligence occasioned a message from the throne to both houses of parliament, wherein appeared the greatest anxiety, and the warmest zeal. This message set forth, that unwarrantable practices were carried on in North-America, and that violent proceedings had lately been pursued at the town and port of Boston, with a view of obstructing the commerce of this kingdom, upon grounds and pretences immediately subversive of its constitution. It was also signified that his majesty confided in his parliament for the support of his authority, and trusted in their attachment to the common interest and welfare of his dominions, and that they would not only enable him effectually to take such measures as might be most likely to put an immediate stop to these disorders, but also take into their consideration what further regulations, and permanent provisions, should be necessary for the better securing the execution of the laws, and the just dependence of the colonies upon the crown and parliament of Great-Britain.

This message was attended with a great number of papers relating to the transactions in the colonies, containing copies of extracts from the several governours; the commander in chief of the forces; from the admiral in Boston harbour; from the persons to whom the tea had been consigned; to one of the ring-leaders of the faction in Boston, with the votes and resolves of the town previous to the landing of the tea, and narratives of the transactions which followed that event; a petition from the consignees to the council of Massachusetts-Bay, praying that their persons and property might be taken under the protection of government, with the refusal of the council to interfere in any manner of business: a proclamation issued by the governour to forbid factious assemblies of the meetings of the inhabitants; and the transactions of the Massachusett's council, condemning the measures of destroying the tea, and advising legal prosecutions against the perpetrators, none of whom were known, nor were there any possibility of their discovery. These papers also contained details from the different governours, of all the transactions relative

tive to the tea, which took place in their respective governments, from the first intelligence of their being shipped in England, to the date of their letters; as also the threatenings, and prophetical informations, which had been often sent to the gentlemen to whom the tea was consigned: copies of printed papers, inflammatory hand bill, alarms, illegal proceedings of committees, and extraordinary minutes of council, had all been transported across the Atlantic, to the government in England, and were now laid before the parliament. In these papers the uniformity of stile, language and sentiment, fully discovered that the colonists were generally of the same opinion, and that not only the Massachusett's-Bay, but all America were offended at the proceedings of the ministry.

When these papers were laid before the house, they were aggravated by ministerial comments, which set them forth in the most attrocious and criminal point of view, particularly those which related to the transactions of Boston. In these the conduct of the governour was represented in the most favourable and shining point of light; to which was contrasted, the vicious, factious, and rebellious behaviour and disposition of the colonies. In behalf of the governour it was said, that he had taken every measure which prudence could suggest, or good policy justify for the security of the property of the East-India company, the safety of the consignees, and the preserving of order and quiet in the town. Every civil precaution, to prevent the mischiefs that followed had been used in vain. His majesty's council, the militia, and the corps of cadets, had all been seperately applied to for their assistance in the preservation of the public peace, and the support of the laws, but all without effect; they refused or declined doing their duty. The

sheriff

sheriff read a declaration to the faction of that town, at their town meeting by which they were commanded to break up their illegal assembly; but the proclamation was treated with the greatest contempt, and the sheriff insulted in the grossest manner.

That he had it undoubtedly in his power, by calling in the assistance of the naval force which was in the harbour, to have prevented the destruction of the tea; but as the leading men in Boston had always made great complaints of the interruption of the army and navy, and charged all disturbances of every sort to their account, he, with great prudence and temperance, determined from the beginning to decline a measure which would be so irritating to the minds of the people; and might well have hoped, from this confidence in their conduct, and trust reposed in the civil power, that he should have calmed their turbulence and preserved the public tranquility. Thus, said the ministry, the people of Boston were fairly tried. They were left to their own conduct, and the exercise of their own judgment, and the result has given the lie to all their former professions. They are now, say they, without an excuse; and all the powers of government in that province, are found insufficient to prevent the most violent outrages. The loyal and peaceable people of a mercantile town, as they affect to be peculiarly considered, have given a notable proof to the world of their justice, moderation, loyalty, and affection for the mother country, by wantonly committing to the waves a valuable commodity, the property of another loyal mercantile body of subjects; without the pretence of necessity, even supposing that their opposition to the payment of the duties, could justify such a plea; as they had nothing to do but to adhere to their own resolution of non-consumption

consumption, effectually to evade the revenue laws. It was concluded upon the whole, that by an impartial view of the papers now before them, it would manifestly appear, that nothing could be done by either civil, military, or naval officers, to effectuate the re-establishment of tranquility and order in that province, without addition of parliamentary powers, to give efficacy to their proceedings. That no person employed by government could, in an act, however common or legal, fulfil the duties of his office or station, without being exclaimed against by the licentious, as an infringement of their liberties. That it was the settled opinion of some of the wisest men both in England and America, and those the best acquainted with the affairs of the colonies, that in their present state of government, no measures whatsoever could be pursued, that could, in any degree, remedy those glaring evils which is every day growing to a more enormous and dangerous height. That parliament, and parliament only, was capable of re-establishing tranquility among those turbulent people, and of bringing order out of confusion. And that it was therefore incumbent on every member to weigh and consider with an attention suitable to the importance of the subject, the purport of the papers before them, and totally lay all prejudices aside, to form his opinion upon the measures most eligible to be pursued, for supporting the supreme legislative authority of parliament, and the great interests of the British empire. This is the substance of what was urged by the ministry, when they presented the papers. The grand object which the ministry had in view, and which they coloured with the name of the supremacy of parliament, was the supremacy and dominion of themselves, which they wanted to establish on the authority of

colonists were subjects of the British empire, that they were to be governed by the fundamental statutes of the constitution; and that no new forms of government, or modes of taxation, could be admitted in any part of the British empire, contrary to the fundamental laws, without dissolving the ancient frame of government, and bringing the people again to a state of nature. The supremacy of the parliament of Britain could only *legally* and *reasonably* extend as far as those places where its members represented, or to subjects that had been settled by agreement to be referred to their jurisdiction. To proceed farther was to establish in parliament a despotism over one part of the empire, which is not permitted in other parts, which few people will think reasonable when applied to themselves.

The party in parliament which had strong presumptions that the disorders in the colonies proceeded as much from the mismanagement of government, as from the turbulent temper of the colonies, proposed an examination of the measures that had been pursued for some time past, and that the conduct of the several governours, and the orders that had been sent to them from the ministry, should be examined. This was a very fair and reasonable proposal, which honest men could not decently refuse. But the ministry strongly opposed all retrospect views of their past conduct, alledging that it only tended to inflame the minds of the people, and would exasperate them more against government. The business they said was urgent and important, and required a speedy discussion; and that in the enquiry, some great and important points would come under their consideration. Particularly, is America any longer to be dependent on this country? How far is it to be connected? In

the colonies should not be given up? But if this question is decided in the negative, then it would be necessary to examine in what manner their subordination should be preserved, and the authority of this country inforced? These points required the most serious investigation, in which the retrospect recommended would be unnecessary, and perhaps dangerous, as encouraging those whom it was the business of parliament, by every means, to reduce to obedience. This method of reasoning was sophistical and delusory; for it suggested that there were no other methods of conciliating the affections of the colonies, and securing their dependence on the mother country, except those that were calculated to support the dominion of the ministry, and secure them and their friends in their places and pensions. Instead of any of those questions which have been mentioned, it might perhaps have been much better for the honour and dignity of the nation, and the supreme legislature, never to have called their authority in question, but to have proceeded to reverse the laws complained of, and to rectify those false steps of government which had occasioned the present discontents. It has almost been the case in all ages, with all empires and governments, that have as yet existed, that their power and authority were never called in question, till they began to stretch them beyond their just bounds; and then by making new statutes to inforce the power, they suggested reasons of doubt whether they were possessed of any such authority. It is highly probable, that had the ministry pursued the advice given them by the minority, and made such a reformation as the nature of the subject required, that we should not have heard of the independency of America for a century to come.

Many plausible, but selfish arguments, were used by the

the miniftry to incenfe the nation againft the colonifts; but the ftrongeft, and which had moft effect, was, that our trade to America would ceafe to exift, if the flagrant outrage at Bofton fhould pafs unpunifhed. By ftrong reprefentations of this evil, the people began to be inflamed againft the colonifts, and in the time of this artificial fermentation, the miniftry pufhed on their fchemes of coercion and violence with the greateft rapidity. They knew the minority would not choofe to refift in exprefs terms, what was fo pofitively affirmed to be for the advantage of the nation, or if they did, they would foon lofe all their popularity; they therefore made the beft of this opportunity to carry their points in the houfe of commons. By carrying the vote of addrefs to the king, giving him thanks for the communication of the papers that had been laid before the houfe, the miniftry gained a great advantage; for they found by the difpofition of the houfe, which was ftrongly againft taking any retrofpect view of things paft, that they would confine themfelves to the mere behaviour of the Americans. The violence of the colonifts was manifeft and indifputable, and while no other reafons were produced except what appeared in the face of their actions, it was the moft likely thing in the world, that any propofition againft them would be carried. It was fortunate for the miniftry that no part of the weaknefs and diforderly ftate of fo many governments, was laid before the houfe, for in this cafe they were likely to get clear of feveral years mifmanagement, which would have been a clog to all their motions, and muft certainly have iffued in their difgrace.

It appeared manifeft that the ftorm that was gathering againft the colonies, would fall firft upon that of Maffachufett's-Bay. This made the agent for that colony prefent a petition to the houfe, by way of precaution, desiring that he might be permitted to lay before them the *acta regia* of Queen Elizabeth, and her successors, for the security of the planters and their descendants, and the perpetual enjoyment of their liberties. These proofs he alledged had never been laid before the house, nor had the colonies ever had an opportunity to ascertain and defend them. This petition was received without much opposition, and ordered to ly upon the table.

The minister, after having moved that the king's message of the 7th of March should be read, opened his plan for the restoring of peace, order, justice and commerce, in the province of Massachusetts-Bay. He stated that the opposition to the authority of parliament had always originated in that colony; and that colony had been always instigated by the irregular and seditious proceedings of the town of Boston. That, therefore, for the purpose of a thorough reformation, it became necessary to begin with that town, which, by a late unparalleled outrage, had led the way to the destruction of commerce in all parts of America. That if a severe and exemplary punishment was not inflicted on this heinous act, Great-Britain would be wanting in the protection she owed to her most peaceful and meritorious subjects. That, had such an insult been offered to British property in a foreign port, the nation would have been called upon to demand satisfaction. He would therefore propose that the town of Boston should be obliged to pay for the tea which had been destroyed in their port. That the injury was indeed done by persons unknown and in disguise, but that the town magistracy had taken no notice of it, had never made any search for the offenders, and therefore, by a manifest neglect of a known duty, became accomplices in the guilt. That the fining of communities for their neglect of punishing offences committed within their limits, was justified by several examples. These examples were one in the case of London, one in the case of Edinburgh, and another in the case of Glasgow, with regard to Dr Lamb, Captain Porteus, and Mr Campbell. These examples were said to be strong, and in point for such punishments. It was not a single act of violence. It was a series of seditious practices of every kind, and carried on for several years. He was of opinion, therefore, that it would not be sufficient to punish the town of Boston, by obliging her to make a pecuniary satisfaction for the injury, which, by not endeavouring to prevent and punish, she had in fact encouraged; security must be given in future, that trade may be safely carried on, properly protected, laws obeyed, and duties regularly paid; otherwise the punishment of a single illegal act is no reformation. It would, he said, be proper to take away from Boston the privilege of a port, until his majesty should be satisfied in these particulars, and publicly declare in council, on a proper certificate of the good behaviour of the town, that he was satisfied. Until this should happen, the customhouse officers, which were not now safe in Boston, or safe no longer than when they neglected their duty, should be removed to Salem where they might exercise their functions. By this Boston would certainly suffer. But she ought to suffer; and by this resolution would suffer less punishment than her delinquents fully justified. For she was not wholly secluded from all supply. She was, by this proposition, only to be virtually removed seventeen miles from the sea. The duration of her punishment was entirely in her own power. For when she should discharge this debt to the East-India company, which had been contracted by her own violence, and had given full assurances of obedience in future to the laws of trade and revenue; there was no doubt but that his majesty, to whom he proposed to leave that power, would again open the port, and exercise that mercy which was agreeable to his disposition. He strongly recommended unanimity, and said that this was a crisis that demanded vigour. He was by no means an enemy to lenient measures. Resolutions of warning and censure will avail nothing; now is the time to stand out and defy them; to defy them with firmness and without fear. A conviction must be produced to America that we are in earnest, and will proceed with firmness and vigour. This conviction would be lost if they found us doubting and hesitating. Some friends to British authority may suffer a little, but if with this temporary inconveniency we compare the loss of the country, and its due obedience, it will bear no comparison. It is said the Americans will not pay their debts; this they threatened before the repeal of the stamp act. The act was repealed. What was the consequence. They did not pay. This threatening, if attended to, must disable parliament equally in all her operations. This act will not require a military power to enforce it; four or five frigates will be sufficient. But if they should not be sufficient, he would not scruple to use a military force, which might act with effect, and without bloodshed. The other colonies will not take fire at the proper punishment inflicted on those who have disobeyed the laws. They will leave them to suffer their own punishments. If they do combine with them, the consequence of their rebellion belong not to us, but to them. We are only answerable that our measures be just and equitable. Let us proceed, says he, with firmness, justice, and resolution; which

course

course, if pursued, will certainly produce that due obedience to the laws of this country, and security of the trade of this people, which I so earnestly wish for. These are the arguments of the minister which he used to support his motion for bringing in the Boston Port-bill; and accordingly, leave was given for bringing it in.

In the progress of this a motion was made for an amendment, for the purpose of laying a fine on the town of Boston, equivalent to the damage sustained by the East-India company. If they refused to pay this fine, that the other penalties mentioned in the bill, might be inflicted. This amendment was rejected, and this bill pregnant with so many important consequences, was pushed on with so much vigour and dispatch, that it did not remain long in the house. It is somewhat surprizing that a law so full of direful consequences, should have been received with so much applause and approbation, as this did at the first. Without enquiring into the reason of the behaviour of the people of Boston, they were condemned unheard, and disfranchised without ever having their cause brought before those who pretended to be their judges. The equity of obliging a delinquent and refractory colony to make satisfaction for the disorders which were supposed to have arisen from their factious temper, and negligent police, was taken for granted to be a necessary exertion of the powers of government, and many things exceptionable in the act were, on that account, overlooked. But when these proceedings of parliament are accurately considered, and the speech of the minister seriously analized, they will appear to be pregnant with baneful influence to every species of liberty. The speech of the minister declares, that he took for granted what neither the British constitution

stitution nor the colonists admit to be true, namely, that the parliament of Britain have a right to impose taxes, where the people have no representation; and that resistance to foreign laws is worthy of severe punishment.—That the parliament of Britain has a right to take away what it never had a right to give; namely, a right for men to enjoy the possessions which they had purchased from the original proprietors of a country where Britain had no jurisdiction. The equity and justice which the speech superficially mentions, are only words without any meaning, unless that justice varies with the climate, and equity changes with the longitude and latitude. For what he so warmly recommends as just and equitable in Boston, would be accounted lawless tyranny in any part of Great-Britain.

At this time the friends of the colonies in parliament were divided; one party applauded the present measures as lenient and gentle; others continued to stand upon their old ground, and maintained their constant principles. In the course of the debate in the progress of the bill, they seem to have been truer prophets than the minister; for almost all the events which they foretold have nearly come to pass, but not one word of his prophecies have been accomplished. Opposition to this bill encreased, during the time of the debates. Mr Bolan, agent for the council of Massachusett's-Bay, presented a petition, desiring to be heard for the said council, and in behalf of himself and others, the inhabitants in the town of Boston. The house refused to hear the petition. It was said that the agent of the council was not agent for the corporation, and no agent could be received from a corporate body, except he were appointed by all the necessary constituent parts of that body. Besides the

council

council was fluctuating, and the body by which he was appointed could not be than exifting. This vote rejecting the petition was severely censured. It was certainly very inconsistent to receive a petition from the same person a few days before, and refuse his petition at this time for want of a qualification, they allowed him then to be possessed of. What made this rejection of the petition appear more extraordinary was, that at that very time the house of peers was actually hearing Mr Bolan at their bar upon his petition, as a person duly qualified. The same objection might be made to all American agents, none of them were then qualified as the minister required, and thus all communication between the parliament and the colonies, was than cut off; at the same time they were making laws to oppress them. It will be difficult for a benevolent citizen of the world, in some future period of time, to believe that there were such measures carried on in a parliament of Great-Britain, consisting of men professing the protestant religion, and bearing the Christian name. They will be ready to consider this part of the history of Britain in the light of a fable or romance, contrived by some ingenious person to amuse the reader, without any intention of finding credit, or expecting to be accounted a true historian.

After some softening motions had been proposed and rejected, the minister brought in another bill, to which the Boston Port act was only a prologue; it was intituled a bill for the better regulating the government of this province of Maffachusett's-Bay. This bill was intended to alter the constitution and government of this province, as it stood settled by the charter of King William, and to take all share of government out of the hands of the people, and to vest the nomination of counsellors, judges and magistrates

of

of all kinds, including sheriffs, in the crown, and in some cases in the king's governor, and all to be removeable at the pleasure of the king. This was at one stroke undermining the ancient government of the colony, and leaving the people no share in their own government at all. The supporters of this bill alledged, that the disorders of the province of Massachusett's-Bay, not only distracted that province within itself, but set an ill example to all the colonies. An executive power was wanting. The force of the civil power, it was said, consisted in the *posse comitatus;* but the *posse* are the very people who commit the riots. That there was a total defect in the constitutional power throughout. If the democratical part shew a contempt of the laws, how is the governour to enforce them? Magistrates he cannot appoint; he cannot give an order without seven of the council assenting; and let the military be never so numerous and active, they cannot move in support of the civil magistracy, when no civil magistrate will call upon them for support. It is in vain, it was said, that you make laws and regulations here, when there are none found to execute them in that country. It is therefore become absolutely necessary to alter the whole frame of the Massachusett's government, so far as it relates to the executive and judicial powers. It was also affirmed, that the juries were injudiciously chosen, and that some immediate and permanent remedy ought to be adopted. The bill, which was at last formed into a law, will testify upon what principles it was found. A vigorous but ineffectual opposition was made to the passing of this arbitrary law; the court had a strong majority, which was fit to carry every point, and it does not appear that they would have hesitated at any thing whatsoever.

The minority urged, that to take away the civil constitution of a whole people secured by charter, the validity of which was not so much as questioned at law, upon mere loose allegations of delinquencies and defects, was a proceeding of a most arbitrary and dangerous nature. They said that it was worse than the proceedings against the Americans and English corporations, in the reign of King Charles and King James the second, which were, however, accounted the worst acts of those arbitrary reigns. At that time the charge was regularly made; the colonies and corporations called to answer; time was given, and the rules of justice, at least in appearance, were observed. But here, they said, there was nothing of the kind, not so much as a pretence to the colour of justice; not one evidence had been examined at the bar, a thing done on the most trifling regulation, affecting any franchise of the subject. That the pretence of taking away the charter, in order to give strength to government, could never answer; for this was first doing evil, that good might follow. They asked the ministry, Whether the colonies, which are already regulated nearly upon the plan proposed, were more submissive to our right of taxation, than that of Massachusett's-Bay. If not, what would be gained by the bill, that can be so very material to the authority of parliament, as to risk all the credit of parliamentary justice, by so strong and irregular a proceeding? That the part of the act which affected juries, was made without so much as a single complaint of abuse pretended. They proceeded further, and affirmed, that the case of the late Captain Preston, Mr Otis, and many others, shewed with what justice the juries in that colony acted. They denied that the juries were improperly chosen; that they were appointed by a better method than ours, by a sort of ballot in which no partiality could take place. But by the new regulation the sheriff is appointed, without any qualification, by the governour, and to hold his office at his pleasure. This was a power, they said, given to the governor, greater than that given by the constitution to the crown itself. This they insisted was a great abuse, instead of reformation; and tended to put the lives and properties of the people absolutely into the hands of the governours. It was further urged, that the disorder lay much deeper than the forms of government. That the people throughout the colonies were universally dissatisfied, and that their uneasiness and resistance was no less in the royal government than in others. That the remedy could only be in the removal of the cause of the distemper, and in quieting the minds of the people. That the act had a direct tendency to the contrary; and they feared, that instead of giving strength to government, it would destroy the small remains of English authority which was left in the colonies.

Mr Bolan the agent of the Massachusett's council, made another effort in behalf of his province, and attempted to petition for time to receive an answer from the province, to the account he had sent of the proceeding against them. But the house refused to receive the petition by a large majority. The same natives of America, who petitioned against the Boston Port-bill, again renewed their endeavours, by a petition against this. This petition was written with great spirit, and in a very warm stile, and composed with much judgment; it set forth the apprehensions of the petitioners, what would be the effects of this bill in the place where it was intended to operate, and was a true prognostication of what has since come to pass. It had leave to lie upon the table, but was no more taken notice of. The bill at last was passed by a very great majority, after a very spirited and long debate. The debates in the house of Lords were equally warm, and upon the same principles, and in the end issued in the same manner. When this business was finished, the minister proceeded to give the finishing stroke to the liberties of America. It was moved for leave to bring in a bill for the impartial administration of justice, in cases of persons questioned for any acts done by them in the execution of the laws, or for the suppression of riots or tumults in the province of Massachusett's-Bay, in New England. This bill provides, that in case that any person indicted for murder, or any other capital offence, and that it shall appear to the governor, that the fact was committed in the exercise or aid of magistracy in suppressing tumults and riots; and it shall further appear to the governour, that a fair trial cannot be had in the province, he shall send the person so indicted, &c. to another colony, or to Great-Britain to be tried. The charges on both sides to be paid out of the customs. This act was to continue for four years.

The arguments used to inforce this bill were, that magistracy must be inforced by all possible means; for as these orders would probably be resisted by force, it would lay them under a necessity to use force in the excution of them. In this case blood would be probably spilled. Who would risk this event, though in the excution of his duty, if the rioters themselves, or their abettors, were to sit as judges? The minister alledged, that such an act was not without precedent at home. Where smuggling was known to be notoriously countenanced in one county, the trial of offences of that kind had been directed to be in another. The

rebels

rebels of Scotland, in the year 1746, were tried in England. All particular privileges gave way to the public safety; when that is endangered, even the Habeas Corpus act, the great palladium of English liberty has been suspended. That the act proposed did not establish a military government, but a civil one, by which the former was greatly improved. It gave to the province a council, magistrates and justices, when in effect they had none before. This bill was warmly opposed, and all these reasons fully refuted; but a dead majority carried all before them.

It is impossible not to observe the weakness, as well as the absurdity of the ministerial arguments, used on this occasion, as well as the futility of the precedents brought to confirm them. There had been recent instances of the impartiality of juries in the colonies in the case of Captain Preston and others, when verdicts had been given according to justice, according to the ministers own ideas of that matter, and there could be no reason of fearing justice would not be executed, unless he was designed to promote some conduct which would give reason for setting aside its usual course. His speech suggested that he intended that something would be done, which he would call justice, and which the colonists would have reason to account unjust, and would be obliged in conscience to treat it as it deserved. He was therefore providing against a consequence he foresaw would happen, because he was determined it should happen. In this the old maxim was confirmed, "That the children of this world are wiser than the children of light." But there was no reason for making provision against an evil that never would have happened, unless the minister himself had been the author of it. He appears to have been determined that blood should be shed, and speaks of it with great coolness and indifference; and what bears the most unfavourable interpretation, he wanted to have those he intended should shed it, screened from justice if he possibly could."

The precedents which he mentions, are most unfavourable for his argument; for it is only supporting one act of injustice by another." For though many in a county may countenance smuggling, yet it does not prove that all the county are smugglers, and that an honest jury cannot be found in some counties in England. No man would suppose this unless he were a proficient in the practice of deceit himself.

'The case of the Scotch rebels is still more unfavourable for the case of the colonies, and that of the Jacobites are quite different.' The colonies were acknowledging the sovereignty of the king, and petitioning most humbly for a redress of grievances; they wanted not to have the government changed, nor the revolution set aside, but to have the old laws continued, and their ancient constitution secured against modern invasions of parliament. They were willing to continue in allegiance to the king, and desired no more than that protection which other subjects of the empire enjoined; they claimed, and they prayed for no more than what all British subjects claim as their just and legal right to possess.' But this was not the case of the Jacobites; their greatest grievance was the revolution itself, and their greatest eye-sore the Brunswick family that supported it. They did not come to the throne with petitions, but attacked it with the sword in their hands; they aimed at the destruction of the sovereign, and intended to change the constitution. These Jacobite tribes most voluntarily, and without any new oppression, or any new reasons of rebellion; but what will always be the same to them,

drew

drew the fword againſt the King and the laws, and fought the life of his Majeſty King George, to place a Popiſh Pretender upon the throne of theſe kingdoms. But the coloniſts were praying and befeeching both king and parliament to fupport the common liberties of the empire, which had been ratified by the revolution fettlement, and confirmed by all the fovereigns fince that time. The oppofition which the Americans made to new ſtatutes is fupported by the conſtitution itſelf, and without new laws fetting aſide the old ones, they could not be made rebels.— The violence of the miniſtry drove them to refiſtance, which was determined rebellion, to give fanction to the force that was intended to be ufed to make them fubmit to the new meafures of government. In theſe reſpects the cafe of the colonies and the Jacobites were very different, and no arguments drawn from the one to the other can poſſibly be of any force. The paſſions, prejudices of intereſted perſons may lead them to prevert the cleareſt reaſon; but all difpaſſionate and difintereſted men, who are under the government of right reaſon and common fenfe, will judge in another manner, and determine according to truth. Had the miniſter ſpoken the real fentiments of his mind, he would have declared that he wanted to have a military government in the colonies to inforce obedience to all the arbitrary meaſures that had been purfued: for his words could imply nothing lefs than that he intended to rule by the fword, and therefore wanted to have his agents fecured againſt law and juſtice.

The laſt and moſt remarkable tranfaction of this year was the Quebec bill, which was called a bill for making more effectual proviſion for the government of the province of Quebec in North America.— This bill came down from the Houſe of Lords to the

Commons for their approbation, where it met with strong oppofition, and underwent feveral amendments. The miniftry expected that as the bill paffed the Houfe of Lords fo eafily, that it would have met with no oppofition from the Commons; but in this they were miftaken. What embarraffed the minifter moft in this particular cafe was, that the bill made a great noife without doors, and was altogether unpopular in its nature. It had an article concerning religion in it, which appeared to have a tendency to inflame the nation; and provided there had been as much zeal for the Proteftant religion, as in former times, the minifter durft not have proceeded fo far with his favourite bill, nor would it have at all paffed. This bill took up a good deal of time, and met with a very warm oppofition. Many witneffes were examined to give as much colour as poffible to the fairnefs of the proceeding.—Among thefe were General Carleton, Governor of Canada; Mr Hay, Chief Juftice of that province; Mr Mazeres, Curfitor Baron of the Exchequer, late Attorney General there, and Agent to the Englifh inhabitants of Canada; Doctor Marriot, the King's Advocate General in England; Monf. Lolbiniere, a French gentleman of confiderable property in Canada. The principal objects of this bill were to afcertain the limits of that province, which were extended far beyond what had been fettled as fuch, by the King's proclamation of 1763.—To form a legiflative council for all the affairs of that province, except taxation, which council fhould be appointed by the crown; the office to be held during pleafure; and his Majefty's Roman Catholic fubjects were entitled to a place in it. To eftablifh the French laws, and a trial without jury, in civil cafes; and the Englifh laws, with a trial by jury, in criminal ones.—To fecure to

GENERAL CARLETON.

the Roman Catholic clergy, except regulars, the legal enjoyment of their estates, and of their tythes, from all that are of their own religion. These were the chief objects of this act.

The arguments which were used for the support of this bill were,—That the French, who were a very great majority of the inhabitants of that country, having been used to live under an absolute government, were not anxious for the forms of a free one, which they little understood, or valued. That they even abhorred the idea of a popular representation, observing the mischiefs which it introduced in their neighbouring countries. Besides, it would be unreasonable to have a representative body out of which all the natives should be excluded; and perhaps it would be dangerous to trust such an instrument in the hands of a people but newly taken into the British empire. They were not yet ripe, it was said, for English government. That their landed property had been all granted, and their family settlements made on the ideas of French laws: that the laws concerning contracts and personal property were nearly the same in France as in England; that a trial by jury was strange and disgusting to them. That with regard to religion, it had been stipulated to allow them perfect freedom in that respect by the treaty of Paris, as far as the laws of England permitted. The penal laws of England, with respect to religion, they said, did not extend beyond the kingdom; and though the king's supremacy extended farther, a provision was made in the act to oblige the Canadians to be subject to it; and an oath prescribed as a test against such papal claims as might endanger the allegiance of the subjects. That it was against all equity to persecute those people for their religion, and that people have not the privileges of religion

ligion who have not their own priesthood. And as for the payment of tythes, it was at best only setting down their clergy, where they were found at the conquest. In one respect, it was said, they were worse, as no person professing the Protestant religion was to be subject to them, which would be a great encouragement to conversions.

There is great reason to conclude, that none of these were the true reasons for preferring the bill; but the main reason, though not what is now called the ostensible one, was, to bring over the French colonists to the designs of the ministry, and to persuade them, by pretended favours, to fall upon the back settlements of the English colonies. The minister seems to have been totally ignorant of the disposition of the French Catholics in Canada; for we do not find that ever these papists have been so dutiful as to thank government for the new favours that were granted them; — and it has appeared since that they were not desiring any such change. A few tools of government were persuaded to send a petition to parliament for the French laws, but it was far from the minds of the generality to solicit any such favour. With regard to the promise made in the king's declaration, it extended no farther than a free toleration; whereas the bill gives a legal establishment to popery in Canada, and pledges the faith of king and parliament for the support of the popish religion. The religion of popery in that part of his Majesty's dominions is established upon the same footing as that of the Church of England; upon papists acknowledging the king's supremacy, as appointed by the first of Queen Elizabeth. Whereas the protestants have no other security than the pleasure of the king, nor any right to demand anything, except what he shall please to grant them. But this law the papists

papists are secured in all their religious privileges, and provided for by an act of the British parliament, with a legal security for a maintenance for their clergy. The only favour which is shewn to protestants is that they are freed from paying tythes, which the minister thought would be a powerful means of conversion, to bring over papists to the protestant religion; but though this may appear to be a very strong incentive to a minister of state, or others who pay little regard to any religion, yet to such as have any principles of conscience, some stronger means of conversion are necessary. It appears from the ministerial arguments that the minister wanted only such converts from popery as were swayed by the motives of worldly rewards, which are those most prevalent with many in his station. The giving the Canadian colonists the trial by jury in criminal causes, and the French method of trial in civil causes has a very whimsical appearance; for certainly a man would chuse to trust his property where he would chuse to trust his life. And it is certainly necessary, that people have as good a chance for securing their property as they possibly can. But although government intended to grant a favour to the papists; this was no reason why the protestant subjects of the empire should be stripped of their rights to oblige Roman papists; the protestants in Canada ought to have had the enjoyment of what the law secures to English subjects, whatever the government might be pleased to grant to papists. But by this law they have deprived the protestant subjects of Britain of their just, natural rights, secured to them by the constitution, upon the faith of enjoying which, they settled in that part of the world. The passing of this bill, whereby such favour was shewn to the church of Rome, created more suspicion

H h h

picion on account of the legislature refusing a petition which had been presented some time before by the Protestant dissenters for relief from some penal laws that were standing against them. It was concluded that government shewed this favour to the Catholics, from a persuasion that they were suitable instruments to promote their arbitrary designs, and that they wanted to discourage the the dissenters, because they were friends to liberty, and foes to all sort of tyranny and despotism. Whatever were the motives which determined the legislature to pass this law, it is manifest that it is an infraction of the constitution, by establishing popery in the British empire, which the revolution settlement guarded against. It is a special part of the present infelicity of these nations at present, that there are a number of modern statutes that clash with ancient and constitutional laws, whereby men in defending the one, may be punished for transgressing the others. It is not in the power of the far greater part of British subjects to know and understand the large body of laws that are contained in the statutes, and through ignorance are ready to expose themselves to the sanctions of some standing law of the land; especially as it has been for so many ages an established idea, that all the subjects of the British empire have the same privileges of the laws, and may all be their own legislators, when they become freeholders of the empire. But though it was formerly thought that the subjects of the colonies were freemen, like others at home, yet it has been determined that *colonist* and *freeman* have different significations; and that there can be no legal freedom out of Great Britain. For this is the import of the reasoning upon the subject of colonization in the present times.

C H A P.   VIII.

A View of the Proceedings at Home—Transactions in Massachusetts-Bay—Rhode-Island—New-Hampshire The Affair at Lexington and Concord—The Battle of Bunker's Hill, and its consequences, &c.

BEFORE we proceed directly to the transactions of this year, it may be necessary to take a view of some proceedings of the year 1774, which seem immediately connected with the important transactions of this. After General Gage arrived at Boston, and had, after some altercations on both sides, dissolved the assembly, the committee of correspondence at Boston entered into an agreement, which they entitled a solemn league and covenant, wherein the subscribers bound themselves in the most solemn manner, and in the presence of God, to suspend all commercial intercourse with Great Britain, from the last day of the ensuing month of August, until the Boston port-bill, and the other obnoxious laws were repealed, and the colony of Massachusetts-bay fully restored to all its chartered rights and privileges.— They also bound themselves in the same manner, not to consume, or purchase from any other, any goods whatsoever which arrived after the specified time, and to break off all commerce, trade, and dealings, with any who trade with the importers of such goods, as well as with the importers themselves. They also renounced in the same manner, all future intercourse and connection with those who should refuse to sub-

similar agreement with the dangers, the penalty annexed, of having their names published to the world.

This covenant, accompanied with a letter from the committee at Boston, was circulated with great industry and activity, and the people not only in the New England provinces, but in the other provinces, entered into this new league with the greatest keenness.——What was somewhat remarkable is, that similar agreements had been entered into about the same time, in various parts of the continent, and without any previous concert with one another, any more than with those at Boston. The title of a solemn league and covenant greatly alarmed General Gage, and the friends of the ministry in all parts of the British dominions; its name, as well as its tendency, was ominous and frightful. It brought to the remembrance of his Majesty's governors and ministers, the times of England and Scotland, entering into a solemn league and covenant for the defence of their legal rights and privileges, which have always been remembered by men of arbitrary principles with horror and disgust. The causes and the effects were by some considered at this time to be pretty much similar to those in the time of the long-parliament; and it was no great wonder that General Gage was alarmed at the tidings of a new solemn league and covenant. His proclamation on the 29th of June shews how much he was agitated and alarmed. He stiles it an unlawful, hostile, and traiterous combination, contrary to the allegiance due to the king, destructive of the lawful authority of the British parliament, and of the peace, good order, and safety of the community. All persons, were warned against incurring the penalties due to such aggravated and dangerous offences; and all such as should have any share in the publishing, subscribing, aiding, or assisting the foregoing, or any similar covenant.

This proclamation produced no other effect than to exercise the judgement and pens of those who had knowledge of the laws, in shewing that the association did not come within any of the laws that respected treason, and that the charges made by the Governor were erroneous, unjust, and injurious.—— They said he had assumed a power which the constitution denied even to the sovereign, the power of making those things to be treason, which were not considered to be such by the laws; that the people had a right to assemble to consider of their common grievances, and to form associations for their general conduct towards the remedy of those grievances; and that the proclamation was equally arbitrary, odious, and illegal. Had the Governor considered the history of former times carefully; he might have easily discovered that covenanters are not so easily frightened as to give up what they conceive to be their just rights, for a simple proclamation. The case now between the crown officers and the colonists was much like that between the ancient covenanters and the royalists, in the reign of Charles the first. The partizans of Charles charged the covenanters with treason and rebellion, and the others accused them of tyranny and treason against the constitution. Neither party could convince the other by arguments, they at last appealed to Heaven, and tried to determine their cause by the length of the sword; the determination was fatal to many thousands, and to Charles himself, and ought to be a warning to all future magistrates not to provoke a people too far. Ministers and court favourites ought to consider, that among their friends there are few that are such from principle, and provided that it should happen to be their interest to turn against them, they will soon desert them, and join with their enemies; whereas those that are against them, for the most part, have both *principle* and *interest*, in opposing them, and are determined by the strongest motives. But before we proceed to consider the transactions at home, which relate to the American affairs of this year, we shall take a view of the behaviour of the colonists, and what pass in America.

The determination of the general congress had now confirmed the principles of the timid and cautious, and their fears being removed, they laid aside that moderation which before they affected to observe. The resolves of the congress became now the creed of the colonies in matters of politics, and a perfect compliance with their determinations was every where observed. The unanimity through the whole continent was amazing; the same language was observed by town and provincial meetings, by general assemblies, by judges in their charges, and by grand juries in their presentments; and all their acts tended to the same point. It was surprising and wonderful to see the inhabitants of rich commercial countries, who had acquired a long and established relish for the superfluities of life, and who it might have been supposed, would have acquired irresistible habits in using them, all on a sudden throwing aside the captivating allurements, and confining themselves to what was merely necessary. To observe the merchant forego the advantages of trade and commerce, the farmer submit to the loss of the sale of the produce of his industry, and the seaman, with the numberless other persons dependent upon trade, contentedly resign the very means of their livelihood, and trust to their precarious subsistence, from the public spirit and charity of the opulent, was an uncommon phœnomenon; and what is perhaps more amazing, that the rich should have been disposed to run the hazard of losing their all, and supplying the poor, for the uncertain expectation of obtaining what probability seemed to determine against. Such however was the view that America at that time, since, and at present exhibited to the world.

They had sent a petition from the continental congress to the throne, upon which they placed some hopes of a reconciliation with the mother-country.— It was imagined that a general application to the people of England would have produced a salutary effect, and the colonists had still a greater dependance upon the unanimity of the determinations of the Congress, in influencing the public opinions at home in the mother-country. These hopes however did not prevail so far with them, as to put them off their guard, or to make them abate of their zeal in pursuing such measures as were necessary to provide against the worst that might happen. The principal leaders did not depend much upon these expectations, which some placed in the success of their petition to the throne. The southern colonies began to arm, as those in the north, and to train and arm their militia; and as soon as advice was received of the proclamation issued in England to prevent the exportation of arms and ammunition to America, measures were speedily taken to provide a remedy for that defect. For this purpose, and to render themselves as independent as possible upon foreigners for the supply of these essential articles, mills were erected, and manufactures formed, both in Philadelphia and Virginia,

for

for the making of gunpowder, and encouragement given in all the colonies, for the fabricating of arms of every sort. Great and many difficulties attended these first essays; and the supply of powder, both from home manufacture, and importation, was for a long time scarce and precarious. But such was their resolution and zeal, that they ardently persisted in their undertakings, and success attended their endeavours.

Governor Gage issued a proclamation against the provincial congress of Massachussett's-Bay, but it did not produce the smallest effect in the proceedings of the Congress, nor in the conduct of the people, who paid an implicit obedience to its determinations. It is highly probable that the measures of this provincial assembly were managed by advice of the general congress, which was sitting at the same time, with whom they held a constant correspondence. The critical situation of Boston, the capital of the province, was an object of much consideration, nor was it easy to determine in what manner to provide for the safety of the inhabitants, and to prevent the town becoming a thorn of uneasiness to the province, if matters should come to the last extremity. From its natural advantages of situation, and the works thrown up on the neck, Boston was already become a strong hold, and was capable, with little difficulty, by the protection of a fleet, to be made almost impregnable against any force. It was also at the pleasure of the governor, capable of being made a secure prison for the inhabitants, who would thereby become hostages for the province at large. Several different proposals were made to prevent or remedy these evils.— One was only to remove the inhabitants; another to set a valuation upon the estates, to burn the town,

and

and reimburse them for their losses. Both these schemes were clogged with insurmountable difficulties, which rendered them impracticable. Force was the only expedient that could be pursued with a probability of success; but they were not yet determined to proceed to that extremity. They had still some hopes that Britain would relax in her demands, and think better on the subject; they could hardly persuade themselves that she was determined upon slaughtering the subjects of the empire, for the sake of opinions merely problematical, and which could be no way available to her real interest. They considered the military preparations of the mother country in the same light that they were considered at home, intended to frighten them into a compliance with the measures of government, but that they did not intend to proceed to hostilities. However, in the mean time, many of the principal inhabitants removed out of the town, under the real apprehensions of immediate violence from the troops, or of being secured and sent to England, to stand their trial for supposed offences.

The provincial congress having finished all their business which they thought proper and necessary at this time; dissolved themselves in the end of November, having first appointed another meeting in the ensuing month of February. During this recess, the friends of government began to bestir themselves, and to shew their designs in some few places. They wanted to try their strength and their numbers, and to make a stand against the general current. Some associations were formed for mutual defence, and in some few towns a refusal was made to the orders of the congress; but the opposite temper was so prevalent, that those attempts were soon quelled.

quelled. The diffidents were overpowered by numbers, and all their attempts came to nothing.

The suspicion which the mother country had of the colonies, promoted the grounds of their suspicions; for by prohibiting the exportation of military stores, she suggested the idea of resistance, or at least supposed that something would be done by government, that would tend to provoke the colonists to make use of such stores. When the account of this prohibition was received at Rhode Island, the people seized and carried away all the ordnance belonging to the crown in that province, which lay upon some batteries that defended one of the harbours, and which amounted to above forty pieces of cannon, of different sizes. When a captain of a man of war waited upon the governor to enquire into the meaning of this procedure, he was informed with great frankness, that the people had seized the cannon to prevent their falling into the hands of the king's forces, and that they intended to make use of them to defend themselves, against any power that should attempt to molest them. The assembly of that island also passed resolutions for the procuring of arms and military stores, by all means, and from all quarters from whence they could be obtained, as well as for training and arming the inhabitants.

The province of New Hampshire, which had hitherto appeared to be of a placid and moderate temper, and had behaved with more respect to government than the other provinces of New England, as soon as they heard of the resolutions of Rhode-Island, and received a copy of the royal proclamation that gave rise to them, pursued the same plan. A body of men assembled in arms, and marched to the attack of a small fort called William and Mary, only

considerable

considerable for being the object of the first military operation in that province.——This fort was easily taken, and supplied them with a quantity of powder, by which they were enabled to put themselves in a state of defence. No other acts of hostility or violence happened during the winter, but a firm determination of resistance was however universally spread and encreased every day. The arrival of the king's speech and the addresses of the new parliament, added to the flame that was already kindled. Their former jealousy, which needed no additional fuel, began now to blaze forth with all the expressions of concern and anxiety, attended with the signs of determined resolution to resist every act of violence that government should attempt to commit upon them.

The king's speech, in the opinion of the colonies, cut off all hopes of reconciliation, and made them strain every nerve to provide against the storm they saw gathering against them. It is very remarkable that all the public acts and declarations, which in England were recommended as the means of pacifying the colonies, by intimidating them, constantly operated in a different manner. The more clearly a determination was shewn to inforce an high authority, the more resolutely the colonists seemed to resist it. The assembly of Pennsylvania, which had met by adjournment towards the close of the year 1774, was the first legal convention that ratified unanimously all the acts of the General Congress, and appointed delegates to represent them in the new congress, which was to be held in the ensuing month of May.— The proceedings in other places were similar, and much of the same kind through all the colonies.——— The convention of Maryland appointed a sum of money for purchasing arms and ammunition, and the

provincial

provincial assembly of Philadelphia in the end of January passed a resolution for the encouragement of manufacturing gunpowder.

The assembly of New York, which met in the beginning of the year, differed indeed from the rest of the continent. After several debates upon the question concerning acceding to the general congress, it was rejected upon a division, but by a very small majority. About this time the friends of government, by instructions from Britain, formed a representation of grievances, which they proposed to lay before the king and parliament; in this they were encouraged by the lieutenant-governor, imagining that as they had refused to join the general congress, that their representation and petition would meet with acceptance; but this petition and representation was as ineffectual as many others.

The new provincial congress of Massachusett's-Bay assembled upon the 1st of February at Cambridge, and pursued the same plan that had been marked out for them by their predecessors. Among other resolutions they published one to inform the people, that from the present disposition of the British ministry and parliament, there was real cause to fear that the reasonable and just application of that continent to Great Britain for peace, liberty, and safety, would not meet with a favourable reception; but on the contrary, from the large reinforcement of troops, expected in that colony, the general appearance, and tenor of intelligence from Great Britain, they had reason to apprehend that the sudden destruction of that colony was intended, for refusing with the other American colonies, tamely to submit to what they termed, the most ignominious slavery. They therefore urged in the strongest manner, the militia in general, and the

minute-

minute men in particular, to spare neither time, pains, nor expence, at so critical a juncture, in perfecting themselves in military discipline. They passed other resolutions for the providing and making of fire arms and bayonets, and renewed more strictly the prohibition of the former congress, concerning not supplying the troops at Boston with any of those necessaries which are peculiarly requisite for the military service: The markets of Boston being still open for the supply of provisions. The distinction that is here made between the militia and the *minute* men may perhaps not be understood by some. The meaning of this distinction is, that a select body of the militia were engaged to hold themselves ready upon all occasions, and at the shortest notice, for actual service. That is, according to the phrase, to be ready at a minute's warning. On this account they are stiled minutemen; and they have shewn, by their readiness and activity since, the propriety of their name.

The meetings of the general congress, and the conventions of particular provinces, were a dreadful eye-sore to the government. The secretary of state for the American department, issued a circular letter, forbidding, in the king's name, and under the pain of his displeasure, the election of deputies for the ensuing general congress; but this letter produced no effect. The elections took place every where, and even in the province of New-York, notwithstanding their late promising proceedings. Matters continued very quiet at Boston, which happened on account of the injunctions of the general congress, more than from the ships of war that crowded the harbour, or the force that was stationed in the town. The calm was, however, precarious and fictitious. Abundance of fuel had been gathered on both sides, sufficiently

prepared

prepared to kindle with the smallest spark; more was preparing, and the least touch was likely to kindle a general conflagration. Upon the 26th of February, General Gage sent a detachment of troops, under the command of a field officer, to seize some brass cannon he had been informed were deposited in the town of Salem. These sailed aboard a transport to Marblehead, which lies four miles south of Salem, and about fourteen miles from the town of Boston; from thence they marched to Salem, where they found no cannon. They were, however, suspicious that they had been carried away that morning in consequence of the report of their approach, and from this apprehension marched farther into the country, in hopes of overtaking them. In this pursuit they arrived at a draw-bridge over a small river, where a number of the country people were assembled, and those on the opposite side had taken up the bridge to prevent their passage. The commanding officer ordered the bridge to be let down, which the people peremptorily refused to do, saying, that it was a private road, and he had no authority to demand a passage that way; for both sides still professed to keep the public peace, though war was in their hearts, and till the sword was drawn all resistance was carried on upon legal grounds and pretences. If this was actually a private road, the soldiers had no right to commit a trespass from a pretence of seeking cannon, where they were not likely to find any, and the people had an undoubted right to dispute the passage with the military as they were off the king's highway, and not travelling in the common road where such travellers were wont to pass. The officer, who seems to have considered himself in an enemy's country, and not in a country where he was amenable to the laws, was determined to force his passage, and perceiving a boat near at hand,

determined

GENERAL GAGE.

determined to make use of it to gain the possession of the bridge.—But the country people perceiving his design, several of them jumped into it, and with axes cut holes in its bottom, which occasioned a scuffle between them and the soldiers in and about the boat. Things were now tending to extremities, as the commander seemed determined to force his passage, and the others were as resolutely bent to prevent it. In this situation were matters, when a clergyman in the neighbourhood, who had attended the whole transaction, remonstrated with the officer, who was a lieutenant colonel, upon the fatal consequences that would insue, provided he made use of force; and finding that the officer stood upon a point of honour in making good his passage, more than any other thing, for it was then too late to go in search of the cannon, he persuaded the people to let down the bridge, which the troops took possession of. The colonel having sent a detachment a short way into the country, in exercise of his right which he assumed, they immediately returned, without molestation, on board the transport. Thus ended this first expedition, without producing any material effect, and without much mischief. But it now appeared how small a matter would have produced hostilities, and in what a precarious situation the peace of the empire now was; and that the least exertion of the military would certainly bring matters to an extremity. There was one thing which greatly exasperated the colonists, and that was, the act for taking away their charters, and for protecting the military from any trial in the province; this made them consider themselves as under a military government. Every motion of the military body became suspected, and in the eyes of the people was considered as an exertion of the most hateful and odious tyranny. This appearance of resistance greatly offended and irritated the military, who, from this time,

time, appear to have lived upon worse terms with the people of Boston, than they had done before. Men who have been bred to the profession of arms, and consider all inferiors merely under the command of their superiors, and bound to obey them without asking or giving any other reason of their doing so, than that they are commanded, consider all opposition to their will and pleasure as the most heinous transgression. It becomes natural to them to rule over all whom they have power, according to the military law, for which reason they become very disagreeable neighbours to all those who have just ideas of liberty, and pursue the rights of human nature. The British soldiery imagining, as indeed was the case, that they were sent to Boston to rule the town, and act towards the people as rebels to the king, began to insult the inhabitants, and to behave as in an enemy's country. Several of their outrages were now complained of, and all things seemed to tend to a general rupture. The crisis fast approached when all lesser calamities were to be forgotten, in a general contemplation of those of a greater and more serious nature.

The provincials having collected a considerable quantity of military stores at the town of Concord, where the provincial congress was sitting, General Gage considered it as expedient to detach a party of the troops to destroy them. Lieutenant Colonel Smith, and Major Pitcairn, with the grenadiers and light infantry of the army, were detached for that purpose. It was confidently reported and believed at that time, that this military appointment had another object in view, and that the intention thereof principally was, to seize Messrs. Hancock and Adams, these great obnoxious leaders of what was called the faction, which was against the new form of government. This detachment

tachment is said to have consisted of 900 men, prepared and appointed for the purpose. This body of troops embarked on the night preceding the 19th of April, and landed at a place called Phipps's Farm, about six miles north-west from Charlestown Ferry; from thence they proceeded in their march with great silence and expedition, towards Concord. This town stands on the east side of the river of the same name, sometimes also called Billerika, which runs into the river Mirimak, a little below the falls of Pantucket. On the road to Concord stands Lexington, about five miles towards the east; thither the troops marched with great expedition. Several officers upon horseback secured the country, and secured all the people which they found in their way at that early time, lest they should give the alarm to the inhabitants, who would be ready to rise in arms to oppose their designs. This precaution, though it was abundantly prudent, did not prevent the town and country people from receiving notice of their approach, which they soon discovered by the firing of guns and ringing of bells. They were now assembling in the neighbouring villages before day-light, and making preparations for the event which they feared. Upon the troops arriving at Lexington at five in the morning, they found the company of militia belonging to the town, assembled upon a green near the road; upon which an officer in the van called out, " Disperse ye rebels; throw down your arms and disperse;" the soldiers at the same time, running up with loud huzzas, fired some scattering shot, and then gave a general discharge, by which eight of the militia were killed, and several wounded. This was the first shedding of blood that happened in this unhappy and unnatural contest. Much pains have been taken on both sides of the question to prove the others the aggressors upon this occasion. The gazette affirmed, that the troops were fired upon from some neighbouring houses; but for this there does not appear to be the smallest evidence. The gazettes about that time were so inconsistent and badly composed, often contradicted by the friends of government that were upon the spot, that the public have since given very little credit to them. It appeared from the whole tenor of the evidence, as well as of our own people who were taken prisoners, as from many of the provincials, all whose depositions were taken by proper magistrates, that the firing both at Lexington and Concord, was begun by the king's troops. It is not at all probable that those in the houses would have exposed the lives of their friends in the militia, who were standing in a manner under the muzzles of the guns of the soldiers, by firing upon the troops from their covers. The few militia who were now in the power of the troops, may be conceived as sufficient pledges to prevent any outrage from their friends and neighbours in the adjoining houses.

After this execution, the detachment proceeded to Concord, the commanding officer having previously dispatched six companies of light infantry, to possess two bridges which lay beyond the town, upon the *Sudbury* and North Concord, with a design to prevent any of the stores from being carried away, or the two devoted rebels, Adams and Hancock, from escaping. It happened, however, that they were disappointed in both their views; for they could not find these two obnoxious persons, and except three old cannon, and a small quantity of flour, they found nothing of consequence. They indeed did execution upon the cannon by rendering them unserviceable,

and

and most heroically threw the barrels of flour into the river. About a year after that flour would have been of some service to the same troops, when they were cooped up in Boston. It argues a great malignity of temper to destroy the bounties of providence, for fear that our enemies should enjoy them. We have certainly a right, provided we are in want of provisions, to prefer ourselves to our enemies; but wantonly to destroy corn and flour, for fear others should use it, is a warring with providence, and declaring, we have no confidence in the justice of our cause. Weapons of war, and instruments of hostility, may lawfully be destroyed in the hands of our foes, or taken away from them whether we need them or not, but to destroy that food which is the general support of all men, for fear those we call enemies should use it, affords a different moral reflection. Besides, at this time these colonists had not shewn any acts of enmity against the troops; they were therefore both seeking to starve and murder their friends and countrymen. The colonists appear to have industriously avoided engaging in hostilities on this occasion; for a body of militia, which occupied a hill in the way between Concord and the bridge, retired, and passed along it at the approach of the troops, which immediately took possession thereof. This shews that they did not intend to have begun hostilities at this time, otherwise they would have disputed the passage of the bridge with the light infantry, which they might easily have done. The militia had not retired far till they perceived several fires in the town, which they imagined were houses in flames; they therefore returned towards the bridge which they had passed, which lay directly in their way. Upon this the light infantry retired on the Concord side of the river, and began to pull up the bridge; but

upon

upon the approach of the militia, who seemed industriously to avoid beginning the attack, and made as if they intended to pass as common travellers, the soldiers immediately fired and killed two men. The provincials returned the fire, and a skirmish ensued at the bridge, in which the kings troops were put into some confusion, and were forced to retreat, having several men killed and wounded, and a lieutenant and some others taken prisoners. This fully proves that the provincials had no intention of beginning hostilities at this time; for they might have at first disputed the bridge with the troops, had they designed to have come to blows, more easily than to drive them from the possession of it. The country now arose upon the king's troops; they were attacked on all quarters, and skirmish succeeded skirmish. A continued, though scattered and irregular fire, was maintained through the whole of a long and very hot day. The troops did not find it so easy in marching back as they did in marching from Boston. All the way between Concord and Lexington the houses, walls, and coverts were lined with armed men, who constantly annoyed the troops, and they were pursued and attacked in the rear by the militia which defeated them at the bridge. They were now in a very critical situation, and much distressed, which evils they had brought upon themselves, by their rashness in shedding blood when they had no occasion; they were now likely to suffer severely, when Lord Percy arrived at Lexington with a strong reinforcement for their relief and assistance. General Gage, either through suspicion of what would happen, or from knowing what orders he had given to Colonel Smith, had, early in the morning, sent off Earl Percy with sixteen companies of foot, a detachment of marines, and two pieces of cannon,

to

HUGH Earl PERCY.

to support the operations of the Colonel. This reinforcement was just arrived as the fatigued troops returned to Lexington. This fresh assistance was the more acceptable and seasonable, as the troops are said to have run short of all kinds of ammunition; but suppose that had not been the case, it was impossible for them to have escaped being cut off, or being taken, in the journey of fifteen miles they had to make before they arrived at Boston.

This powerful support gave them a breathing, and the cannon was of great service to them. These kept the pursuers at some distance, as they had no ordnance of the same kind to answer them. But when the troops resumed their march, the attack became more fierce and violent; the country assembled on all sides, and attacked the forces with the utmost fury. Many were killed in the retreat by people that watched the approach of the troops behind walls, hedges, and ditches, and the danger encreased until sun-setting, when they arrived at Charlestown in a most shattered and fatigued situation. All things considered, both officers and men, who did not fall by the way, made an exceeding swift and expeditious march back to Boston. What on this occasion was exceedingly singular was, the troops accused the provincials of cruelty, and upbraided them with cowardice; though their behaviour to their prisoners shewed the accusation to be false, and the defeating the king's troops shewed their assertion of cowardice to be unjust. It had long been the tone of military men, that the colonists were cowards and would not fight, but they began now to experience to their cost, that they had been greatly mistaken. Courage is a thing that may be acquired more ways than one; and is not confined to those who make war a profession. When men are persuaded of the juftnefs of their caufe, and are endowed with equal bodily ftrength, a little practice in arms will render them as courageous as others; and in proportion as they purfue the ideas of juftice and true liberty, their courage will be more fteady, rational, and deliberate. People often miftake madnefs and fury for courage, when, through the heat of paffion, they rifk their lives for what neither their reafon nor confcience can approve; and often neceffity paffes under the fame appellation; when men are obliged, by the force of command, to venture their lives one way, otherwife they will be taken from them in another. Neither of thefe deferve the name of true courage, for both of them may be found in other animals as well as in man. Juftice is the foundation of courage; all other exertions of force is violence and madnefs. There are fome fpecies of courage like that of the gentleman who faid he would chearfully go to hell, provided he could obtain the ruin of a clafs of people he greatly abhorred.—This was daring courage, and wrought up to a great pitch.

This unfortunate beginning of the American war was not attended with fo great lofs of men on either fide as might have been expected from the length, irregularity, and variety of the engagement. This muft be attributed to the provincials having few men at firft, and to their afterwards being kept at a diftance by the cannon of the king's troops. His majefty's forces, as is natural to fuppofe, fuffered moft upon this occafion; though it is not eafy to afcertain the number of killed and wounded in this unfortunate expedition. According to the neareft and beft calculation that has yet been given, of the king's troops there were killed, wounded, and taken, 273. Of thefe 65 were killed, 2 lieutenants, and above 20 private men were taken

prifoners;

prisoners; and Colonel Smith, with another lieutenant-colonel, and several officers were wounded. According to the provincial accounts, which gave the names and places of abode of those who fell on their side, their loss in killed and wounded, including those that were killed in the morning at Lexington, amounted only to about 60, of which near two-thirds were killed.

By the best accounts, there were near 2000 of the best troops in his majesty's service, that were at this time stationed at Boston, employed in this expedition. The event proved to a demonstration, how ill informed many people at home were, who affirmed, that 500 men would force their way through the whole continent of America, and the sight of a grenadier would be sufficient to put the whole American army to flight. Such idle and unguarded assertions, even after this unfortunate expedition, were frequently uttered by the friends of the government, as they called themselves; and the cowardice of the provincials was still insisted on, by persons who either through ignorance or prejudice, were disposed to persist in their mistake.

After this expedition was over, each party charged the other with the most inhuman acts of cruelty. This has always been common in civil wars, and on such occasions it is not easy to ascertain the exact point of truth on either side. Sometimes the worst part of the charge is too true, which is no argument in favour of the purity of human nature. On this occasion both parties were no doubt ready to give strong colourings to the conduct and transactions of each other, and to exaggerate their actions and their criminality. The colonists were charged by the king's troops of being guilty of the most shocking barbarity to the soldiers that fell into their hands; whereas, some

officers

officers and men, who were wounded and taken prisoners, gave public testimonials of the humanity with which they were treated. And the provincial commanders sent an offer to General Gage, to admit his surgeons to come and dress his wounded men.

The colonists, on the other hand, charged the troops with killing the old and infirm, the unarmed and the wounded; with burning houses, and plundering every thing that came in the way. Considering the character of soldiers in these modern times, this is not at all unlikely; for though in our army there are both officers and common men that have honour and humanity, yet there are such a great number of officers that are mere soldiers of fortune, and common men collected from the dregs of mankind, that it is next to impossible to restrain them from evil when it is in the power of their hands to do it. It would have been a greater wonder if no such cruelties had happened, than that they should have fallen out in the time of action, when such a number of wicked people were concerned. But this is more to be imputed to the impossibility of restraining bad men in the time of action, than to the intentions of government, or of the principal commanders in the army. There is no doubt that the provincials would be ready to give strong colourings to every appearance of severity, which the troops might proceed to, from the consideration that they were in a state of rebellion. We must therefore, after examining all circumstances, determine according to the nearest degree of certainty, or the highest degree of probability.

This affair at Concord put the whole province in motion, and also alarmed the whole continent of America. All New-England was now almost in arms; for although a sufficient number were assembled to

invest

invest the king's troops in Boston, it was with difficulty that those who were hastily marching from different parts, could be prevailed upon to return to their respective places of abode. Every road that directed to Boston was crouded with men in armour, marching to the assistance of their friends in distress. General Washington, with the Virginia horse and riflemen, were marching from the south, the New-Hampshire troops and rangers advancing by two ways from the north, and those of Connecticut and Rhode-Island were posting from the south by another way. Along with these last were a company of artillery, and waggons with stores and provisions. The body of militia assembled in the province of Massachusett's-Bay before the arrival of the troops from the other provinces, amounted to near 20,000, under the command of the Generals Ward, Pribble, Heath, Prescot, and Thomas. These gentlemen were before only colonels, but now acted in the capacity of generals; who, having fixed their head quarters at Cambridge, seven miles north-west from Boston, formed a line of encampment, which on the right extended to Roxbury, towards the south about the same distance from Boston as Cambridge; on the south west, along the side of Charles' River, opposite to Watertown, about ten miles from Boston; and on the north, along the side of Mystic River, near to the same distance from the town. The distance between the points was very near thirty miles. These were joined by General Putnam, an old officer, who had acquired exprience and reputation in the two last wars. He encamped, with a body of Connecticut forces, in such a situation as to be ready to support those who were before the town.

The affair of Concord and Lexington greatly excited the indignation of the other colonies, and they prepared for war with as much zeal as if an enemy had already appeared at their doors. It was a circumstance which gave spirit to the rest of the colonies, that the militia of New-England had been able to make such a good defence, and in a manner even beat the king's troops; this was reported and published with great exultation, and it must be allowed that it was an event that neither themselves, nor any others, expected to have fallen out at that time. Those who fell in the action were lamented with deep concern, and honoured not only as patriots, but as martyrs for the cause of liberty, who had nobly sacrificed their lives for the freedom of their country, and died like heroes in that great cause. The cruelties and outrages of the king's forces were now painted in such a light at the funerals of those who were slain in this action, that the speeches and reports which were made, however justly or unjustly founded, produced a great effect, and encreased like a violent flame throughout the whole continent.

The provincial congress, which was now removed to Watertown, drew up an address to the inhabitants of Great Britain, in which they stated the most material particulars that related to the engagement at Concord, and endeavoured to shew that hostilities were first begun by the king's troops, and that blood was first shed at Lexington by the regular forces. They also complain of the ravages committed by the troops in their retreat, and seem to place much confidence in the honour, wisdom, and valour of Britons, from which they expect their interference in preventing measures which they represent as equally ruinous to the mother country and the colonies. They also made great professions of their loyalty, but at the same time declare, that they will not tamely submit to the tyranny of a cruel ministry; and they appeal to heaven, that they
are

are determined to be free. The provincial congress also passed a vote for marshalling and supporting an army; fixed the pay of the officers and soldiers, and published rules and orders for its regulation and government. For this purpose they passed a vote for issuing a considerable sum in paper currency, which was to be received in all cases as money, and the faith of the province pledged for its payment; this was appointed for the payment of the troops. The term for which they were chosen was to expire on the 10th of May, so they gave notice for a new election for members to the next congress, which was to meet on the 31st of that month, at the same place, and to be continued for six months and no longer. They also passed a vote, declaring General Gage utterly disqualified and incapable of serving the colony as governor, or in any other capacity, and that in future no obedience was due to him; but on the contrary, that he ought to be guarded against, and considered as a most inveterate enemy to the country.

As one thing generally brings on another, and the colision of parties, for the most part, breaks in the end into outrage, the opposition to government at last issued in seizing the revenues and magazines that belonged to the king. In New-Jersey they seized the treasury, and applied it against government, and for the purpose of their own defence. There was at this time a considerable sum of money in Jersey for the purposes of government, which was now appropriated for paying the new levies which were carrying on for the defence of the colonies. At the same time without consulting with one another, a stop was made almost every where to the exportation of provisions; and in some places all kind of exportation was kept till the sentiments of the general congress was taken concerning

concerning that subject. Lord North's conciliatory plan, or the resolution founded upon it, was totally rejected by the assembly of Philadelphia and New-Jersey; nor was it regarded or received in any place.

While things were going on in this manner, the governor and forces in Boston, as also the inhabitants, continued closely blocked up by land, and being shut out from provisions and vegetables, which could easily have been afforded from the neighbouring counties, they began to feel and experience a real distress. The inhabitants were in the same situation with the forces, and had no other resources for subsistence; this made the provincials watch the more carefully to keep out any supply, thinking the soldiers would suffer the inhabitants to depart for fear of an absolute famine; or at least that the woman and children would be suffered to depart, which was repeatedly required and applied for. There is some reason to imagine that the governor considered the inhabitants as necessary hostages for the security of the town at least, if not for the safety of the troops. This had as much the appearance of cowardice as any thing that appeared in the conduct of the provincials; for it argued that they were afraid either to fight the colonists in the open field, or to defend the town against their force. To keep women, old men, and children confined for a security for their own safety, argued that they were either afraid to fight, or believed they were not able to conquer the force that was before the town. It had often been asserted at home, that a few regular troops would go through all America, but now a general, with a number of the best troops in the service, was cooped up in a town, and durst not even stay in it without old women, men, and children, to guard them. This had a very bad appearance, and gave confiderate people reason to conclude that the miniftry were greatly mistaken in their conjectures.

The general at laft entered into an agreement with the towns-people, that if they would deliver up their arms, they should have liberty to go where they pleased, and carry their effects where they had a mind. This they accordingly did; but to their amazement and furprize, the governor refufed to fulfil the conditions on his fide. This was matter of great complaint againft General Gage; and it muft be allowed, that it favoured both of cowardice and difhonefty; for though he had ftripped the towns-people of all their weapons of defence by means of treachery, he durft not ftay in it without them, for fear of the force that lay encamped in the neighbourhood. Many, however, were fuffered afterwards to quit the town at different times, but they were obliged to leave all their effects behind them; fo that thofe who had hitherto lived in affluence, were at once reduced to extreme indigence and mifery. The general congrefs complained loudly of this conduct of the general, and ranked the fufferings of the inhabitants of Bofton among the moft grievous and the moft bitter of their complaints. They faid that paffports were granted in fuch a manner that families were broken, and the neareft connections feparated; part being compelled to leave the town, and part retained againft their will. This was very difhonourable to General Gage, and one could wifh that it had never happened; but as it was pofitively affirmed by the provincials, and never contradicted, the truth of hiftory requires it to be fairly ftated. The poor and the helplefs were all fent out. It is pofible that the ideas which General Gage had of the Americans being rebels, made him conclude that they were a political

fort

sort of heretics, with whom no faith was to be kept, which made him break his promise in such a flagrant manner: It is certain that no man who believed that promises are sacred would have so palpably violated a voluntary contract, when it was in his power to have performed it.

The continental congress assembled on the 10th of May at Philadelphia, and soon adopted such measures as established the people in their conduct and resolution. One of their acts was for raising an army, and establishing a large paper currency for its payment; the security of the United Colonies, which title they now assumed, was given for realizing the nominal value of this currency. They also prohibited the supplying the British fisheries with any kind of provisions; and to enforce this prohibition the more effectually, they stopt all exportation to these colonies and islands which still remained in their obedience to Great Britain. This was a home stroke which the ministry and people in the mother country were not thinking upon; it was a measure they never apprehended the colonists would have fallen upon in their then situation. It greatly distressed the people of Newfoundland, and all those who were employed in the fisheries; insomuch, that to prevent an absolute famine, several ships were obliged to return light from that station, to carry out cargoes of provisions from Ireland. When the tidings of this resolution came to Britain, it was considered as a mere chimera, and it was said that the colonists would not continue in this resolution, because it would greatly injure themselves; but these persons afterwards found a steadiness in the resolutions of the colonists, which they never expected would have happened. The ministry at home seem to have been either ill informed concerning the temper of the colonists, or willing to be deceived; for nothing fell out according to their professed hopes and expectations. In the progress of future events in this contest, they always found themselves disappointed.

The city and province of New York, from which government had the greatest hopes, on account of their former resolutions, upon receiving the news of the action at Concord and Lexington, began to depart from their moderation, and seemed to have received a liberal portion of the common temper and spirit that operated in the other colonies. A most numerous association was formed, and a provincial congress was chosen. The situation of this city and province was at this time very critical; for some regiments of troops were expected from Ireland, and as New York is exposed to the sea, it was not probable that it would be able to abide an attack. However a body of men from Connecticut arrived in the neighbourhood of that city, avowedly for its protection, and with an intention to support the disposition of the people. But as there were suspicions of the insufficiency of this force in case of an attack by sea, they applied to the general congress for advice how to behave upon the arrival of the troops. The congress, with a prudence which would in some assemblies have been accounted great wisdom and sagacity, advised them for the present to act defensively with respect to the troops, as far as it could be done consistently with their own security and safety;—to permit them to occupy the barracks, so long as they behaved quietly and peaceably, but not to suffer them to erect any fortifications, or in any manner to cut off the communication between the city and the country. If they attempted hostilities they should defend themselves, and repel force by force.

force. They also advised them to provide for the worst that might happen, by securing places of retreat for the women and children; by removing the arms and ammunition from the magazines; and by keeping a sufficient number of men embodied for the protection of the inhabitants in general. The departure of such a number of helpless objects from the places of their habitation, was a very affecting sight, and an unusual spectacle. That once flourishing and trading city was now almost become a wilderness. It was, by its own inhabitants devoted to the flames. It was one happy circumstance for New-York, that the troops were more wanted at Boston, and did not at this time land at that place. It was probably not in the favour of government that the troops did not arrive at New-York at this time; for it both gave the town and the province time to form, and to confirm their resolutions, and to drink more deep in the same sources of disaffection with the rest of the colonies.

While Boston was in the possession of the king's troops, and surrounded with the provincial armies, a few private adventurers attempted an enterprize which was astonishing to all Europe. Some persons belonging to the back parts of Connecticut, Massachusetts, and New-York, undertook at their own risk, and without any public command or authority, or without communicating their designs, an expedition of the utmost importance, which not only in its consequence most materially affected the interest of government in the colonies, but brought the question to a point of critical nicety, whether Britain should have a single possession left in all North America. This was the surprizing of Ticonderago, Crown-Point, and other forts situated on the Great Lakes, and which commanded the passes between the British colonies

colonies and Canada. Some of those who had formed this design, and were set out upon this expedition with the greatest secrecy, met others upon their march, who, without any previous concert, were set out upon the same design, and embarked in the same project. These adventurers, amounting to 240 men of Colonel Easton and Colonel Ethan Allan's, with great perseverance and address surprized the small garrisons of Ticonderago and Crown-Point. They took these two fortifications without the loss of a single man on either side. In these forts they found a considerable quantity of artillery; amounting, as was reported, to 200 pieces of cannon, besides some mortars, howitzers, and quantities of other stores; they also took two vessels, which gave them the command of Lake Champlain, and materials provided at Ticonderago for the building and equipping others. This was as daring an act of intrepidity as had been known for a long time, and shewed that the colonists were now in earnest in their opposition. Such an enterprize performed by British forces, would have been accounted an act heroism, and was no less a bold action when performed by those provincials.

While these things were transacting, the Generals Howe, Burgoyne, and Clinton, arrived at Boston from England, together with a reinforcement of marines, and draughts from other regiments, to supply the vacancies that were in the troops at Boston. Several regiments from Ireland soon followed these, so that the forces at Boston, with respect to number, the goodness of the troops, and the character of the commanding officers, were become very respectable, and it was now thought that matters could not remain long in the situation they were then in. No remarkable achievements had for some time been performed on either side; the blockade was continued, but nothing material attempted, except some small skirmishes for provisions, which happened in the islands which lye in the bay, in which the king's troops were worsted. In the last skirmish which happened at Noddle-island, a small island which lies east from Boston, they destroyed a schooner belonging to government, which had been left by the tide, in spite of all opposition.

Matters continued still in the same situation at Boston, notwithstanding of the new generals, and reinforcement of fresh troops. Both parties appear to have been doubtful of the event of an engagement, and industriously avoided coming to action as long as they could. It is highly probable, that the provincials would have made an attempt to storm the town, immediately after the affair of Lexington, had not they been determined to spare it for the sake of their friends who were in it; this prevailed over every other consideration. It must be granted, that from the number of ships of war which almost surrounded the peninsula, as well as the vast artillery by which it was protected, and the goodness of the troops, that such an attempt would have been attended with great danger and difficulty, and that the destruction of the town must have been the certain consequence. There were other causes that operated on this occasion, in determining the provincials not to attack the town. A repulse, or even a victory, attended with much bloodshed in so arduous a struggle, might have been attended with fatal consequences. The people were not yet accustomed to war; their situation was new and critical; they were entering into a contest of a

singular

singular nature, untried, unthought of, and unnatural; loaded with the most fatal consequences, without a precedent to direct them, or experience to guide them: nor had they as yet given up all hopes of an accommodation. They were therefore afraid that those who were not fully established in their principles of opposition, would totally condemn any violent measures which might exclude them from such a desirable event. In this state of anxious hope and fear much caution was necessary to be used, lest any unsuccessful event might suddenly damp the spirit and ardour of the people, stagger their resolution, and dissolve their confederacy.

The continental congress upon the 8th of June, resolved that the compact between the crown of England, and the people of Massachusetts Bay was dissolved, by the violation of the charter of William and Mary; and recommended to the people of that province, to proceed to the establishment of a new government, by the electing a governor and assistants, according to the powers contained in the original charter. They passed another resolution, that no bill of exchange, draught, or order, of any officer in the army or navy, their agents or contractors, should be received or negociated, or any money supplied to them by any person; and prohibited the supplying of the army or navy, or ships employed in the transport service, with provisions or necessaries of any kind. They at the same time erected a general post-office at Philadelphia, which extended through the United Colonies; and some time after placed Dr Franklin, who had been disgraced and removed from that office by government, at the head thereof. The congress had now, under the soft idea of recommendation and advice,

advice, assumed the power of a supreme government.

General Gage, nearly about the same time, issued a proclamation, in which was offered, in the king's name, a free pardon to all those who should forthwith lay down their arms, and return to their respective occupations and peaceable duties, excepting only from the benefit of the pardon, Samuel Adams, and John Hancock, whose offences were considered to be so atrocious as to be beyond the reach of forgiveness. All such as did not accept of this offered mercy, or who should protect, assist, conceal, or correspond with them, were to be treated as rebels and traitors. It was also declared, that as a stop was put to the due course of law and justice, that the martial law should take place till the laws were restored to their former course, and justice executed in its usual channel. This proclamation produced no effect. Mr Hancock was chosen president of the congress at the very season that this proclamation was intended to operate. Such a proclamation at this time was considered as a preliminary to immediate action; accordingly, from this time both parties held themselves in readiness for it. The post of Charlestown had been neglected by both parties, though it was a post of much consequence; for by having the command of the rock which joins the peninsula to the continent, those that are in possession thereof, have it in their power to stop the passages to the north and north-west, and to prevent the communication between Boston, the west parts of Massachusett's-Bay, New Hampshire, and the other parts towards the west and north-west. The neck of the peninsula is not much above half a mile in breadth, and by being properly fortified, may

command

command Charles' river on the south, and Mystic river on the north, and interrupt the communication between Boston and those parts of the Bay on both sides, in a great measure. It would have been an easy matter for the king's forces, who had the command of the river, to have fortified this neck, and rendered it exceedingly serviceable to them. They found afterwards their mistake in neglecting it. The provincials considered it of service for them, whether they should chuse to act on the defensive or offensive. There is a rising ground, called Bunker-Hill, just within the neck, that joins the peninsula to the continent. This neck is very like that on which Boston stands; except the isthmus is considerably wider, and Bunker-hill higher than any hill in the other. The towns are only separated by Charles' river, which, in that part, is only about the breadth of the Thames between London and Southwark; so that Charlestown seemed to hold the same connection with Boston, that the Borough does with London. West from Bunker-hill lies another rising ground called Winter-hill, and on the right hand, at a small distance, another called Prospect-hill; all these being contigious, were advantageous posts, and were by this step in the possession of the provincials.

The party that was sent in the night to fortify Bunker-hill, carried on their work with so much secrecy and expedition, that though the peninsula was surrounded with ships of war and spy boats, they were not heard during the night, and such extraordinary dispatch had they used, that in the morning by day-break, they had a small redoubt, considerable entrenchments, and a breast-work, that in some parts was cannon proof, very near compleated. The sight

of

of thefe works was the firft notice that alarmed the Lively man of war in the morning, and her guns called the town, camp, and fleet to behold a fight which appeared little lefs than a prodigy. A heavy and continued fire of cannon, howitzers, and mortars, was now carried on upon the works, from the fhips, floating batteries, and from the top of Cop's-hill in Bofton. Such an inceffant and prodigious roar of artillery, would have been a trial to the courage and firmnefs of the oldeft foldiers, and muft have undoubtedly greatly interrupted the finifhing of the works; it was however faid, that the provincials bore this fevere fire with wonderful firmnefs, and feemed to go on with their bufinefs as if no enemy had been near, nor any danger in the fervice. General Gage now perceived that the provincials were not to be frighted merely with the found of cannons and mortars, and that fome more effectual method behoved to be ufed to make them give over their undertaking. About noon, June 21ft, the fame day that the works were begun, and brought to the condition that has been mentioned, he ordered a confiderable body of troops under the command of Major Gen. Howe, and Brigadier Pigot, to drive the provincials from their works. This detachment confifted of 10 companies of grenadiers, as many of light infantry, and the 5th, 38th, 43d, 51ft, and 52d battalions, with a fuitable artillery, landed and drawn up without oppofition from the fhips of war. The two generals found the enemy fo advantagioufly pofted, and in fuch a pofture of defence, that they thought it neceffary to fend back for a reinforcement before they began the attack. They were accordingly joined with fome companies of light-infantry and grenadiers, by the 47th regiment, and by the

1st battalion of marines, amounting in the whole, as represented by Gen. Gage's letter, to something more than 2000 men.

The attack was begun by a heavy discharge of cannon and howitzers, under which the troops advanced in a slow march towards the enemy, and halted several times to afford time for the artillery to destroy the works, and to throw the provincials into confusion. But this did not happen according to their expectations; for the enemy remained steady, and the troops were unusually staggered in this attack. The provincials threw some men into the houses of Charlestown, which covered their right flank, by which means General Pigot, who commanded the left wing, and who behaved with great bravery and firmness, was at once exposed to the fire of the lines, and to that from the houses. In this attack Charlestown was set on fire, and burnt to ashes. It remains a point yet undetermined how and by whom this town was set on fire; whether by bombs from the ships, or by the troops. It is most probable that the troops set it on fire, for their own defence against the attack that was made from the houses, and with a design to dislodge the provincials that were in it. Whatever way it happened, that fine town, consisting of 400 houses, was reduced to ashes. The provincials were still unmoved, notwithstanding the continual fire of small arms and artillery. They behaved like veterans, and troops of the greatest experience. All this, while they did not return a single shot, until the king's forces had almost approached their works, when a dreadful fire took place, by which a number of brave British officers fell. Some officers who had served in the most distinguished actions in the last war, declared,

that

that this action, for the time it lasted, was the hottest engagement they ever saw. It is no wonder, if under so heavy and destructive a fire, our troops were thrown into disorder. It was reported that General Howe was for a few seconds left almost alone; and it is certain that most of the officers that were near his person were either killed or wounded. He deserves the greatest praise for his coolness and intrepidity on this occasion; he fully discovered that solid and rational courage that has appeared so conspicuous in the family of the Howes. General Clinton, who at this time had just arrived from Boston, during the time of the engagement, is said to have rallied the troops, and led them on again to charge the enemy. After a most dreadful carnage, they attacked the works with fixed bayonets, and dislodged the provincials. This would have been a work of much more slaughter, provided the colonists had been sufficiently provided with bayonets; for though many of them had no bayonets, and their ammunition was expended, they fought desperately within the works, and were with difficulty drove from them. They, however, retreated over Charlestown neck, which was enfiladed by the guns of the Glasgow man of war, and of two floating batteries. These did but small execution, though the dread of it had prevented some regiments, who were ordered to support that post from fulfilling their duty.

The battle of Bunker's-hill was one of the most bloody actions that has happened this long time, in which there were more British officers killed and wounded, according to the proportion of the number engaged, than were in any engagement last war. According to the public accounts, published by authority, the whole loss in killed and wounded amounted to 1054, of whom

226 were killed; of these 19 were commissioned officers, including a lieutenant-colonel, 2 majors, and 7 captains; 70 other officers were wounded. Among those who were most lamented on this occasion were lieutenant-colonel Abercromby, and Major Pitcairne of the marines. The majors, Williams and Spendlove, the last of which died of his wounds some time after the action, had distinguished themselves in such a manner as to make their loss more sensibly felt. The king's troops behaved with much bravery, as was manifest by the event; for there was scarce a single officer who had not an opportunity of signalizing himself, and the generals and field officers used the most extraordinary efforts. All these things concur to shew the dangerous and difficult service in which they were engaged. The battle of Quebec in the last war, with all the glory and vast consequences that attended it, was not so destructive to our officers as this entrenchment, thrown up in a few hours. It was a matter of grievous reflection, that such brave men, many of whom had contributed to exalt the dignity of their country in subduing her enemies and enlarging her territories, should have fallen in supporting a power that was seeking to enslave and ruin the British empire. These brave British officers found to their sad experience what wonderful exertions the spirit of liberty will produce even in unexperienced and raw troops. The provincials, who had been rated as cowards and poltroons in the ministerial vocabulary, under the influence of the powerful spirit of liberty shewed instances of wisdom, courage and intrepidity, that would not have disgraced troops of more experience and reputation. The consequences of this action were of more advantage to those that were supposed

to be vanquished, than to the conquerors; for the provincials began to find that they could face the king's troops and also to make some impression upon them; and they also discovered, that they could retreat without being pursued by the king's troops, which had confirmed them in the opinion that their enemies had suffered severely. What was the loss on the side of the provincials could not be learned by our troops; for unless 30 wounded men which were left on the field, the British forces took no prisoners. According to the account published by the congress of the province, their loss was comparatively small, amounting to about 450 killed, wounded, and missing. They affirm that on our side the slaughter was much more considerable; but of this our accounts said nothing. It was affirmed that the provincials buried a great number of their dead in the time of their engagement; but this is an extraordinary circumstance, which does not appear very credible; or if it was true, it shews that they had plenty of time, and were not hardly charged by our troops.

The person among the provincials that was most lamented, who was slain in this action, was Doctor Warren, who acted as a major-general and commander on this occasion; he was killed fighting bravely at the head of his troops, in a little redoubt to the right of the lines. This gentleman, who was generally esteemed for his merits, eloquence, and other abilities, had been one of the delegates to the first general congress, and was at this time president of the provincial congress. He is said to have been an eminent physician, and a person of an amiable character. When he saw his country going to be enslaved, as he judged, he fired with indignation at the thought, and broke thro'
all

all the endearing ties of family satisfaction, and devoted himself to the public service of the community, and fell gallantly in the cause of freedom and liberty. —They lost some other officers of character, one of whom, a lieutenant-colonel, died of his wounds, in the prison of Boston.

It is not easy to settle the different claims of parties, with respect to this action. Each side claimed much honour to themselves. The king's troops said the defeated three times their own number, out of a strong fortified post, and under many disadvantages. On the other side, they represented the regulars as amounting to 3000 men, and rated themselves at the number of only 1500; and affirmed that this small body not only withstood their attack, and repeatedly repulsed them with great loss, notwithstanding the powerful artillery they had brought with them, but that they had at the same time, and for several hours, sustained a most severe and intolerable fire from the ships, floating batteries, and fixed battery at Boston, which prevented them from being able to finish their works. In cases of this sort, great allowances must be made for the prejudice of parties; for it is very common for each side of a question to say the most favourable things of themselves that they can. The number of the provincials were perhaps neither so many as our accounts set them forth, nor so few as they themselves pretended. It is however manifest that the colonists were not casten down nor dispirited by this defeat; and it appears that they both had some judgment of the power of our troops, and of their own strength. It is highly probable that our troops on this occasion, though they pretended to despise the provincials, as inferior to them in courage and military discipline, received

received such an impression of what they would and could do, which made them more cautious afterwards. Had some of our boasting heroes at home been in the situation of General Howe and his officers, they would have been more cautious in talking of American cowardice. The provincials shewed a great degree of activity and skill in the construction of their works, and of steadiness and constancy in defending them, under many great disadvantages. They said, tho' they had lost a post, they had almost all the effects of a compleat victory; as they entirely put a stop to the offensive operations of a large army sent to subdue them; and which they continued to block up in a narrow town. They now triumphed that their actions had refuted those reproaches which had been thrown upon them in England, of being deficient in courage and resolution. The advantages of this engagement did not counterbalance the loss to the King's troops; for all that could be said to have been obtained in lieu of 1054 men killed and wounded was 5 pieces of cannon, and 30 wounded men.

The provincials after the action at Bunker's-hill, threw up works upon Winter-hill, on their side Charlestown neck, so that the troops were as closely invested in that peninsula, as they had been in Boston. They were also indefatigable in securing the most exposed posts of the lines with redoubts covered with artillery, and advanced their works close to the fortification on Boston-neck, where with equal boldness and address they burnt a guard-house belonging to the king's troops. As the army was abundantly furnished with all manner of military stores, and artillery; the troops were not sparing in throwing shells and maintaining a great cannonade upon
the

the works of the provincials, which had no other effect than to accustom them to that sort of service, and to wear off the dread of those noisy messengers of death. The provincials, on the other side, seemed to be cautious in expending their ammunition.

The melancholy effects of this battle appeared most manifest in the ruins of the town of Charlestown, which was now an affecting spectacle to the serious and unprejudiced of all parties. It was the first settlement made in this colony, and was considered as the mother of Boston; for the town of Boston was first built by a number of emigrants from Charlestown some short time after the year 1630. Charlestown was large, handsome, and well built,—both with regard to its public and private edifices; it was about half as large as Boston, and was capable of being made as strong, for it stood upon a peninsula, much in the same manner as Boston does, and had nearly the same natural advantages. It was both a market and county town, being the county town of Middlesex, in Massachusett's-Bay. It had a good large church, a market-place in a handsome square by the river side, supplied with all necessary provisions, both of flesh and fish,—and two large streets leading down to it, which were both regular and elegant. It carried on the greatest trade of any town in the province, except Boston. It is said that the two ports cleared out a thousand vessels annually for foreign trade, exclusive of a vast number of coasters. Such is the end of human labour, wisdom and industry—and such the effects and fatal fruits of civil dissention and discord! The work of a day will ruin the labour of ages, and lay riches, grandeur, magnificence, and splendor in ruins.

His Majesty's forces were now in a very ineligible situation;

situation; they were deprived of provisions from the country, by two causes;—they were hedged in by the provincial troops by land, and the colonies had agreed to send them none by sea. They had nothing but what they had from the ships, or what they took at the hazard of their lives; and their duty was now doubled, by being both obliged to guard their encampment and defend the town. This evil had one advantage attending it, it enlarged their quarters, and afforded them more room, and more fresh air.— They were more dreadfully incommoded in the town during the excessive heat of the summer, which was ready to bring on distempers and crowd the hospitals: This encampment was therefore a sort of relief for the present, tho' it was attended with more fatigue. —Their wants were at the same time very grievous, their situation irksome and degrading: they were insulted by an enemy whom they had been taught to despise, and in continual alarm from a people whom they had sufficiently provoked. Their provisions were both salt and bad; and, like other things that are derived from government contracts, were pernicious in their effects, and exorbitant in their price. The heat of the climate, the badness of provisions, and confinement, naturally brought on diseases, and filled the hospitals. The number of sick and wounded, at a moderate computation, amounted now to 1600. Considering all circumstances, it was a wonder there were not more in this distressed situation. It was however fortunate, that few, in comparison of the numbers that were sick, died.

A regiment of light cavalry arrived from Ireland,— which, instead of affording aid to their friends, were rather a grievance; for they were never able to set a

foot

foot out of the garrison, and only helped to confume the provifions which were in the town; by which means both the foldiers and the town's people were more diftreffed. Almoft all circumftances concurred to diftrefs and render the troops uneafy; they found from experience that the provincials were not fuch cowards as they had been reprefented, and that it was dangerous to prefume too far upon that hypothefis, and that many of thofe things which they needed greatly could not be obtained without encountering a defperate enemy. They were conftantly witneffes of the moft daring adventures performed by perfons whom they had been told were mean, daftardly poltroons, and who would run at the fight of a grenadier, —They were now not only obliged to rifk their lives for fupplies of neceffary food to themfelves, but to venture them for fupplies to their horfes; for hay, as well as bread, corn, and flefh, was become an article of very great importance. The hay, fheep, and cattle in the iflands were now as much the reafons of war, as the rights of the Britifh parliament over America; and they were heartily in earneft to fight for their food, who were indifferent about fighting for the dominion of others. The provincials knew the fituation and circumftances of the troops, and underftood what neceffity would fuggeft to them; having therefore procured a number of whale boats, and being mafters of the fhore and inlets of the bay, they burnt, deftroyed, and carried away, in fpite of all the fhips of war and armed veffels, thofe neceffary articles which the king's troops ftood moft in need of.———Thefe enterprifes brought on fundry fkirmifhes, and the provincials grew fo daring at length as to burn the light-houfe, which was built upon an ifland at the entrance of the

harbour,

harbour, tho' a man of war lay within a mile of them at the time. Some carpenters were sent afterwards, under the protection of a small party of marines, to erect a temporary light-house, when they killed and carried off the whole detachment. All these actions were at home represented as deeds of cowardice, and we heard nothing from ministerial demagogues, except, coward, rebel, or poltroon. Such is the infatuation of prejudiced minds, when set upon a favourite project, that they not only will not perceive the truth, but wilfully pervert it. Even when appearances were strongly against us, we still interpreted them in our own favour; from whence the public news became the vehicles of falshood, mifmformation, and deception. We were promised that in one campaign the war would be ended, the Americans obliged to submit to the will and pleasure of the minister, and Britain indemnified for all her expences by the wealth of the colonies. So far will blinded mortals proceed, when pride, interest, and passion put out their eyes.

While the troops were thus blockaded in Boston, a war of plunder commenced, or in more polite terms, it became prædatory. It was carried on between the ships of war and the inhabitants in different parts of the coast. The first being refused the provisions and necessaries which they wanted for themselves or the army, endeavoured to obtain them by force, and in these attempts were frequently opposed, and sometimes repulsed by the country people. The seizing of ships according to the new laws, or at the commands of the admiral, was also a continual source of animosity, the proprietors naturally hazarding all dangers, in defence, or for the recovery of their property. These contests brought the vengeance

geance of the men of war, upon several of the small towns upon the sea coast, some of which underwent a severe correction. On these occasions the argument concerning cowardice appeared to have as much force on the one side as the other; for if the provincials took the advantage of the country, and did not expose themselves unnecessarily to the violence of our men, our troops were cautious to keep within reach of their ships, and did not venture to penetrate into the country. It might have been expected while the war was hanging in this kind of suspence, and both parties seemed afraid to venture a general engagement, that some sparks of wisdom would have sprung up in the minds of the British ministry, and that they would have tried some softening measures, to have prevented the further shedding of blood.—— But either pride or revenge operated strongly upon their temper, and the blood they had shed was only a sort of a whet which made their appetites keener for slaughter, that they might glut their revenge. It was generally believed, that at this time the sovereign was greatly abused, and matters were misrepresented to him, otherwise he would not have given countenance to a war, which could have no good effect in its prosecution, and might issue in dismembering the empire. The friends of the revolution and the Hanoverian succession, could not prevail upon themselves to believe, that a King of the family of Brunswick could be so blind to his own interest, and that of his people, as to listen to the counsels of men that were advising him to ruin his own family. They at last had reason to fear that a great infatuation had seized the moving powers of the body politic, and the head as well as the members, were greatly infected. This they

they could only lament; for all the remedies which they tried proved ineffectual. Petitions and remonstrances were constructed disrespectful to his Majesty, and insults to government; and those who had ventured their lives and fortunes in quelling an actual rebellion against the sovereign, were accounted disloyal for pleading the cause of *magna charta* and the *revolution*; while some who had drawn their swords against their king and the laws, were preferred to high honours, and suffered to bask in the warm sunshine of royal favour.——The true lovers of English liberty were stigmatized with the opprobrious names of factious disturbers of the peace, and mock patriots, and venal scriblers were privileged to blacken their cause, and abuse their characters. Their opposition to violent measures, for supporting what at best was problematical, was termed indirect rebellion; and those who had once actually rebelled, were loudest in the cry against them.

The policy of the ministry at this time was as unsuccessful as it was absurd in its principles; the Canada bill, which is commonly called the Quebec act, operated in a manner directly opposite to its first and true intention. Its pernicious consequences were now displayed in a manner and degree beyond what its most sanguine opposers ever imagined could happen. Instead of gaining the French Canadians to the interests of government, by this absurd and inconsistent law, the ministry lost their affections, and they were found as much averse to this act, and as much disgusted at its operations as the British settlers. General Carleton, the governor of this province, who had placed much confidence in the raising a considerable army of Canadians, and being enabled to march at

their

their head to the relief of General Gage, found himself sadly disappointed; for tho' government relied much upon the hope of this manœuvre, and had sent 20,000 stands of arms, and a great quantity of military stores for this wise and gracious purpose, the Canadians were not disposed to make any use of them. The people said they were now under the British government; that they could not pretend to understand the causes of the present disputes, nor the justice of the claims on either side; that they did and would shew themselves dutiful subjects, by a quiet and peaceable demeanor, and due obedience to the government under which they were placed; but that it was totally inconsistent with their present state and condition, to interfere or in any degree render themselves parties in the contest that might arise between the government and its ancient subjects. The governor issued a proclamation for assembling the militia, and for the execution of the martial law, but it was in vain, for it produced no effect: they said they would defend the province if it was attacked; but they absolutely refused to march out of it, or to commence hostilities against their neighbours. When all earthly arguments failed, the governor had recourse to spiritual injunctions. He applied to the Bishop of Quebec to use his spiritual authority and influence with the people towards disposing them to the adoption of this favourable measure, and particularly that he would issue an episcopal mandate to be read in all the parish churches, by the priests, in the time of divine service; — but the Bishop excused himself from a compliance with this proposition, by representing, that an episcopal mandate on such a subject would be contrary to the canons of the church of Rome. The ecclesiastics, tices, in the place of this, issued pastoral letters which almost were generally disregarded. The noblesse alone, who were chiefly considered in the Quebec act, shewed a zeal against the English colonists; but as they stood separated from the great body of the people, they shewed no formidable degree of strength. These proceedings fully shew the real intention of this popish, absurd, and unconstitutional law; that it was formed with no other design than to make popery, as far as its professors would comply with the orders of state, subservient to arbitrary government. It was by no means to ease the consciences of catholics, nor to serve the purposes of their religion, nor those of any other form of godliness, but to serve the ends of the minister in subduing and enslaving the colonies. —The catholics in Canada perceived the design, and were far from thanking government for the new favour that was pretended to be conferred upon them; they despised the idea, and inferred, that government would make the same use of all religions to serve the ends of their ambition. This was such a coarse spun thread of human policy, that it was easily perceived by every eye, and the ministry greatly exposed both their weakness and malice in fabricating such an absurd law. It will in some after ages be considered as a strange political phænomenon, to find that a British parliament should have given sanction to a law so exceedingly contrary to the constitution of the empire. As this act was publicly complained of, and exposed in the several publications, the friends of the ministry set their hirelings to work to defend it; that if they could not altogether lick it into the form of truth, they might as far as was possible conceal, or varnish its deformity. His Majesty's promise in his

declaration

declaration at the peace 1763 was insisted upon as a reason for this new law; but it was affirmed that there was a wide difference between the promise of permitting the free exercise of any religion, and ingrafting it upon the states as a legal establishment: that the government had now established popery, and left the protestant subjects of the empire no more than a precarious toleration, depending upon his Majesty's will and pleasure, while popery was not only secured by law, but its clergy supported by the authority of parliament. This bill, like many other things which proceed from evil principles and springs of action, neither answered the design of the contrivers, nor pleased any party that was concerned in it.

This endeavour, which was expected to have great efficacy, not succeeding according to the wishes of the contrivers, the ministry proceded to another, equally absurd, cruel, and pernicious. Agents were employed who were supposed to have influence among the Indian tribes, which border upon the back settlements of the colonies, to stir them up to war, and make them fall upon the colonists with that fury that is peculiar to them when they engage.———But neither presents nor persuasions were capable of producing this effect. From whatever cause it proceeded, those savage warriors, who had at other times been ready to take up the hatchet, without support or engagement, now turned a deaf ear to all proposals and solicitations, and declared for a neutrality. They used much the same reasons that the Canadians had done: they said they did not understand the subject, and were sorry for the present unfortunate disputes; but it was not fit nor becoming for them to take any part in quarrels between Englishmen,

men, for all of whom, on both sides of the water, they had a great affection. This reply might have been sufficient to have made an impression upon consciences that were not altogether hardened;—it was a plain testimony that the Indians did not imagine that the claims of the ministry were a sufficient foundation for war, and that the dispute ought not to have been determined by the sword. The congress on this occasion did not neglect their own interest, nor lose an opportunity of so much consequence to their cause;——they accordingly employed proper persons to cultivate the favourable opinion of the Indians, and by degrees took such measures as made the agents for government think it proper to provide for their own safety. It is said that some of the Indians made proposals to take up arms on the other side; but the colonists only requested them to observe a strict neutrality. Candour must oblige an historian to confess that this was a very different temper from that of the ministry, who wanted the Indians by all means to fall upon the colonists: it would have had some appearance of reason for the colonists to have desired the Indians to have taken up the hatchet, because the government had shewn an intention to employ them in that manner; for it could only have been accounted self-defence to have made use of their enemies instruments against them. But this they did not do, which must be considered as a wise and prudent part of their conduct. It is a most disagreeable task in going over this part of our history, to be obliged to determine in many instances against the conduct of our government,—which in former times has been so remarkable for justice, mercy, and benevolence. General Gage's late proclamation tended much to increase

crease the animosity, indignation, and rage, which were already so prevalent in the colonies; and brought forth a declaration from the congress, which in the nature of these appeals that are made to mankind, as well as Heaven, in a declaration of war, set forth the causes and necessity of their taking up arms. Among the long list of the causes which they offer, besides the late hostilities, they state endeavours used to stir up the Indians and Canadians to attack them, and severely reproach General Gage for what they call his perfidy, cruelty, and breach of faith, in breaking the conditions which he had engaged to observe with the inhabitants of Boston; they also freely censure the army, whom they charge with the burning of Charlestown wantonly and unnecessarily.

When they state their resources, they consider foreign assistance as undoubtedly attainable if it were necessary. They however say, that lest this declaration should disquiet the minds of their friends and fellow subjects in any part of the empire, they assure them that they meant not to dissolve that happy union which had so long subsisted between them, and which they earnestly wished to see restored: and necessity had not yet driven them to that desperate measure, or induced them to excite any other nation to war against them; they had not raised armies with ambitious designs of separating from Great Britain, and establishing independent states; they fought not for conquest or glory.——This declaration was read with great seriousness, and even religious solemnity to the different bodies of the army who were encamped around Boston, and was received by them with loud acclamations of applause and approbation.

This declaration was followed by an address to the inhabitants

inhabitants of Great Britain; another to the people of Ireland; and a petition to the King. All these writings were drawn up in a very masterly manner; and in respect to art, address, and execution, equal to any public declarations made by any powers, upon the greatest occasions. The congress had in their declaration, without mentioning it particularly, reprobated the principles of Lord North's conciliatary proposition, which they called an insidious manœuvre, adopted by parliament. They sometime afterwards took the resolution more formally into consideration. It had been communicated to them by direction, or at least by permission of the minister, in the hand writing of Sir Grey Cowper, one of the two principal secretaries of the treasury. In the course of a long and argumentative discussion, they condemn it as unreasonable and insidious: that it is unreasonable, because, if they declare they will accede to it, they declare without reservation, that they will purchase the favor of parliament, not knowing at the same time at what price they will estimate their favour: that it is insidious, because, individual colonies having bid and bidden again, till they find the avidity of the seller too great for all their powers to satisfy, are then to turn into opposition divided from their sister colonies, whom the minister will have previously detached by a grant of easier terms, or by an artful procrastination of a defensive treaty. They conclude upon the whole, that the proposition was held up to the world to deceive it into a belief, that there was nothing in dispute except the *mode* of levying taxes; and that parliament have now been so good as to give up that, the colonies must have been unreasonable in the highest degree if they were not perfectly satisfied.

The

GENERAL PUTNAM.

The colony of Georgia at length joined in the general alliance. A provincial congress assembled in the beginning of the month of July, which speedily agreed to all the resolutions of the two general congresses, in the utmost extent, and appointed five delegates to attend the present. To make an amends for their delay, they entered into all the spirit of the resolutions formed by the other colonies, and adopted similar ones and declared that tho' their province was not included in any of the oppressive acts lately passed against America, they considered that circumstance as an insult rather than a favour, as being done only with a view to divide them from their American brethren. They also addressed a petition, under the title of 'An humble petition and address to his Majesty;' which, however trite the subject was now become, was not deficient in a certain freshness of colouring, which gave it the appearance of novelty. Upon the accession of this province, the colonists assumed after this period the appellation of *The Thirteen United Colonies*. Such was the progress of the general spirit of liberty, which we at home called rebellion, that it surmounted difficulties of the most grievous nature, and produced such an union among the colonies, which few would have expected to have happened for some ages to come.

The general congress, in compliance with the general wishes of the people, and the particular application of the New England provinces, appointed George Washington, Esq; a gentleman of affluent fortune in Virginia, and who had acquired considerable military experience in the last war, to be general and commander in chief of all the American forces. They also appointed Artemus Ward, Charles Lee, Philip Schuyler, and Israel Putnam, to be major-generals;

rals; and Horatio Gates, Esq; adjutant-general.—
The congress also fixed and appointed the pay of
both officers and soldiers; the latter of which were
much better provided for than those upon our establishment.

About the beginning of July, the Generals Washington and Lee arrived at the camp before Boston, and were treated with the greatest honours in all places thro' which they passed. They were escorted by large detachments of volunteers, composed of gentlemen in the different provinces; and received addresses from the provincial congresses of New-York and Massachussett's Bay. The military spirit and disposition was now so high and general, that war and military preparations employed the minds and hands of all orders of people throughout the continent.—— Men of the highest rank and fortunes, who were not appointed to public offices in the army, entered chearfully as private men, and served as volunteers in the ranks. Many of the younger Quakers, that peaceable and inoffensive denomination of Christians, when they saw their rights and liberties at stake, forgot their passive principles of forbearance and non-resistance, took up arms, and formed themselves into companies at Philadelphia, and applied with assiduity to study the military exercise and discipline. It was reported, though not with any degree of certainty, that there were not fewer than 200,000 men in arms and training this year throughout the continent of America.

Boston continued to be shut up by the provincial troops, and matters continued much in the same situation all the rest of this year, and a considerable part of the next: the king's forces, and the remaining inhabitants suffered prodigiously by fevers, fluxes, and the

scurvy,

scurvy, brought on thro' confinement, heat of weather, and bad provisions. Some things which were begun this year in Canada, will fall more properly under the history of the transactions of the following year, which shall be considered after we have finished the political history of this.———The ministry notwithstanding their zeal in pursuing measures to bring the colonists to subjection, shewed a real want of system and design in their whole proceedings.——— Tho' they saw the opposition in the colonies every day gathering strength, and encreasing in force, they seemed not to regard it, but formed their estimate wholly upon a peace establishment. The land-tax was continued at three shillings in the pound, and no vote of credit was required: the army remained upon its former footing, and a reduction was made of 4000 seamen, only 16000 being required for the ensuing year. This had the appearance of great inconsistency; for as the speech from the throne announced the American affairs to be in a most critical and alarming situation, and seemed to call for the most vigorous measures, yet in appearance there was nothing but supineness and want of attention prevailing upon the conduct of government. It was said by the opposition that this was only a ministerial stratagem to form estimates which were designed for no other purpose than to waste paper, but was never intended to be pursued; that under colour of this, the house would be surprized, and driven into grants of an enormous nature. That it was fit the ministry should explain their real intention, that gentlemen might be able to inform their constituents concerning what future burdens were to be imposed, or whether compulsive measures were intended against America; for that to talk

of

courage. He affirmed that they were not disciplined, nor capable of discipline, and that formed of such materials, and so indisposed to action, the numbers, of which such boasts had been made, would only add to the facility of their defeat.——From what has been shewn above, in the affairs of Lexington and Bunker's-hill, we may see how ill informed this minister of state was concerning the character and disposition of the colonists. He seemed to affirm a real falshood by declaring he knew what he did not know, and what experience has fully proved was in no respects the truth. It appears exceedingly strange to honest men, to hear persons in such exalted stations of life, so far degrading their characters, as to expose their own ignorance and folly in such a public manner. A nation is in a very critical situation when it is under the management of such ignorant persons.

Altho' on these grounds the establishment stood, or seemed to stand as reduced, the ministers did not disclaim any farther arrangement of a political nature. By being frequently pressed, some explanation was drawn out on that subject in the House of Commons. A member of the Commons called publicly upon the minister in that House, to know whether he had any information to lay before them, or any measures to propose concerning America; for if he had not, he thought it the duty of parliament to interpose, to call for papers, and to proceed on such information, however defective, as they could obtain. He conluded his speech by totally condemning the measures adopted by the late parliament, as equally impolitic and impracticable; and said that they never could be prudently or effectually carried into execution.

The minister did not enter into a defence of the measures

of inforcing acts upon a reduced eſtabliſhment, either naval or military, was a ſort of language only fit to amuſe children. It had undoubtedly the appearance of great inconſiſtency to pretend to diminiſh the ſea forces, when the king's ſpeech declared that the affairs in America were in a critical and dangerous ſituation.

The conduct of the miniſtry was greatly complained of on this occaſion; becauſe when they were leading the nation into war, they were taking every ſtep they could to make that war ruinous, by neglecting thoſe preparations that were neceſſary for carrying it on with honour and ſucceſs. That they would neither make peace, by making reaſonable conceſſions, nor war, by any vigorous military arrangements; but fluctuating between both, deprived the nation of a poſſibility of deriving benefit from either. It was ſaid, that this delay was ſo far from ſaving any thing for the public, that it would increaſe the future expence which the nation would aſſuredly feel in due time.—The oppoſition ſaid they were far from deſiring war, and as far from deſiring large peace eſtabliſhments; but if againſt their will, war muſt be carried on, that common ſenſe dictated that it ought to be carried on with effect; and that if a peace eſtabliſhment, and even lower than a peace eſtabliſhment, was ſufficient to ſupport a war, this was a demonſtrative proof that the peace eſtabliſhment had been ſhamefully prodigal, and the ſubſtance of the nation profuſely waſted.

In anſwer to this charge, the miniſter of the naval department publicly aſſerted in the Houſe of Lords, that he knew the low eſtabliſhment propoſed, would be fully ſufficient for reducing the colonies to obedience. He ſpoke with great contempt of the Americans, and ſeemed to deſpiſe both their power and courage.

measures of the late parliament. He pretended that the subject required the greatest attention and diligence, as being a matter of the greatest consequence ever disputed within the walls, and that he would not agree to condemn measures hastily, which had been taken up upon such weighty motives; that at that time it was impossible to tell how they might answer, but that they should have a fair trial before they were reprobated; and that the wisdom and policy of them could only be known in the event. That he had information which he would lay before the House soon after the holidays, and that he would adopt the gentleman's ideas so far, who had called upon him, as to propose the appointment of a committee, for taking the affairs of America under the consideration. This delay was the cause of much altercation, and many severe reflections against the ministry. To pursue the debates in parliament on this occasion, would be both tedious and uninteresting to many of our readers;— we shall conclude the history of this year by laying in one view before them, the substance of all those debates in the following state-papers.

The humble Address of the Right Honourable the Lords Spiritual and Temporal, and Commons, in Parliament assembled; presented to his Majesty on Thursday the 9th of February, 1775.

"Most Gracious Sovereign,

"WE, your Majesty's most dutiful and loyal subjects, the Lords Spiritual and Temporal, and Commons, in parliament assembled, return your Majesty our most humble thanks for having been graciously pleased to communicate to us the several papers relating to the present state of the British colonies in America,

America, which, by your Majesty's commands, have been laid before us: We have taken them into our most serious consideration; and we find, that a part of your Majesty's subjects, in the province of the Massachusett's-Bay, have proceeded so far as to resist the authority of the supreme legislature; that a rebellion at this time actually exists within the said province; and we see, with the utmost concern, that they have been countenanced and encouraged by unlawful combinations and engagements, entered into by your Majesty's subjects in several of the other colonies, to the injury and oppression of many of their innocent fellow-subjects, resident within the kingdom of Great Britain, and the rest of your Majesty's dominions: This conduct, on their part, appears to us the more inexcusable, when we consider with how much temper your Majesty and the two houses of parliament, have acted in support of the laws and constitution of Great Britain. We can never so far desert the trust reposed in us, as to relinquish any part of the sovereign authority over all your Majesty's dominions, which, by law, is vested in your Majesty and the two houses of parliament; and the conduct of many persons, in several of the colonies, during the late disturbances, is alone sufficient to convince us how necessary this power is for the protection of the lives and fortunes of your Majesty's subjects.

We ever have been, and always should be, ready to pay attention and regard to any real grievances of any of your Majesty's subjects. which sha'l, in a dutiful and constitutional manner, be laid before us; and whenever any of the colonies shall make a proper application to us, we shall be ready to afford them every just and reasonable indulgence: At the same time, we consider it as our indispensible duty humbly to beseech
your

your Majesty, that you will take the most effectual measures to enforce due obedience to the laws and authority of the supreme legislature;' and we beg leave, in the most solemn manner, to assure your Majesty, that it is our fixed resolution, at the hazard of our lives and properties, to stand by your Majesty, against all rebellious attempts in the maintenance of the just rights of your Majesty and the two houses of parliament."

His Majesty's most Gracious Answer.
" My Lords and Gentlemen,
"I thank you for this very dutiful and loyal address, and for the affectionate and solemn assurances you give me of your support in maintaining the just rights of my crown, and of the two houses of parliament; and you may depend on my taking the most speedy and effectual measures for inforcing due obedience to the laws, and the authority of the supreme legislature.

" Whenever any of my colonies shall make a proper and dutiful application, I shall be ready to conclude with you, in affording them every just and reasonable indulgence; and it is my ardent wish, that this disposition may have a happy effect on the temper and conduct of my subjects in America."

Protest of several of the Lords, on its being resolved in their House, on Tuesday, the 7th of February, 1775, to put a main question, viz. To agree with the Commons in the foregoing address, sent by them to their Lordships for their concurrence, by filling up the blank left in it for that purpose, with the words, " Lords Spiritual and Temporal;" as likewise another Protest of

several

several of the Lords, on their House's agreeing with the Commons in the said Address.

Dissentient,

1st. The previous question was moved, not to prevent the proceedings in the address communicated at the conference with the Commons, but in order to present the petitions of the North American merchants, and of the West India merchants and planters, which petitions the House might reject if frivolous, or postpone if not urgent, as might seem fit to their wisdom; but to hurry on the business to which these petitions so materially and directly related, the express prayer of which was, that they might be heard before "any resolution may be taken by this right honourable House respecting America:" To refuse so much as to suffer them to be presented, is a proceeding of the most unwarrantable nature, and directly subversive of the most sacred rights of the subject. It is the more particularly exceptionable, as a Lord, in his place, at the express desire of the West-India merchants, informed the House, that if necessitated so to do, they were ready, without councel or farther preparation, instantly to offer evidence to prove, that several islands of the West-Indies could not be able to subsist after the operation of the proposed address in America. Justice, in regard to individuals, policy, with regard to the public, and decorum, with regard to ourselves, required that we should admit this petition to be presented. By refusing it, justice is denied.

2dly. Because the papers laid upon our table by the ministers, are so manifestively defective, and so avowedly curtailed, that we can derive from them nothing like information of the true state of the object on which we are going to act, or of the consequences of the resolutions which we may take. We ought, as we conceive, with gladness to have accepted that information from the merchants, which if it had not been voluntarily offered it is our duty to seek. There is no information concerning the state of our colonies (taken in any point of view), which the merchants are not far more competent to give than governors or officers, who often know far less of the temper and disposition, or may be more disposed to misrepresent it than the merchants. Of this we have a full and melancholy experience, in the mistaken ideas on which the fatal acts of the last parliament were formed.

3dly. Because we are of opinion, that in entering into a war, in which mischiefs and inconveniences are real and certain, (but the utmost extent of which it is impossible to foresee), true policy requires that those should be thoroughly satisfied of the deliberation with which it was undertaken: and we apprehend that the planters, merchants, and manufacturers will not bear their losses and burthens, brought on them by the proposed civil war, the better for our refusing so much as to hear them previous to our engaging in that war; nor will our precipitation in resolving add much to the success in executing any plan that may be pursued.

We protest therefore against the refusal to suffer such petitions to be presented, and we thus clear ourselves to our country of the disgrace and mischief which must attend this unconstitutional, indecent, and improvident proceeding.

Richmond,	Portland,	Ponsonby,
Camden,	Archer,	Fitzwilliam,
		Rock-

Rockingham, Scarborough, Wycombe,
Abergavenny, Effingham, Abingdon,
Torrington, Craven, Stanhope,
Courtenay, Cholmondeley, Tankerville.

Then the main question was put, whether to agree with the Commons in the said address, by inserting the words; (Lords Spiritual and Temporal) and

It was resolved in the affirmative.

    Contents 87
    Non-Contents 27

Dissentient, 1st. Because the violent matter of this dangerous address was highly aggravated by the violent manner in which it was precipitately hurried through the House. Lords were not allowed the interposition of a moment's time for deliberation, before they were driven headlong into a declaration of a civil war. A conference was held with the Commons, an address of this importance presented, all extraneous information, although offered positively refused, all petitions arbitrarily rejected, and the whole of this most awful business received, debated, and concluded in a single day.

2dly. Because no legal grounds were laid in argument or in fact, to shew that a rebellion, properly so called, did exist in Massachussett's-Bay, when the papers of the latest date, and from whence alone we derive our information, were written. The overt-acts, to which the species of treason affirmed in the address ought to be applied, were not established, nor any offenders to be marked out: but a general mass of the acts of turbulence, said to be done at various times and places, and of various natures, were all thrown together to make out one general constructive treason. Neither was there any sort of proof of the continu-
              ance

ance of any unlawful force, from whence we could infer that a rebellion does now exist. And we are the more cautious to pronounce any part of his Majesty's dominions in actual rebellion, because the cases of constructive treason, under that branch of the 26th of Edward the Third, which describes the crime of rebellion, have been already so far extended by the judges, and the distinctions upon it so nice and subtle, that no prudent man ought to declare any single person in that situation, without the clearest evidence of the uncontrovertible overt-acts, to warrant such a declaration. Much less ought so high an authority as both houses of parliament, to denounce so severe a judgment against a considerable part of his Majesty's subjects, by which his forces may think themselves justified in commencing a war, without any further order or commission.

3dly. Because we think that several acts of the late parliament, and several late proceedings of administration, with regard to the colonies, are real grievances, and just causes of complaint; and, we cannot, in honour, or in conscience, consent to an address which commends the temper by which proceedings, so very intemperate, have been carried on; nor can we persuade ourselves to authorize violent courses against persons in the colonies who have resisted authority, without, at the same time, redressing the grievances which have given but too much provocation for their behaviour.

4thly. Because we think the loose and general assurances given by the address of a future redress of grievances, in case of submission, is far from satisfactory, or at all likely to produce their end, whilst the acts complained of continue unrepealed, or unamended.

ed, and their authors remain in authority here, because these advisers of all the measures which have brought on the calamities of this empire, will not be trusted whilst they defend as just, necessary, and even indulgent, all the acts complained of as grievances by the Americans; and must, therefore, on their own principles, be bound in future to govern the colonies in the manner which has already produced such fatal effects; and we fear that the refusal of this House so much as to receive, previous to determination (which is the most offensive mode of rejection) petitions from the unoffending natives of Great Britain, and the West-India islands, affords but a very discouraging prospect of our obtaining hereafter any petitions at all from those whom we have declared actors in rebellion, or abettors of that crime.

Lastly, Because the means of enforcing the authority of the British legislature, is confided to persons of whose capacity, for that purpose, from abundant experience, we have reason to doubt; and who have hitherto used no effectual means of conciliating, or of reducing those who oppose that authority:—this appears in the constant failure of all their projects, the insufficiency of all their information, and the disappointment of all the hopes, which they have for several years held out to the public. Parliament has never refused any of their proposals, and yet our affairs have proceeded daily from bad to worse, until we have been brought, step by step, to that state of confusion, and even civil violence, which was the natural result of these desperate measures.

We therefore protest against an address amounting to a declaration of war, which is founded on no proper parliamentary information; which was introduced

ced by refusing to suffer the presentation of petitions against it, (although it be the undoubted right of the subject to present the same) which followed the rejection of every mode of conciliation; which holds out no substantial offer of redress of grievances; and which promises support to those ministers who have inflamed America, and grossly misconducted the affairs of Great Britain.

Richmond,	Cholmondeley,	Craven,
Abingdon,	Archer,	Portland,
Abergavenny,	Camden,	Rockingham,
Effingham,	Wycombe,	Stanhope,
Courtenay,	Scarborough,	Torrington,
Fitzwilliam,	Ponsonby,	Tankerville.

Message of his Majesty to the House of Commons, on Friday, the 10th of February, 1775.

"George R.

"HIS Majesty being determined, in consequence of the address of both houses of parliament, to take the most speedy and effectual measures for supporting the just rights of his crown, and the two houses of parliament, thinks proper to acquaint this house, that some addition to his forces by sea and land will be necessary for that purpose; and doubts not but his faithful Commons, on whose zeal and affection he entirely relies, will enable him to make such augmentation to his forces as the present occasion shall be thought to require.

"G. R."

Petition of the Lord Mayor of the city of London, &c. presented to the House of Commons, on Friday, the 24th of February, 1774. To

To the Honourable the Commons of Great Britain, in Parliament assembled.

The humble Petition of the Lord Mayor, Aldermen, and Commons of the city of London, in Common-Council assembled,

Sheweth.

"THAT although your petitioners bear all due respect to the policy of those acts of parliament, which have anciently preserved Great Britain a necessary and beneficial commerce with our colonies, yet they are exceedingly alarmed at the consequences that must ensue, if the bill now depending in this honourable house should pass into a law, entitled, "A bill to restrain the trade and commerce of Massachusett's Bay and New Hampshire, and colonies of Connecticut and Rhode Island, and Providence Plantations in North America, to Great Britain, Ireland, and the British islands in the West-Indies, and to prohibit such provinces and colonies from carrying on any fishery on the banks of Newfoundland, or other places therein to be mentioned, under certain conditions, and for a time to be limited;" the said bill, as your petitioners conceive, being unjustly founded, because it involves the whole in the punishment intended for the supposed offences of a few.

"That it must, in its consequences, overwhelm thousands of his Majesty's loyal and useful subjects with the utmost poverty and distress, inasmuch as they will be thereby deprived of the fisheries, which are the natural means of supporting themselves and families.

"That the extensive commerce between Great-Britain and her colonies will, by this bill, be greatly injured, as a capital source of remittance will be stopt, which

which will not only disconnect the future commercial intercourse between those colonies and this country, but will eventually render them incapable of paying the large debts already due to the merchants of this city,

"That the utmost confusion will probably ensue from enforcing this bill, if it is passed into a law, as it cannot be supposed that a great number of men, naturally hardy and brave, will quietly submit to a law which will reduce them almost to famine, they not having within themselves provisions sufficient for their subsistence.

"That it will induce the French to extend their fisheries, and by that means increase the wealth and strength of our rivals in trade, to the great prejudice of this country.

"That your petitioners feel for the many hardships which their fellow-subjects in America already labour under, from the execution of several late acts of parliament, evidently partial and oppressive; and which seem to be extended and continued by this bill; inasmuch as it confirms those acts, which in particular cases deprive the American subject of trial by jury, prohibit the Americans from carrying provisions from one colony to another, invite a contraband trade, under military protection, prevent any subject of Great-Britain or Ireland from being part owner of certain American ships or vessels, and vest an undue and dangerous authority in the governor and council of Massachusett's Bay.

"Your petitioners, therefore, humbly pray this honourable house, that the said bill may not pass into a law."

Articles of confederation and perpetual union entered into by the Delegates of the several colonies of New Hampshire, Massachusett's, &c. &c. &c. &c. &c. &c. &c. &c. &c. &c. in General Congress, met at Philadelphia, May 20th, 1775.

ARTICLE I.

The name of the confederacy shall henceforth be, The United Colonies of North America.

II. The United Colonies hereby severally enter into a firm league of friendship with each other, binding on themselves and their posterity, for their common defence against their enemies, for the security of their liberties and properties, the safety of their persons and families, and their mutual and general welfare.

III. That each colony shall enjoy and retain as much as it may think fit of its own present laws, customs, rights, privileges, and peculiar jurisdictions, within its own limits; and may amend its own constitution, as shall seem best to its own assembly or convention.

IV. That for the more convenient management of general interests, delegates shall be elected annually, in each colony, to meet in general congress, at such time and place as shall be agreed on in the next preceding congress. Only where particular circumstances do not make a deviation necessary, it is understood to be a rule, that each succeeding congress is to be held in a different colony, till the whole number be gone through, and so in perpetual rotation; and that accordingly, the next congress after the present shall be held at Annapolis, in Maryland.

V. That the power and duty of the congress shall extend to the determining on war and peace, the entering into alliances, the reconciliation with Great Britain, the settling all disputes between colony and colony, if any should arise, and the planting new colonies where proper. The Congress shall also make such general ordinances thought necessary to the general welfare, of which particular assemblies cannot be competent, viz. those that may relate to our general commerce or general currency, to the establishment of posts, the regulation of our common forces; the congress shall also have the appointment of all officers civil and military, appertaining to the general confederacy,—such as general treasurer, secretary, &c. &c. &c.

VI. All charges of war, and all other general expences to be incurred for the common welfare, shall be defrayed out of a common treasury, which is to be supplied by each colony, in proportion to its number of male polls between 16 and 60 years of age; the taxes for paying that proportion are to be laid and levied by the laws of each colony.

VII. The number of delegates to be elected, and sent to the congress by each colony, shall be regulated from time to time, by the number of such polls returned; so as that one delegate be allowed for every 5000 polls. And the delegates are to bring with them to every congress an authenticated return of the number of polls in their respective colonies, which is to be taken for the purposes above-mentioned.

VIII. At every meeting of the congress, one half of the members returned, exclusive of the proxies, shall be necessary to make a quorum; and each delegate at the congress shall have a vote in all cases; and if necessarily absent, shall be allowed to appoint any other delegate from the same colony to be his proxy, who may vote for him.   IX.

IX. An executive council should be appointed by the congress out of their own body, consisting of 12 persons, of whom in the first appointment one-third, viz. four, shall be for one year, four for two years, and four for three years; and as the said terms expire, the vacancies shall be filled up by appointments for three years, whereby one-third of the members will be chosen annually; and each person who has served the same term of three years, as counsellor, shall have a respite of three years, before he can be elected again. This counsel, of whom two-thirds shall be a quorum, in the recess of the congress is to execute what shall have been enjoined thereby; to manage the general continental business and interests, to receive applications from foreign countries, to prepare matters for the consideration of the congress, to fill up, *pro tempore*, continental offices that fall vacant, and to draw on the general treasurer for such monies as may be necessary for general services, and appropriated by the congress to such services.

X. No colony shall engage in an offensive war with any nation of Indians, without the consent of the congress or great council above mentioned, who are first to consider the justice and necessity of such war.

XI. A perpetual alliance, offensive and defensive, is to be entered into, as soon as may be, with the six nations; their limits ascertained and secured to them; their lands not to be encroached on, nor any private or colony purchase to be made of them hereafter to be held good, nor any contract for lands to be made but between the great Council of the Indians at Onondega and the general Congress.——The boundaries and lands of all the other Indians shall also be ascertained and secured to them in the same manner;

and

and persons appointed to reside among them in proper districts, who shall take care to prevent injustice in the trade with them; and be enabled at our general expence, by occasional small supplies, to relieve their personal wants and distresses; and all purchases from them shall be by the congress, for the general advantage and benefit of the united colonies.

XII. As all new institutions may have imperfections, which only time and experience can discover, it is agreed that the general congress, from time to time, shall propose such amendments of this constitution, as may be found necessary, which being approved by a majority of the colony assemblies, shall be equally binding with the rest of the articles of this confederation.

XIII. Any and every colony from Great Britain upon the continent of North America, not at present engaged in our association, may, upon application, and joining the said association, be received into the confederation, viz. Quebec, St. John's, Nova-Scotia, Bermudas and the East and West Floridas, and shall thereupon be entitled to all the advantages of our union, mutual assistance, and commerce.

These articles shall be proposed to the several provincial conventions or assemblies, to be by them considered; and if approved, they are advised to empower their delegates to agree and ratify the same in the ensuing congress; after which the union thereby established is to continue firm, till the terms of reconciliation proposed in the petition of the last congress to the king are agreed to; till the acts, since made, restraining the American commerce and fisheries, are repealed; till reparation is made for the injuries done to Boston by shutting up its port; for burning Charlestown,

town, and for the expence of this unjust war; and till all the British troops are withdrawn from America. On the arrival of these events, the colonies are to return to their former connections and friendship with Great Britain; but on failure thereof, this confederation is to be perpetual.

 WHEREAS it hath pleased God to bless these countries with a most plentiful harvest, whereby much corn and other provisions can be spared to foreign nations who may want the same:

Resolved, That after the expiration of six months, from the 20th of July inst. being the day appointed by a late act of parliament of Great Britain, for restraining the trade of the confederate colonies, all custom-houses therein (if the said act be not first repealed) shall be shut up, and all the officers of the same discharged from the execution of their several functions; and all the ports of the said colonies are hereby declared to be thenceforth open to the ships of every state in Europe that will admit our commerce, and protect it, who may bring in and expose to sale, free of all duties, their respective produce and manufactures, and every kind of merchandize, excepting teas, and the merchandize of Great Britain, Ireland, and the British West-India islands.

Resolved, That we will, to the utmost of our power, maintain and support this freedom of commerce for two years certain after its commencement, any reconciliation between us and Great Britain notwithstanding, and as much longer beyond that term as the late acts of parliament for restraining the commerce and fisheries, and disallowing the laws and charters of any of the colonies, shall continue unrepealed.

Address,

Address, &c. of the Lord Mayor of the city of London, &c. presented to his Majesty, on Friday the 14th of July, 1775.

To the King's Most Excellent Majesty.

The humble Address and Petition of the Lord Mayor, Aldermen, and Commons of the city of London, in Common Council assembled.

"Most gracious Sovereign,

YOUR Majesty's most loyal and dutiful subjects, the Lord Mayor, Aldermen, and Commons of the city of London, in common council assembled, with all humility beg leave to lay themselves at your royal feet, humbly imploring your benign attention towards the grievous distractions of their fellow-subjects in America.

The characteristic of the people, Sire, over whom you reign, has ever been equally remarked for their unparalleled loyalty to their Sovereign, whilst the principles of the constitution have been the rule of his government, as well as a firm opposition whenever their rights have been invaded.

Your American subjects, Royal Sire, descended from the same ancestors with ourselves, appear equally jealous of the prerogatives of freemen,—without which they cannot deem themselves happy.

Their chearful and unasked for contributions, as well as willing services to the mother-country, whilst they remained free from the clog of compulsory laws, will, we are sure, plead powerfully with the humanity of your disposition, for graciously granting them every reasonable opportunity of giving, as freemen, what they seem resolutely determined to refuse under the injunction of laws made independent of their own consent.

The abhorrence we entertain of civil bloodshed and confusion will, we trust, Sire, if not wholly exculpate us in your royal mind, yet plead powerfully in our favour, for the warmth with which we lament those measures, whose destructive principles have driven our American brethren to acts of desperation.

Convinced of the earnest disposition of the colonists to remain firm in all duteous obedience to the constitutional authority of this kingdom, permit us, most gracious sovereign, to beseech you that those operations of force, which at present distract them with the most dreadful apprehensions, may be suspended; and that, uncontrouled by a restraint incompatible with a free government, they may possess an opportunity of tendering such terms of accomodation, as, we doubt not, will approve them worthy of a distinguished rank among the firmest friends of this country."

Signed by order of court,

WILLIAM RIX.

To which address and petition, his Majesty was pleased to return the following answer:

"I AM always ready to listen to the dutiful petitions of my subjects, and ever happy to comply with their reasonable requests; but while the constitutional authority of this kingdon is openly resisted by a part of my American subjects, I owe it to the rest of my people, of whose zeal and fidelity I have had such constant proofs, to continue and enforce those measures by which alone their rights and interests can be asserted and maintained."

His Majesty's most gracious Speech to both Houses of Parliament, Friday, May 26, 1775.

"My

"My Lords and Gentlemen,

I cannot, in justice to you, forbear to express my intire satisfaction in your conduct, during the course of this important session.

You have maintained, with a firm and steady resolution, the rights of my crown, and the authority of parliament, which I shall ever consider as inseparable: you have protected and promoted the commercial interests of my kingdoms, and you have at the same time, given convincing proofs of your readiness, as far as the constitution will allow you, to gratify the wishes, and remove the apprehensions, of my subjects in America; and I am persuaded, that the most salutary effects must, in the end, result from measures formed and conducted on such principles.

The late mark of your affectionate attachment to me, and to the Queen, and the zeal and unanimity which accompanied it, demand my particular thanks.

I have the satisfaction to acquaint you, that, as well from the general dispositions of other powers, as from the solemn assurances which I have received, I have great reason to expect the continuance of peace: nothing on my part, consistent with the maintenance of the honour and interest of my kingdoms, shall be wanting to secure the public tranquility.

Gentlemen of the House of Commons,

It gives me much concern, that the unhappy disturbances in some of my colonies have obliged me to propose to you an augmentation of my army, and have prevented me from completing the intended reduction of the establishment of my naval forces. I cannot sufficiently thank you for the chearfulness and public spirit with which you have granted the supplies for the several services of the current year.

My

"My Lords and Gentlemen,

I have nothing to desire of you but to use your best endeavours to preserve and to cultivate, in your several counties, the same regard for public order, and the same discernment of their true interests, which have in these times distinguished the character of my faithful and beloved people; and the continuance of which cannot fail to render them happy at home, and respected abroad."

Then the Lord Chancellor, by his Majesty's command, said,

My Lords and Gentlemen,

It is his Majesty's royal will and pleasure, that this parliament be prorogued to Thursday the twenty-seventh day of July next, to be then here held; and this parliament is accordingly prorogued to Thursday the 27th day of July next.

A Declaration by the Representatives of the United Colonies of North America, now met in General Congress at Philadelphia, setting forth the causes and necessity of their taking up arms.

IF it were possible for men, who exercise their reason, to believe that the Divine Author of our existence intended a part of the human race to hold an absolute property in, and unbounded power over others, marked out by his infinite goodness, and wisdom, as the objects of a legal domination, never rightly resistable, however severe and oppressive; the inhabitants of these colonies might at least require from the parliament of Great Britain some evidence, that this dreadful authority over them has been granted to that body. But a reverence for our Great Creator, principles of humanity, and the dictates of common sense, must convince all those who reflect upon the subject, that government was instituted to promote the welfare of mankind, and ought to be administered for the attainment of that end. The legislature of Great Britain, however stimulated by an inordinate passion for a power not only unjustifiable, but which they know to be particularly reprobated by the very constitution of that kingdom, and desperate of success in any mode of contest where regard should be had to truth, law or right, have at length, deserting those, attempted to effect their cruel and impolitic purpose of enslaving these colonies by violence, and have thereby rendered it necessary for us to close with their last appeal from reason to arms. Yet, however blinded that assembly may be, by their intemperate rage for unlimited domination, so as to slight justice and the opinion of mankind, we esteem ourselves bound, by obligations of respect to the rest of the world, to make known the justice of our cause.

Our forefathers inhabitants of the island of Great Britain, left their native land, to seek on these shores a residence for civil and religious freedom. At the expence of their blood, at the hazard of their fortunes, without the least charge to the country from which they removed, by unceasing labour and an unconquerable spirit, they effected settlements in the distant and inhospitable wilds of America, then filled with numerous and warlike natives of Barbarians. Societies or governments, vested with perfect legislatures, were formed under charters from the crown, and an harmonious intercourse was established between the colonies and the kingdom from which they derived their origin. The mutual benefits of this union became in a short time so extraordinary, as to excite astonishment.

astonishment. It is universally confessed, that the amazing increase of the wealth, strength, and navigation of the realm, arose from this source; and the minister, who so wisely and successfully directed the measures of Great Britain in the late war, publicly declared that these colonies enabled her to triumph over her enemies. Towards the conclusion of that war, it pleased our sovereign to make a change in his councils. From that fatal moment the affairs of the British empire began to fall into confusion, and, gradually sliding from the summit of glorious prosperity, to which they had been advanced by the virtues and abilities of one man, are at length distracted by the convulsions that now shake it to its deepest foundations. The new ministry, finding the brave foes of Britain, though frequently defeated, yet still contending, took up the unfortunate idea of granting them a hasty peace, and then of subduing her faithful friends.

These devoted colonies were judged to be in such a state, as to present victories without bloodshed, and all the easy emoluments of statutable plunder. The uninterrupted tenure of their peaceable and respectful behaviour, from the beginning of colonization; their dutiful, zealous, and useful services during the war, though so recently and amply acknowledged in the most honourable manner by his Majesty, by the late king, and by parliament; could not save them from the mediated innovations. Parliament was influenced to adopt the pernicius project, and, assuming a new power over them, have in the course of eleven years, given such decicive specimens of the spirit and consequences attending this power, as to leave no doubts concerning the effects of acquiescence under it. They have undertaken to give and grant our mo-

ney

ney without our consent, though we have ever exercised an exclusive right to dispose of our own property. Statutes have been passed for extending the jurisdiction of courts of Admiralty and Vice-Admiralty beyond their ancient limits, for depriving us of the accustomed and inestimable privileges of trial by jury, in cases affecting both life and property; for suspending the legislature of one of the colonies; for interdicting all commerce of another, and for altering fundamentally the form of government established by charter, and secured by acts of its own legislature, solemnly confirmed by the crown; for exempting the murderers of colonists from legal trial, and, in effect, from punishment, for erecting in a neighbouring province, acquired by the joint arms of Great Britain and America, a despotism dangerous to our very existence; and for acquainting soldiers upon the colonists in times of profound peace. It has also been resolved in parliament, that colonists, charged with committing certain offences, shall be transported to England to be tried.

But should we enumerate our injuries in detail?— By one statute it is declared, that parliament can 'of right make laws to bind us in all cases whatever.'— What is to defend us against so enormous, so unlimitted a power? Not a single man of those who assume it is chosen by us, or is subject to our controul, or influence; but, on the contrary, they are all of them exempt from the operation of such laws; and and American revenue, if not diverted from the ostensible purposes for which it is raised, would actually lighten their own burthens, in proportion as they increased ours. We saw the misery to which such despotism would reduce us. We for ten years incessantly ly and ineffectually besieged the throne as supplicants; we reasoned, remonstrated with parliament in the most mild and decent language. But administration, sensible that we should regard these oppressive measures as freemen ought to do, sent over fleets and armies to enforce them. The indignation of the Americans was roused, it is true; but it was the indignation of a virtuous, loyal, and affectionate people. A congress of delegates from the united colonies was assembled at Philadelphia, on the 5th day of last September. We resolved again to offer an humble and dutiful petition to the king, and also addressed our fellow subjects of Great Britain. We have pursued every temperate, every respectful measure; we have even proceeded to break off our commercial intercourse with our fellow-subjects, as the last peaceable admonition, that our attachment to no nation upon earth would supplant our attachment to liberty.——— This we flatter ourselves, was the ultimate step of the controversy; but subsequent events have shewn how vain was this hope of finding moderation in our enemies.

Several threatening expressions against the colonies were inserted in his Majesty's speech. Our petition, though we are told it was a decent one, that his Majesty had been pleased to receive it graciously, and to promise laying it before his parliament, was huddled into both houses amongst a bundle of American papers, and there neglected. The Lords and Commons in their address, in the month of February said,—' that a rebellion at that time actually existed within the province of Massachusett's-Bay; and that those concerned in it had been countenanced and encouraged by unlawful combinations and engagements,

entered

entered into by his Majesty's subjects in several of the other colonies; and therefore they besought his Majesty that he would take the most effectual measures to enforce due obedience to the laws and authority of the supreme legislature.' Soon after the commercial intercourse of the whole colonies, with foreign countries and with each other, was cut off by an act of parliament; by another, several of them were intirely prohibited from the fisheries in the seas near their coasts, on which they always depended for their sustenance; and large reinforcements of ships and troops were immediately sent over to Gen. Gage.

Fruitless were all the intreaties, arguments, and eloquence of an illustrious band, of the most distinguished peers and commoners, who nobly and strenuously asserted the justice of our cause, to stay or even to mitigate the heedless fury with which these accumulated and unexampled outrages were hurried on. —Equally fruitless was the interference of the city of London, of Bristol, and many other respectable towns in our favour. Parliament adopted an insidious manœuvure, calculated to divide us, to establish a perpetual auction of taxations, where colony should bid against colony, all of whom uninformed what ransom should redeem their lives; and thus to extort from us at the point of the bayonet the unknown sums that should be sufficient to gratify, if possible to gratify, ministerial rapacity, with the miserable indulgence left to us of raising in our mode the prescribed tribute. What terms more rigid and humiliating could have been dictated by remorseless victors to conquered enemies?— In our circumstances, to accept them would be to deserve them.

Soon after the intelligence of these proceedings arrived

rived on this continent, General Gage, who, in the course of the last year had taken possession of the town of Boston, in the province of Massachusett's-Bay, and still occupied it as a garrison, on the 19th of April, sent out from that place a large detachment of his army, who made an unprovoked assault on the inhabitants of the said province, at the town of Lexington, as appears by the affidavits of a great number of persons, some of whom were officers and soldiers of that detachment; murdered eight of the inhabitants of the said province, and wounded many others.--------
From thence the troops proceeded in warlike array to the town of Concord, where they set upon another praty of the inhabitants of the same province, killing several and wounding more, until compelled to retreat by the country-people suddenly assembled to repel this cruel aggression. Hostilities thus commenced by the British troops, which have been since prosecuted by them without regard to faith or reputation. The inhabitants of Boston being confined within that town by the general, their governor; and having, in order to procure their admission, entered into a treaty with him; it was stipulated that the said inhabitants having deposited their arms with their own magistrates, should have liberty to depart, taking with them their other effects. They accordingly delivered up their arms; but, in open violation of honour, in defiance of the obligation of treaties, which even savage nations esteem sacred, the governor ordered the arms deposited as aforesaid, that they might be preserved for their owners to be seized by a body of soldiers; detained the greatest part of the inhabitants in the town, and compelled the few, who were permitted to retire, to leave the most valuable effects behind.

By

By this perfidy wives are separated from their husbands, children from their parents, the aged and sick from their relations and friends, who wished to attend and comfort them; and those who have been used to live in plenty, and even elegance, are reduced to deplorable distress.

The General further emulating his ministerial masters, by a proclamation bearing date on the 12th day of June, after venting the grossest falshoods and calumnies against the good people of these colonies, prodeeds to 'declare them all, either by name or description, to be rebels and traitors, to supersede the course of the common law, and instead thereof to publish and order the use and exercise of the law martial.'—His troops have butchered our countrymen; have wantonly burnt Charlestown, besides a considerable number of houses in other places; our ships and vessels are seized; the necessary supplies of provision are intercepted; and he is exerting his utmost power to spread destruction and devastation around him.

We have received certain intelligence, that General Carleton, the governor of Canada, is instigating the people of that province and the Indians to fall upon us; and we have but too much reason to apprehend, that schemes have been formed to excite domestic enemies amongst us. In brief, a part of those colonies now feel, and all of them are sure of feeling, as far as the vengeance of administration can inflict them, the complicated calamities of fire, sword, and famine. We are reduced to the alternative of chusing an unconditional submission to the tyranny of irritated ministers, or resistance by force. The latter is our choice. We have counted the cost of this contest, and find nothing so dreadful as voluntary slavery.

Honor,

Honour, justice, and humanity forbid us tamely to surrender that freedom which we received from our gallant ancestors, and which our innocent posterity have a right to receive from us. We cannot endure the infamy and guilt of resigning succeeding generations to that wretchedness which inevietably awaits them, if we basely entail hereditary bondage upon them.

Our cause is just: Our union is perfect: Our internal resources are great; and, if necessary, foreign assistance is undoubtedly attainable. We gratefully acknowledge, as signal instances of the divine favour towards us, that his Providence would not permit us to be called into this severe controversy, until we were grown up unto our present strength, had been previously exercised in warlike operations, and possessed the means of defending ourselves. With hearts fortified with these animating reflections, we most solemnly before God and the world declare, that, exerting the utmost energy of those powers which our beneficent Creator hath graciously bestowed upon us, the arms we have been compelled by our enemies to assume, we will, in defiance of every hazard, with unabated firmness and perseverence, employ for the preservation of our liberties, being with one mind resolved to die freemen rather than live like slaves.

Lest this declaration should disquiet the minds of our friends and fellow-subjects in any part of the empire, we assure them, that we mean not to dissolve that union which has so long and so happily subsisted between us, and which we sincerely wish to see restored. Necessity has not yet driven us into that desperate measure, or induced us to excite any other nation to war against them. We have not raised armies with ambitious designs of separating from Great Britain, and establishing independent states. We fight not for glory or for conquest. We exhibit to mankind the remarkable spectacle of a people attacked by unprovoked enemies, without any imputation, or even suspicion of offence. They boast of their privileges and civilization, and yet proffer no milder conditions than servitude or death.

In our own native land, in defence of the freedom that is our birthright, and which we ever enjoyed till the late violation of it; for the protection of our property, acquired solely by the honest industry of our forefathers, and ourselves; against violence actually offered, we have taken up arms. We shall lay them down when hostilities shall cease on the part of the aggressors, and all danger of their being renewed shall be removed, and not before.

With an humble confidence in the mercies of the supreme and impartial judge and ruler of the universe, we most devoutly implore his divine goodness to conduct us happily through this great conflict, to dispose our adversaries to reconciliation on reasonable terms, and thereby to relieve the empire from the calamities of civil war.

By order of the Congress,
JOHN HANCOCK, President.

Attested,
CHARLES THOMPSON, Secretary.

Philadelphia, July 6, 1775.

A Second Petition from the General Congress in America to his Majesty.

The following is a true copy of the Petition from the General Congress in America to his Majesty, which

The Honble JOHN HANCOCK.

we delivered to Lord Dartmouth the first of this month, and to which, his Lordship said, no answer would be given.

Richard Penn.

Sept. 4, 1775.   Arthur Lee.

To the King's most Excellent Majesty.

Most Gracious Sovereign.

WE your Majesty's faithful subjects of the colonies of New Hampshire, Massachusett's-Bay, Rhode Island and Providence Plantations, Connecticut, New-York, New Jersey, Pennsylvania, the counties of New-Jersey, Kent and Sussex in Delaware, Maryland, Virginia, North and South Carolina, in behalf of ourselves and the inhabitants of these colonies who have deputed us to represent them in General Congress, entreat your Majesty's gracious attention to this our humble petition.

The union between our mother country and these colonies, and the energy of mild and just government, produced benefits so remarkably important, and afforded such assurances of their permanency and increase, that the wonder and envy of other nations were excited, while they beheld Great Britain rising to a power the most extraordinary the world had ever known. Her rivals observing that there was no probability of this happy connection being broken by civil dissentions, and apprehending its future effects, if left any longer undisturbed, resolved to prevent her receiving so continued and formidable an accession of wealth and strength, by checking the growth of these settlements, from which they were to be derived.

In the prosecution of this attempt, events so unfavourable to the design took place, that every friend to the interest of Great Britain and these colonies,

entertained

entertained pleasing and reasonable expectations of seeing an additional force and extension immediately given to the operations of the union hitherto experienced, by an enlargement of the dominions of the crown, and the removal of ancient and warlike enemies to a greater distance.

At the conclusion, therefore, of the late war, the most glorious and advantageous that ever had been carried on by British arms, your loyal colonies having contributed to its success by such repeated and strenuous exertions as frequently procured them the distinguished approbation of your Majesty, of the late king, and of parliament, doubted not but that they should be permitted, with the rest of the empire, to share in the blessings of peace, and the emoluments of victory and conquest. While these recent and honourable acknowledgments of their merits remained on record in the journals and acts of that august legislature, the parliament, undefaced by the imputation, or even the suspicion of any offence, they were alarmed by a new system of statutes, and regulations adopted for the administration of the colonies, that filled their minds with the most painful fears and jealousies; and to their inexpressible astonishment, perceived the dangers of a foreign quarrel quickly succeeded by domestic dangers, and in their judgment of a more dreadful kind.

Nor were their anxieties alleviated by any tendency in this system to promote the welfare of the mother country: for though its effects were more immediately felt by them, yet its influence appeared to be injurious to the commerce and prosperity of Great-Britain.

We shall decline the ungrateful task of describing

ing the irkfome variety of artifices practifed by many of your Majefty's minifters, the delufive pretences, fruitlefs terrors, and unavailing feverities, which have from time to time been dealt out by them in their attempts to execute this impolitic plan, or of tracing through a feries of years paft the progrefs of the unhappy differences between Great Britain and thefe colonies, which have flowed from this fatal fource.— Your Majefty's minifters perfevering in their meafures, and proceeding to open hoftilities for enforcing them, have compelled us to arm in our own defence, and have engaged us in a controverfy fo peculiarly abhorrent from the affections of your ftill faithful colonifts that when we confider whom we muft oppofe in this conteft, and if it continues, what may be the confequences; our own particular misfortunes are accounted by us only as parts of our diftrefs.

Knowing to what violent refentments and incurable animofities civil difcords are apt to exafperate and inflame the contending parties, we think ourfelves required, by indifpenfible obligations to Almighty God, to your Majefty, to our fellow-fubjects, and ourfelves, immediately to ufe all the means in our power, not incompatible with our fafety, for ftopping the further effufion of blood, and for averting the impending calamities that threaten the British empire. Thus called upon to addrefs your Majefty on affairs of fuch moment to America, and probably to all your dominions, we are earneftly defirous of performing this office with the utmoft deference to your Majefty; and we therefore pray that your royal magnanimity and benevolence may make the moft favourable conftructions of our expreffions on fo uncommon an occafion.

Could

Could we represent, in their full force, the sentiments which agitate the minds of us, your dutiful subjects, we are persuaded your Majesty would ascribe any seeming deviation from reverence, in our language, and even in our conduct, not to any reprehensible intention, but to the impossibility of reconciling the usual appearances of respect with a just attention to our preservation against those artful and cruel enemies, who abuse your royal confidence and authority for the purpose of effecting our destruction.

Attached to your Majesty's person, family, and government, with all the devotion that principle and affection can inspire, connected with Great Britain by the strongest ties that can unite societies, and deploring every event that tends in any degree to weaken them, we solemnly assure your Majesty, that we not only most ardently desire the former harmony between her and these colonies may be restored, but that a concord may be established between them on so firm a basis as to perpetuate its blessings uninterrupted by any future dissentions to succeeding generations in both countries; to transmit your Majesty's name to posterity, adorned with that signal and lasting glory that has attended the memory of those illustrious personages, whose virtues and abilities have extricated states from dangerous convulsions, and by securing happiness to others, have erected the most noble and durable monuments to their own fame.

We beg leave further to assure your Majesty, that notwithstanding the sufferings of your loyal colonists, during the course of the present controversy, our breasts retain too tender a regard for the kingdom from which we derive our origin, to request such a reconciliation, as might in any manner be inconsistent with

with her dignity or her welfare. These, related as we are to her, honour and duty, as well as inclination, induce us to support and advance; and the apprehensions that now oppress our hearts with unspeakable grief being once removed, your Majesty will find your faithful subjects, on this continent, ready, and willing, at all times, as they have ever been, with their lives and fortunes to assert and maintain the rights and interests of your Majesty, and of our mother country.

We therefore beseech your Majesty, that your royal authority and influence may be graciously interposed to procure us relief from our afflicting fears and jealousies, occasioned by the system before-mentioned, and to settle peace through every part of your dominions; with all humility submitting to your Majesty's wise consideration, whether it may not be expedient, for facilitating those important purposes that your Majesty be pleased to direct some mode by which the united applications of your faithful colonists to the throne, in pursuance of their common-councils, may be improved into a happy and permanent reconciliation; and that in the mean time measures may be taken for preventing the further destruction of the lives of your Majesty's subjects, and that such statutes as more immediately distress any of your Majesty's colonies be repealed. For by such arrangements, as your Majesty's wisdom can form, for collecting the united sense of your American people, who are convinced your Majesty would receive such satisfactory proofs of the disposition of the colonists towards their parent state, that the wished for opportunity would soon be restored to them of evincing the sincerity of their professions, by every testimony of devotion becoming the most dutiful subjects, and the most affectionate colonists.

That your Majesty may enjoy a long and prosperous reign, and that your descendants may govern these dominions, with honour to themselves and happiness to their subjects, is our sincere and fervent prayer.

JOHN HANCOCK.

Colonies of New Hampshire. John Langdon, T. Cushing.

Massachusetts-Bay. Samuel Adams, John Adams, Robert Treat Paine.

Rhode Island. Stephen Hopkins, Samuel Ward, Eliphant Dyar.

Connecticut. Roger Sherman, Silas Deane.

New York. Philip Livingston, James Duane, J. Alsop, Francis Lewis, John Jay, Robert Livingston, junior, Lewis Morris, William Floyd, Henry Wisner.

New Jersey. William Levingston, John Dehart, Richard Smith.

Pennsylvania. John Dickinson, Benjamin Franklin, George Ross, James Wilson, Charles Wilson, C. Humphreys, Edward Biddle.

Delaware Counties. Cæsar Rodney, Thomas M'Kean, George Read.

Maryland. Matthew Tilghman, Thomas Johnson, junior, William Pace, Samuel Chase, Thomas Stone.

Virginia. P. Henry, junior, R. Henry Lee, Edmund Pendleton, Benjamin Harrison, Thomas Jefferson.

North Carolina. William Hooper, Joseph Hewes.

South Carolina. Henry Middleton, Thomas Lynch, Christopher Gasden, J. Rutledge, Edward Rutledge.

The

The Address, Memorial, and Petition, of several of the Gentlemen, Merchants, and Traders of the city of London, presented by a deputation to his Majesty, on Wednesday the 11th of October, 1775.

To the King's most Excellent Majesty.

The humble Address, Memorial, and Petition of the Gentlemen, Merchants, and Traders of London.

May it please your Majesty;

WE your Majesty's most dutiful and loyal subjects, the Gentlemen, Merchants, and Traders of London, beg leave to approach your Majesty with unfeigned assurances of affection and attachment to your Majesty's person and government, and to represent, with great humility, our sentiments on the present alarming state of public affairs.

By the operation of divers acts of the British parliament, we behold, with deep affliction, that happy communion of interests and good offices, which had so long subsisted between this country and America, suspended, and an intercourse (which, augmenting, as it grew, the strength and dignity of your Majesty's dominions, hath enabled your Majesty to defeat the natural rivals of your greatness in every quarter of the world) threatened with irretrievable ruin.

We should humbly represent to your Majesty, if they had not been already represented, the deadly wounds which the commerce of this country must feel from these unfortunate measures; for that it has not yet more deeply felt them is owing to temporary and accidental causes, which cannot long continue.

But we beg your Majesty to cast an eye on the general property of this land, and to reflect what must be be its fate when deprived of our American commerce.

It fills our mind with additional grief to see the blood and treasure of your Majesty's subjects wasted in effecting a fatal separation between the different parts of your Majesty's empire, by a war, uncertain in the event, destructive in its consequences, and the object contended for lost in the contest.

The experience we have had in your Majesty's paternal regard for the welfare and privileges of all your people, and the opinion we entertain of the justice of the British parliament, forbids us to believe that laws, so repugnant to the policy of former times, would have received their sanction, had the real circumstances and sentiments of the colonies been thoroughly understood, or the true principles of their connection with the mother country been duly weighed: we are therefore necessarily constrained to impute blame to those by whom your Majesty and the parliament have been designedly misled, or partially informed of those matters, on a full knowledge of which alone, determinations of such importance should have been founded.

We beg leave further to represent to your Majesty, that, in questions of high national concern, affecting the dearest interests of a state, speculation and experiment are seldom to be justified:—That want of foresight is want of judgment; and perseverence in measures which repeated experience hath condemned, ceases to be error.

We might appeal to the histories of all countries to shew, that force had never been employed with success, to change the opinions or convince the minds of freemen; and, from the annals of our own in particular,

cular, we learn, that the free and voluntary gifts of the subject has ever exceeded the exactions of the sword.

Restraining, prohibitory, and penal laws have failed to re-establish the public tranquility; and the present state of this unfortunate dispute affords reason to believe, that, as it commenced without policy, it must be prosecuted by means which the natural and constitutional strength of Great Britain cannot supply.

In your Majesty's justice we confide for a fair construction of an apprehension we have conceived, that your Majesty hath been advised to take foreign troops into British pay, and to raise and discipline Papists, both in Ireland and Canada, for the purpose of enforcing submission to laws which your Majesty's Protestant subjects in America conceive to be destructive of their liberties, and against which they have repeatedly petitioned in vain.

Anxious to vindicate the national honour, we would willingly discredit reports of slaves incited to insurrection, and barbarous nations encouraged to take up arms against our American brethren if they had not prevailed without refutation, and filled the minds of your Majesty's faithful subjects with indignation and horror.

If to these circumstances of peril and distress, our fears could suggest any addition, we might justly expect it from the resentment of those powerful enemies, who have ever shewn a readiness to take advantages of our internal commotions, and will joyfully embrace the occasion of avenging that disgrace they sustained, during the late glorious war, from the united arms of Great Britain and America;—and we should indeed be reduced to despair, but that we are

encouraged

encouraged to look up to your Majesty, the common father of all your people, as the happy instrument in the hands of Divine Providence, which bringeth good out of evil, for restoring to this distracted empire the blessings of mutual confidence, liberty and peace.

For the speedy effecting of which, we most humbly beseech your Majesty to cause hostilities to cease in your Majesty's colonies in America, and to adopt such a mode of reconciling this unhappy controversy, as may best promote the interest of commerce, and the welfare of all your people.

(Signed by 1171 persons.)

Address of a very numerous body of the Merchants and Traders of the city of Lodon, presented by a deputation of them to his Majesty, on Saturday the 14th of October 1775, which Address his Majesty was pleased to receive very graciously; and the Gentlemen of the deputation had the honour to kiss his Majesty's hand.

To the King's most Excellent Majesty.

Most Gracious Sovereign,

WE your Majesty's faithful and loyal subjects, merchants and traders of the city of London, filled with the deepest concern at the unjustifiable proceedings of some of your Majesty's colonies in America, beg leave to approach your royal throne to testify our entire disapprobation and abhorrence of them, with the most solemn assurances that we will support your Majesty with our lives and fortunes, in maintaining the authority of the legislature of this country, which, we conceive, does and ought to extend over and pervade every part of the British dominions.

With regret and indignation we see colonies,
which

which owe their existence, and every blessing that attended their late prosperous situation, to this their parent country, unnaturally regardless of the fostering hand that raised and supported them, and affecting distinctions in their dependence, not founded in law, or in the constitution of Great Britain.

We are convinced by the experienced clemency of your Majesty's government, that no endeavours will be wanting to induce our deluded fellow-subjects to return to their obedience to that constitution which our ancestors bled to establish, and which has flourished, pure and uninterrupted, under the mild government of the house of Hanover.

May that Being, who governs the universe, so direct your Majesty's councils and measures, that, from the present confusion, order may arise, and peace again be restored.

That your Majesty may long reign over an happy and united people is the earnest prayer of.

    May it please your Majesty,
    Your Majesty's most faithful and loyal subjects.
       (Signed by 941 persons.)

His Majesty's most gracious Speech to both Houses of Parliament, on Thursday the 26th day of October, 1775.

My Lords and Gentlemen,

THE present situation of America, and my constant desire to have your advice, concurrence, and assistance on every important occasion, have determined me to call you thus early together.

Those who have long too successfully laboured to inflame my people in America by gross misrepresentations, and to infuse into their minds a system of opinions

nions repugnant to the true constitution of the colonies, and to their subordinate relation to Great Britain, now openly avow their revolt, hostility, and rebellion. They have raised troops, and are collecting a naval force; they have seized the public revenue, and assumed to themselves legislative, executive, and judical powers, which they already exercise, in the most arbitrary manner, over the persons and properties of their fellow-subjects; and although many of these unhappy people may still retain their loyalty, and may be too wise not to see the fatal consequence of this usurpation, and wish to resist it; yet the torrent of violence has been strong enough to compel their acquiescence till a sufficient force shall appear to support them.

The authors and promoters of this desperate conspiracy, have, in the conduct of it, derived great advantage from the difference of our intentions and theirs. They meant only to amuse us by vague expressions of attachment to the parent state, and the strongest protestations of loyalty to me, whilst they were preparing for a general revolt. On our part, though it was declared in our last sessions, that a rebellion existed within the province of the Massachusett's-Bay, yet even that province we wished rather to reclaim than to subdue. The resolutions of parliament breathed a spirit of moderation and forbearance; conciliatory propositions accompanied the measures taken to enforce authority; and the coercive acts were adapted to cases of criminal combinations amongst subjects not then in arms. I had acted with the same temper; anxious to prevent, if it had been possible, the effusion of the blood of my subjects, and the calamities which are inseparable from a state of war;

war; still hoping that my people in America would have discerned the traiterous views of their leaders, and have been convinced that to be a subject of Great Britain, with all its consequences, is to be the freest member of any civil society in the known world.

The rebellious war now levied is become more general, and is manifestly carried on for the purpose of establishing an independent empire. I need not dwell upon the fatal effects of the success of such a plan. The object is too important, the spirit of the British nation too high, the resources which God hath blessed her too numerous, to give up so many colonies which she has planted with great industry, nursed with great tenderness, encouraged with many commercial advantages, and protected and defended at much expence of blood and treasure.

It is now become the part of wisdom, and (in its effects) of clemency, to put a speedy end to these disorders by the most decisive exertions. For this purpose, I have increased my naval establishment, and have greatly augmented my land-forces; but in such a manner as may be the least burthensome to my kingdoms.

I have also the satisfaction to inform you, that I have received the most friendly offers of foreign assistance; and if I shall make any treaties in consequence thereof, they shall be laid before you. And I have, in testimony of my affection for my people, who can have no cause in which I am not equally interested, sent to the garrison of Gibraltar and Port-Mahon, a part of my Electoral troops, in order that a larger number of the established forces of this kingdom may be applied to the maintenance of its authority, and the national militia planned and regulated with equal regard

regard to the rights, safety, and protection of my crown and people, may give a farther extent and activity to our military operations.

When the unhappy and deluded multitude, against whom this force will be directed, shall become sensible of their error, I shall be ready to receive the misled with tenderness and mercy; and, in order to prevent the inconveniences which may arise from the great distance of their situation, and to remove, as soon as possible, the calamities which they suffer, I shall give authority to certain persons upon the spot, to grant general or particular pardons or indemnities, in such manner, and to such persons, as they shall think fit, and to receive the submission of any province or colony which shall be disposed to return to its allegiance. It may be also proper to authorise the persons so commissioned to restore such province or colony, so returning to its allegiance, to the free exercise of its trade and commerce, and to the same protection and security, as if such province or colony had never revolted.

Gentlemen of the House of Commons,

I have ordered the proper estimates for the ensuing year to be laid before you; and I rely on your affection to me, and your resolution to maintain the just rights of this country, for such supplies as the present circumstances of our affairs require. Among the many unavoidable ill consequences of this rebellion, none affects me more sensibly than the extraordinary burthen which it must create to my faithful subjects.

My Lords and Gentlemen,

I have fully opened to you my views and intentions. The constant employment of my thoughts, and the most earnest wishes of my heart, tend wholly to
the

the safety and happiness of all my people, and to the re-establishment of order and tranquility through the several parts of my dominions, in a close connection and constitutional dependence. You see the tendency of the present disorders, and I have stated to you the measures which I mean to pursue for suppressing them. Whatever remains to be done, that may farther contribute to this end, I commit to your wisdom. And I am happy to add, that, as well from the assurances I have received, as from the general appearances of affairs in Europe, I see no probability that the measures which you may adopt will be interrupted by disputes with any foreign power.

CHAP. IX.

A short View of American Affairs, 1775.—The Invasion of Canada by the Colonists.—The Forts of Chamblee and St. John taken.—Montreal taken.—Arnold appears before Quebec. - General Montgomery joins him. The Siege.—An Attempt to Storm the Town.—Montgomery killed—Arnold wounded.—The Provincials retire.

THE colonists in proportion as their hopes of accomodation with the mother country decreased, grew more daring in their enterprises, and extended their views to more distant and remote consequences. The parliament of Great Britain having passed a law establishing the Popish religion in Canada, greatly alarmed the colonists.——They considered this law, which went by the name of the Quebec Act, as a stratagem of state, intended to seduce the Papists in Canada into the designs of government; which were to excite the Canadians to take up arms, and fall upon the back settlements of the New England provinces. It appeared even to the people at home to have this intention, and was greatly complained of by the true friends of the constitution. It was said to be an infringement of the revolution settlement, and a violation of the King's coronation oath, as well as a palpable system of partiality to Popery in the framers of that law. The whole of the dispute upon this subject is so well known, and has been so often reviewed in various publications, that I shall take no more notice of it on this occasion. The intentions of the British government were perfectly understood by the colonists, who pursued such measures as they thought were most proper to render the schemes of the ministry of none effect. It was the apprehension of the consequences of this bill that made the colonies in opposition, so warmly address the French inhabitants of Canada; which has been already taken notice of.

As the good success of a former expedition to the Lakes, had given spirits to the Americans, and Ticonderago and Crown-Point was now in their hands, the congress was resolved to make a bold push for the possession of all Canada; the way to it was open by their possessing the command of the Lakes, and they thought that if they could accomplish this grand design they would in a great measure emancipate themselves from the tyranny of the British government.—Such a measure, of so extraordinary a magnitude required the most serious consideration. They had hitherto been only standing upon the defensive, and endeavouring to support what they believed to be their just rights and privileges, against the invasion of an arbitrary power, that seemed determined to wrest that from them; but this was a new project, and carried the matter a great deal farther. It was making the war offensive, and attacking the power of the Sovereign in those parts where they were not immediately concerned. The conduct of the colonies in their former proceedings was supported by very strong authority, and precedents the most respectable, oppression and injustice in many governments had been opposed and resisted. But this new proceeding of the colonists was said to be without precedent. To flying in the face of the Sovereign, carry on war in his dominions, and invade a province to which they could lay no claim, nor pretend to any right, appeared such an outrage as not only to overthrow every plea of justifiable resistance, but militated with the established opinions, principles, and feelings of mankind in general.

It was alledged on the other side, that the danger was pressing and great. General Carleton had received powers from government of an alarming nature, and was authorized to arm the Canadians, and to march them out of the country, against the other colonies, with a design to reduce them to a state of bondage and slavery; and was impowered to proceed even to capital punishment, against all those, and in all places, whom he should judge rebels and opposers of the laws. The powers he had received within his own province were equal to those of the most arbitrary princes in Europe, and had been already felt both by the English and French subjects. Tho' the Canadians had hitherto refused to be embodied, or to march upon any terms out of the province, it was easily perceived, that as soon as the Governor's authority was inforced by the arrival of troops from England, that the Canadians would be obliged to obey him implicitly, as well in that as in other matters.

He had already engaged a confiderable number of Canadians, and other Indians, in his service; and if his arms once became predominant, the defire of fpoil would bring the favages in crouds from the remoteft defarts to affift him. Befides, they were perfectly acquainted with, and therefore had every thing to dread from the zeal and fpirit of enterprize,
and

and talents of that able and resolute officer. In such circumstances they considered it contrary to all the rules of reason and prudence to wait till they were attacked by a formidable force at their backs, in the very instant that it would require all their power and force to defend their coasts and protect their capital cities against the resentment of a mighty power, which they had so much provoked and offended, and with whom they were entering into a contest, arduous and hitherto untried. They alledged that it was as just to prevent a known enemy from gathering strength to destroy them, when they knew that he intended their ruin, as it was just to defend themselves against them, when they assaulted them; and that the principles of self-defence allowed them to take every step which their reason suggested to prevent their own ruin; and that it was less cruel to prevent such an evil than to suffer it, if they possibly could prevent it. They said that there was no law of nature, of reason, nor convention among mankind, by which a person was bound to be a simple spectator while his enemy was loading his gun for his destruction, was he to wait till the execution was over, for fear he should be considered as an aggressor? Cases and questions of this nature, however entertaining in other occasions, have no weight in circumstances on which the fate of nations depend. Were they only to seek a redress when the savages had penetrated into their country, and the fury of the flames which had consumed their settlements were only retarded by the blood of their wives and infants?

The congress were sensible that they had now proceeded so far as could only be justified by the force of arms; for force of argument had no influence upon on those they had to dispute with. They had already drawn the sword, and the appeal was made. It was now too late to turn back, and to waver was certain destruction. Their success now depended upon vigorous measures, which could alone give sanction to their resistance, and dispose the government of Great Britain to an accomodation upon lenient terms; without this they knew that they would not only lose those liberties for which they contended, but all their other privileges would be at the mercy of a jealous and provoked government. In such a situation, their moderation in the instance of Canada they imagined would be but a poor plea for compassion or indulgence.

They were well informed of the state of affairs in Canada, and understood the temper of the people: this last gave them encouragement in the enterprize they were about to engage in. They knew that the French inhabitants, excepting the noblesse and clergy, were generally as much discontented at the setting aside the English laws, and the introduction of the new system of government, as the British settlers themselves. It appeared exceeding probable that this new discontent co-operating with their rooted aversion which they had to their ancient, proud, and oppressive tyrants, the noblesse, or lords of the manors, and the mortal dread which they had of being again reduced to their former state of vassalage, would incline them to consider the provincials rather as friends than invaders, and make them embrace so favourable an opportunity of obtaining a share of the common liberty, which they were contending for.— Though the Canadians were unacquainted with the nature of the controversy, and very little interested in

it,

GENERAL MONTGOMERY.

it, yet as it appeared to be for liberty, and American freedom, the name was pleasing, and likely to engage their attention. I was also in favour of the colonies, of which Canada was a part.

It was determined not to lose the opportunity of pursuing this measure, while the British arms were weak, and shut up within the town of Boston: this was considered as a proper time for attempting the reduction of the province of Canada. A body of New York militia and New England troops, and some others, to the amount of 2000 men, under the command of the Generals Schulyer and Montgomery, were appointed for this service. Batteaus and flat-boats were built at Ticonderago and Crown-Point, to convey the troops along Lake Champlain to the river Sorrel, which forms the entrance into Canada, and is composed of the surplus waters of the Lakes, which it discharges into the river St. Lawrence, and would afford an agreeable communication betwixt that river and the Lakes, were it not on account of the rapidity in some parts that obstructs the navigation. The Sorrel runs a course of 69 miles, and falls into the river St Lawrence in latitude 46. 10. lon. 72. 25.

General Montgomery, who was at Crown-Point, had received intelligence, that a schooner of some considerable force, with other armed vessels which lay at St. John's on the river Sorrel, were making ready to enter the Lake, and were intended to obstruct the passage of the provincials. Upon receiving this information, tho' he had not the half of the forces that were intended for this expedition, he proceeded with those which he had to the Isle of Noix, which lies in the entrance of the river, and took necessary measures

measures to guard against the passage of these vessels into the Lakes. General Schuyler, who was at that time chief in command, having arrived at Albany, the two generals published a declaration to encourage and persuade the Canadians to join them, and with this expectation marched on to the Fort of St. John, which lies only about twelve miles from the above mentioned island. Having taken a view of the fort at some small distance, they peceived signatures of strong resistance, which made them land at a considerable distance in a woody country, full of deep swamps, and intersected with creeks and waters. In this situation they were attacked by a considerable body of Indians, who did not neglect to take hold of the advantages which the situation afforded them.— These two circumstances concurring, namely the apparent strength of the fort, and the resistance of the Indians, determined them to return to their former station in the island, and wait till the arrival of the artillery and reinforcements, which were expected.

Schuyler upon this returned to Albany, to conclude a treaty with the Indians in these parts, which he had been negociating for some time past; but being thro' illness unable to return, the whole weight of the war fell upon General Montgomery. This gentleman was most eminently qualified for military service; though perhaps this expedition required the utmost reach of all his abilities. His first measure was to detach from the service of General Carleton those Indians who had joined them, and being strengthened by the arrival of his reinforcements and artillery, he prepared to lay siege to the fort of St. John. This fort was garrisoned by the greater part of the 7th and 26th regiments, being nearly all
the

the regular troops then in Canada; and was well provided with stores, ammunition, and artillery.

The parties of the provincials were spread over the adjacent country, and were every where well received by the Canadians, who, besides joining them in great numbers, gave every possible assistance, whether in carrying on the siege, removing their artillery, or supplying them with provisions and necessaries. While matters were in this situation, the famous Ethan Alen, who without any commission from the congress had a principal share in the original expedition to the lakes, and the taking of the forts; and who since, under the title of colonel, seems rather to have acted as one of the party, than as a person obedient to any regular command, had a mind to signalize himself, by surprizing the town and garrison of Montreal. He undertook this hazardous enterprize at the head of a small party of provincials and Canadians, without the knowledge of the commander in chief, or the assistance which he might have procured from some of the other detached parties. The event was unsuccessful as the undertaking was rash. The militia, supported by a few regular troops under the command of some English officers met the adventurer at some distance from the town, defeated his troops, and took himself prisoner, with forty others: the rest of his party escaped into the woods. Allen and his fellow-prisoners were by the orders of General Carleton loaded with chains, and in that condition sent a-board a man of war to England. They were however afterwards sent back to America, for what reason is not particularly affirmed.

The progress of the siege of St. John was for some time retarded for want of ammunition sufficient for such an operation. Of all which none were more necessary than powder and ball.——The fort of St. John's, which commands the entrance into Canada, could not be reduced without a suitable provision of this fort. General Montgomery by a fortunate event was delivered from this difficulty. A little fort called Chamble, lay deep in the country, and seemed covered by St. John's. It was garrisoned by a small detachment of the seventh regiment, and was in a state not fit for enduring a siege. The General turned his attention first to this fort, and by pushing forward a party joined by some Canadians, he easily became master of the place. Here he found considerable store, but the article of the greatest consequence was gun-powder, which they were greatly distressed for, and of which they took about 120 barrels.——This acquisition facilitated the siege of St. John's, which had been for some time in a great measure interrupted for want of ammunition.

The garrison of St. John's under the command of Major Preston, amounted to between 6 and 700 men, of which about five hundred were regulars, and the rest Canadian volunteers. They endured the difficulties of a very hard siege, and suffering the hardships attending it, augmented by a scarcity of provisions, with unremitted steadfastness and resolution.— In the mean time General Carleton was indefatigable in his endeavours to raise sufficient forces for its relief. Attempts were also made by Colonel M'Clean for raising a Scotch regiment, under the title of Royal Highland Emigrants, to be composed of natives of that country, who had lately arrived in America, and who in consequence of the troubles had not obtained settlements. The colonel with these and some Canadians,

dians, to the amount of a hundred men, was posted near the junction of the Sorrel with the river St. Lawrence. General Carleton used his utmost diligence to effect a junction with Colonel M'Clean, and then to march to the relief of St. John's; but his purpose was frustrated, and his design rendered abortive by the activity and vigilance of the provincials. —He was attacked at Longueil, in attempting to pass over from the island of Montreal, by a party of provincials, who easily repulsed the Canadians, and frustrated his whole design. Another party had pushed M'Clean towards the mouth of the Sorrel, where the Canadians having received advice of the Governor's defeat, immediately abandoned him to a man, and he was under the necessity of making the best of his way to Quebec with his Royal Scotch Emigrants. —The provincials on this occasion were extremely active, and took every opportunity that might be thought necessary to crown this expedition with success; their contrivances, and their attempts to execute them, were equally surprising. Upon M'Cleans retreat to Quebec, the party who had reduced him to that necessity, immediately erected batteries on a point of land at the junction of the Sorrel with the river St. Laurence, with a design to prevent a number of armed vessels which General Carleton had at Montreal, from escaping down the river. They also constructed armed rafts, and floating batteries for the same purpose. These measures effectually prevented the passage of General Carleton's armement to Quebec, which were not only defeated in several attempts, but pursued, attacked, and driven from their anchor up the river by the provincials; so that as General Montgomery approached Montreal immediately

ately after the surrender of St, John's, the governor's situation, whether in town or a-board the vessels, became dangerous and critical. General Carleton on this occasion needed all his military sagacity and fortitude ; his condition was truly critical and alarming, for it appeared scarcely possible that he could escape the strict watch of a people whose interest depended so much in the ruin of so inveterate an enemy.

This danger was increased by the arrival of General Montgomery at Montreal, where a capitulation was proposed by the principal French and English inhabitants, including a sort of general treaty, which Montgomery refused, as they were in no state of defence to entitle them to a capitulation, and were on their side unable to fulfil the conditions. He however sent them a written answer, in which he declared that the continental army having a generous disdain of every act of oppression and violence, and having come for the express purpose of giving them liberty and security;—he therefore engaged his honour to maintain in the peaceable possession of their property of every kind, the individuals and religious communities of the city of Montreal. He also engaged for the maintenance of all the inhabitants in the free exercise of their religion, and expressed his hopes, that the civil and religious rights of all the Canadians would be established upon the most permanent footin by a provincial congress. He promised that courts of justice should be speedily established upon the most liberal plan, conformable to the British constitution; and he in general complied with other articles, so far as they were in his power, and consistent in him to grant. This security being given to the people, his troops

troops took possession of the town upon the thirteenth of November.

It was now that season of the year when troops instead of marching to invest formal sieges, usually go into winter quarters; and in such a climate as Canada this step appeared more especially necessary.—The snows here are generally deep and the frosts severe, that it is impossible for an army to carry along with them all those implements of war which are necessary for besieging castles or storming cities. It is even a task beyond the ordinary efforts of nature, for troops to march in that season of the year in such a wild and uncultivated country, where the woods are so extensive, the thickets almost impenetrable, and the swamps so numerous. It required an uncommon resolution, as well as an extraordinary strength of body to endure the toil and fatigue that attended such an expedition.——Nothing but an ardent inclination to support the cause of liberty could have supported this small army under the many disadvantages that were in their way. The inhabitants of Canada must have in general wished well to this enterprize, otherwise it was in their power to have crushed it in its first opening; tho' they did not enter heartily into it, yet it is manifest that they wished it to succeed, rather than desired it might fail of success.

Nothing now could afford the slightest hope of the preservation of Canada, except the season of the year; it was this which alone gave hope of its preservation to government. It appears somewhat extraordinary that the provincials did not begin their operations sooner in the summer, for had they had three months of good weather before them, there was the greatest reason to conclude that they would have become

come masters of all Canada. It has not yet been ascertained whether this neglect happened thro' want of ability, or proceeded from difference in opinion in the managers of public affairs; it was however unfortunate for their design of becoming masters of Canada, that they did not set out three months sooner upon this expedition. As a balance to this disadvantage, there were but few forces belonging to the government in Canada; and the taking of General Carleton, which seemed almost certain, would have rendered the reduction of Canada exceedingly easy.— A particular accident, which was fortunate for General Carleton, determined this matter otherwise.— At that time all hopes of armed vessels being able to get down the river were given up; and when Montgomery was preparing batteaus with light artillery at Montreal to attack them on that side, and force them down upon the batteries, means were successfully used to convey the Governor in a dark night in a boat with muffled paddles past the enemies guards and batteries, to Quebec, where he arrived in safety.— This was a forunate incident for government, but a most unlucky one for the provincial adventurers, who provided they had got the Governor into their power, would have easily brought over all Canada to their views of liberty.

But to return to the siege of St. John's, which was carried on with great vigour, and had been attended with better success than the adventurers had reason to expect. The works were advanced near the body of the fort, and all things prepared for a general assault. This would have probably been a very dangerous as well as a fruitless enterprise, considering the goodness of the troops within the fort, and the

weakness

weakness of the assailants. Major Preston was a good officer, and his men were regular troops, and understood the military exercise to a great exactness;—he was determined to defend the fort to the last extremity, which would have made the capture dear to the besiegers. In this situation of affairs, an account of the success at Longueil, accompanied with the prisoners arrived at the camp, upon which General Montgomery sent a flag and a letter by one of them to Major Preston, wherein he signified his hopes that as all means of relief were cut off by the Governor's defeat, he would by a timely surrender of the fort, prevent the further effusion of blood, which a fruitless and obstinate defence must necessarily occasion——This greatly staggered the major's resolution, and brought him to a parley, which had he been as well acquainted with the state of the country and his enemy's force, as he might have been, he would certainly have refused; for as he had near 700 regular troops in the fort, well appointed and furnished with a sufficient quantity of ammunition, he might have resisted the force of double the number of his own troops, especially as the besiegers were but raw and inexperienced, and not well appointed for carrying on a siege. It appears to have been the general misfortune of the British Governors in America, and the officers serving under them, that they were unacquainted with the state of the country, and the disposition of the inhabitants. This must have proceeded either from want of capacity, or from want of attention to their duty. It would have certainly been an easy matter for the servants of government to have been acquainted with the whole proceedings of the inhabitants within the circle of their administration, and by that means have had

had it in their power to have guarded against and prevented being surprized by any attack from the assembling of the subjects. When government intended to impose such obnoxious laws upon the colonists, they ought first to have known their dispositions, and in case that they found them averse to compliance, have secured their obedience by such sound steps of policy as would have answered their own intentions. To be surprized by their own subjects, argued a real want of understanding of the disposition of the people, and a deficiency of political forecast with regard to the means of executing their new laws.—— Both General Carleton and Major Preston, ought to have informed themselves of every step that the colonies were taking, and to have acquainted government with the real situation of the country. Two things appear obvious in the history of the proceedings of government, that they either never intended to inforce their new laws, or that they were totally infatuated with regard to the means of rendering them effectual; for if they had studied for an age to expose their own weakness, they could not have taken more effectual methods to have done it than those they pursued. The troubles in America have principally arisen from either the selfishness or incapacity of the Governors in those parts, who either were constantly pursuing their own interests without minding either the affairs of government or the people, or were persons preferred to those posts by the interest of friends, without having a single qualification for the office they were preferred to. It has long been a mistaken opinion prevailing in the mother country, that such as are not qualified for offices at home, may answer the purpose of colony administration;

tion; from this idea has the governments abroad in the colonies been supplied with both the weakest and the worst of men.

Major Preston endeavoured to obtain a few days time in hopes of some relief; but this was refused, on account of the lateness and severity of the season: he also endeavoured in settling the terms of capitulation, to obtain liberty for the garrison to depart for Great Britain, which proved equally unsuccessful, and they were obliged, after being allowed the honours of war, on account of their brave defence, to lay down their arms, and surrender themselves prisoners.—— They were allowed their baggage and effects, the officers to wear their swords, and their other arms to be preserved for them till the troubles were at an end. ——General Montgomery in all transactions with the King's troops, writ, spoke, and behaved with that attention, regard, and politeness, to both private men and officers, which might be expected from a man of honour, and integrity, who found himself involved in an unhappy quarrel with his friends and countrymen. Such behaviour was no more than what all who were personally acquainted with that officer, would always have expected of him. All the prisoners who were taken at this time, were sent up the Lakes, by way of Ticonderago, to those inland parts of the colonies, which were best adapted for their reception and provision. The provincials found in this fort a considerable quantity of artillery and useful stores, necessary for carrying on the enterprise they were now engaged in. The success of this expedition had hitherto proceeded beyond the most sanguine hopes of the adventurers, and their good fortune in what they had attempted pushed them on to achievements altogether beyond their strength. Their success upon the lakes seduced them into an opinion of reducing the city of Quebec to the obedience of the congress, and they seem to have both forgotten and despised the dangers and fatigues of an inclement season, thro' the hopes of finishing with glory so important an enterprise. The provincials had now the whole command of the lakes. General Prescot had been obliged to enter into a capitulation with them, by which the whole of the river's naval force, consisting of eleven armed vessels, was surrendered into their hands. General Prescot, with several officers, and some gentlemen of the civil department, Canadian volunteers, with 120 English soldiers, all of whom had taken refuge on board the vessels upon the approach of General Montgomery, were made prisoners of war. Tho' the rapid success of Montgomery was not at that time blazoned with ministerial figures of embellishment in the Gazette, yet there has nothing during the course of this unfortunate war been carried on with more address, and supported with greater energy, than this enterprise. The humanity of the commander, and the regularity of the troops, would have done honour to the most legal military corps, and their fortitude in combating dangers and fatigues, sets them forth in a point of view which heroes need not be ashamed of. Feats of a much inferior nature have been in our government accounts extolled with the highest strains of hyperbole, while the epithets of cowardice and rebellion have been given this bold and daring expedition. It is not the province of an historian to determine what is rebellion; this must be left to the judgment of after ages, who will determine with more impartiality than the

present

GENERAL ARNOLD.

present concerning the character of American resistance. There have been some grand rebellions in times past recorded in the English history, which have changed their names into those of Revolutions, and are now adorned with the epithet *glorious*, which according to the principles now in vogue among courtiers, would have been stigmatized with the name of rebellion had they been unsuccessful.—It is time that must declare which of the two this American resistance belongs to.—Perhaps an hundred years hence what we account rebellion, will in the history of America be yclept *a Revolution*. Should it prove in the end unsuccessful, it must continue in the language and stile of state politicians, a grand rebellion.

While Montgomery and his troops were carrying on the war in upper Canada, from New York, by the old beaten course of the Lakes, an expedition, distinguished by its novelty, spirit of enterprise, the difficulties that opposed it, and the constancy maintained in its execution, was undertaken directly against the lower part of the province of Quebec, from the New England side, by a rout that had hitherto been unexplored, and considered as impracticable. About the midst of September, Colonel Arnold, at the head of two regiments, consisting of about 1100 men, marched from the camp near Boston to Newport, at the mouth of the river Merrimack, where vessels were ready to carry them to the mouth of the river Kennebec, in New Hampshire, a voyage of about forty leagues. Upon the twenty second of the same month, they embarked their stores and troops at Gardiner's Town, on the Kennebec; and proceeded with great difficulty up that river. The Kennebec has a rapid stream, and its bottom and shores in many places are rocky,

rocky, the navigation is continually interrupted by falls, and the carrying places are exceedingly difficult.—— In this paſſage the batteaus were frequently filled with water, and overſet, in conſequence of which a part of their arms, ammunition, and proviſions, were ſometimes loſt. Beſides the labour of loading and reloading at the carrying places, they were obliged to carry the boats upon their ſhoulders. The great carrying place was about twelve miles a-croſs, which was attended with much labour and fatigue. That part of the detachment which was employed in managing the batteaus, marched along the banks of the river, and the boats and men being diſpoſed in three diviſions, each diviſion encamped together every night.—— The march by land was not more eligible than the paſſage by water.——They had thick woods, deep ſwamps, difficult mountains and precipices, alternately to encounter, and were upon occaſions obliged to cut their way through the thickets for miles together. At the carrying places they were obliged to traverſe the ſame ground twice over heavy loaded. From all theſe impediments their progreſs was of courſe very ſlow, travelling in general only from four or five to nine or ten miles a day. The conſtant and ſevere fatigue cauſed many of them to fall ſick, which added to their hardſhips;—and proviſions grew at laſt ſo ſcarce, that ſome of the men eat their dogs, and whatever elſe of any kind could be converted into food.— When they arrived at the head of the Kennebec, which is upwards of an hundred and fifty miles from Gardiner's Town, and according to their way of travelling muſt have been much more, they ſent back their ſick, and one of the colonels took that opportunity of returning with his whole diviſion, under the pretence

pretence of the scarcity of provisions. This was done without the consent of the commander in chief, who had marched forward to explore the way. By this desertion, and the sick that were returned, Arnold's detachment was reduced about one third from its original number. They however proceeded with their usual constancy, and having crossed the heights of land, which are ridges of mountains that extend quite thro' the continent called heights, they at last arrived at the head of the river Chaudiece, which runs thro' Canada, and falls into the river St. Lawrence near Quebec.— This ridge of little hills seems to be the middle of the continent in those parts; for as soon as you come to the top of the heights, the river runs towards the north, as they do on this side towards the south. This little army had still a great way to march, though the greatest hardships were now over; they were now arrived at the inhabited part of Canada, where they found provisions. On the third day of November, an advanced party returned with provisions, and they soon after came to an house, which was the first they had seen for thirty-one days; having spent the whole time in traversing an hideous wilderness, without ever seeing an human face, except those of their own party. Their march from the mouth of the Kennebec, was almost streight north where they were aproaching nearer to the pole every stage, and encountering a severe winter in a cold climate. They had from their taking ship at Boston, in the middle of September travelled 365 miles directly north, supposing they had travelled in a direct line,—but considering the many turnings and windings in their journey, it may well be supposed that they marched near double that number of miles.

The

The Canadians received them with the same good will that Montgomery and his corps were received in the neighbourhood of Montreal; they supplied them liberally with all sorts of provisions and necessaries, and rendered them every other assistance in their power. Arnold published immediately an address to the people signed by General Washington, of the same nature with that which had been issued before by Generals Schuyler, and Montgomery. They were invited to join with the other colonies in an indissoluble union, and to range themselves under the standard of liberty. They were informed in this address that the armament was not sent into the province to plunder, but to protect and animate them;—that they themselves were enjoined to act, and to consider themselves as in the country of their best friends; that they were therefore requested not to desert their habitations, nor to fly from their friends, but to provide them with such supplies as their country afforded; and he pledged himself for their safety and security, as well as for an ample and satisfactory compensation. The reception which these adventurers met with from the Canadians, shews plainly that the English governors and new laws were not popular nor acceptable among them; that provided the scale should have preponderated in favour of the colonists, they would not have been averse to join the association. This is very unlike the substance of the petition that was sent from Canada to obtain an establishment of the French laws, and a repeal of the English trials by juries.

7 The city of Quebec was at this time in a state of great weakness, as well as internal discontent and disorder. The British merchants and inhabitants had been for a long time much disgusted and dissatisfied. They

They had opposed the Quebec act, and sent petitions to England upon that subject, which had been grievously resented by their own government, and from that period they said they had been not only slighted and treated with indifference but even regarded with an apparent eye of distrust and suspicion. They complained that as the great political object in that country was to attach the native Canadians inviolably to government, so the French noblesse and civil officers became, except the British military, the only favourites, and these having acquired the manners and affections of all other courtiers and favourites, suffered no occasion to pass of insulting the English as malecontents, with the violence of their zeal and the outrageousness of their loyalty. They presented that these new courtiers industriously brought in questions upon public affairs and discourses upon government in their company, and then construed that freedom, which the native English had derived from nature and habit, as well from the present discontent, as proceeding from ill design and disaffection.—— Their complaints upon this head appear to have had a real foundation, and it is a proof how little they were either trusted or regarded, that when the troops were sent off to Montreal and the Sorrel, to oppose the other colonists, notwithstanding the very alarming state of public affairs, and that city, together with the property which they possessed in it, were left exposed without a garrison, yet when they applied for leave to be embodied as a militia for its defence, so far were government from complying with their request, that they even did not judge them worthy of an answer. There seems to have been an uniformity to the measures of government in all parts of the empire,

pire in difobliging and offending all fuch as either whifpered or hinted their regard to liberty and the conftitution. The nobleffe and the popifh clergy, thefe *dupes* to tyranny, and *flaves* to princes, were now become the favourites of the British government, becaufe they were known to be friends to arbitrary power, and enemies to the common rights of the people. The policy of our court in this predilection to creatures of its own principles, was far from anfwering the ends which it had in view; the defigns of the miniftry were even perceived and difapproved by the meaneft French peafant in Canada. Nature, notwithftanding all its corruptions, difpofes mankind to love and purfue liberty, as foon as they perceive it, through all the ranks and degrees of fociety; and it requires a very deep draught of corruption fo to intoxicate the mind as to make men love flavery and oppreffion, when they know that it is their right to be free. Penfioned cafuifts, and fuch as for the fake of lufts or worldly interefts, have given up confcience and have loft the feelings of the moral fenfe, may varnifh the rights of fovereings, and the power of princes with all the fine colourings of fophiftry and deceit, and dignify tyranny and oppreffion in the hands of monarchs with the divine epithets of the *powers that be*, or the ordinances of God: but common fenfe will teach every unprejudiced fubject, that there can be no powers or ordinance derived from divine authority that authorifes a few to gratify their own paffions or appetites, at the expence of the commonweal of fociety. What on all occafions would determine the truth of this point, would be, for the difputants to change fituations, and the friends of arbitrary power to become fubject to it in the hands of others.

A

A very short trial would soon alter their sentiments.—If the Deity had ever intended a certain form of government to have been universally adopted, he would have certainly pointed it out in such a manner as it could not have been mistaken, and given infallible marks of the persons who were to superintend it.—But as this is not the case, we have no other method of judging concerning governments, but that of their answering the end of the common-weal. When they answer this end, they are from heaven;—but when they destroy it, they proceed from another source.

When Arnold arrived at Quebec, the inhabitants were in a wavering situation; the English subjects were disgusted, and the French were not to be trusted with the defence of the city. There were no troops of any sort in the place till M'Clean's new raised emigrants arrived from the Sorrel. Some marines, whom the Governor had sent for from Boston, were refused by a naval council of war, on account of the lateness of the season, and the danger of navigation. The militia had been lately embodied by the Lieutenant-governor, and this was the condition of Quebec whem Arnold arrived with his party, and appeared at Point Levi, opposite to the town. The river was fortunately between them, and the boats secured, otherwise it appeared highly probable that they would have become masters of it in the first surprise and confusion. This defect in a few days was supplied by the alacrity of the Canadians, who supplied them with canoes, and they effected their passage in a dark night, notwithstanding the vigilance of the armed vessels and frigates of war in the river. The critical moment was now over, and the inhabitants began to think of securing their property; the discontented, both English and Canadians, when the danger pressed them, united for their common defence. Had the city been taken by surprise, it is highly probable that the malecontents would have joined the conquerors; but as it was now doubtful whether they should succeed in their enterprise, they considered it as the wisest course to hold with those who had the possession. The inhabitants were embodied and armed, and the sailors landed from the ships to attend the batteries and serve the guns. The besieged were considerably superior in number to the besiegers, and Arnold had no artillery.

It is probable that Arnold depended upon the disaffection of the inhabitants, which in case he had been able to have taken the town by surprise, might have been of service to his undertaking: but being disappointed in this view, there was nothing that remained practicable for him but intercepting the roads, and cutting off the supplies till Montgomery should arrive. He made a shew for some days upon the heights near the town, and sent two flags to summon the inhabitants, but they were fired at, and no message admitted. Upon which he withdrew his troops into quarters of refreshment. Considering their long and wearisome march, it must be supposed that they were in much need of some rest and refreshment: but when we reflect upon their present situation, it must suggest that their rest would be far from being very refreshing.

After Montgomery had received large supplies of all necessaries for his men at Montreal, and clothed and refreshed his little army, he set forward to Quebec. 'Tho' appearances were greatly on his side at this

this time, his situation was far from being agreeable.
Continual difficulties, and encreasing hardships attended him, that nothing less could have surmounted than his own enterprising genius. The difficulty of governing an army composed wholly of new soldiers, and these led directly from their civil employments to the field, even supposing them raised in old countries, and where subordination is the most perfectly established, will be conceived by those who are the least conversant in military affairs. Montgomery's troops were composed of men the most unaccustomed, and who from principles and habit, and manner of life, were the most averse to our ideas of military subordination, of any people whatsoever. I cannot however agree with those who affirm, that they are a people from habit and principle, and manner of life the most averse to every idea of subordination, of any civilized people in the world. This certainly is not the case, for they *then* did and have *since* voluntarily submitted to all the rules of military order and discipline. Had not the army which followed Montgomery been influenced with some more powerful principle than it was possible for his genius to inspire them with, they would never have endured the fatigues, undergone the hardships, and encountered the dangers which they voluntarily went through.— It was the spirit of liberty, the animating influence of freedom, and love of independency of a government which they conceived tended to enslave them, that operated more powerfully than the genius of Montgomery. It can easily be conceived that as they joined Montgomery freely and voluntarily, and knew the nature of the expedition they were going upon, that they had resolved to undergo the dangers and hardships

ships which atttended it, in hopes of promoting the great end which the colonists had in view. When military men serve from principle, and are actuated by conscience, there will be little need for that severe discipline which is necessary to be practised among those that are either forced into the service, or enter into it from principles of idleness, love of plunder, or other similar base principles. The Roman soldiers, in the time of the common-wealth, while virtue was predominant in the empire, without force or constraint, served their country, and maintained good dicipline from mutual choice: the soldiers, who were free Romans, and had an interest in the happiness of their country, as well as as the officers, endured hardships and encountered dangers, not from force, but because they considered themselves members of the common-wealth, and mutual sharers of the honours and privileges which they were fighting for, with the greatest senators of Rome. The provincial troops did not follow Montgomery to Canada for the sake of plunder, or from any wanton desire of laying waste the country, but to prevent government from making use of the forces in that quarter, in distressing the back settlements of the New England provinces, they had therefore determined with themselves before their setting out, to observe a strict discipline, as true friends of liberty, avoiding all licentiousness and disorders.

General Carleton arrived at Quebec near about the time that Arnold's detachment had retired from its neighbourhood, and immediately took such measures for its defence, as were suitable to that character, which he had sustained as a military officer.—He first obliged all those with there families to leave the town who refused to take up arms in its defence.———

The

The garrison including all orders who did duty, consisted of about 1500 men, a number totally unequal to the defence of such extensive works, provided they had been attacked by a powerful force, supported with things necessary for a siege. The besiegers were not more numerous than the besieged, and were but ill provided for such an arduous undertaking; their artillery was too light and trifling to demolish such works as defended Quebec. Nothing could have rendered their success probable, except a division among the inhabitants of the town, or a sudden attack to have thrown them into confusion.

The troops in the town, except one company of the 7th regiment, which had escaped being taken, and were principally recruits, were only a new raised militia, unacquainted with, and scarcely trained to any form of military discipline; so that the troops on both sides might have been considered as nearly equal in their characters. The principal defence of the town rested in some marines and about 450 seamen, belonging to the King's frigates, and the merchant ships that wintered in the harbour. These being accustomed to the management of the great guns, and the ready manœuvre of that sort of exercise, were the real strength of the garrison. There was however a great difference in the intrepidity of both the troops and officers of the parties; the towns-men were not all well affected to the Governor; for though they had through necessity taken up arms, for fear of some ill consequences, or because they thought it impossible for the provincials to take the town, yet in their hearts they wished well to their cause, and would not have been ill pleased if they had succeeded. The other had marched with the strongest resolution to fulfil the end for which they were sent, and were in general of an intrepid and daring disposition.

Montgomery, having left some troops in Montreal and the forts, and sent detachments into the different parts of the province to encourage the Canadians, as well as to forward supplies of provisions and necessaries, pushed on with as many men as could be spared, and such artillery as he could procure, to join Arnold. Their march was in winter, through bad roads, in a severe climate, beneath the fall of the first snows, and therefore made under great hardships; which they however encountered with equal resolution, and arrived with incredible expedition at Quebec.

It was upon the twenty-fifth day of December when Montgomery appeared before the town, when he wrote a letter to the Governor, magnifying his own strength, stating the weakness of the garrison, shewing the impossiblity of relief, and recommending an immediate surrender, to avoid the consequences which must attend a storm, from victorious troops irritated with the injurious treatment which they had in various instances received at their hand. The flag which carried this letter was fired at, as well as every other which was sent, so that all communication was totally forbidden between the besiegers and the inhabitants, by the Governor. Notwithstanding of this strict guard, Montgomery found other means to convey a letter of the same nature and import into the town; but this had no effect upon the Governor, who remained firm and inflexible, in spite of all threatenings. It appears somewhat of a strange adventure in Montgomery, to invest a fortified place with a number of troops not superior to those that defended it, either in quantity or quality. His only prospect of
success

success seems to have depended upon the effect which his warlike preparations and the violence of his attack might have upon the inhabitants of the town, who being hastily embodied were but a very motley garrison; or in case he should fail in an assault to weary them out with continued and false alarms.—— He accordingly commenced a bombardment with five small mortars, which continued for some days, and might have been supposed to have struck terror into the minds of the people, and to have intimidated the town into a surrender; but the intrepidity of the Governor, supported by the bravery of the general officers, and the activity of the seamen and marines, prevented this effect. The garrison in general behaved with great bravery, and nobly followed the example of their officers, and endured incommodities, wants and distresses incident to so long a siege, with wonderful steadfastness and resolution.

General Montgomery in a few days opened a six gun battery, about 700 yards distance from the walls, but this metal was too light to produce any considerable effect. The walls of Quebec were not so easily battered down as to give way to such a feeble force as that of a few small pieces, more adapted to the field than fitted for a siege. Meanwhile the snow lay deep upon the ground, and such was the severity of the climate, that human nature seemed incapable of withstanding its force in the open field.———The hardships of the provincials, both arising from the season and the smallness of their numbers, seemed incredible, and could only be endured through an enthusiastic adherence to their cause, and the affectionate esteem they had for their general, who bore fatigue and encountered danger equally with themselves. This constancy

stancy was likely to fail, provided the evil should encrease or continue too long, human nature must have yielded to difficulties which were totally unsupportable in their then situation. An excuse for relinquishing this project was soon likely to happen, as the time was near expired for which every man of the soldiers had been lifted; and it was most likely that the feelings of nature, and the future prospect of danger would prevail over their enthusiasm, and make them take the advantage of the opportunity of returning home according to their agreement. This would have totally broke up Montgomery's little army. The New York troops felt the severity of the climate, and did not shew so much steadiness and perseverence, as the hardy New Englandmen who had traversed the desart with Arnold. These shewed an amazing constancy and intrepidity. Montgomery in these circumstances found that something decisive behoved immediately to be done, otherwise the benefit of his past success and labour, would be in a great measure lost to the cause he was engaged in, and his fame and reputation, which now shone with the greatest lustre, would be dimmed, if not totally obscured. He knew that the Americans depended greatly upon his conduct and valour, and would consider Quebec as good as taken as soon as they heard that he was arrived before it, and that the higher their expectations were raised, the more grievous the disappointment would be to them, in case the undertaking was frustrated. Their confidence of success was founded upon the high opinion which they held of his courage and ability: to forfeit that opinion was to him the worst of all possible consequences. To storm the city with an army not superior to the garrison which

defended

defended it, considering also the natural strength of the place, which, in the common way of speaking, was reckoned impregnable, was a desperate undertaking. But persons who have their minds possessed with the romantic ideas of honour in war, seldom estimate danger by the strict rules of prudence; but provided the honours in view be great, seldom attend minutely to the dangers which lye in the way of the object. In the history of military achievements in all ages we find that the success of great attempts have depended upon a noble contempt of forms and ordinary calculations. Providence, in contempt of human pride, ever was, and ever will be, the great arbiter in war. Montgomery depending much upon fortune, and also upon the nature and disposition of the garrison, determined on a desperate attempt to carry the place by scaling the walls.

As in the most perfect society upon earth there have been found traitors, so in this army of provincials there were some who betrayed the purposes of the general to the garrison of Quebec.——Some deserters, either through design, or to make their peace with the governor, informed the besieged of the design of the general. This he was fortunate enough to perceive, from the motions of the townsmen, who had not only been informed of his design In general, but of the particular manner of carrying it into execution. This unfortunate circumstance disconcerted his whole plan, and made him change his dispositions, which had a considerable influence on the succeeding events. Had he succeeded in his first scheme, and made good a lodgment in the city in any part that was unguarded, there would have been a severe struggle for the possession of it, and it is not improbable

bable that Quebec would have been taken, notwithstanding the vigilance and activity of the Governor. Montgomery being fruſtrated in his plan of operation, proceeded to attack the town according to a new plan. Upon the laſt day of the year 1775, and under the cover of a violent ſtorm of ſnow, he proceeded to this arduous attempt. Having diſpoſed his little army into four diviſions, of which two carried on falſe attacks againſt the upper-town, whilſt himſelf and Arnold conducted two real ones againſt oppoſite parts of the town. By this means the alarm was general, in both towns, and might have diſconcerted the moſt experienced troops. From the ſide of the river St. Lawrence, and round to the Baſon, every part ſeemed equally threatened and equally in danger.

About five o'clock, Montgomery, at the head of the New York troops, advanced againſt the lower town, at a place called Aunce de Mere under Cape Diamond: but for ſome difficulties which had intervened in his approach, the ſignal for engaging had been given, and the garriſon alarmed before he could reach the place. He notwithſtanding preſſed on in a narrow file upon a ſcanty path, with a precipice to the river on one ſide, and an hanging above him which in a manner projected over him. Having ſeized and paſſed the firſt barrier, accompanied by a few of his braveſt men and officers, he marched boldly at the head of his detachment to attack the ſecond. This was much ſtronger than the firſt, and had ſeveral cannon loaded with grape ſhot. From this much execution was done upon the aſſailants; both the cannon and muſketry were well directed, and from this barrier or battery Montgomery was killed, and finiſhed

his

his military career; he fell together with his aid-de-camp, and several officers; and the most of those that were near his person lay dead upon the spot. Upon the fall of Montgomery, the command devolved upon one Campbell, who retired immediately, without making any further attempt to proceed.———It was thought by the colonists that Campbell yielded too easily to the first impression, and that had he continued the attack as resolutely as Montgomery began it, as they were now close at the battery, and might have taken it with little loss, that the town would have fallen into their hands.———For as Arnold was gaining ground in that quarter which he attacked, had Campbell pushed the attack as he might have done, it would have prevented the Governor from employing the forces in that part of the town against Arnold's division, which were already victorious, and would have distracted the townsmen, that they would not have had time to have paid attention to the progress of the other division of the provincials.

While things were carried on in this quarter as has been mentioned, Arnold was not idle in pushing matters as far as he could in the department assigned to him. With an intrepidity that would have done honour to the most veteran troops, this division attacked that part of the town called the Saut aut Matelot, and having penetrated through St. Roques, they attacked a well defended battery, which they carried after an hour's sharp engagement with considerable loss. It was here that their commander was wounded, his leg was shattered by a shot, and they were obliged to carry him to the camp; but these troops did not retreat hastily upon the departure of the commander, as the New-York detachment did; his place

was

was supplied by other officers, who with no less intrepidity carried on the attack, and the men shewed a resolution on that occasion equal to the oldest and most regular forces. They were as yet ignorant of Montgomery's misfortune, and were so far from being dejected with their own, that they pushed on with greater vigour, and made themselves masters of another battery. Had all the provincial troops on this occasion been equal to those of New England, notwithstanding all the misfortunes they sustained by the loss of their general officers, they would certainly have taken the town that very day. The New York forces certainly behaved but ill in precipitately retreating upon the death of their General, for had they continued to have made a diversion in that part of the town where they were appointed to serve, they would have prevented the garrison from attacking Arnold's party in the rear, which would have been of great consequence.

Upon Campbell's retreat, the garrison had now time to turn their whole attention to Arnold's division, and perceived they had now an occasion offered of cutting their retreat off. The situation of the assailants was now such that in attempting a retreat, they had to pass a considerable way within fifty yards of the walls, exposed to the whole fire of the garrison. And what rendered their fate inevitable was, a considerable detachment with several field pieces issued thro' a gate which commanded that passage, and attacked them furiously in the rear, while they were already fully employed in every other part, by the troops which poured upon them in every other quarter. In these desperate circumstances, without a possibility of escape, attacked on all sides, and under every disadvantage

vantage of ground, as well as numbers, they obstinately defended themselves for three hours, and at last surrendered prisoners of war. A greater instance of bravery has not been exhibited by any veteran troops on almost any occasion, and provided they had not been under the predicament of rebellion, would have had the honour of being extolled as the greatest heroes in the Gazette. The governor treated the prisoners with great humanity, and it was thought a thing more extraordinary that he pursued such lenitive measures, seeing he had been long habituated to the severity of a military life. This observation suggests an idea in no wise friendly to those who assume a military character, and pursue war as a profession;—such a manner of life hardens the human heart, and renders the feelings of the soul callous to the pains and distresses of our fellow-creatures. The profession of arms ought certainly only to be occasional, when there is a special call to defend ourselves and property against unjust claims and assaults;—but it ought never to be the study of a man's life, and the constant theme of his practice. Such as go volunteers to foreign wars, in which they are in no wise interested, only for the sake of learning to shed blood, can only be considered as professional butchers, going abroad to learn their business.——After the death of Montgomery, all enmity against him arising from party animosity ceased, and respect to his private character prevailed over every other consideration; his dead body received every possible mark of distinction from the victors, and was interred at Quebec with all the military honours due to a brave soldier. By comparing the different accounts and circumstances subsequent to the engagement, the provincials in killed,

killed, wounded, and prisoners, did not lose fewer than half of their number. This appear from a letter of General Arnold, written soon after,—which states their remaining number at only 700 men.

Thus fell Richard Montgomery in the cause of liberty, fighting as he believed, and as unbiassed reason will in after ages determine, for the rights of human nature and of his country, against the illegal encroachments of a British ministry, who by misleading their most gracious Sovereign, the rightful prince and monarch of a vast empire, procured by the energy of some invisible influence, the sanction of legislative authority, to oppress the subjects, contrary to the fundamental statutes of a noble and well-poised constitution.—He died in modern stile, a rebel, but no otherwise deserved that character than Russel and Sidney, names which will ever live, while there are any persons living who value the glorious Revolution, and love liberty. He was a gentleman of a good family in the kingdom of Ireland, and served with reputation in the last war with France and Spain: He fell in the prime of life, much lamented by his friends, and even praised by his enemies. His many and excellent qualities, and agreeable disposition, had procured him an uncommon share of both public and private esteem, and there was perhaps no person engaged on the same side, and few on either, whose loss would have been more regretted both in Britain and America.— He was a real and firm lover of liberty; and his enemies could never with justice accuse him of being a friend to licentiousness; he had studied and understood the true principles of liberty, believed their real value, and counted nothing too dear in supporting of them. . He married a lady, and purchased an

estate

estate in New York, and on this account was induced to consider himself as American. When he perceived the measures of the British ministry with regard to his country directly overturning what he believed to be the colony constitution, he joined in opposing them, not from wrath, but principle. He was led from sentiment and full persuasion, that it was his duty to quit the sweets of an easy fortune, the enjoyment of a loved and philosophic rural life, with the highest domestic felicity, to take a share in all the miseries and dangers of those troubles which have been already so baneful to the empire. He had undoubtedly great military abilities, though in the attempt in which he fell he was unsuccessful. It is much to be lamented that a man of so great abilities, and so well formed to support the glory of his country, should have fallen in a most unnatural civil contest. In America he was revered and extolled as a martyr to the cause of human nature and the liberties of mankind. What was more extraordinary, the most eminent orators in the British senate, displayed their eloquence in praising his virtues and lamenting his fate. A great speaker, whose eloquence has often been admired, a veteran fellow-soldier of Montgomery in the late war, shed abundance of tears whilst he expatiated on their past friendship and participation of service in that season of enterprise and glory. Even the minister extolled his virtues, whilst he condemned the rebellious cause they were employed in, and the fatal effects which their mistaken application had produced. In this praise of the minister there is something exceedingly mysterious, for it supposes what can never happen, namely, that virtue can be applied to rebellious purposes. When a man is really engaged in what is

truly

truly rebellion, that which some people call virtue is no more than vicious exertions of the mind against truth. If Montgomery's application of the powers of his mind and body was employed in supporting rebellion, in the true sense of the word, instead of being reckoned virtuous, he ought to have been accounted a person destitute of all true sense of moral virtue. But it would appear that the minister had a different opinion, and must have had some suspicion of the existence of Montgomery's rebellion.

Governor Carleton and his officers acquired great honour by the defence they made, and the behaviour of the garrison would have done honour to veteran troops. It shews how far the example of a few brave officers will operate to render the rawest and worst formed troops respectable. The Governor is allowed on all hands to be one of the first military characters of the age, and on this occasion he by no means tarnished the reputation he had formerly acquired.

After the unsuccessful attack of Quebec, the besiegers immediately quitted their camp, and retired about three miles out of the city, where they secured and strengthened their quarters as well as they were able, being apprehensive of an attack from the garrison; but the one was as unfit for pursuing, as the others were to have endured a severe attack. The Governor wisely contented himself with the unexpected advantage he had obtained, without hazarding the fate of the province, and perhaps of America, by a rash and uncertain enterprise. The city was now out of danger, and the great succours which were expected would not fail to relieve the whole province. Arnold, who now commanded in chief, upon the death of Montgomery was far from being in an eligible situation; the climate was uncommonly cold and the weather severe; the hope of assistance was distant, and the arrival of succours of consequence slow. Notwithstanding the provincials with an astonishing perseverance bore every hardship.—— They had lost their commander in chief, the best of their officers, and some of the bravest of their men, with a part of their small artillery; they could not depend upon the Canadians, who fickleness rendered it unsafe to depend upon, and whom success or disappointment were equally ready to influence. In such a situation, it required no small share of address and activity to keep together such an army, where their hopes were small and their danger multiplying. General Arnold, who had hitherto displayed uncommon abilities in his march into Canada, discovered on this occasion the utmost vigour of a determined mind, and a genius full of resources. Wounded and defeated as he was, he put his troops in such a condition as to keep them still formidable; and instead of appearing as one who had met with a defeat, he continued to threaten the city, by turning the siege into a blockade, and effectually to obstruct the arrival of all supplies of provisions and necessaries into the town. He dispatched an express to General Wooster, who was at Montreal, to bring succours, and take upon him the command; but as this was not immediately to be done, he supported himself against the difficulties that surrounded him with the force which he had. It appears from the whole of his operations, that the Governor considered it as a dangerous expedient to attack Arnold in the open field, though he had near double the number of his forces, and that provided it had been in the power of General Wooster to have sent

sent a suitable reinforcement, the fate of Quebec would have still been doubtful. Had not Arnold been wounded, notwithstanding the death of Montgomery, it is not improbable that Quebec would have been taken that evening. It was certainly a bold adventure for so few troops to make such a daring attack upon a fortified place, by many reckoned impregnable against any force whatsoever.

The march of the New England troops from Gardiner's Town to Quebec, may be considered as one of those amazing exertions of conduct and intrepidity, which could only be undertaken by a great mind, and executed by a people willing to submit to every hardship for the sake of freedom and liberty. A multitude of men, possessed of such ideas, disposing them voluntarily to encounter such hardships and difficulties, can never be subdued by any power on earth, without first conquering their existence, and extirpating them from the face of the ground. The most romantic notions of military glory and honour will never determine a multitude of persons, freely and voluntarily, without any hope of present advantage, to encounter such great immediate hardships and difficulties. The famous retreat of Xenophon with ten thousand Greeks, which is famous in history, was an effort of necessity, which is the parent of invention, and the long and dangerous march which was conducted with so much wisdom and intrepidity was undertaken and pursued for immediate self-preservation. But the march of Arnold through the American deserts was undertaken for the sake of the general cause of liberty, as they believed, and with a design to prevent a power which they thought inimical to the rights of mankind from enslaving their country.——
Men

Men of different opinions concerning the policy of nations, will judge differently with regard to this expedition; but whether they determine the ends of it good or evil, all must allow, that it was a great undertaking, and conducted with much intrepidity. After the fermentation of party zeal has subsided, and men cooly consider the actions of others, and their principles, they will be obliged to confess that the march of Colonel Arnold and his troops is one of the greatest exploits recorded in the annals of nations; when the way in which they marched, the season of the year, the severity of the climate, and the many other disadvantages and hardships which attended them are considered. They were only new soldiers, who had but lately taken up arms for the defence of their liberties, and had never been accustomed to the hardships of war; they were led through a wilderness, unexplored by human eye, where there was no paths, and through thickets almost impenetrable, and swamps next to impossible. They had no possibility of obtaining any more provisions than they carried with them, till they came to Canada, either by force or otherwise, and it was uncertain when they should arrive there. It required an amazing resolution to determine men to engage in such evident and unavoidable hardships already foreseen, and presented to their minds.

A VIRGINIA

A
VIRGINIA CHARTER,

KING JAMES I's Letters Patent to Sir Thomas Gates, Sir George Somers, and others,——— for two several Colonies and Plantations, to be made in Virginia, and other parts and territories of America. Dated April 10, 1606.

1. JAMES, by the grace of God, King of England, Scotland, France, and Ireland, Defender of the Faith, &c. Whereas our loving and well disposed subjects, Sir Thomas Gates, and Sir George Somers, Knights, Richard Hacklut, Clerk, Prebendary of Westminster, and Edward Maria Wingfield, Thomas Hanham, and Relegh Gilbert, Esqrs. William Parker, and George Popham, Gentlemen, and divers others of our loving subjects, have been humble suitors unto us, that we would vouchsafe unto them our licence, to make habitations, plantations, and to deduce a colony of sundry of our people into that part of America commonly called Virginia, and other parts and territories in America, either appertaining unto us, or which are not now actually possessed by any Christian prince or people, situate, lying, and being all along the sea coasts, between four-and-thirty degrees of northerly latitude from the equinoctial line,

line, and five-and-forty degrees of the same latitude, and in the main land between the same four-and-thirty and five-and-forty degrees, and the islands thereunto adjacent, or within one hundred miles of the coast thereof.

II. And at that end, and for the more speedy accomplishment of their said intended plantation and habitation, they are desirous to divide themselves into several colonies and companies; the one consisting of certain knights, gentlemen, merchants, and other adventurers, of our city of London and elsewhere, which are, and from time to time shall be, joined unto them, which do desire to begin their habitation and plantation in some fit and convenient place, between four-and-thirty and one and-forty degrees of the said latitude, along the coasts of Virginia and coasts of America aforesaid; and the other, consisting of sundry knights, gentlemen, merchants, and the other adventurers, of our cities of Bristol and Exeter, and of our town of Plymouth, and of other places, which do join themselves unto that colony, which do desire to begin their plantation and habitation in some fit and convenient place, between eight-and-thirty degrees and five-and-forty degrees of the said latitude, all along the said coast of Virginia and of America, as that coast lieth.

III. We, greatly recommending, and graciously accepting of, their desires for the furtherance of so noble a work, which may, by the providence of Almighty God, hereafter tend to the glory of his divine Majesty, in propagating of Christian religion to such people as yet live in darkness and miserable ignorance of the true knowledge and worship of God; and may in time bring the infidels and savages living in those parts, to human civility, and to a settled and quiet government: Do, by these our letters patents, graciously accept of, and agree to their humble and well intended desires.

IV. And do therefore grant to the London company liberty to settle any where on the coast of North America, between latitude four-and-thirty degrees and latitude one-and-forty degrees, and of the sea-coast near their place of settlement to the distance of fifty miles from it, each way, and to the depth of one hundred miles into the main land.

V. And we do also grant to the Plymouth company liberty to settle any where on the coast of North America, between latitude eight-and-thirty degrees and latitude five-and-forty degrees, and of the sea-coast near their place of settlement to the distance of fifty miles from it, each way, and to the depth of one hundred miles into the main land.

VI. Provided that the settlements that shall be last made shall be no more than one hundred miles distant from the first.

VII. And we also ordain, that each of these colonies shall be governed by a council of thirteen persons appointed by the King.

VIII. And there shall also be a superior council of thirteen persons residing in England, appointed by the King.

IX. And moreover we do grant liberty to work all mines of gold and silver in the said colonies, paying to the King a fifth part of the gold and silver, and a fifteenth of the copper.

X. And a power is hereby given to establish coins for those colonies.

XI. And we do likewise give full power and authority

thority to carry out the King's subjects to settle the said colonies.

XII. Moreover, we grant power and licence, to resist and expel all intruders into the said colonies.

XIII. We give and grant power to raise two and a half per cent. upon all goods imported thither by the King's subjects, and five per cent. upon those imported by strangers.

XIV. And we do further give and grant liberty to carry goods into the said colonies, from the King's other dominions, free from custom for seven years.

XV. Also we grant a general denization of all such persons as shall be born in these colonies.

XVI. Moreover, we declare, that all persons, who, under pretence of trading to these colonies, shall send goods into foreign countries, shall forfeit their ships and goods.

XVII. Provision in case of any of the inhabitants of those colonies shall rob or injure any other of the King's subjects, or the subjects of any prince or state in amity with England.

XVIII. And finally, we promise to grant the lands that shall be occupied by the first colony, to such persons as shall be appointed for that purpose by the council of that colony.

XIX. And do in like manner, grant the like promise with respect to the lands that shall be occupied by the second colony.

LUKIN.

Per breve de privato Sigillo.

END OF VOLUME FIRST.

www.ingramcontent.com/pod-product-compliance
Lightning Source LLC
Chambersburg PA
CBHW031932290426
44108CB00011B/531